THE HISTORY
FASHION JOU.....

THE HISTORY OF
FASHION JOURNALISM

Kate Nelson Best

Bloomsbury Academic
An imprint of Bloomsbury Publishing Plc

B L O O M S B U R Y
LONDON · OXFORD · NEW YORK · NEW DELHI · SYDNEY

Bloomsbury Academic

An imprint of Bloomsbury Publishing Plc

50 Bedford Square	1385 Broadway
London	New York
WC1B 3DP	NY 10018
UK	USA

www.bloomsbury.com

BLOOMSBURY and the Diana logo are trademarks of Bloomsbury Publishing Plc

First published 2017

© Kate Nelson Best, 2017

British Library Cataloguing-in-Publication Data
A catalogue record for this book is available from the British Library.

ISBN:	HB:	978-1-8478-8656-9
	PB:	978-1-8478-8655-2
	ePDF:	978-1-4742-7972-7
	ePub:	978-1-4742-8517-9

Library of Congress Cataloging-in-Publication Data
Names: Best, Kate, author.
Title: The history of fashion journalism / Kate Nelson Best.
Description: London ; New York : Bloomsbury Academic, an imprint of Bloomsbury Publishing Plc, 2017. | Includes bibliographical references.
Identifiers: LCCN 2016025282| ISBN 9781847886569 (hardback) | ISBN 9781847886552 (paperback) | ISBN 9781474279727 (epdf) | ISBN 9781474285179 (ePub)
Subjects: LCSH: Fashion writing--History. | BISAC: DESIGN / Fashion. | LANGUAGE ARTS & DISCIPLINES / Journalism.
Classification: LCC TT503.5 .B47 2017 | DDC 808.06/674692--dc23 LC record available at https://lccn.loc.gov/2016025282

Cover design: Adriana Brioso
Cover image © Nat Farbman /The LIFE Picture Collection/Getty Images

Typeset by Fakenham Prepress Solutions, Fakenham, Norfolk NR21 8NN
Printed and bound in India

To my family

CONTENTS

ILLUSTRATIONS

PLATES

1   *Le Cabinet des Modes*, January 1, 1786. © Bibliothèque nationale de France. (The *Cabinet*'s plates pioneered very detailed and high-quality engravings.)

2   Pelisse Turque Garnie de Martre. *Journal des Dames et des Modes*. Paris, France, 1812. © Victoria and Albert Museum, London. (Note that the illustration is still not branded at this stage.)

3   *La Mode Illustrée*, June 14, 1868. Two Women in a Carriage. © Victoria and Albert Museum, London. (The figures' luxurious shiny fabrics, extravagant costumes, and presence at Le Bois suggest the aspirational lifestyle of *La Parisienne*. By now, the plate is branded.)

4   *Le Follet*, *Journal du Grand Monde.19th Century.* Jules David. © Victoria and Albert Museum, London. (The mother's dark fabrics, modest style, and demeanor mediate her function as moral custodian. The yellow bonnet is uncharacteristically bright, suggesting artistic license.)

5   "La Marseillaise." Etienne Drian. *La Gazette du Bon Ton*, July 1914. © Victoria and Albert Museum, London. (The title and the use of Tricolor colors suggest nationalism, but the whimsical artistry denotes it as a fashion plate, imbricating patriotism with the creativity of French fashion.)

6   Erté cover for *Harper's Bazaar*, January 1923. © Sevenarts Ltd/DACS 2016. Image courtesy of the Advertising Archives/Harper's Bazaar/ Hearst Magazines UK. (Like others of the period—*Vogue* and *Fémina*, for example—Erté's covers function as artifacts, conveying mood rather than clothing.)

7   *Vogue Paris*, December 1939. Christian Bérard. © DACS/London 2016/ *Vogue Paris*. (Christian Bébé Bérard was a regular contributor to *Vogue*. As in Drian's plate, fashion is imbricated with patriotism.)

FIGURES

ACKNOWLEDGMENTS

would first like to thank Lisa Armstrong, Jane Bruton, Vanessa Friedman, Masoud Golsorkhi, Betty Jackson, Dylan Jones, Colin Mcdowell, Penny Martin, Leandra Medine, Eric Musgrave, and Saskia Wilkins who gave of their precious time to be interviewed for this book and offered such valuable insights.

It was Anna Wright of Bloomsbury who had the faith to commission this book, and my editor Hannah Crump who had the faith to stick with it through endless domestic and scholarly vicissitudes. I would like to thank them both.

I am extremely grateful to the staff of all the libraries I have used, particularly those from The British Library and The National Art Library, who have been especially accommodating. Thanks also to all those who have spent hours putting periodicals online: while there is no substitute for the feel and look of the thing in one's hands, for an editorial overview it has been most helpful.

I owe heartfelt thanks to Julia Harris Voss, my patient picture researcher, for her indispensable assistance and tolerance of my indecision over visuals; to my dear friend Tim Cooke for lending his professional expertise to the editing of the original manuscript—twice the size of this one; to my equally dear friend Liz Gunewardena for her hard work on German translation; to Tallulah Bullock for her significant research contribution to Chapter 9; and to my lovely husband Tony for his technical and emotional support.

This book was inspired by my students, and I am particularly grateful to Katie Landsdown for the phrase "camera culture" and to Michelle Chai (aka Daisy Park) for her illumination of the blogosphere.

Last but not least, thanks to my friends, especially Anita, for keeping things in perspective; and to my family, especially dear Nancy, Alice, and Iris, for *really* keeping things in perspective—with apologies to them and to Mum for my long periods of emotional absence while writing.

1 INTRODUCTION

I have before me a series of fashion engravings dating from the Revolution and finishing about the time of the Consulat. These costumes, which cause much amusement amongst many thoughtless people—solemn people who lack real gravitas—have a dual charm both artistic and historical. They are often beautiful and drawn with wit but what matters as much to me and what I am happy to find in all, or almost all of them, are the moral and aesthetic values of their time.

(BAUDELAIRE, *THE PAINTER OF MODERN LIFE* 1968 [1863]: 547)

I confess, I am as charmed by the sight of fashion on the page as Baudelaire. I have spent many hours writing about fashion journalism, even more time researching it, and more time than I care to remember consuming and enjoying it. I am not alone in this: artists from Manet, Cocteau (figure 1.1), and Klimt to Damien Hirst, photographers such as Man Ray and Deborah Turbeville, and writers from Honoré de Balzac and Oscar Wilde to Dorothy Parker, Angela Carter, and Linda Grant have all been fascinated by writing about and images of fashion. This is no mystery to me because, as I will endeavor to show, fashion journalism cannot be seen as being separate from fashion itself. The two are symbiotic. As an integral part of the fashion system, fashion journalism reflects all of the variety and creativity of fashion. Indeed, if fashion is the creation of the symbolic value of clothing, then the fashion media—dedicated magazines, fashion columns in newspapers, women's "service" magazines, Sunday supplements, hybrid or niche magazines, television, and blogs and other online platforms—have been, since the outset, at the very heart of the process. This is the argument proposed by Roland Barthes in his seminal work on French fashion journalism, *The Fashion System* (1990 [1967]). Although Barthes was not an enthusiast of fashion journalism, his exploration of late 1950s' magazines provides a useful point of departure for an analysis of the fashion discourse. Barthes suggested that fashion journalism has shaped, and possibly even created, the concept of fashion and its symbolic value.

FIGURE 1.1 Cocteau Illustration of Schiaparelli Dress, *Harper's Bazaar* 1937.
© ADAGP, Paris and DACS, London 2016. Image courtesy of Fashion Institute of
Technology/SUNY, Gladys Marcus Library Department of Special Collections.

Furthermore, if fashion is a protean and ambivalent subject, fashion journalism has, since *Le Cabinet des Modes* in the eighteenth century, been responsible for harnessing this mercurial goddess into a comprehensible and desirable system. Fashion functions paradoxically as a marker both of individual identity and of an individual's relationship to the group. Fashion journalism has from the beginning served to bridge this gap, democratizing fashion but at the same time upholding its discriminatory and symbolic value (Bourdieu 2010 [1984]).

Nor is fashion journalism simple writing about fashion. As Baudelaire observes, it holds up a mirror to broader culture, acting as a hinge between the fashion industry and public consciousness (Wilson 2003 [1985]: 157). Fashion journalists thus function as 'gatekeepers' who often identify and anticipate dramatic shifts in the broader culture (McCracken 1986: 77), as was the case with the Kate Moss cover of *The Face* (plate 14), which signaled a shift away from glossy designer imagery. In addition, since the appearance of *Le Mercure Galant* in the seventeenth century, fashion writing has also made a significant contribution to ideological history and cultural norms, particularly where women are concerned. It has helped shape not only views of beauty and femininity but also attitudes toward consumerism and even national identity. The fashion media have also been at the forefront of developments in marketing, image making, and publishing.

Fashion journalism is increasingly recognized as a discipline. Today it is the subject of professional courses and degrees at the likes of Pennsylvania State, the University Of Michigan, and Rutgers University, as well as specialist fashion institutions such as FIT and The London College of Fashion. Fashion journalism is also the most popular specialism on more broadly based media studies courses (Bradford 2015: xii). However, there has never been a study dedicated solely to an analysis of the historical form and content of the fashion discourse. This is the gap *The History of Fashion Journalism* aims to fill.

For some critics, writing about fashion lacks journalistic integrity because of its close link with the fashion industry itself (Robin Givhan is the only fashion journalist to have been awarded a Pulitzer Prize). In this view, fashion writers and magazines are little more than what Friedman calls "cheerleaders" (2014) or others, less generously, "PR poodles": their job is to encourage readers to buy clothes and thus to keep the fashion industry—and themselves—in business. As sociologist Brian Moeran has noted, fashion magazines are both cultural products and commodities (2008: 269) and therefore inevitably mediate tensions between their artistic, ideological, and commercial agendas. As we will see, however, this has not precluded aesthetic innovation, ideological insight, and cultural influence in fashion journalism. Again, I would argue that it is precisely the inherent tensions born of its close relationship with the fashion industry that makes fashion journalism so rewarding a subject of study.

Above all, when considering the value of fashion journalism, I think it is worth considering this question. If it really is as trivial as its critics allege, why did Hitler work so hard to muzzle the French fashion press during the German occupation in World War II (1939–45)?

A crisis of identity?

Fashion is a $1 trillion global industry (Tungate 2012 [2005]: 1). The fashion media are just as global and have their own impressive figures. In 2015 *Vogue* had an international print audience of 12.7 million and 31.1 million monthly unique users of its website (condenast.com), while the Louis Vuitton 2015 cruise collection, which was showcased at Bob Hope's Palm Springs mansion, nearly crashed Instagram. Fashion has arguably become *the* global discourse, with more media coverage than any other similar subject (Polan 2006: 154), stretching from the blog of America's First Lady, Michelle Obama, to coverage of emerging fashion centers such as Nigeria. Fashion is the subject of movies and TV shows and webcasts of "behind the scenes" films, while designers have crossed disciplines to open hotels (Missoni, Armani), collaborate with food manufacturers (Coca Cola, Pepsi), and open art foundations (Prada, Louis Vuitton).

As the reach of fashion has grown, so has that of the fashion media: 'Today newspapers, fashion magazines, television programmes, and the internet bombard us with information and advice on dress and appearance. We are saturated with images of fashion' (Wilson 2003 [1985]: 248). Traditional print journalism has been challenged by cinema, television, blogs, live streaming of catwalk shows, celebrity and designer social media, fashion film, and online retailers as sources of fashion information and inspiration. Commercial pressures and conglomerate power have left some journalists feeling 'just garnish for PRs and designers' (Cronberg 2016). For some observers, such developments—combined with the increasingly rapid fashion cycle whereby clothes are on the high street before fashion journalists have a chance to opine on them—have brought traditional fashion journalism to a crisis point. As early as 2004 Stéphane Wargnier, then director of communications at Hermès, argued that contemporary fashion journalism was weakened by a 'loss of identity' (Wargnier 2004: 164–5). This begs the question of exactly what that identity is, and what has been the historical function of the fashion media.

Toward an approach: Key themes

Despite widespread academic and public interest in fashion itself, fashion journalism—with the exception of fashion photography and illustration—has remained somewhat marginalized.[1] However, there has recently been more engagement with the development of the fashion media, most notably: Breward

(2003: Chs 4 and 5); Polan (2006); Bartlett et al. (2013); Bradford (2015) and McNeil and Miller (2014). *The History of Fashion Journalism* forms part of this engagement by providing a historical overview of the industry and its development from its origins up until the present day. Focusing on the specialist fashion media, it will also look at the expanded coverage of fashion in newspapers since World War II and the advent of color supplements in the 1960s—many of the industry's "grande dames," such as Eugenia Sheppard, Hebe Dorsey, Ernestine Carter, and Suzy Menkes, were and are newspaper based—as well as its expansion to television and the internet. It does not claim to be exhaustive but aims to cover the highlights and major changes in both format and content, and to act as a reference and springboard for more detailed research.

Such an overview suggests that the principal functions of fashion journalism have remained largely unchanged since the seventeenth century, although their reach and scale have developed alongside the industry.

Cultural arbiters

Vogue's website claims that the brand's authority is founded on its role as a "cultural barometer for a global audience" (2015). The starting point of this history is this relationship between fashion, its media, and culture, as examined also by commentators as varied as Baudelaire and Barthes. So successful has journalism been as a "cultural barometer" that some observers, such as Gilles Lipovetsky (1994 [1991]), would argue that fashion is at the heart of modern culture and, indeed, Western democracy.

The traditional role of fashion journalists has been as cultural arbiters who "review aesthetic, social and cultural innovations as they first appear and then classify these innovations as either important or trivial" (McCracken 1986: 77). Journalists then pass on their views to readers (ibid.), making them what Wargnier calls "social mediators" or "spokespersons for the spirit of the time" (2004: 165). This link between fashion and culture is the mechanism journalists use to create what Barthes calls "the fashion effect": in other words, fashion (1990 [1967]: 17). Indeed, Barthes argues that it is only from this dialogue with broader ideological values that fashion acquires its meaning (ibid.: 218). Of course, neither this meaning nor fashion's symbolism within culture has remained stable: at certain points, such as the mid-nineteenth century in France, for example, fashion has come to symbolize everything that is happening in society. Furthermore, it does not always translate across national boundaries. Shifts in values are reflected in both imagery and text and, indeed, in the shifting relationships between them.

In their 2014 book, *Fashion Writing and Criticism*, historians Peter McNeil and Sanda Miller explore the importance of "taste" as a criterion for judging fashion in the eighteenth century. The notion of taste later disappeared as the key signifier in fashion judgment, replaced by a new lexicon that reflected changing cultural values. The new touchstones included "smart" and "chic" in the 1920s, "elegant" in the 1950s, and "style" in the 1980s. For some observers, the fact that contemporary fashion writing lacks such recognized touchstones is a sign of a lack of evaluative appraisal.

A symbiotic relationship

As noted earlier, the relationship between the fashion media and the industry is symbiotic: as the industry changes so does its journalism, and sometimes vice versa. Essentially, however, it remains commercial in nature: "Fashion, the described garment encourages the purchase" (Barthes 1990: 17), or as Anna Wintour once put it, "Vogue's not here to burst the bubble; it's here to sell, sell, sell." The eighteenth-century use of advertorial—advertising masquerading as editorial—was an early example of this business agenda. Later in the nineteenth century magazines both supported and were supported by department stores, in the 1950s and 1960s by fabric manufacturers, and in the 1980s by the menswear business.

The promotional relationship between the industry and its media is one of the central themes of this book, but as we shall see, there are conflicts between the commercial, the ideological, and the magazine as cultural artifact. The tension between commercial and editorial considerations is common to all forms of consumer journalism but, arguably, has been most pronounced in fashion journalism, as Shinkle notes in relation to the fashion photograph: "If there is one characteristic shared by all fashion photographs, it is their simultaneous placement within the artistic and commercial realms" (2010 [2008]: 2).

Nationhood and cultural imperialism

Since its inception, fashion journalism has been laced with nationalism, whether in Louis IV's cultural imperialism, the tussle for cultural supremacy through the fashion industry between France, Germany, and the U.S. during the world wars (see Chapter 4), or the cheerleading of the British press during the "Cool Britannia" period of the 1990s (see Chapter 8).

The focus of this book is the history of fashion journalism in America, Britain, and France in particular because, in my opinion, these countries have until the twenty-first century produced many of the innovations in the field. Fashion has been far from homogeneous, however, and nor have the fashion media.

Democratization and distinction

Fashion journalism has to walk a fine line between creating fashion as a group phenomenon while retaining the symbolic discriminating value or cultural "distinction" of fashion (Bourdieu 2010 [1984]). Lipovetsky sees this paradox of mass democracy and discriminating individualism as being inherent in the fashion system (1994 [1991]).[2] The "elitest" value of fashion is central to the arguments of commentators such as Veblen (2009 [1899]) and Simmel (1971 [1904]), who have seen it as closely aligned to money and hierarchies of social class. At other times, as in the 1960s, it has been related to "being in the know" and subcultural knowledge. The dynamics of this contradiction between democracy and distinction are central to the history of the fashion media, as it is also a key function of fashion journalism to constantly redress the balance. As importantly, it is fashion journalism that Barthes claims "creates the fashion effect," placing it at the heart of the symbolic meaning of fashion in history.

One result of fashion journalism's commercial remit has been the systematic democratization or what we might call demystification of fashion, bringing it to a wider audience. The historian Anne Higonnet estimates, for example, that fashion prints reached an audience of more than one million in France by the end of the nineteenth century (Higonnet 1992: 91). Since the nineteenth century, magazines have used patterns as means of disseminating fashion more broadly, including haute couture (figure 1.2).

This expansion of the market, however, also threatens the symbolic value of fashion as being distinctive and desirable, whether in class, taste, or subcultural value. As we will see, journalism attempts to limit this effect through regulatory discourses, but new forms of commentary and presentation also appear to reassert these discriminatory values (for example, in *La Gazette du Bon Ton*, which in 1912 sought to uphold the artistic merit of couture in the face of mass production and plagiarism [see Chapter 4], or the many niche magazines of the new millennium that provided an antidote to the growing ubiquity of celebrity fashion: in February 2004 the American magazine *Sleaze* featured a burning picture of Victoria Beckham on the cover to accompany an article entitled "Celebrity Burnout" [see Chapter 9].

However, over history these new discriminatory or avant-garde elements have often been assimilated into the mainstream fashion media—Condé Nast bought *La Gazette du Bon Ton* and appropriated its artists and illustration for *Vogue*, thus continuing the cycle of democratization following heightened discrimination. Such has also been the case with the democratizing discourse of the bloggers, which has been recuperated, to some extent, into a more privileged viewpoint.

FIGURE 1.2 *Le Petit Echo de la Mode*, March 22, 1953. © Kharbine-Tapador/British Library. (Patterns were used from the nineteenth century to democratize the fashion press. In the 1950s they gave ordinary women access to haute couture styles.)

Fashion leaders and celebrity

Meanwhile, there have always been fashion leaders who have epitomized and asserted the acme of fashion's discriminatory values. The link between "celebrity" and fashion is therefore another key theme of the book. Fashion journalism has on occasion co-opted these figures from other mass media, such as 1930s' Hollywood or pop music in the 1960s, or created them itself, as was the case with the "Dames de Vogue" in the 1920s. In her book *Fashion on Television* (2014), Helen Warner argues that fashion programming has an important function in educating women in life skills and competencies. She sees celebrity icons as cultural intermediaries who embody these competencies. For others, such as Robin Givhan, celebrities' millennial dominance of fashion discourse has devalued fashion and fashion journalism as mass entertainment (Aguilar 2013). Such figures reflect broader culture values as much as fashion but they also speak to definitions of gender.

Gender ideologies

In her writings on gender, feminist scholar Judith Butler argues that gender is expressed in "styles of the flesh" (1999 [1990]: 177) and that dress is an important component of these gendered identities (1993: 33). The fashion media have been central in teaching their readers, to paraphrase Simone de Beauvoir, "how one becomes a woman" and, especially recently, "how to become a man." As Butler points out, following de Beauvoir, these identities are multiple and often conflict with each other, as some are idealized and others degraded (1993: 86–7). They shift across time (1999: 177). Such modulating identities mark the history of fashion journalism and form another key component of this book.[3]

Gender ideals or "identifactory fantasies" (Butler 1993: 86) have been a feature of fashion journalism since its outset. In the nineteenth century fashion magazines established the link between femininity and consumption, mainly of clothes, but also of home furnishings and other luxury items. Already different publications posited competing versions of the "ideal" woman, highlighting types such as *La Parisienne*, The Mother, and The Young Lady, or *Jeune Fille* (see Chapter 3). Although gender identities have shifted over time, the tension between childish innocence and repressed sexuality inherent in the figure of the *Jeune Fille* may be recognized, albeit in a different guise, in the more contemporary teenage figure produced by *Seventeen* magazine, as identified by McCracken (1993: 144).

Fantasy and regulation

Although some, including feminists, have seen the fantasies and ideals of the fashion press as pernicious and oppressive to women, others such as Elizabeth

Wilson see them as more playful and as stimuli to active, self-fashioned cultural identities. As Cavallero and Warwick point out, dress's role lies "in organizing and constructing lifestyles" that are central to our desire for a stable identity (2001 [1998]: 98). The fact that such stability is itself a fantasy leads us to search for new expressions of ourselves through fashion and in the fashion media.

The History of Fashion Journalism will also explore the ways in which the fashion media have sought to regulate behavior in line with social norms as much as inspire through fantasy. Part of this is related to limiting any tendency toward democratization and is best summed up in the fear of wearing the wrong thing or making fashion *faux pas*. According to philosopher Michel Foucault, this type of self-regulatory function is implicit in all discourses relating to care of the self (1988 [1966]). He points out that self-discipline and control underlie even upbeat injunctions on appearance, such as when consumers are encouraged to sunbathe naked—but accompanied by imagery that implies they should do so only if they are "slim, bronzed and beautiful" (Foucault 2001). While the injunctions of the early fashion press were more direct and insistent (for example, warning women that overly extravagant outfits would lead to marital estrangement), even in today's era of apparent individualism the contemporary discourse contains regulatory rhetoric, as in the very title of the television series *What Not to Wear*.

Image and text

The relationship between image and text is central to these functions of fantasy and regulation, with imagery the main receptacle for fantasy. In *The Fashion System*, Barthes examines the relationship between image and text, and concludes, principally, that the role of the text is to direct the reading of the image (1990 [1967]: 16–17). He also ascribes a more important role to the editorial, perhaps more justifiable in the late 1950s. Writing in 1999, Paul Jobling argues for a more "in tandem" approach in analyzing text and image. This inter-textual approach is central to this book. However, it does not intend to provide a detailed examination of fashion iconography, a subject well covered elsewhere.[4] It is the shifting dynamics between the two elements that reveal both the changing functions of fashion journalism and shifts in cultural values which are the focus here.

While early fashion writing played an important descriptive role (for example, it provided seamstresses with detailed information for making garments) it also manufactured the desirability of fashionable clothing by describing the glamorous situations where such garments could be seen. At the same time, fashion plates in magazines increasingly portrayed desirable lifestyles that they suggested might be accessible through clothing (see Chapters 2 and 3). Later plates linked fashion with the symbolic value of the visual arts, a process that continues in the creation of new aesthetic values in fashion photography.

Fashion and the arts

The relationship between fashion and the broader arts and the role of fashion journalism in forging this link is another theme central to this book. Some observers argue that fashion magazines have been an important means by which movements such as Cubism and Surrealism have reached a wider public "and as such are key disseminators of taste" (Hall-Duncan 1979: 12) (figure 1.3). The configuration of fashion as art has been a paradigm of fashion journalism since the late nineteenth century, when magazines such as *L'Art et La Mode* and *La Mode Artistique* used artistic references to connote cultural and social superiority in clothing. Meanwhile, new types of hybrid publication emerge at times of what Walter Benjamin calls "cultural dislocation," when fashion often finds itself at the center of a broader artistic milieu.

A vector for criticism

As we will see, there have always been those who see fashion journalism, as pernicious. Its rapid expansion in the nineteenth century was blamed by the French writer Charles du Pouey in 1869, for example, for turning economical home-loving women into extravagant, power-hungry monsters (du Pouey 1869: 14–15), although ultimately his criticisms were more about changes in society than about fashion. In the twenty-first century, the fashion press has been held responsible for the dramatic rise in eating disorders among young women, although this association has effectively been challenged by the fashion scholar Pamela Church Gibson, who points out that the virtual media world is so fragmented that there is no longer a monolithic high-fashion "ideal" to which young women aspire (2012 [2010]: 29). From a historical perspective, it seems to me that—while fashion journalism has undoubtedly contributed to gender ideals, consumerism, and the obsession with celebrity, among other reproaches—its position at the nexus of culture often makes it a vector for general criticism of society's perceived ills. Indeed, its long association with women might make it an easy target, while at the same time assuming a lack of agency among its consumers.

Fashion future

Fashion has been pronounced moribund on a number of occasions. In September 1968 the British magazine *Nova* announced, "Fashion is Dead"; *Wall Street Journal* reporter Teri Agins came to the same conclusion in her 1999 book *The End of Fashion*. But in commercial and cultural terms fashion, as we have seen, continues

FIGURE 1.3 Schiaparelli Beach Wear. George Hoyningen-Heuné. Published in British *Vogue*, April 8, 1928. © Richard Horst. Photo courtesy Staley/Wise Gallery NYC. (Hoyningen-Heuné was very influenced by Surrealism, as reflected in the half-seen mannequin's legs.)

to thrive. One of the most important contributions to its success, as identified by Barthes and others, is the role of the fashion media in creating fashion's symbolic value and, through their dissemination of information and aspiration, turning that somewhat magical value into hard financial profit.

Today, the mechanisms of fashion journalism have changed and its function faces challenges, particularly from fast fashion and social media. As we will see, however, the fashion media have been here before and have successfully survived developments such as the advent of television. Arguably, today's unfiltered circulation of fashion discussion and fashion images may make the role of the fashion journalist as mediator and stylist of dreams more important than ever. By looking into the past, we can see more hope for the future.

Notes

1   Women's media have a number of published histories, including: Sullerot (1966); White (1970); Adburgham (1972); Bonvoisin and Maignien (1986); Shevelow (1989); Ballaster et al. (1991); Damon-Moore (1994); Scanlon (1995); Braithwaite and Barrell (1988 [1979]); Beetham (1996); Zuckerman (1998); and Walker (2000). Although these publications offer valuable insights into fashion journalism and its relationship to consumption and gender ideology, it is not their primary focus. There have been two detailed histories of the German fashion press (Völkel 2006; Zika 2006) and a few exhibitions dedicated to the wider subject, including "Fashion Magazines" (Manchester: 1976) and "Glossy: modes et papier glassé" (Marseille, Musée de la Mode: 2004). Histories of individual publications such as *Vogue*, *Elle*, *Blitz*, *Purple*, *i-D*, *Another Man*, and *Dazed and Confused* exist but do not necessarily cover a wider cultural, geographical, and commercial context.

2   Dani Cavallero and Alexandra Warwick put a cogent argument on the paradox of how dress works in relation to the body and society in *Fashioning the Frame: Boundaries, Dress and The Body* (2001 [1998]).

3   The role of the women's press in mediating feminine identities has been explored elsewhere (e.g., Ferguson [1983]; Winship [1987]; Ballaster et al. [1991]), as has the function of the fashion press as a primary site for the construction of the identity of the "new man" (Mort 1996; Nixon 1996; Benwell 2003; Jobling 2005).

4   See Hall-Duncan (1979); Devlin (1979); Harrison (1991); Blackman (2007); Downton (2010); Shinkle (2010 [2008]).

2 A SYMBIOTIC RELATIONSHIP: THE ORIGINS OF THE MODERN FASHION PRESS

There will soon be only one form of dress in the West, in the South and in the North – ours.

(*FASHION-THÉORIE*, FEBRUARY 1863)

Introduction

The fortunes of the fashion industry and fashion journalism have been inextricably linked since the seventeenth century, when France and its court assumed fashion leadership among the Western aristocracy as part of Louis XIV's wider pretentions to cultural domination. The epicenter of women's fashion was Paris, where fashion media developed to disseminate its innovations.

During the eighteenth century, the appetite for fashion grew as the increasingly urbanized and expanding middle class sought to create an identity distinct from court dominance. As the fashion industry developed to meet this demand, the first magazine devoted to fashion, *Le Cabinet des Modes*, appeared in France in 1785. It was imitated in Britain, Germany, and Italy.

By the mid-nineteenth century French women's fashion mesmerized the Western world. The active promotion of the French fashion industry at the Great Exhibitions in London and Paris—France was the only country to exhibit women's ready-made clothes in 1852, 1855, and 1867—and the status of Paris as the apotheosis of fashionable culture created a desire for French fashion across Europe and America. The first edition of *Harper's Bazaar* in America in 1867 boasted that its fashion news was as up-to-date as that of Paris, while acknowledging the popularity of all things Parisian (*Harper's Bazaar*, November 2, 1867: 2).

By 1860 France was Europe's leading industrial power thanks to fashion and its ancillary industries (Mermet 1879: 710), and the economic, political, and cultural importance of the fashion industry meant that the French dominated the fashion media until the last quarter of the century. While countries such as Britain and Germany had their own fashion magazines from the end of the eighteenth century, they were largely derivative of the more innovative French models, particularly in their use of patterns and advertising. These publications also lacked the international impact of the French fashion press. French was widely spoken among educated Europeans and Americans, and French fashion magazines such as *Le Follet* and *Le Moniteur de la Mode* had as many as eight foreign editions and were circulated in more than twenty countries (Best 2007: 15). French fashion plates were also highly sought after in the foreign fashion press (Gaudriault 1983: 122) and became a selling point.

The nineteenth century brought an explosion in the number of fashion magazines. The sector grew from a handful of titles at the turn of the century to perhaps a hundred by its end: some 180 new fashion magazines were launched between 1871 and 1908 in France alone (Gay-Fragneaud and Vallet 2004a: 180). The rise reflected many factors, such as the development of railways, growth in female literacy, rising consumer prosperity, technological advances in printing, the development of the lithograph print, and innovations in the magazines themselves.

Above all, the expansion of the fashion press was linked to the growth of the French fashion industry itself, which industrialized rapidly. There was widespread adoption of mechanization, from weaving looms to stocking knitting frames; aniline dyes, discovered in 1856, which led to the speedier production of colored fabrics; the development of ready-made clothing for women, a sector worth 100 million francs by 1866; and the advent of department stores such as Le Bon Marché, which opened in 1852.[1] The development of the fashion industry expanded the market and created advertising support for the fashion press.

Fashion was the key signifier of France's industrial superiority, reflected in the ubiquity of references to "notre génie industriel" in the fashion press. Unsurprisingly, the government had a vested interest in promoting the business of fashion and the fashion press. Unlike the rest of the heavily censored French press, fashion publications were largely immune from prosecution and taxation, which undoubtedly encouraged their expansion. In Britain, in contrast, taxes on advertising and paper—not abolished until 1853 and 1861, respectively—contributed to the relatively slower development of the fashion press.[2]

The importance of fashion in France went beyond the purely economic and political, however. It was also at the forefront of a cultural revolution, and became important for the artistic community as an expression of *modernité*.

In part, fashion's *modernité* was linked to its broader symbolism as the emblem of democracy and consumer choice. While similar cultural changes were occurring elsewhere—the growth of the middle class and consumerism, in particular—in France the democratic symbolism of clothing was linked to the formation of the post-revolutionary nation and therefore, arguably, had an especially deep resonance. The edict of October 29, 1793 overthrew the sumptuary laws of the *Ancien Régime*, which had restricted many types of clothing and fabrics to the aristocracy: "No-one can constrain any citizen male or female from dressing in a particular fashion." Indeed, the writer Ernest Feydeau argued that the right to luxury goods, particularly fashion, was one of democracy's greatest attainments (Feydeau 1866: 64).

Meanwhile, of course, there were those who were unhappy with fashion's increasing importance and the type of society it represented. Fashion and the fashion press provoked antagonism in France and elsewhere.

The seventeenth century and *Le Mercure Galant* (1672–1832 [1724])

The first vehicles of the fashion media were the dolls regularly sent by the shops in Rue Saint-Honoré to the courts of Europe at the beginning of the seventeenth century in order to encourage business for the Paris guild of tailors and seamstresses.[3] These "Pandoras" were presented in the Hotel Rambouillet once a month and sent to all the major European cities (Kleinert 1980: 22) and even to the "New World" (Roche 1996 [1989]: 475). The dolls were so important to the French fashion trade that in times of war they were accompanied by an armed escort. Shortly thereafter the tailors and seamstresses began distributing engraved plates in the same way, although these became collectors' items as much as fashion inspiration (Dolan 2011). The "Pandoras" helped spread French culture as well as clothing and were prominently displayed in Europe's town squares and shops by the eighteenth century (Roche 1996: 475). They remained in circulation until the beginning of the nineteenth century, when they were banned by Napoleon, who was concerned that they could be used to conceal messages from spies (Völkel 2006: 27).

Louis XIV, who saw fashion as a means of dominating European culture, encouraged the commercialization of the French industry. Engraved plates were part of a "royal imperative in creating the art of fashion as an essential part of cultural propaganda" (Ribeiro 2005: 19).

The first magazine to publish reports on fashion was also part of Louis' cultural offensive. It was at Versailles that Jean Donneau de Visé, a nobleman and author of popular farces, created *Le Mercure Galant* (1672–4) (figure 2.1).

LE
MERCVRE
GALANT.

CONTENANT PLUSIEURS
HISTOIRES VERITABLES,

Et tout ce qui s'eft paffé depuis
le premier Janvier 1672. jufques
au Depart du Roy.

A PARIS,

Chez CLAUDE BARBIN, au Palais,
fur le Second Perron de la S.Chapelle.

M. DC. LXXII.
AVEC PRIVILEGE DV ROY.

FIGURE 2.1 *Le Mercure Galant*, 1672. Tome 1 title page. © Bibliothèque nationale de France.

The inaugural issue promised that the publication would report on theater, court events, and the King's armies, would include poetry and would describe "new fashions," with plentiful information provided by the "coquettes of Paris" (first issue: 10). Initially the magazine was a postcard-sized pamphlet with text in two columns like a newspaper that intermittently published features on court fashion together with black-and-white engravings advertising the names and addresses of suppliers. Taking the form of letters addressed to the female reader, it set out "to entertain" but also to inform provincial readers, who were, according to *Le Mercure*, particularly interested in fashion (ibid.). Thus the first fashion magazine was already closely allied to the spread of fashion culture. *Le Mercure Galant* was short-lived—six issues—but it re-emerged in 1677 as *Le Nouveau Mercure Galant*, which remained in print[4] until 1724. It continued intermittently and under various guises until 1832.[5]

Appearing monthly, *Le Nouveau Mercure* included book and play reviews, poems, songs, court gossip, marriages and deaths, and a lively letters page. It also covered the new season's *toilettes* for spring and autumn, especially in the biannual "Extraordinaires"—special editions of thirty or forty pages that focused exclusively on fashion, fabrics, and home furnishings (Jones 2004: 26)—although some regular editions lacked any fashion at all. The information given on suppliers was sometimes so detailed that the magazine resembled a mail order catalog. *Le Nouveau Mercure* was aimed at both sexes and covered both men's and women's fashions.

Given its court origins, the magazine's key fashion arbiters were the King and Queen, although "gens de qualité" were also important, and *Le Mercure* also served Louis XIV's propaganda goals by overtly linking national identity to fashion superiority: "Everyone must agree that nothing pleases more than the fashions born in France" (*Mercure Galant*, 1673 t.3: 315).

Le Mercure depicted fashion as a fickle goddess, a representation that continued until the emergence in the nineteenth century of individual dressmakers, such as Victorine and Palmyre. It divided clothes into what was "à la mode," what was "much worn" ("on en porte beaucoup"), or what is "no longer worn"—the term *démodé* did not yet exist, because the rapid cycles of industrialized fashion had yet to begin—and described each new fashion in great detail, giving styles terms or names that often derived from popular plays.

Fashion and fashion magazines already faced criticism. This ranged from anti-fashion pamphlets by the French *frondeurs* (political rebels), such as De Fitelieu's "Le Contre Mode" (1642), to fashion leaflets (*modeflugblätter*) from the German middle classes intended to turn people against fashion by caricaturing prevailing trends, such as a farmer's maid taking her poultry to market flaunting a ridiculous hairstyle (Völkel 2006: 29–31). In these debates, fashion was a weapon not only for criticism of the court but also for antagonism toward the commercial and urban culture that was emerging, particularly in Paris (Jones 2004: 15–17).

The eighteenth century: A feminine fashion press

In the eighteenth century, this mercantile culture brought increased affluence to a growing middle class and increasing leisure time to women who could afford servants. Together with the expansion of female education and literacy, this led to an increased appetite for reading material, as reflected in the rise of the novel, mobile libraries, and later reading rooms in both France and Britain. The growing populations of cities and towns also created a new market for fashionable clothing as sartorial display became ever more significant in fashioning identity for the bourgeoisie in these more mobile and impersonal societies, both as a group and as individuals, and as people simply had more opportunity to experience changes in clothing.[6]

Fashion became a hot topic: "All of Europe was focused on fashion," according to Henri Bidou, editor of *La Gazette du Bon Ton* in 1912 (Preface: 3). The first French newspapers, *Le Journal de Paris* and *La Feuille sans titre*, both reported on fashion, reflecting the widespread interest in the subject (Jones 2004: 181).

As interest in fashion grew, so did interest in fashion plates, which unlike previous costume plates gave information on current or coming fashion (Langley-Moore 1971: 10). The number of plates produced in France quadrupled between 1700 and 1799 to approximately 1,275 (Roche 1996: 477). A parallel development was a huge increase in the number of almanacs and pocket books published throughout Europe (Langley Moore 1971: 12–14; Adburgham 1972: 159–76). These diaries, often given as New Year gifts, usually contained at least one fashion plate as well as poetry, puzzles, songs, and even recipes. Almanacs were not strictly speaking fashion magazines, as they only came out once a year and thus lacked the timely element or "actualité" that Balzac, for one, saw as an essential component of fashion (Lehmann 2009: 304). However, their popularity spoke to an increasing appetite for fashion information, and the plates themselves were viewed as art and often used for interior decoration or placed in albums—a practice that continued with the hand-colored plates of the nineteenth century.[7]

In 1778 a more extensive collection of plates appeared that bridged the gap between the almanacs and the fashion magazine. Published on a more regular basis, *La Gallerie des Modes* (1778–87) contained six prints in each edition and was very expensive (Gay-Fragneaud and Vallet 2004a: 178). In addition to its black-and-white and colored engravings, it contained detailed reports on the origin of the costumes featured, including information from Rose Bertin, dressmaker to Marie Antoinette, and descriptions of the fabrics used (ibid.).[8]

As advances in technology made printing easier, cheaper, and of better quality, the second half of the eighteenth century saw the emergence of a regular women's press.[9] In Britain, the first issue of *The Lady's Magazine* (1759–63; 1770–1832) in 1759 carried a black-and-white engraving entitled "Habit of a Lady" and promised to "inform its readers of every innovation in fashion" (Adburgham 1972: 121). The magazine was, however, somewhat apologetic about its coverage of "a subject of such frivolous importance", and it took several years before there was fashion information every month. Reports on British and Paris fashion did not appear until 1790 (Adburgham 1972: 121–9), although Langley Moore and others credit *The Lady's Magazine* with producing the first colored fashion plate (1971: 14).

Meanwhile, French society was already being affected by the divisions that led to the Revolution of 1789. There were profound shifts in the fashion industry, where royal control of production and distribution was undermined by the increasingly powerful mercantile culture (see Jones 2004: Part II; Roche 1996). In spite of a growing number of sumptuary laws, Versailles was increasingly challenged as the arbiter of fashion.

Most significantly, perhaps, debate raged about the unstable nature of fashion and its unwelcome effeminate influence on French culture, although some observers saw fashion as being emblematic of democratic progress and it featured prominently in Diderot's *Encyclopaedia* (Jones 2004: 114).[10]

"Taste" emerged as a stabilizing anchor for fashion and a yardstick for judging its aesthetic value. As scholars Peter McNeil and Sanda Miller have argued, the notion of "*goût*" also formed the basis of the first journalistic criticism of fashion (2014: Chs 3 and 4) and began increasingly to feature in the fashion press, where Miller argues that it helped raise the status and intellectual profile of magazines (2013: 13–21).

Le Cabinet des Modes (1785–93)

It was against this backdrop that the first regular magazine devoted entirely to fashion appeared, namely *Le Cabinet des Modes* (1785–6). The brainchild of editor Jean Antoine Brun (also known as LeBrun Tossa) and the publisher Bosse, *Le Cabinet* was published every fifteen days, ran to eight pages, and contained three plates at a cost of 21 livres, much cheaper than *La Gallerie*. Its first edition announced its intention to describe clearly and precisely all the clothing and new adornments of both sexes in order to give "an exact and timely knowledge" (Preface, October 15, 1785). The magazine also covered home furnishings, decoration, and jewelry, but it ultimately promoted itself as a cheaper and superior replacement for the costly "Pandoras" and expensive commercial agents (Preface, October 15, 1785: 2 and 3).

The finely detailed engravings (see plate 1) did indeed offer precise information about new fashions (Gaudriault 1983: 17). Briefly under new editorship, the magazine was renamed *La Magasin des Modes Nouvelles Françaises et Anglaises*

(November 1786 to December 1789), but when Brun regained control in February 1790, he renamed it *Le Journal de la Mode et du Goût*, as it remained until it ran into financial trouble in April 1793.

Despite changes of title, the format and function of the magazine remained constant and created the model of modern publications. It was instrumental in defining and disseminating the new fashion industry but also in promoting the culture of fashion. It made it clear that the King and Queen were no longer the sole arbiters of fashion. Within the growing mercantile, democratic culture, new figures originated trends, including actresses and the *marchandes de modes*.

Le Cabinet sought to present "la mode" as a more organized system. It traced the origins of trends and sought to define the fashion season: "This journal will henceforth be divided into four sections or time periods relating to the seasons; because each season has its fashions and costumes" (November 1, 1786: 186). All this was designed to rationalize fickle fashion (Roche 1996: 499), but it also had benefits for the industry. An etiquette of dressing was created in which certain clothes were deemed suitable for certain occasions or times of day: "I should add that the *caraço* is only suitable as a morning outfit when it is too early to have got properly dressed but one needs to go out and walk before midday" (*Cabinet*, June 15, 1786: 115). Such rules expanded the requirements for and therefore the consumption of new clothes, but also created a role for the magazine as a guide to these rules. The etiquette of dressing formed a staple of fashion magazines until the 1960s.

Le Cabinet viewed itself as a "business." It also sought to justify its price compared to other magazines on the basis of the quality of its illuminated engravings and editorial (November 1, 1786: 186). According to Brun, *Le Cabinet* was in profit by 1785 (Roche 1996: 486, 46). The fashion magazine as a commodity was born.

As well as helping structure the fashion system, *Le Cabinet* also acted as an intermediary between the industry and its consumers. It feted the creativity of Paris *marchandes* but also contained publicity for them in both *announces* (small-space advertising) and, just as often, advertorial, advertising masquerading as editorial: "This bonnet, already taken up by a large number of our Ladies, is a creation of *Mlle Roussand* whose taste our subscribers are capable of judging from the number of bonnets that we have shown from her" (*Magasin des Modes Nouvelles*, November 1, 1786). Although tailors and dressmakers were by now sending out *prix courants*—simple brochures of their wares—*Le Cabinet* also functioned as a mail order catalog, blurring the distinction between advertising, retailing, and editorial.

Le Cabinet promoted itself as a guide and counselor for its readers, inaugurating the fashion magazine as a fashion advisor and arbiter of taste:

A woman who is attending to her toilette always needs someone whom she can consult to know whether this hairstyle, or this bonnet is well suited to her and whether she can present herself advantageously on the Promenades or other public places: why shouldn't we make ourselves her advisor and why shouldn't she read the opinions she's looking for in our issues? (June 15, 1786: 113)

Part of this advisory role involved initiating the reader into the fashion culture and its language. While much of the appeal of *Le Cabinet* lay in its plates, as both Jones (2004: 191) and Kleinert (2001: 3) have noted, the text was equally important in explaining correct terminology for fashionable items. *Le Cabinet* points out in its Preface that all its italicized words are "des termes techniques." In fact, they changed as often as the fashions themselves. Keeping up with them gave upper-class eighteenth-century European readers social standing, in the same way that knowledge of luxury brands gives Chinese consumers "face" today (Reinarch 2013: 145). In this way, *Le Cabinet* was responsible for producing fashion culture as much as reporting it.

This culture was becoming increasingly feminine, and by 1788 *Le Cabinet* was addressed solely to a female readership (Lehmann 2009: 300). Shopping and fashionable "taste" became seen as an exclusively feminine expertise—an ideology that *Le Cabinet* worked hard to promote (Roche 1996: 487–94) as middle-class men sought to define themselves in terms of work, in contrast to the leisured aristocrat.

Nationalism and support for French industry were integral to *Le Cabinet* from the outset and it promoted Paris, "this modern Athens," as the center of fashionable culture. *Le Cabinet* also linked fashion with democratic ideals. Its editorial emphasized the notion that "everyone" could now "satisfy that passion which they carry from birth for the objects which will present them to the best advantage." This democratic symbolism reverberated across Europe and beyond among the growing upper-middle classes. In the new social order, self-definition and luxury consumption replaced absolutist and aristocratic controls.

Le Cabinet was highly successful: it already had 846 subscribers in its first year (Roche 1996: 486). It was also popular abroad, and imitations appeared all over Europe.

In 1789 the French Revolution disrupted Paris's pre-eminence as a fashion center. This allowed other countries to venture into fashion publishing, creating new networks for the circulation of fashion in London, Germany (Weimar), and Austria (Leipzig) (Breward 2003: 118). In addition, the Revolution sparked a wave of emigration that, together with Louis' earlier expulsion of the Protestant Hugenots, spread French skills across the West.

Germany's first fashion magazine, *Journal des Luxus und der Moden* (1786–1827 [1808]) (figure 2.2), was modeled on *Le Cabinet* and was rushed into print by Friedrich Justin Bertuch to stop the French magazine gaining a foothold in Germany (Purdy 1998: 8–9).[11]

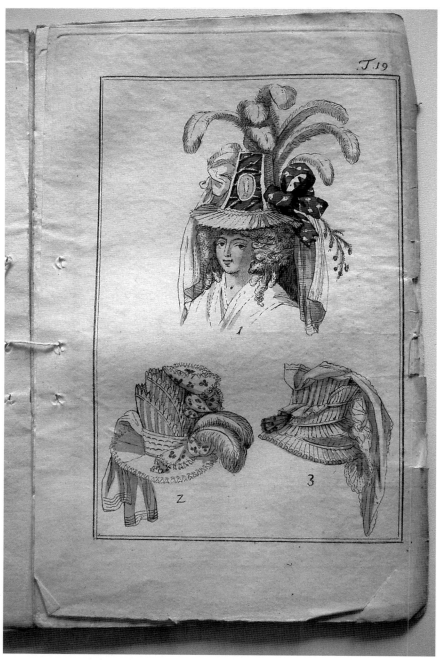

FIGURE 2.2 *Journal des Luxus und der Moden* Mode, a.d. Jahre 1789, ff.
© Kurptälzisches Museum der Stadt, Heidelberg. Photo: Dr. Kristine Scherer.

In Italy, the *Giornale delle Dame e delle Mode di Francia* (1786–94), which was published in Milan, and the *Giornale Dedicato al Bel Sesso* in Venice reproduced plates and directly translated articles from *Le Cabinet* (Sama 2004: 400).

The first British publication devoted to fashion, the *Gallery of Fashion* (1794–1803), was started by the French émigré Nicholas Heideloff, again using *Le Cabinet* as a model. Created using French engravers and illustrators, it was designed to appeal to the displaced French aristocracy in London as much as to the British.[12]

Le Cabinet had set the pattern for the modern fashion journal. Its imitators and foreign editions created a new appetite for fashion culture and fashion magazines throughout Europe:

> Now a new universal fashion literature, one more powerful than any of its predecessors, has really spread not only across Germany but across all of Europe, drawing all ranks and classes of society and driving out almost every other kind of literature. (*Journal des Luxus*, cited in Purdy 1998: 42)

The nineteenth century: Democratization and expansion of the fashion press

Despite the Revolution, French women's fashion soon reasserted its dominance, which continued for most of the nineteenth century. As a corollary, the French fashion press expanded exponentially, both domestically and internationally. As well as the plates—which "possess as much merit as a picture" (*Godey's Lady's Book*, January 1850)—magazines throughout the world retained French terms for fabrics and styles of clothing and expressions such as "*plus recherché*" ("the most sought after"). The italicization of such terms not only helped draw attention to their value as cultural capital for the reader but worked as an affirmation of the fashion credentials of the magazine itself.[13]

Napoleon, international expansion, and *Le Journal des Dames et des Modes* (1797–1839)

The beginning of the nineteenth century saw much political turmoil in France and little technological or industrial change in the fashion industry. Nevertheless, in spite of the disruption created by the Revolution and the Napoleonic Wars (1803–15), a powerful new international fashion magazine appeared. This was *Le Journal des Dames et des Modes*, which for thirty-two of its nearly forty years was edited by college professor Pierre de La Mesangère, who was also its primary journalist.

Despite his draconian press laws, Napoleon supported the magazine, which he called "Le Moniteur officiel de la mode." Napoleon saw fashion as an important industry for France, and banned the import of foreign fabrics (Cage 2009: 209). He also banned the dispatch of fashion dolls, which incidentally boosted fashion magazines. By 1820 French style was established once more as the "elegance" of Europe (Adburgham 1972: 208)—despite the patriotic promotion of domestic fashion industries in both German and British magazines during the Napoleonic Wars (Beetham 1996: 32)—and *Le Journal des Dames et des Modes* was instrumental in renewing the French dominance.

The magazine came out every five days, with eight pages of text and one or two colored copperplates (see plate 2). Its regular publication and its format of color plates, texts describing the clothes and lifestyles of the society elite, poetry, theater reviews, musical scores, and later serialized fiction reflected the model of *Le Cabinet* but had a wider editorial remit, prefiguring the more mainstream press of the nineteenth century and beyond. Highly commercial, it carried much advertising for fashion and beauty products in particular, and ran a mail order service that also offered credit. Relatively inexpensive—initially 10 livres a year— *Le Journal des Dames* was popular as far afield as Boston and Philadelphia, as well as in Britain, Holland, Italy, Belgium, Germany, and Russia. At its peak its circulation globally was 2,500, with less than half in Paris, although readership would have been much higher (Kleinert 2001: 111–16). New editions were produced, including one in Germany from 1799 to 1848, while other publications plagiarized its plates, style, and format.

In addition to its breadth of editorial and lively debates on subjects such as divorce, its fashion content changed from an imitative "reporterly" model to one of fantasy and identification. Although the magazine's focus, like that of the fashion industry, was the society elite—"des élégantes du haut rang" (January 25, 1824)—many of its readers lived outside Paris (Sullerot 1966: 98). What Siobhan McIlvanney has called "a relatively undistorted reflection of [a society] woman's life" (2010: 6) had little connection with readers' own lives. The magazine's detailed descriptions encouraged readers to fantasize about a life which they themselves did not necessarily enjoy, thus creating aspirational dreams that linked fashionable clothing and lifestyle:

> In the morning to do her errands, an elegant lady has a black satin coat or at the art gallery or the Tuileries, a black or violet velvet one, trimmed with mink; in her calèche or Tilbury, a coat of cashmere with large tartan checks and at the end of the day to leave the theatre a feather cloak lined with fur and ornamented with a black velvet collar with a band of gold at each corner. (December 20, 1824)

Despite its embrace of aspiration, fashion remained a relatively closed world. The editorial of *Le Journal des Dames* is full of unidentified protagonists and half-explained anecdotes clearly aimed at those in the know. Ulrich Lehmann suggests that this tone helped create an intimacy that echoed the discussion of fashions among affluent friends.

Until around 1830, fashion magazines were a shared part of soirees or afternoon visits (Lehmann 2009: 300). Such occasions allowed non-subscribers to share the latest novelties but also created the concept of the fashion magazine as a community. This sharing of magazines was instrumental in the growth of the fashion press in the nineteenth century. In Britain and France, reading rooms were also an important source of new readers (Rappaport 2001: 108), while in America shared subscriptions or "clubbing" was a popular way of building circulation for more mainstream journals, including *Godey's Lady's Book* (Zuckerman 1998: 6).[14]

The phenomenal success of *Le Journal des Dames* was due in part to the fact that it lacked much competition. One exception was the British publisher John Bell's *La Belle Assemblée* (1806–32) which, Breward argues, was influenced by French models and "affected a certain gallic sophistication" (2003: 119). *La Belle Assemblée* was as much a literary as a fashion magazine until 1810, when Mrs. Mary Ann Bell took control of the fashion department. Unusually for a British publication of the time, she introduced an advertorial approach,[15] making the magazine an advertising vehicle for her own shop, Le Magazin des Modes.

The expansion of the fashion press

Although the first half of the nineteenth century had seen the beginnings of a fashion industry,[16] it was the mechanization of clothing production and textiles, the development of ready-to-wear clothing, and the advent of the department store in the second half of the century, along with the expansion of the railways, that brought fashion into middle-class culture.[17] These changes coincided with a growing market and appetite for fashion as an expanding and increasingly wealthy, mobile capitalist society used clothing to define itself. Fashion epitomized nascent bourgeois values, which, according to writers the Goncourts, focused on materialism.

Fashion was also becoming important to definitions of gender. John Harvey argues that among the new middle classes the increasingly black-clad male signified economic productivity and strength (both physical and intellectual) and the fashion-conscious female the leisured and emotional excluded from power (Harvey 1995). In the new mobile society, fashion magazines both spoke to and circulated this definition of femininity. As the century progressed, they also increasingly linked femininity to the consumption of fashionable things.

In the first half of the century, aided by increasing literacy and cheaper printing costs, a host of new French fashion titles appeared—Gaudriault claims there were as many as 100 (1983: 64)—inspired by the success of *Le Journal des Dames et des Modes* and supported by speculators and advertising. Subscribers were invited to invest 100 francs for a stake in a journal (Lehmann 2009: 306).

With a few notable exceptions, including *Le Journal des Demoiselles* (1833–1922) and *Le Moniteur de la Mode* (1843–1913),[18] however, many new titles did not survive or were absorbed by others. Despite an increasing readership, particularly in provincial towns—the most successful new title, *Le Petit Courrier des Dames*, had 7,000 domestic subscribers by 1840 (Tétart-Vittu 1992: 63)—there was not yet enough of a clothing industry or consumer market to support so many publications.

Although fashion coverage expanded in newspapers—every French paper had a fashion column—the specialist fashion press solidified its influence on the culture and discourse of fashion. In the second half of the nineteenth century, fashion journalism—like the industry itself—moved from being a parochial, elitest concern to a more mainstream one: it expanded and became more democratic with the advent of cheaper new publications. In France there were about twenty established titles in the 1840s and sixty by 1870 (Best 2007: 14). In Britain, *May's Press Directory* of 1875 listed twenty titles concerned primarily with women's dress, although a number were French imports, such as *Le Follet* and *La Mode Illustrée* (Breward 1995: 74).[19] Despite more frequent publication—weekly as well as bi-monthly or monthly—circulations increased dramatically: by the mid-1860s *La Mode Illustrée* had 50,000 French subscribers and more abroad; by 1876 it had more than 100,000 in France alone. *Godey's Lady's Book*, the most significant American fashion magazine of the period, had 150,000 subscribers by 1860 and around 500,000 readers by 1869 (Aronson 2002: 201). Magazines also became larger, moving from octavo (6 x 9 inches) to quarto (9.5 x 12 inches) format and increasingly using columns rather than being written across the page like a book.

From a literary to a consumerist model

In France and elsewhere, particularly in England, the fashion periodicals of the first half of the nineteenth century remained fairly elitist and were as literary as they were sartorial. Serialized novels, which had been mixed with fashion since *The Lady's Magazine* in 1759 (Adburgham 1972: 129), appeared around 1815 in the French fashion press (Lehmann 2009: 302) and proved highly popular. As well as fashion and literature, most fashion journals included educational material on science, history, and geography, as well as coverage of court society.

Fashion was widely viewed in bohemian Paris as a symbol of modern aesthetics—if not modernity itself—a symbolism articulated by Baudelaire in "The Painter of Modern Life" (see McNeil and Miller 2014: 65). For artists and writers fashion assumed a value "that explained and embraced everything" (Simon 1995: 9). When poet Mallarmé launched *La Dernière Mode*, he set out to "study fashion as art" (December 20, 1874: 2).

Numerous contemporary writers embraced fashion: Balzac wrote for *La Mode* and Flaubert for *Les Modes Parisiennes*, for example. Indeed, fashion journalists often came from literary backgrounds until the 1920s, when they instead often came from advertising (Breazeale 2000: 241). Both the French poet Stéphane Mallarmé and the British aesthete Oscar Wilde actually edited fashion magazines—*La Dernière Mode* and *The Woman's World*, respectively—while Edgar Allen Poe guest-edited *Graham's Magazine* in America, although his contribution was literary rather than fashion related.

La Mode (1829–54)

The magazine *La Mode* epitomized the fusion of art, fashion, and modernity of the literary publications. Owned by Émile de Girardin, who was also proprietor of the national newspaper *La Presse*, and aimed at the aristocracy of Saint Germain, *La Mode* sought not only to showcase the latest fashions but also to elevate the quality of fashion illustration and fashion writing. Its plates by Paul Gavarni (1806–44) were noted by Baudelaire for the modernity of their animated figures, social interaction, and influence: "He has considerable effect on manners [...] many people force themselves into the likeness of the fashion plates" (1995 [1863]: 182–3). The magazine also included such literary contributors as Victor Hugo, George Sand, Alexandre Dumas, and Eugène Sue, as well as Balzac, whose commentary in *La Mode*—including "Traité de la Vie Elégante" ("Treatise on an Elegant Life") in 1830, a lengthy treatise on dandyism[20]—formed part of a more general intellectualization of fashion and a new philosophy of dress: "The Art of Dress is not so much in the clothing but in a certain way of wearing it."

La Mode was enormously popular: by June 1830 it had 2,600 subscribers (Morienval 1934: 31). Ultimately it was a commercial failure, however, in part because the aristocratic ladies of Saint Germain objected to its attempts to include advertorial for celebrated tailors and dressmakers (ibid.: 30). However, such commercialism was becoming the norm.

As the century progressed, the philosophical and educational elements of fashion magazines dropped significantly or disappeared, except in those journals aimed at younger women. Many upmarket magazines became more overtly fashion and lifestyle based. *Le Moniteur de la Mode* focused on the society elite, especially the court at Compiègne. Its column "Critical Revue of Fashion" covered outfits seen in high society; it included rules and regulations for dressing by the aristocratic Comtesse de Bassanville, well known for her manuals on the subject, and a "Review of Shops" by La Vicomtesse de Renneville.

While editorial filled in the descriptive detail of what the fashion plates could not show, such as cut and fabric in particular, and even price, the commentary, like the plates themselves, focused increasingly on fashionable clothing as a way to access a specific and desirable lifestyle. As we have seen, it promoted the idea that feminine identity could be found in the purchase of fashionable things.

The fashion press played a key role in making fashion and its consumption central to feminine identity. It promoted the "new" with ever greater vigor and became what Foucault would term a "regulatory discourse." The idea of "à la mode" was now linked to the notion of "*démodé*" and the threat of social exclusion or embarrassment due to a lack of knowledge of current trends generally being "worn" or "admitted" in society. As early as 1826, *Townsend's* warns against cambrics printed with black checks, which "have become too common to be seen now upon the head of an *élégante*" and *Le Moniteur de la Mode* points out that leather belts "used by society women for their morning outfits" are now "abandoned to their maids" (June 1860: 88). While the fashion magazine circulated these rules and regulations, it was also the guide to avoiding being "à la banal"—mainly by following the elite as aspirational role models and arbiters of fashions: "Lace is always the most highly prized by those who really know how to dress. At the Asile-Fénelon ball, which was unquestionably one of the most brilliant if not the most beautiful of the season, lace was everywhere" (*Moniteur de la Mode*, February 15, 1853: 158).

By the time Mallarmé published *La Dernière Mode* in 1874, the consumerist model was so established that he was able to parody it by assuming the guise of stereotypical editorial *personae* with female pseudonyms. While Mallarmé was almost certainly experimenting with language,[21] he also criticized the commodification of the fashion press:

> Go to M. Worth's establishment—in a two horse carriage, attracted by the news of the master's three new creations; or to the Malle des Indes for cashmeres— thyme-coloured, otter-fur or heron-lined, you will find the same crowd, quite desperate to spend money. ("Miss Satin," November 1, 1874, trans. Furbank and Cain 2004: 124)

Segmentation and the new practical journals: *La Mode Illustrée* and *The Englishwoman's Domestic Magazine*

Meanwhile, new magazines emerged aimed at a middle class and, later in the century, working-class public, due to the mechanization of the printing process and increased consolidation of resources (of which more later) which led to cheaper and tiered subscription rates: *La Mode Illustrée* had subscriptions

FIGURE 2.3 Women's Fashion Editorial from *La Mode Illustrée*, June 25, 1899. © De Agostini/British Library Board.

that ranged from 4 francs a year for illustrated patterns to 24 francs a year for the deluxe *album coloré*, complete with numerous color plates. The press also became more segmented, with different magazines and patterns of consumption depending on whether the reader was a *jeune fille*, a mother, or a society hostess (see Chapter 3).

The new, cheaper publications, meanwhile, sought to educate readers on fashion matters rather than merely chronicle trends. Mixing home-making with fashion, they tended to favor black-and-white lithographs that featured groups of women interacting in domestic situations: in the park with children or at home having tea. Both *La Mode Illustrée* (figure 2.3) and *The Englishwoman's Domestic Magazine* were important early examples of these more mainstream domestic magazines, as advertising commentator Mermet notes: "*La Mode Illustrée* is completely different from other fashion magazines in that it principally contains very practical subjects. So although this magazine reports all the changes in fashion, its principal aim is to educate" (Mermet 1879: 70). A new tone helped increase the circulation of the magazines by both creating a less intimidating editorial environment and showing the reader ways to access fashion at a lower cost.

The magazines focused on economy as well as style: "Dresses with low bodies and pelerines are very much in vogue. This is a very useful and economical way of making a dress as it can be worn either for morning or evening toilet" (*EDM*, November 1860: 45).

La Mode Illustrée (1860–1937)

Launched in 1860 by the publishers Firmin-Didot, *La Mode Illustrée* described itself as a "journal de famille" and was the first fashion weekly. Under the editorship of the redoubtable Emmeline Raymond, who wrote most of the content, it covered all aspects of the middle-class housewife's life, from crochet and embroidery designs and clothing patterns for women and children to recipes, table plans, and advice on parenting and gardening. It suggested how last year's fashions could be remodeled or dyed, and explained the benefits of certain types of fabrics and garments and their appropriate usage. It also contained literature and moral advice dispensed in response to "readers' letters" on such subjects as hygiene (April 5, 1868), avoiding boredom (July 9, 1865), and appropriate behavior during mourning (September 19, 1869).

La Mode Illustrée had high-quality colored plates created by the renowned illustrators Anaïs Toudouze and her sister Héloïse Leloir (see below), featuring aspirational social settings and activities (see plate 3). The black-and-white woodcuts that formed the majority of its imagery were more detailed and informative. The magazine was phenomenally successful. It was sold abroad, including in America, and was widely imitated both in France and elsewhere.

The Englishwoman's Domestic Magazine (1852–79)

Another magazine in the mold of *La Mode Illustrée* was *The Englishwoman's Domestic Magazine*, originally launched by Samuel Beeton in 1852 as a cheaper monthly at a cost of tuppence. Its main focus was the metropolitan middle-class housewife and her domestic environment, and it described itself as "An Illustrated Journal combining Practical Information, Instruction and Amusement." It offered a new vision of domestic skills as something desirable to be acquired (Beetham 1996: 66) and included a practical manual of instruction that may in turn have influenced the editorial approach of Raymond. *The Practical Dress Instructor* was the first pattern service included in a British magazine, but fashion coverage was limited to this and a black-and-white woodcut. By 1856 Beeton claimed to be selling 500 copies a month (de Ridder and Van Remoortel 2012: 25).

In 1860, Beeton launched a new edition of *The Englishwoman's Domestic Magazine*. This version was larger (8 x 5 inches), thicker (48 pages), and more fashion oriented than its predecessor, although it still included serialized fiction, recipes, and household advice. Following the lead of *La Mode Illustrée*, its mission was to make "dressing in accordance with the latest fashions easy and not too expensive" (1864: 378). Beeton experimented with modulated subscriptions for two years, selling a basic sixpenny version and a one-shilling edition with additional plates (figure 2.4), patterns, and fiction. Other economical—and popular—features in the magazine included "The Englishwoman's Exchange," a Victorian precursor to eBay where women offered garments and accessories for sale or replacement.[22]

Advertising and the impact of the department stores

Segmentation was not the only factor in the expansion of the press. Advertising was also important:

> Among the numerous collections of magazines that we had to flick through for our research, it is in the annals of the fashion magazine that we came across the most unusual advertising and examples that are of the most interest to the history of the industry. (Mermet 1879: 71)

French fashion magazines carried more advertising for the fashion industry than their counterparts elsewhere. British publications, for example, relied more on cover price and shares for income until the last quarter of the nineteenth century (Ballaster et al. 1991: 77–8), when advertising was first mixed with editorial (Beetham and Boardman 2001: 4).[23] French magazines were also more

THE FASHIONS

Expressly designed and prepared for the

Englishwoman's Domestic Magazine.

JULY 1860

FIGURE 2.4 Plate from *The Englishwoman's Domestic Magazine*. Jules David. ©
Victoria and Albert Museum, London. (Beeton bought David's plates from Goubaud in
return for publicity.)

innovative. Henri de Villemessant, founder of *La Sylphide*, perfumed the covers of the magazine with free sachets of scent from Guerlain—sachets that were given in exchange for editorial publicity (Mermet 1879: 374).

French magazines appear to have worked on a commission basis and fashion plates carefully listed details of every supplier, down to hat-pins, handkerchiefs, and lingerie. *Psyché* seems to have worked on a commission basis for Blech-Steinbach & Mantz, whose redingote dresses it advertised under its masthead. Indeed, by the 1850s the commercial exploitation of the fashion editorial had reached such a point in French magazines that *Le Moniteur de la Mode* felt obliged to issue an apology to its readers for promoting its patrons (June 1853).

This type of advertorial only became a prominent feature of the British press in the 1860s with "Spinnings in Town" in the *Englishwoman's Domestic Magazine* where "The Silkworm"—Matilda Brown—gave a shop-by-shop guide to fashionable novelties.[24] Similarly, American magazines tended to focus on direct advertising until after 1850.[25]

An increasing source of finance for the growth of fashion magazines, particularly in France, was advertising from department stores. Retailers inserted *annonces* (classified advertisements), catalogs, and store brochures into magazines in return for commission on sales or fashion plates. By 1860, most French fashion magazines had formed relationships with a few preferred retailers: *La Mode Illustrée* circulated a catalog of the seasonal fashions of Les Grands Magasins du Louvre, for example.

Department store advertising became equally important in other countries. In return, magazines served the stores with advertorial endorsements: "If our readers will refer to cuts from the Stewart establishment in New York, they will have a very good idea of some of the latest styles of robe dresses" (*Godey's*, July 1865). Department store shopping was promoted as an essential part of women's new leisured lifestyle and the culture of consumerism: "Just like a walk in the Tuileries garden, or a tour of the Bois (de Boulogne), a visit to a department store is the height of fashion" (*Moniteur de la Mode*, March 1860).

Patterns

Another French innovation that broadened access to fashion and added to the appeal of the magazines—particularly after the arrival of the sewing machine—was the dressmaking pattern (initially diagrams rather than the paper patterns we know today). By combining the aspirational fashion plate with the practical pattern, the magazines gave women the opportunity to re-create the leisured ideal. *Le Journal des Demoiselles* included pattern drafts from 1833 (Emery 2014: 21–2). After 1850, patterns became widespread in France, but patterns were still available in only one size until the invention of the graded pattern by Ellen Curtis Demorest in America in the late 1850s (Millbank 1989: 18).

Patterns were crucial in the fortunes of later nineteenth-century magazines in America, where the home sewing machine was adopted more quickly than in France (Millbank 1989: 25). *Godey's Lady's Book* included a Practical Dress Instructor from around 1855 and mail order paper patterns became the norm from the 1860s, when Demorest featured them in her magazine. Patterns were also the basis of other magazines: *The Delineator*, *The Pictorial Review*, and *McCall's* were all set up to sell their founders' patterns.[26]

Press barons, Goubaud, and *Le Moniteur de la Mode* (1843–1914)

The publishers behind the fashion magazines were overwhelmingly male. Some were speculators, but the trend was toward consolidation and monopoly as publishers exploited the commercial opportunities offered by female consumers. In France the most powerful press magnate was Adolphe Goubaud, who by 1874 owned twenty titles under the auspices of the Société des Journaux de Mode Réunis, which also included a school of dressmaking and two brochure workshops, and which employed 250 colorists, illustrators, and engravers, and six printers. Goubaud's empire, like others, was founded on reusing resources, particularly fashion plates. Goubaud created a whole series of sub-brands of *Le Moniteur de la Mode*, including the cheaper *Le Petit Echo du Moniteur de la Mode* (1879–1977) and eight foreign editions, which meant that even as early as 1856 a plate by the illustrator Jules David had a circulation of 35,000. By the 1870s the magazine styled itself "Le Journal de Mode du Monde" (Guy-Fragneaud and Vallet 2004a: 78).

Le Moniteur de la Mode began life as a glorified catalog under the title *Le Journal Spécial des Nouveautés de la Maison Popelin du Carre*. Even after it became independent in 1843, it continued to include a twice-yearly brochure of the store's latest fashions. From the first, Goubaud promoted the magazine as an artifact, prefiguring Condé Nast's vision by more than fifty years: "*Le Moniteur de la Mode* is the only fashion magazine that merits being made into an art album, as well as being a specialized fashion magazine with luxurious production values" (Gaudriault 1983: 70).

By 1869 *Le Moniteur de la Mode* was published in twenty foreign cities, including New York, St. Petersburg, and London. Later in the century, British fashion publishing was dominated by large companies with a number of titles, such as Weldon & Co. and Myra & Son. In America and elsewhere, monopolies did not emerge until the twentieth century.

Fashion plates

Much of the consumer appeal of the fashion magazines lay in their visual content. Although at the beginning of the nineteenth century plates often circulated separately from the text, they gradually became integrated into the publications. Although earlier fashion plates had credited the engraver more than the artist, magazine readers had long seen fashion illustrations as a form of art: nineteenth-century American fashion plates were torn from magazines to decorate middle-class homes (Lehuu 2000: 103). Indeed, tiered subscriptions that charged more for editions of magazines with plates encouraged the view of the fashion plate as an item of artistic merit and value. The earliest plates were hand-colored and many early illustrators were more general artists: Héloïse Leloir (Colin), for example, painted miniature portraits and illustrated popular novels (Higonnet 1992: 97).

Plates provided not only visual interest but also practical information for dressmakers and readers.[27] Their circulation increased enormously after the widespread adoption of the lithograph (Higonnet 1995). Fashion plates became a major selling point for magazines from Paris to Philadelphia and became clearly branded by publications (earlier plates did not carry the magazine's name). Fashion plates themselves became commodities. In 1854 new French laws on artistic property allowed magazine proprietors to control their illustrators' work, increasing commercial opportunities for publishing monopolies in France.

From the 1840s onward fashion illustration became a recognized profession in France, with Gavarni's plates for *La Mode* being one of the first credited examples (Gaudriault 1983: 65). The most influential illustrators included the Colin sisters, whose widely used plates helped *Le Follet* (1829–82*)* gain international success in England (1843), Germany (1848), and Italy (1851). Later their illustrations and those of their offspring, Isabelle Desgrange, graced publications such as *The Queen* in Britain and *Godey's Lady's Book* and *Harper's Bazaar* in America.[28]

French plates, as we have seen, functioned largely as a form of advertising, but they also promoted consumption as part of an idealized self, according to art historian Anne Higonnet: "Fashion prints functioned as harbingers of a self that might be constructed with the commodities they displayed" (1995: 95). From about the 1830s onward, plates depicted women in specific and aspirational social settings that linked consumption to lifestyle (see Chapter 3).

A feminine press, female journalists, and *Godey's Lady's Book*

By the middle of the nineteenth century this aspirational lifestyle, like the fashion press itself, had become exclusively aimed at women—a male fashion press was not to re-emerge until the 1920s (Breward 1995: 71)—and was a key concern of the middle-class woman. Sartorial *savoir-faire* was both a woman's duty and her expected area of expertise. Failure to learn one's fashion lessons could result in scorn and ridicule, or even marital discontent. Fashion magazines both circulated these ideas and created a role for themselves as a guide to avoiding such perils.

In France, although women were legally barred from publication, writers and editors of the fashion press were increasingly women, such as the founder of *Le Petit Courrier des Dames* Donatine Thierry, Louise d'Alq (*Les Causeries Familières*), and Emmeline Raymond (*La Mode Illustrée*), who appear to have published with legal impunity. Indeed, Raymond capitalized on her renown to publish numerous guides to housekeeping and fashion.

In America, female editors were also important to fashion magazines, including Mary Louise Booth at *Harper's Bazaar* and the first, Sarah Josepha Hale, at *Godey's Lady's Book*.

Godey's Lady's Book (1830–96)

In 1837 Philadelphia publisher Louis Godey merged his own fairly elitest magazine—a cornucopia of plagiarized articles, his own editorial, and fashion plates—with a more literary and educational journal, *The Boston Ladies Magazine*. He put Hale, the journal's founder, in charge of the new publication *Godey's Lady's Book*, beginning a partnership that was to last for forty years (figure 2.5).

A monthly publication with eighty-four pages by the 1850s, *Godey's* covered many of the same topics as magazines in Europe, including fiction, recipes, handicrafts, patterns, beauty, gardening, interior decoration, musical scores—apparently the second most popular feature after the fashion plates (Finley 1931: 254)—and fashion "Chit-Chat".

Thanks to Hale, *Godey's* was "the first avowed advocate of the holy cause of women's intellectual progress" (January 1850), championing campaigns such as rights for married women (see Finley 1931). Hale took a similarly pedagogical view on fashion. She advised readers against tight lacing—to little effect—and suggested that the engravings were not published for slavish imitation "but as a study for each reader to examine and decide how far this costume is appropriate to her figure, face, and circumstances" (ibid.: 153). Her fashion judgments were trenchant and often ironic: in February 1850 a figure is described as wearing "An indescribably ugly costume; but *new*, very new, which may throw a charm around it." While lauding the quality of French fashion, Hale also sought to engender a native American style: plates state that they are "Paris Fashions Americanized" and by 1865 there was monthly "Chit-Chat upon New York and Philadelphia Fashions."

Hale made *Godey's* less elitist and more pragmatic. She included "The Practical Dress Instructor" and later Demorest's patterns, and made economy a central

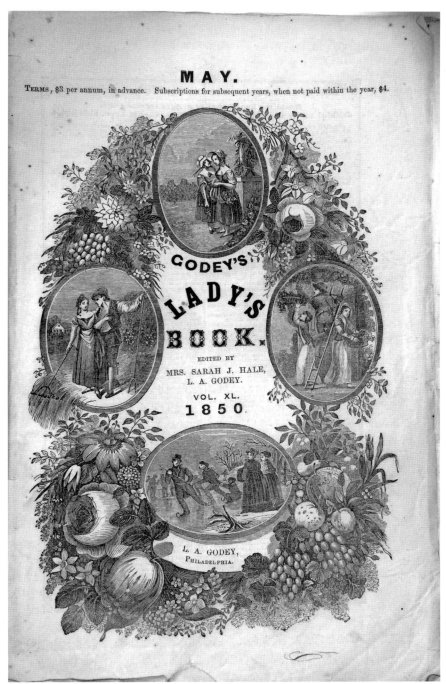

FIGURE 2.5 Cover of *Godey's Lady's Book*, May 1850. Courtesy of the Collection of Hope Greenberg. Used by permission.

component, as well as praising dressing gowns for their "comfort" and "convenience" (April 1850). She promoted clubs as a way of expanding readership—10 dollars could obtain six copies (May 1850)—and introduced a highly successful shopping service in 1852 which boasted: "Bridal wardrobes, bonnets, dresses, jewellery, cake boxes, envelopes [...] will be chosen with a view to economy as well as taste and forwarded to any part of the country."

In the latter part of the century *Godey's* was eclipsed by cheaper pattern publications, such as *McCall's*. It finally closed in 1896.

New press centers and American expansion (1875–1900)

The last quarter of the nineteenth century saw the first use of photography in a fashion magazine—*L'Art de La Mode* in 1880—and the ability to integrate images into the text rather than on plates. It also brought further expansion of the fashion press. Not only did French department stores start to produce their own magazines (Gaudriault 1983: 101), but much growth also came from outside France. The French were distracted by the Franco–Prussian War (1870–1), once more allowing the development of the fashion press in other centers. Germany was unified in 1871 and its emerging ready-made clothing industry needed press support, including Vienna-based *Die Modenwelt* (1865–1911), which was translated into fourteen languages and exported as far afield as South America, and the long-running Berlin-based *Brigitte* (1886–), originally titled *Dies Blatt Gehört der Hausfrau* ("This Newspaper Belongs to The Housewife").[29]

The latter part of the century witnessed a rapid expansion of magazines in America, where by 1880 there were at least eighteen established women's fashion titles (Seebohm 1982: 37). In part this growth mirrored the circumstances elsewhere, especially the expanding ready-made industry and department stores—*Harper's Bazaar* reported in its first issue that Americans spent $300 million annually on dry goods—but continuing emigration from Europe and the development of a significant domestic pattern industry were also key factors. New York became the major publishing and fashion center of the time.

The expansion of the American market and particularly the arrival of the mass-market women's magazines that Zuckerman calls the "Big Six"—including the more fashion-oriented *The Delineator* (later *Delineator*) and *McCall's*—were to have profound implications for the journalistic balance of power. By 1902 *The Delineator* appeared in five languages and claimed to have the largest paid subscription of any fashion magazine in the world (Zuckerman 1998: 14–15); by 1909 its publisher, Butterick, owned thirty magazines, all of which promoted its patterns (Gaudriault 1983: 124). The power of fashion publishing, like that of the fashion market, had shifted across the Atlantic. Two launches summed up this shift: the 1867 launch of *Harper's Bazar* (it changed its name to *Bazaar* in November 1929) and Arthur Baldwin Turnure's 1892 launch of *Vogue* as a weekly.

Harper's Bazaar (1867–)

Harper's Bazar, published by Harper & Brothers in New York, started as a weekly—it became monthly in 1901—and described itself as "A Repository of Fashion, Pleasure and Instruction." It was newspaper sized, cost 4 dollars for a year's subscription (10 cents for a single copy), and had black-and-white fashion woodcuts on its front cover, like *La Mode Illustrée*. Its first edition explained its role as a repository of luxury goods:

> A Bazar in Oriental parlance is not in fact a vulgar marketplace for the sale of fish, flesh and fowl, but a vast repository for all the rare and costly things of earth—silks, velvets, cashmeres, spices, perfumes and glittering gems; in a word whatever can comfort the heart and delight the eye is heaped there in bewildering profusion.
>
> Such a repository we wish *Harper's Bazar* to be, combining the useful with the beautiful and aiming to include everything that will be interesting to the family circle, for whose use it is designed. (November 1867: 2)

The magazine was, in fact, modeled on the German publication "the celebrated *Bazar* of Berlin."

Aimed at upper-middle-class "ladies," *Harper's* contained literature, art, science, gardening, society news, architecture, and "household literature," but fashion and literary works were its mainstay. The publishers aimed "to make the *Bazar* a first class weekly newspaper of fashion, the only one in existence in this country" (November 2, 1867: 2). It included patterns for clothing and "fancywork," two colored fashion plates, and seven pages of news of "Paris modes," as well as a "chronicle of the fashions most in vogue in New York, which in this respect may be styled the Paris of America" (ibid.). It adopted a new patriotic editorial tone to support the domestic industry and the American way of life: "The double skirt always popular in Paris has found a rival here in single skirts with trimmings arranged to simulate an upper skirt" ("New York Fashions," November 2, 1867: 3). In 1885, however, the magazine announced a Parisian shopping service, with none other than Emmeline Raymond of *La Mode Illustrée* as its agent (January 1885: 31).

Vogue (1892–)

Vogue's first issue appeared in New York on December 17, 1892, also priced at 10 cents. Like *Bazar*, it explained its own title—tellingly borrowed from the French—"as, a particular style of dress was then *in vogue*." Highly Eurocentric, its creator Arthur Turnure was a wealthy Manhattanite who mixed with and got investment for *Vogue* from the city's aristocracy: the renowned "Four Hundred" who could fit into Mrs. Astor's ballroom, including the Vanderbilts, the Whitneys, and of course the Astors themselves. In his introductory letter to readers Turnure promised to reflect "the ceremonial side of life" of this elite: the first cover has an illustration of a debutante. This high-society remit included an exclusive focus on European, and particularly Paris, fashion.

Vogue was divided into separate departments, as continued into the 1970s. As well as reviews of books, theater, music, and art, and articles on social etiquette "For the Hostess" and elite gatherings in "Society Snapshot," the magazine carried a number of popular fashion features: "Seen in the Shops," "Vogue Designs for the Seamstress," and "The Paris Letter." It also carried male fashion "As Seen By Him." Although it was briefly read by both sexes, by 1895 it was becoming more feminine and more fashion focused (Matthews David 2006: 24).

Vogue's illustrated covers were often by recognized artists, and from around 1900 were frequently in color. Its female editor, Josephine Redding, adopted an authoritarian stance on dress and etiquette. By 1909, when Condé Montrose Nast purchased the magazine, *Vogue* had a weekly circulation of 14,000 copies and an annual revenue of $100,000.[30]

A vector for criticism

As it expanded, fashion journalism, like fashion itself, was increasingly seen as a corrupting influence on women. It was said to encourage profligacy, for example. In 1865, M. le Procureur Général Dupin spoke against the increasing circulation of feminine fashion in a petition against prostitution: "Every woman wants to have the same outfit whoever they are" (cited in Feydeau 1866: 195–205). Dupin's conflation of fashion with a loss of virtue seems to be as much about the regulation of female sexuality as class politics. The increased circulation of novels at around the same time produced a similarly antagonistic moral response, as noted by Beetham (1996) among others. Fashion magazines began to define the parameters of consumption and femininity more tightly, but tensions existed between these ideological aims and their commercial ambitions.

Notes

1   See Perrot (1996 [1981]) in particular on this.

2   See Beetham (1996: 24–6) and Breward (1995: 72).

3   These dolls had been sent from France to the European courts since the Elizabethan era but it was in the seventeenth century that they were linked to and created by the clothing trades.

4   It changed its name several times during this period, including back to *Mercure Galant*.

5   For more on *Le Mercure* see Jones (2004: 25–39), Roche (1996 [1989]: 478–9), and Vincent (2005).

6   See Wilson (2003 [1985]: Ch. 7).

7   See Dolan (2011), Higonnet (1992: 93), and Ribeiro (2005: 18–19).

8   For more on *Gallerie des Modes* see Miller (2013: 17).

9   See Sullerot (1966), Adburgham (1972), White (1970), Shevelow (1989), and Zuckerman (1998).

10   See esp. Jones (2004: Ch. 4), and Roche (1996: Ch. 15) for more on this.

11   Much of its appeal came from the three or four hand-colored plates included in each issue, which Christopher Breward argues were much more naturalistic than those of *Le Cabinet* (2003: 118). Although Germany lacked a domestic fashion industry, it tried to stimulate demand for domestic goods and home-made clothing (Purdy 1998: 3–5) and in February 1786 even asked whether Germany should have a national dress. It also debated the value, meaning, and dangers of fashion and luxury, declaring that its approach would be *wissenschaftlich*, or "learned" (Wurst 1997: 171). The magazine was very successful, with a circulation of around 2,500 at its peak. For more on *Journal des Luxus* see Purdy (1998) and Völkel (2006: 56–68).

12   Each monthly issue contained two colored plates with descriptions in French, German, and English, and despite being expensive, the magazine had a number of foreign subscribers, including the Empress of Germany (Adburgham 1972: 205). The plates were more whimsical and sociable than those of *Le Cabinet*, but they were identifiably French, as were the fashions depicted. However, the plates were not linked to any suppliers, so were less commercial than those of *Le Cabinet*: See Adburgham (1972), White (1970), and Beetham (1996: Ch. 2).

13   German magazines, however, seem to have resisted this French domination. *Die Modenwelt* (1865–1932) favored the German *Anzug* (outfit) over the more universally accepted term "toilette," for example.

14   For a detailed history of *Le Journal des Dames et des Modes* see Anne-Marie Kleinert's 2001 monograph, *Le Journal des Dames et des Modes—ou la conquête de l'Europe féminine*.

15   For more on *La Belle Assemblée* and other contemporaneous British fashion publications see Adburgham (1972: 220–7), Beetham (1996: Ch. 2), and Ballaster et al. (1991).

16   This period witnessed the advent of mechanical fabric production with the Jacquard weaving machine in around 1831, and the launch of ready-made clothing by Pierre

Parisot at his store La Belle Jardinière in 1824. For more details on the fashion industry, see Perrot (1996, esp. Ch. 4), Coffin (1996: esp. 25–7), and Tétart-Vittu (1992).

17 Les Grands Magasins du Louvre in 1855, Printemps in 1861, Bainbridge's in Newcastle in 1838, and John Lewis in Oxford Street in 1864, for example. For more on the impact of the department store see Perrot (1996), Miller (1981), Rappaport (2001), and Howard (2015).

18 *Le Caprice* (1841–1905), *Le Petit Courrier des Dames* (1821–68), *Le Follet* (1821–2), *Le Bon Ton* (1834–84), *Psyché* (1834–54), *La Sylphide* (1840–85), and *La Mode* (1829–54).

19 *La Mode Illustrée* (1860–1937), *Le Journal des Dames et des Demoiselles* (1841–1902), *The Englishwoman's Domestic Magazine* (1852–79), and *The Queen* (1861–2006) were all launched at this time.

20 See Lehmann (2009).

21 Lehmann argues that *La Dernière Mode* "moved on to constitute fashion in the abstract" (2009: 309).

22 For more on *EDM* see Beetham (1996: Chs 5 and 6), Freeman (1977) and Hughes (2006).

23 While *La Belle Assemblée* included an advertising supplement for small space advertisements "literary, fashionable and domestic," these were often for products unrelated to fashion and bore no relationship to the editorial. Indeed, Bell conceived of the supplement as a directory of products and services akin to today's telephone directories. Similarly, *Townsend's Monthly Selection* functioned from its inception as an advertising almanac for everything from candles to "emollient almond oil soap," with ten pages of advertising in the September 1826 issue. Neither, however, used editorial or plates to advertise fashion products or retailers.

24 For more on Browne see Beetham (1996) and Rappaport (2001).

25 For more on advertising and commercialism in the French fashion press see Hahn (2009: Ch. 3).

26 See Seligman (1996), Burman (1999), and Emery (2014) for more on patterns.

27 *Le Petit Courrier des Dames* was among the first to introduce back views into its plates.

28 For more on the Colin sisters see Steele (1998: 102–11), and Gaudriault (1983: 75–8).

29 For more on *Brigitte* see Völkel (2006: 113–27).

30 For more details on early *Vogue* see Angeletti and Oliva (2006: 1–13) and Matthews David (2006: 13–25).

3 *LA PARISIENNE*: EARLY FASHIONABLE ICONS

The Parisienne isn't fashionable, she is fashion.
(ARSÈNE HOUSSAYE, *LES PARISIENNES*, VOL. IV, 1869: 286)

One sometimes wonders—this year more than others, probably—why when one arrives in Paris dressed in the latest fashion why one is not, however, dressed like the Parisiennes? The observer notes the difference without being able to pinpoint its origin.
(*L'ART ET LA MODE*, OCTOBER 26, 1889)

Introduction

By the middle of the nineteenth century, the fashion magazine had become a key part of the idealized lifestyle of the bourgeois (upper-middle-class) woman: "At 10 o'clock the ravishingly elegant woman is at home in her housecoat watering her flowers whilst unfolding her fashion magazine" (Chapus 1855: 5). In addition, fashion and a preoccupation with one's appearance had become essential elements in defining femininity: Baudelaire sees a woman's beauty as inseparable from her dress (1995 [1863]: 31) and journalist Eugène Pelletan argues, "As far as clothing, which is tantamount to exterior beauty, is concerned I do not believe that woman can dream of further progress" (1869: 12).

Appearance became a feminine type of study from which women could accrue cultural capital—"Women's detailed knowledge of dress is understood as a sort of mathematical science" (Chapus 1855: 51)—and the fashion press promoted appearance, and more particularly Paris fashion, as the acme of feminine knowledge, as did numerous etiquette manuals. From 1850 onward the fashion media inextricably linked definitions of upper-middle-class and increasingly middle-class femininity to clothing and its consumption.

The commercial icon of this fashionable femininity at home and abroad was, as art historian Tamar Garb notes, the figure of *La Parisienne*: "France's fashion industry and all its ancillary enterprises depended on the credibility of the Parisienne as a living monument to modern femininity" (1998: 87). This idealized figure was arguably the first in a series of feminine role models that have shaped fashion commentary ever since. *La Parisienne* is still an important figure in today's fashion press, particularly *Vogue Paris*, where the word *Parisienne* is used as both a noun and an adjective "to signify fashion" (Rocamora 2009a: 94). There were tensions, however, between *La Parisienne's* femininity as a fashion consumer and more domesticated views of women as economical home-makers. The contradiction between these feminine ideals was played out in fashion magazines and other parts of the women's press.[1]

Meanwhile, the "cover girl" appeared at the turn of the century, as magazine covers became a selling tool: "The face of a woman could represent both a specific type of female beauty and a 'style' that conveyed model attributes—youth innocence, sophistication, modernity, upward mobility" (Kitch 2001: 5). Although some used photographs of "celebrities," most fashion magazines used illustration to depict the new feminine ideals, creating dreams for "aesthetic imitation" (Orvell 1989, cited in Kitch 2001: 7). The impact of this multitude of commodified images of femininity, with the magazines of the "Big Six" reaching millions of readers, had an effect as dramatic as the advent of television in the 1960s, or social media, particularly Instagram, in the twenty-first century.

As we have seen, the fashion press and its feminine ideals provoked criticism from many quarters, including novelist George Sand:

> The devil entered the bedroom of the young woman in the form of the seamstress, the hairdresser, the piano teacher, the friend leaving school, the fashion magazine borrowed from the seamstress and in particular the descriptions in it of glamorous parties, duchesses and marchionesses. (Sand 1868: 74)

Similar antagonism is found in Fox Linton's diatribe against "The Girl of the Period," discussed later in this chapter.

The latter part of the century saw the emergence of other ideals of fashionable femininity, such as "The Gibson Girl," "The New Woman," and a new breed of fashion leaders from milieux such as the stage which challenged the Parisian hegemony.

Kings and courtly icons

The earliest icons of the fashionable world were part of the closed elite of the European courts, particularly in France. Even after the French Revolution, the focus of early fashion journals such as *Journal des Dames et des Modes* was still very much on "des élegantes du haut rang." Magazines in the 1830s and 1840s continued to focus on this closed aristocratic group, recognizing clothes as fashionable when they were adopted by "the best society" (Greimas 2000: 11). It was around this time that the term "bien," or "acceptable," entered fashion editorial, as did "comme il faut," which suggests both superior social standing and moral character. The meaning of fashion writing became more specialized "to allow those of the restricted circle of Saint Germain to recognize each other" (Greimas 2000: 11).

Individuals with aristocratic connections, such as Beau Brummel and Lord Byron in Britain—Brummel being an intimate of the Prince of Wales—and later Le Comte D'Orsay in France, emerged as icons of dandyism. Their style was eulogized in magazines such as *La Mode* and *Le Fashionable*, and Barbey D'Aurevilly wrote a study of them, but dandyism was not commercially exploited until the end of the nineteenth century and even then not frequently: male fashion magazines had all but disappeared.[2]

As the century progressed, new royal figures emerged in Britain and France as fashionable role models. The patronage of the British royal family became important in denoting fashionable desirability: "The Ordinances of our ABSOLUTE QUEEN are at length published, and our fair fashionables hasten to obey them. She wills that the attire of her subjects should be at once magnificent and tasteful" (*World of Fashion*, December 1832: 274, discussing Queen Mary). In 1885 the trousseau of Queen Victoria's youngest daughter, Princess Beatrice, was covered in great detail in the British and American fashion press. *Harper's Bazaar* had extensive coverage in January 1885, including of the wedding dress. However, the most influential female in matters of nineteenth-century fashion was undoubtedly Empress Eugénie of France (figure 3.1), as *The Queen* acknowledged: "I must conclude with the most dazzling beauty in the room, for the Empress is still exceedingly beautiful" (*The Queen*, January 10, 1869: 37).

Fashion magazines continued to chronicle the courtly elite, but as the fashion industry became more democratized a broader range of more commodified feminine figures emerged. Such developments did not entirely destroy the notion of fashion as a sign of social discrimination, however.

FIGURE 3.1 "Her Majesty Empress Eugénie dressed as an amazon (in riding dress)" by Jules David (Château de Compiègne). *Le Moniteur de la Mode*, Plate 358, March 1853. © Victoria and Albert Museum, London.

Paris as the center of fashion

As has already been noted, women's fashions became a recurrent theme of the propaganda of the Great Exhibitions from 1855 onward[3] and the statue that greeted visitors to the Exposition Universelle in Paris in 1900 was *La Parisienne*, dressed in a Paquin-inspired gown, with a ship, the symbol of Paris, on her head. Fashionable ladies displayed miniature bronze sculptures of this *Parisienne* in their salons after the Exhibition (Rocamora 2009a: 92).

Women's fashion became the standard bearer of France's cultural artistry as well as its national superiority:

> The prohibition of luxury fashions! That would be suicidal for France not only economically but artistically too. (*Réponse d'une femme à Monsieur Dupin*, 1865: 260)

Fashion was commercially vital to Paris, not only because of the city's department stores but also because of its many industry workers: seamstresses, milliners, embroiderers, and, following the launch of Charles Frederick Worth's business, couturiers. As Emmeline Raymond, editor of *La Mode Illustrée,* put it in 1867: "In Paris, half the female population lives off fashion, while the other half lives for fashion."

The whole physical landscape of Paris had changed in the nineteenth century, especially during Baron Haussmann's rebuilding program under Napoleon III. The city's broad new boulevards became an urban catwalk, showcasing the ever-changing fashions.[4] Paris and the new haunts of the fashionable, such as the Bois de Boulogne, Longchamp, and the new spa and beach resorts, were hailed in the fashion media as the height of fashionable culture: "The rendezvous of all celebrities, the dream-star of all young and ardent imaginations, the paradise of luxury and pleasure, the capital par excellence of the fashionable world, the queen of civilisation" (*La Corbeille*, December 1, 1854, cited in Steele 1998 [1988]: 145). Numerous guidebooks appeared which reinforced the sartorial and cultural supremacy of the city.

The mythologized status of Paris as the heart of the fashionable world is reflected in Flaubert's novel *Madame Bovary*, in which Emma fantasizes about the city's material and, to a lesser extent, cultural sophistication. Her fantasies are shaped by reading two elite fashion magazines: *La Corbeille* (1840–55) and *Le Sylphe des Salons* (1829–82):

> She devoured every single word of all the reviews of first nights, race meetings and dinner parties, took an interest in the debut of a singer, the opening of a shop. She knew the latest fashions, the addresses of the best tailors, the days to go to the Bois or the Opera. (Flaubert 2003 [1856]: 54)

As Flaubert suggests, the fashion magazines did, indeed, report on the outfits worn at fashionable rendezvous such as the Bois de Boulogne or court balls: "The reception at the Tuileries was one of the most brilliant, her Majesty the Empress had an outfit of a richness that went marvellously with the diamonds in which she was covered" (*Les Modes Parisiennes*, December 1859: 1262).

Elsewhere the press were equally focused on the fashionable Parisian world. *Townsend's Monthly Selection of Parisian Costumes* reports in February 1850 that "There have been three grand balls given in the Faubourg St Germain (that quarter of Paris inhabited by the Ancient Noblesse) at which all the aristocracy of France were assembled."

Of course, the mythologizing of Paris was as much politically as commercially motivated. The French fashion press acknowledged Napoleon's implicit support by lauding the prestige of his sumptuous court. Later, the Empress Eugénie was apparently single-handedly responsible for the shift in fashionable hair color to blonde during the mid-nineteenth century—a shift reflected not only in fashion plates but also in the numerous advertisements for hair dyes to achieve "golden tresses" and the "FASHIONABLE TINT."

Increasingly, the adjective "parisien" was used as a shorthand to suggest the desirability and fashionability of new items of clothing both in France and elsewhere. *Harper's Bazaar* acknowledges the supremacy of Paris, despite its promotion of New York fashions:

> On examining what is generally worn as well as what is in preparation, it is impossible not to recognize that Paris is still the laboratory of taste, which transforms even what it assimilates, so that outlandish fashions, that are brought from further north and south are converted by its magic touch into graceful and acceptable styles. (*Harper's Bazaar*, January 10, 1885: 31)

In September 1860, *The Englishwoman's Domestic Magazine* turned to capital letters to emphasize the desirable provenance of a "few PARISIAN DRESSES (*sic*) which have been very much admired" (237).

The vogue for all things Parisian was such that fashion retailers in London and elsewhere created false identities for themselves in an attempt to benefit from the city's status. Lois Banner notes the importance of ersatz as well as genuine Parisian identities to the early garment industry in America: "They [dressmakers] remained votaries of fashion who often assumed false identities (such as French names and backgrounds) to indoctrinate American women into an overweening concern with physical appearance and dress" (Banner 1983: 32).

By the middle of the century, a large number of new French fashion periodicals with more or less longevity had appeared with Paris or *Parisienne* in their titles. They included, for example, *La Toilette de Paris* (1849–73), *La Mode de Paris*

(1859–82), *Les Modes Parisiennes* (1843–85), as well as the satirical revue *La Vie Parisienne* (1863–1939).

La Parisienne

As part of the mythology of Paris, the figure of *La Parisienne* came to embody fashionable femininity. *La Parisienne* had signified the sophisticated follower of fashion long before the nineteenth century (Steele 1998 [1988]: 19). In the nineteenth century she featured in literature: Arsène Houssaye wrote a series of novels under the title *Les Parisiennes* and Balzac included *La Parisienne* as a character in novels such as *La Duchesse de Langeais* and *La Fille aux Yeux d'Or*. "La Parisienne" was the equivalent of the French national anthem in the first half of the century, while the figure was also a favorite subject of painters, from Impressionists such as Manet through to Americans such as John Singer Sargent.

The fashion media were quick to exploit the commercial potential of *La Parisienne* by making her a more tightly codified fashionable icon. While Gavarni's fashion plates had previously featured Parisian women, in the later plates of Jules David and the Colin sisters *La Parisienne* became the epitome of a specific elegant lifestyle (plate 3):

> With a repertoire of precise motifs (we find with less frequency an unknown race course, a Suisse chalet or a Henri II sideboard), Jules David recreates the scenes of a stylish lady's very varied life. The activities of this woman (who represents the stylish women of the world), who lives in the city in the winter, in her castle in the summer, are codified and repeated endlessly from 1850 to 1890. (Tétart-Vittu 1992: 13–14)

As *La Parisienne* became more tightly codified, her rituals of dress became more complicated and elaborate. According to *Le Moniteur de la Mode's* etiquette correspondent La Comtesse de Bassanville, elegant Parisiennes needed to change seven or eight times a day:

> A society woman who wants to be well dressed for all occasions at all times needs to make seven or eight changes of outfit a day: a morning dressing gown, a riding outfit, an elegant simple gown for lunch, a day dress for walking, an afternoon dress for visiting by carriage, a smart outfit to drive through the Bois de Boulogne, a gown for dinner and gala dress for evening or the theatre. There is nothing exaggerated about this and it could become even more complicated still at the beach in the summer, with bathing costumes, and in autumn and winter with hunting and skating costumes if she shares with men in such healthy pursuits. (De Bassanville 1859, cited in Perrot 1996 [1981]: 91–2)

This etiquette inevitably encouraged readers to buy more clothes, which in turn benefitted all elements of the fashion industry. Women were co-opted into these rituals with the promise of more renown and social standing: "A tasteful woman aided by a skilful dressmaker should never dread comparison with the fashion leaders, the variety of fashions and accessories give much scope for society advantage" (*Le Moniteur de la Mode*, August 1867: 2).

As Jennifer Craik has remarked, the disciplining of the female body in Western culture has specific moral connotations (2003 [1993]: 65). The body of *La Parisienne* became more flawless and erotic: her white skin, small hands, beautiful shoulders, delicate teeth, slim waist, flowing locks, and small feet were all regularly emphasized. Increasingly invasive advertising appeared for products that promised to correct the body that failed to fulfill the ideal: depilatories (the verb épiler first appeared in the nineteenth century), electric baths that whitened and perfumed the skin, corsets that manipulated the body's contours, slimming pills, dental creams, hair dyes, hair pieces, and unlimited creams and cosmetics. *Le Moniteur de la Mode* recommends the products of La Maison Séguy, 17 Rue de la Paix, including the "famous Pompadour cream" which it links to "women of high society" and an elite lifestyle: "It prevents the complexion from changing as the result of late nights and bright lights" (January 1868: 38).

The "famous Pompadour cream" reflects another important theme underlying the erotic desirability of *La Parisienne*. The idealized figure was more than a mere clothes horse; she also served to reinforce class and social hierarchies. The fabrics she wore, such as lace and cashmere, and the profusion of diamonds she owned were all traditional possessions of the aristocracy, passed to women as a marital gift through the *corbeille* (wedding basket) (see Hiner 2010: 45–76; Best 2007: 78–85). The *corbeille* was an important feature of the French magazines, which encouraged a groom to buy the expensive contents for his wife-to-be if he did not yet have them in his family. Not only did this again lead to further fashionable consumption, it also made both the gift and the aristocratic lifestyle it represented desirable commodities.

This aristocratic coding lies at the center of *La Parisienne*, symbolizing not only the prototype of desirable femininity but also social superiority, the notion of "bon genre" and "comme il faut." Indeed, an editorial in *Le Moniteur de la Mode* (November 25, 1852) describes "La Femme comme il Faut" in terms analogous to those used to depict *La Parisienne*. The same physical attributes—particularly white skin, small hands, and lustrous hair—define both figures (Best 2012b). However, the fashion press presented the social hierarchy as being based on buying rather than birth. *La Parisienne* became the mythical representative of this consumerist dream, even as Princess Eugénie and her circle were promoted as living representatives of the aristocratic fantasy. The reader could enter into this idealized lifestyle through the latest fashionable purchases, as promoted by *La Parisienne*. In an advertorial for the Parisian department store La Ville De

Lyon, *Le Moniteur de la Mode* links the store's gloves with the aristocracy and the Napoleonic empire: "Their Josephine glove, which is created in a specialized way and bordered with a row of waffled, cut-out dahlias, is worn by the finest aristocratic hands" (March 1861: 34).

Anxieties, distinction, and eccentricity

Just as *La Parisienne* both reinforced the elitist quality of fashionable clothing while at the same time suggesting that fashionability could be bought, anxiety grew about whether it was possible to control consumption and prevent the erosion of class distinction in a more inclusive fashion world. As Roland Barthes argues, it is the discourse of fashion itself that creates the value of the fashion object. If part of this value relates to an object's inaccessibility and mystique, then a wider availability of fashion would threaten the value of the object itself. Although much of this concern was voiced by those critical of the fashion industry, fashion magazines also started to try to limit the accessibility of the fashionable aristocratic lifestyle.

As how individuals dressed became a less reliable sign of their social standing, focus shifted to the etiquette of fashion: the manner of dressing became as important as the clothes themselves. The upmarket fashion press focused increasingly on the nebulous discriminator of "distinction" (see Bourdieu 2010 [1984]) and a complex and tautologous set of rules—as seen above—to define fashionable clothing and its wearers. As part of this, even greater emphasis was placed on fashion leaders—the Empress and other members of the European aristocracy—as custodians of sartorial knowledge. According to *Le Moniteur de la Mode*, only those most accomplished in the art of dress were included in the ideal: "We have often said in the columns of this magazine, the official mouthpiece of French fashion, that high fashion is only for the most tasteful" (August 1867: 2). Implicit in such a sentiment was that any attempt at high fashion by the aspirant middle classes would fail, thus revealing their class origins—and so conformity was encouraged.

The magazines became more constrictive in what they proposed as normal or acceptable dress. Clothes that fell outside of their rules were decried as "grotesque," "bad taste," and "excentrique." (Interestingly, "excentrique" had been a positive attribute of fashion earlier in the century but increasingly came to be used to describe the clothing of prostitutes and other women of ill repute.) In a vein similar to contemporary editorial scorn for the "fashion victim," eccentric outfits were associated with those who consumed fashion excessively or whose appearance was overly individualistic:

As for those country hats, which have a slightly irritating flirtatiousness and have been tried out by some [...] we are not aware that this eccentricity has been adopted by any one of those privileged women whose example leads in matters of fashion and good taste. (*Le Moniteur de la Mode*, September 1860: 113)

Fashion journalists themselves seem to have recognized the contradictory nature of their position, as Louise de Taillac acknowledged: "In spite of all the exaggerations of dress that I describe, readers should adopt a great simplicity in their outfits" (*Le Moniteur de la Mode*, April 1865: 124–5).

Critics were also concerned that women were using the erotic spectacle of dress to gain inappropriate attention, especially as they were supposed to be paradigmatic female trophies for their male protectors (see Veblen 2009 [1899]). In September 1869, an anonymous author named Maxine wrote a polemic against *La Parisienne* in *L'Aquarelle Mode*, in which he represented the figure as a mostly foreign feminist who usurps male control and capital with an overt sexuality that is again close to prostitution (Best 2007, 2012b). By 1893, even *La Mode Illustrée* was complaining about young women's incessant quest for notoriety and celebrity (Davray-Piekolek 1990a: 11–12). The fashion magazines themselves were in part responsible through their promotion of high-profile *Parisiennes* as fashion icons, but they nevertheless sought to undermine over-innovative or exaggerated fashions by associating them with courtesans: "Let honest women not complain if their extravagant costume exposes them to perceptions that are highly unflattering to their self-esteem" (*Le Moniteur de la Mode*, October 1865: 338).

As the century progressed, other negative figures emerged to express criticism of the modern fashionable woman, such as "The New Woman" and "The Decadent Artist." "The New Woman," along with other characters such as the "Revolting Daughter" or the "Girton Girl," were, as Beetham notes, a response to women's desires for emancipation (1996: 116).

Culture and chic

From the 1880s, tensions between maternal and erotic figures of femininity (see below) led to the creation of a new hybrid model of femininity, expressed in a somewhat redefined figure of *La Parisienne*. The French fashion press increasingly configured her as a fusion of domestic and public display whose fashionability was signified by her artistic discernment. By 1887, *Le Moniteur de la Mode* described itself as being for the mistress of the house as much as for the "femme élégante" (Tiersten 2001: 199). A new discriminator emerged in the term "chic," which was included in eight titles launched between 1883 and 1908 (Tétart-Vittu 1990: 93). This new notion was as nebulous as that of "distinction"—or indeed "taste"—but as Lisa Tiersten notes: "Fashion magazines emphasized the notion that chic was an aesthetic expression of the private individual that had little to do with money or rank" (2001: 102). In 1889, *L'Art et La Mode* allied fashionable taste with art:

The safest means for a woman to dress with distinction, is a sense of line and colour etc. For this she should ask advice from our great masters of painting whilst giving herself the opportunity to admire their masterpieces. (January 26, 1889)

The chic of *La Parisienne* now came from taste and discernment in all forms of fashionable consumption, including culture. In 1903 *La Revue de la Mode* ran a feature entitled "The Route to Happiness. The Culture of Taste" (April 18: 191) and publicity for department stores allied shopping and intellect: "Today one goes to the Louvre Department Store as one goes to the museum or an exhibition" (Falluel 1990: 75–91).

La Parisienne remained the most desirable manifestation of this ideal and became increasingly identified with the celebrity of society women who dominated the fashionable scene. This was a new incarnation of *La Parisienne*: more than fashion's muse, she created her own fashionable style. However, she was also an icon of the growing couture industry, representing the symbolic mystique and superiority of French fashion, particularly in the American market.

In the late 1880s a new magazine, *L'Art d'Être Jolie*, put photographs of contemporary society beauties on its covers; it was soon followed by *Fémina*. Increasingly, "cover girls" became the norm as magazines sought to define feminine ideals and their readers' aspirations grew: from 1901 *Harper's Bazaar* shifted from having the same cover to a new cover each month (White 2009: 56).

"The Lady"

Meanwhile, new ideals were also emerging in other countries. Although Paris remained the source of fashion and the home of couture, fashion magazines in other parts of the world were endeavoring to create new identities for their domestic markets. In late nineteenth-century Britain, Erika Rappaport points out,

> Advertising, fashion plates, fiction and editorials projected a range of femininities in addition to that of the consumer, and even that identity had many faces. They all promised readers that buying and reading leading magazines would improve their "natural" femininity. (Rappaport 2001: 111)

A key figure to emerge in the fashion press was "The Lady", in many ways the British equivalent of the leisured figure of *La Parisienne*. Idealized feminine beauty was primarily associated with blondeness (Beetham 1996: 28) and, as in France, the British ideal was originally based on a reconfigured aristocratic template. However, "The Lady", unlike *La Parisienne*, was not defined solely by her fashion sense: *The Queen* included a regular and lengthy feature on "The Housekeeper," as well as political news and lengthy discussions about employment and women's education. Indeed, "The Lady" was frequently pitted against the extravagance and eroticism of *La Parisienne* (Beetham 1996: 28).

The aristocratic figure of "The Lady" was particularly central to the identity of *The Queen*—subtitled "The Ladies Newspaper." Defining its readership as the "Upper Ten Thousand," *The Queen* included news of the court and society as well as the latest fashions "from Paris," describing clothes at the Parisian Opéra and other fashionable haunts in the column "Causerie de Paris" (Gossip from Paris). *The Queen* and "The Lady" still looked to Paris and its court for inspiration:

> I have come to the conclusion that the small French *capote* is the most popular among the Parisians who as a rule have small faces, and rarely patronise the eccentricities of attire and that it is the foreigners who adopt the Laurence, the Rembrandt, the Directoire, the Clarissa Harlowe, the Frondeuse, the Isabey, and other fantastic headgear. (January 3, 1880: 7)

The Englishwoman's Domestic Magazine also used "The Lady" as its sartorial and social ideal: "Foulard silk is so essentially ladylike, that it can never become common; ladies alone wear this fabric, which is not appreciated by vulgar minds, who imagine a robe is not rich unless it stands alone" (July 1870: 42).

Anxious to maintain class boundaries and the discriminatory power of dress, magazines also began to use "individual taste" as an arbiter in consumption: "No sensible woman in England in the nineteenth century need be a martyr to any particular fashion, as she can so easily adapt it to her own individual taste" (*The Queen* October 23, 1880: 353). The artistic and discerning nature of "The Lady" was mediated through the visual culture of the magazine, which included recent paintings and portraits alongside its many illustrations.

Like their French counterparts, the editors at *The Queen* were anxious to convey the importance of the increasingly complex rituals of costume, in which the season, the age of the wearer, and the activity helped determine the appropriate fashion, to which end an etiquette column appeared in the 1880s. There were also regular features under the title of "The Tourist" describing destinations as diverse as Biarritz and Saltburn and the appropriate attire in each case.

As a style icon, "The Lady" soon suffered from the same commercial ubiquity as *La Parisienne*. In the 1890s some department stores put portraits of aristocratic beauties in their windows, while, in publications from *Myra's Journal of Dress and Fashion* to the penny weeklies that rose to prominence at the end of the century, "The Lady" was the key figure in the promotion of fashionable clothing.

As in France, the promotion of fashionable consumption as an arbiter of status provoked anxiety and criticism. *The Englishwoman's Domestic Magazine* (EDM) complained about the democratization of fashionable clothing: "The servant-girl and her mistress step the ground in the same high-heeled boots, and try on and wear the self-same bonnets figured in Regent Street and Cranbourne Alley" (January 1873: 45). It sought to distance "The Lady" from the masses: "The lace effect is extremely rich and delicate, and will exactly suit ladies of refined taste; it will not become a favourite with the oi-polloi" (*EDM*, July 1870: 45). As in French magazines, the fashion "rules" focused on taste and moderation rather than on eccentricity: "To dress in really good taste, extremes should always be avoided, and a little moderation exercised in seeking for fashionable novelties" (*EDM*, January 1861: 190).

The mother, morality, and economical fashion

The rules of fashion were not the same for everyone, and one of the key anxieties surrounding *La Parisienne* and her later incarnations was the effect she might have on other, more domesticated ideals. As the fashion press became more segmented, it promoted different feminine ideals to suit different readerships, although such identities were not always mutually exclusive. As Simone de Beauvoir famously noted, women have long been under pressure to respond to many different and conflicting ideals.

The second half of the nineteenth century saw the proliferation of middle-class family journals such as *La Mode Illustrée*, aimed at a new, domestically oriented, maternal ideal, often referred to simply as "woman." These journals suggested that the clothing of the mother figure should be sober and restrained to reflect her moral probity (see plate 4). Outfits and fabrics were frequently described as "simple" and fabrics such as silk were rejected in favor of the cheaper and less showy *foulard* (silk mixed with wool), while lace and embroidered cashmere were to be avoided in favor of grey or brown wool, which was deemed more suitable for housework. In fact, unobtrusive colors (brown, dark purple, black, and white) and simple fabrics such as wool, velvet, linen, and plain cashmere were consistently promoted as being more suitable for "women" than more ostentatious and erotic ones, which suggests that sexuality and social distinctions were as much at stake here as practicality.[5]

There was an increased emphasis on function and practicality in dress, rather than on erotic ostentation:

The style of costume which appears to me practical for travelling is that in which all elaborate trimmings in the way of flutings and ruches are eschewed. Trimmings are liable to catch dust, very liable also to get caught in odd nails and cracks about railway platforms or steamboat decks and cabins. (*EDM*, July 1870: 34)

In a lengthy editorial warning of the dangers of old, dirty clothing and lack of propriety, Emmeline Raymond counsels that the paramount virtue of the wife and mother is to present herself "in a neat and attractive way" and that "the unkempt and unclean woman will quickly become an object of disgust and scorn no matter what other virtues she possesses." She also argues that "order" and "cleanliness" rather than erotic "elegance" should govern her readers' clothing, thus justifying fashionable purchases on the grounds of moral probity (April 5, 1868). Raymond also highlights the role of the mother in setting a good example to her children, especially her daughters. A similar stance is taken in *The Queen* (January 1874: 2), where a mother "whose dress combines economy and good taste" is contrasted with her slovenly nemesis, who neglects her children and home in favor of gadding about.

The morally upstanding figure was also a significant force in American fashion magazines. *Harper's Bazaar*, for example, also invoked propriety and cleanliness as an ideal in justifying sartorial expenditure:

> The sage has told us that the consciousness of being well-dressed imparts a greater tranquillity to the mind than the consolation of religion can afford and there is surely nothing that so completely divests the average woman of dignity and self-respect, or the capacity to do herself justice, as to be keenly alive to the hole in her elbow, the shininess of her silk, or the rustiness of her boots that the best blacking has failed to medicine; she has in this case a pertinacious [*sic*] conviction of her own unworthiness and insignificance. (January 10, 1885: 2)

The maternal icon was a figure of middle-class domestic labor, in contrast to the leisured *Parisienne*. Her cleanliness had a socio-political motive, as hygiene was a key differentiator between the middle and the working classes. Magazines promoted home dressmaking and embroidery, in particular, as salutary activities for the reader, thus marrying fashionable aspirations with domesticity.

As noted earlier, another key aspect of the domestic figure was economy, reflecting her management of the household budget, a role likened by Beeton to "the commander of an army" (Beetham 1996: 67). Magazines persistently promoted economy, both indirectly in articles devoted to refashioning old garments and trims, and directly in the recurrent use of the adjective "economical" to denote desirable clothing.

This domesticated ideal was the centerpiece of the first series (1852–60) of *The Englishwoman's Domestic Magazine* (see Beetham 1996: 62–8). It was also emphasized in *The Queen*, despite the magazine's focus on the aristocratic model of "The Lady" and its support for women's employment. Indeed, *The Queen* suggests that domesticity was considered essential to the English reader: "Homework, however, is the first and most important thing in such a nation as ours, where the home life is so jealously and rightly cherished" (January 5, 1867: 3).

In cheaper publications such as *Myra's Journal of Dress and Fashion* the feminine ideal was also a synthesis of the "useful" with the "economical" and "ladylike." The *Myra* reader was a good housekeeper with regard to her dress as well as her home and was encouraged to seek out "value." Fashions were praised not only for their beauty but overtly for their cost: "nice and cheap"; "I could not have believed without seeing them that anything half so good could have been produced at the prices charged" (May 1893: 8).

Meanwhile, both fashion articles and fiction repeatedly threatened women who failed to fulfill the domestic ideal with the specter of male rejection: "How many women can only blame themselves, their idleness, their disorder for the outcomes they find so upsetting: marital rows, unending reproaches, unhappiness, coldness, disgust and ultimately abandonment" (*La Mode Illustrée*, April 5, 1868).

Commercial tensions and the threat of the erotic

As Christopher Breward has pointed out, as the fashion press became more commercial a tension grew between "the transcendental innocence of the model wife and mother" and the more erotic ideal embodied by *La Parisienne* of "material fashionable display" (1995: 165). These anxieties reached their peak in a diatribe by Eliza Lynn Linton in *The Saturday Review* (March 14, 1868: 339–40), "The Girl of the Period." Notwithstanding the irony that she was herself a journalist on *The Queen*, Linton argued that the pursuit of fashion was turning the contemporary young woman into a French courtesan who neglected her domestic duties (see Breward 1994; Beetham 1996):

All men whose opinion is worth having, prefer the simple and genuine girl of the past, with her tender little ways and pretty bashful modesties, to this loud and rampant modernization [...] but all we can do is to wait patiently until the national madness has passed and our women have come back again to the English ideal, once the most beautiful, the most modest, the most essentially womanly in the world. (339–40)

Some magazines, such as *The Englishwoman's Domestic Magazine*, tried to bring together domestic values and practical skills with the erotic side of fashion implicit in the figure of *La Parisienne*. This hybrid model was inherently unstable, however, and its instability came to the fore in the "tight lacing" controversy and the ensuing debate in the "Conversazione" pages of the magazine.

The debate centered on the ubiquitous corset and how tightly it should be laced, particularly among young women and children. The subject was not unique to the *EDM* or even the British press: articles decrying the practice of tight lacing had appeared in the French press as early as the 1850s.[6] By 1874, however, an *EDM* editorial entitled "The Ideal Woman" suggests that the emphasis has returned to the quintessentially British "beauty of goodness." A new icon of domestic altruism brought together the moral and the fashionable: "She avoids being outré, but she does not object to being in the fashion. Her object in dress, as in all else, is to please others rather than herself" (*EDM*, February 1874: 103).

La Jeune Fille and other young ladies

The figure of *La Jeune Fille*, or marriageable young lady, was another key consumer group catered to by specific French magazines in particular (figure 3.2), most notably *Le Journal des Demoiselles*. The French magazines favored a correspondence model—usually an aunt writing to a niece—and *Le Journal des Demoiselles* featured a long-running "advice" column between Florence and her niece Juliette. Like the domesticated mother figure, *La Jeune Fille* was denied the ostentatious fabrics and accessories of *La Parisienne*—"flee the showy," advised *Le Journal des Demoiselles*—and was counseled to leave lace and diamonds "to the young wives." Her clothing should be circumscribed by modesty, chastity, and naivety: pastels and white were the favored colors, ribbons and daisies were preferred to erotic camellias, and fashion should not be a priority until its wearers are educated enough to "withstand its allurements" (*The Queen*, January 2, 1847: 2).

Central to *La Jeune Fille* was her appeal as a marriage partner, which the fashion press highlighted by devoting large amounts of editorial to wedding dresses and the *trousseau*. The latter became increasingly commodified during the nineteenth century as it moved from being something home-made to shop bought. *La Jeune Fille*'s marital eligibility was linked to her virginal status (Freud 1991 [1977]: 265), and fashion magazines counseled against eroticism and expressions of sexuality. *The Englishwoman's Domestic Magazine* urged "young ladies" to wear a chemisette under a dress whose "body does not close to the throat" (July 1860: 141). "Think less of showing a dainty foot than of conserving your health," counsels *Le Journal des Demoiselles* in January 1856, stressing the importance of a healthy body to marriage prospects. It would seem, however, that "health" here refers to the pure virginal body, as the prohibited items of dress—loose sleeves, dainty shoes—are those most commonly associated with the erotic figure of *La Parisienne*. Tight lacing was also deemed unhealthy: one "coquette" (flirtatious) *Jeune Fille* dies from having tried to achieve too slim a waist (*Le Conseiller des Dames et des Demoiselles*, March 1855).

Despite celebrating the erotic consumption of *La Parisienne* and, indeed, counseling young ladies on cosmetics and hair preparations, fashion magazines were permeated by anxiety over the corruption of young women and their

Modes
Toilettes d'Hiver.

1858.

Bureaux de l'Administration, 68, rue de Richelieu.

FIGURE 3.2 "Toilettes d'Hiver," from *Le Journal des Jeunes Personnes*. The seated figure is in bridal wear. © Victoria and Albert Museum, London.

bodies, even blaming fashionable diets for their pernicious effects on fertility. Marital rejection was once again raised as a specter: *Harper's Bazaar* argued that young women "will not be likely to risk their chances of marriage for the sake of indulging in extra show" (November 2, 1867: 2). Self-containment was required and *La Jeune Fille* is frequently advised to "content herself." There was in France, however, another threat to the virtue of a young lady who was perceived by the editorial to be less constrained and more visible: "la jeune fille américaine."

The Gibson Girl and her antecedents

Although Paris fashion was the mainstay of American magazines, it was not universally approved. Only New Yorkers wore unadulterated Parisian couture and fashion, and French fashion in particular was "like forbidden fruit" for Protestant America, which judged clothing it by its "hygiene and virtue" (Coleman 1990: 136–7). There were a number of attempts to produce an American figure of fashionable femininity. At *Godey's Lady's Book* Hale sought to create an ideal that was less consumer-driven and more radically intellectual than the European equivalent: the magazine focused on "chaste literature" and Hale was a vociferous supporter of women's education.

Despite the magazine's praise for French fashion, however, the ideal *Godey's* Lady looks to herself rather than to the French or the aristocracy for her fashion sense: white skin, small hands, and décolleté necklines are noticeably absent, reflecting in part the more modest values of the American reader. Scanlon notes that the first erotic advertisement in America did not appear until 1910—it was for Woodbury Soap—suggesting a more prudish consumer (1995: 175). Furthermore, Hale is anxious that her readers develop their own American style rather than slavishly adopting the less tasteful elements of European design. Indeed, she suggests that America has become the rubbish bin of European fashion:

> We seem willing to adopt almost any and every frippery or ornament invented by French and English milliners in order to dispose of old or antiquated materials to the "Universal Yankee nation". The refined and elegant women of Paris and London would not wear such things. (Hale, cited in Finley 1931: 152–3)

This American version of "The Lady" is "pretty" and "becoming" but also values "comfort" and "convenience." American "good taste" and "refinement" extended to home decorating and even architecture: the column "The Fine Arts Applicable to Useful Purposes" was a forerunner of the artistic discernment of the "Chic" House Manager discussed earlier.

While magazines such as *Godey's, Harper's Bazaar*, and especially *Ladies' Home Journal* began to fashion an American fashionable ideal, the most powerful fashion icon to emerge in America in the nineteenth century was created not by the fashion press but by an illustrator, Charles Dana Gibson, who allegedly based the figure on Mrs. Wallace Astor: "Between 1895 and World War I, the Gibson Girl came to dominate standards of beauty in women" (Banner 1983: 154.) The Gibson Girl represented elite society and social distinction in clothing—she was frequently pictured, like *La Parisienne*, at balls, the opera, on ocean liners, or at court—and she still fashioned herself around the prevailing Parisian form, with small corseted waist, ample bust, bustled hips, and long skirts. But she was also less formal, with her simple and practical tailored skirt and shirt. Furthermore, she reflected a new kind of youthful elite who shopped at U.S. department stores and patronized American designers rather than visiting Paris.

Where *La Parisienne* was coy, the Gibson Girl's stance and gaze were direct, suggesting her greater independence. The emphasis of the Gibson figure was again on taste, but in the arena of consumer choice and material discrimination rather than the artistic discernment of her French equivalent:

> Gibson's drawings anticipate the vast potential that the United States will contribute to the new century when he creates a national alternative to the European model of femininity and in that he celebrates the American girl who pays special attention to the quality of being young, thus preparing the ground for a dominant cultural phenomenon of the twentieth century. (Köhler 2004: 164)

The French fashion press soon responded to the threat from this new type of femininity to their hegemony and an article in *La Mode de Paris* of February 8, 1885 decries the "simplicité ruineuse" of the tailored shirtwaister and woman's suit, which it calls unpatriotic, although largely due to its English origins (Duvray-Piékolek 1990b: 45). However, by March 1898 the practicality of American fashion embodied in the Gibson Girl was grudgingly accepted by *L'Art et La Mode*: "We have borrowed the suit from American women because it simplifies everything" (March 10, 1898: 30).

The Gibson Girl quickly became the dominant fashionable marketing icon in America. In a similar vein to the French expositions, the Chicago Columbian Centennial of 1893 featured the Gibson Girl as the model of American femininity—Gibson clothing, shoes, wallpaper, and posters were all popularized (Craik 2003 [1993]: 73)—and she appeared in advertising for everything from Coca-Cola to lingerie. Such populist marketing was in sharp contrast to the increasingly elite representation of Parisian chic and haute couture.

While the mainstream women's press in America adopted the Gibson Girl—she featured frequently on the cover of *Ladies' Home Journal*, for example (figure 3.3)—she was less prominent in the more elite fashion magazines, except in advertising. *Harper's Bazaar* has only one Gibson Girl cover, for example, reflecting her populist rather than elite status. The influence of the persona, however, may be seen in the poses and activities of fashion illustrations: in 1900 *Harper's Bazaar* has a woman playing hockey on its cover (White 2009: 56), and *Vogue* covers feature various artistic interpretations of the figure, particularly for Special Fashions issues (see Winter Fashions 1901 and 1904). Editorially, *Vogue* references the Gibson Girl mostly in budget dressmaking features ("Whispers to The Girl with Nothing a Year," July 7, 1904: 23) and "Smart Fashions For Limited Incomes," reporting in May 8, 1902 under the headline "Gibson Lines Growing In Fashion" "One is obliged to report the growing success of the Gibson Lines on bodices and even on this season's new cloth jackets" (479). Later that year it simply referred to the "Gibson Waist."

Dress reform, "The New Woman", and Oscar Wilde's *The Woman's World* (1887–9)

As Martha Patterson points out, Charles Dana Gibson often used the Gibson Girl as a figure of protest—criticizing child labor, for example (2008 [2005]: 29). More generally, his creation represented a strong emancipatory desire that linked her to the more politically motivated "New Woman."[7] The New Woman was linked to increasing demands for female emancipation during the latter part of the century: while 1889 was the year of another Exposition Universelle, for example (it showcased the Eiffel Tower), it was also the year of a women's congress in Paris, *Congrès des Femmes* (Davray-Piekolek 1990a: 11–12).

Some magazines became enthusiastic supporters of calls for political freedom—*L'Art de La Mode* promoted a "divorce dress," for example (Davray-Piekolek 1990b: 40)—but the dress reform movement did not find much sympathy in the wider French press, which was busy promoting poufs, leg-of-mutton sleeves, and ornate "tapageur" styles, nor in French politics: in 1892 the Minister of the Interior limited the wearing of bloomers to cycling (Davray-Piekolek 1990b: 46).

Dress reform took hold more strongly in America and Britain. In 1851 feminists Elizabeth Cady Stanton and Amelia Bloomer started their campaign against fashionable dress and its perceived repression of women by adopting a costume of short dresses worn over baggy trousers or "bloomers". Even Sarah Josepha Hale at *Godey's Lady's Book* remained silent about bloomers, and the costume was largely unsuccessful because it was not connected to or endorsed by Paris and was never promoted in the mainstream fashion press. (In 1893,

FIGURE 3.3 "Gibson Girl," from *Ladies' Home Journal*. © The British Library Board/ HIU.A303, February cover, 1903.

however, *Vogue* did cover a tennis match in which socialite Ava Willing Astor played in bloomers [Banner 1983: 146].)

New magazines such as *Aglaia: The Journal of the Healthy and Artistic Dress Union* (1893–4) were launched to promote less constrictive clothing. As Hilary Fawcett points out, however, reformers were always in a minority (2004: 145) and most mainstream British and American fashion magazines ignored dress reform. "The New Woman," meanwhile—the name was coined by the British writer Sarah Grand in the *North American Review* in 1894—emerged only in the English-speaking press (Richardson 2004: 243). While she later became synonymous with the flapper (see Chapter 4), she initially represented the radical feminist or suffragette. "The New Woman" favored the suit and the shirtwaister, like The Gibson Girl, rather than the radical fashions of the dress reformers (Fawcett 2004: 146), but the fashion press often treated the two as being one and the same.

Perhaps the magazine that most directly addressed this "New Woman" was Oscar Wilde's *The Woman's World*. Wilde was no stranger to the world of fashion or fashion journalism. He had lectured on "dress" in the early 1880s, both at home and in the U.S., linking art with cosmetics, fashion, and home decoration, and his views were similar to those of contemporary female aesthetes whom he knew, such as Mary Eliza Haweis, who had written both *The Art of Dress* (1878) and *The Art of Beauty* (1879) (Fortunato 2007: 40).[8]

Wilde had also already contributed to fashion magazines, including *Lady's Pictorial* and *Paris Illustré*. However, when he took over editorship of *The Woman's World*—it had been in existence for six months as a "standard one-shilling middle-class monthly" (Fortunato 2007: 41), albeit featuring theoretical articles—he decided that it should be different from other fashion-focused magazines: "We should take a wider range, as well as a high standpoint, and deal not merely with what women wear, but with what they think, and what they feel" (letter to Wemyss Reid at Cassell's, cited in Fortunato 2007: 42).

Under Wilde, *The Woman's World* now described itself as "A Magazine of Fashion and Society." Wilde cut out theatrical and musical coverage, society marriages and gossip columns, and discontinued fashion coverage from Berlin and Vienna, keeping only two large reports from Paris and London, the former written by "Violette" and the latter by "Mrs. Johnstone," and both covering children's and men's fashion as well as women's. The magazine also adopted an educational and intellectual stance and contained costume and fashion history— "Muffs" (February 1889: 174); "Boots and Shoes" (April 1889: 313); "Beauty from The Historical Point of View" (June 1879: 454)—as well as sheet music, fiction, and geography. Mrs. Johnstone's "London Fashions" were prefaced with quotes from Longfellow and Shakespeare. Most radically, it promoted women's education, suffrage, and employment (Green 1997).

As editor, Wilde saw fit to comment on his own writers' fashion views as well as the general fashions of the day, and in a series of lengthy editorials promoted an individualistic style of dress that should reflect the wearer's artistic taste and refinement. Later, the magazine contained articles with titles such as "Dressing as a Duty and an Art" or "Dressing in Character": "Life in one respect is a huge fancy dress ball, a ball in which everyone [...] is dressed in harmony with his character" (July 1889: 482).

Although *The Woman's World* did not survive Wilde, the following century saw publishing collaborations which continued his theories that fashion was both art and an iconic symbol of consumer Modernism.

The Queen, meanwhile, also developed a more intellectual component to the fashionable ideal: it reported on The National Strategy for Women's Suffrage, for example. Although it did not become embroiled in the suffrage debate itself, the magazine openly supported women's access to education and entry to Oxford and Cambridge Universities (January 16, 1869: 31) and also debated new employment laws, chastising its readers:

> Ladies seem to have no conscience about the employment of milliners and dressmakers. They will say—giving an order on Friday—it does not matter how late on Saturday we have bonnets or dresses, but we must have them. Ladies are very inconsiderate. (January 9, 1869: 15)

The Queen ran a series in the 1890s promoting different types of employment for women, from typist to private detective. It also debated dress reform (October 23, 1880: 353) and acknowledged alternative fashions: "Artistic dresses are on the increase" ("London Fashions," July 3, 1880: 7). However, it did not truly embrace transvestism—a practice, as noted earlier, outlawed in France—and argued in an article of 1895 on "Rational Dress for Women" that while the "innovations in modern costume, advanced, and in some instances adopted, by that section of society popularly known as "The New Woman"" were, perhaps, acceptable for sport, "we have not yet seen or even heard of the woman who has had the temerity or bad taste, except on stage to display her attractions at a dinner party or a concert, or theatre in male evening dress" (March 16, 1895: 442).

Similar features emerged in America in *Harper's Bazaar*, which introduced "Women and The Law" in 1901 and increased coverage of women's education and careers in articles such as "The New Order of Work" (White 2009: 61–74).[9] There was also a growing emphasis upon independent female activity, particularly sports (figure 3.4). Bicycling, golf, and swimming all became part of the fashionable ideal promoted by the magazines: Condé Nast's first *Vogue* cover (June 24, 1909) has a woman dressed for fishing complete with rod.

FIGURE 3.4 *Margherita*, June 1880. "Two Women Playing Croquet." © Victoria and Albert Museum, London.

The actress

The latter part of the nineteenth century also witnessed the emergence of a new, less politicized type of feminine icon that was to form a crucial part of fashion culture and the business of haute couture. Although the fashion press did not create her as an ideal, elite magazines quickly realized the commercial potential of the actress as a purveyor of fashion's symbolic value (figure 3.5).

French fashion magazines began to reflect the growing interest in the stage as a source of trends after the middle of the century, creating hairstyles in the manner of performers such as singer Adeline Patti, but it was not until the last quarter of the century that they actively promoted actresses as fashion icons. Inspired by Mallarmé's *La Dernière Mode* and its column "Chroniques de Paris," the new "chic" style magazines reported extensively on the fashions worn by actresses such as Sarah Bernhardt and Lillie Langtry, and dancers such as Isadora Duncan (Breward 2003: 104), particularly on the "costume" designs of couturiers such as Paquin and Worth. Couturiers also recognized the promotional value of the actress, and many plays, including period pieces, were performed in contemporary couture. In the fashion press, leading illustrators such as Nada and Marie de Solar re-created the costumes as enigmatic cultural artifacts that were substantially different from the detailed technical engravings of earlier fashion illustration. *L'Art et la Mode* ran a regular feature entitled "A Travers les Theatres," which reviewed the costumes and performances of actresses alongside its profiles of leading aristocratic figures, and both types of figure appeared in the column "Chronique Mondaine." In 1898 the magazine introduced a profile of leading actresses of the day—"Portraits d'Actrices"—with photographs. The actress was often portrayed surrounded by her favorite objects, positioning her as a commodified figure with further commercial and advertising potential. With the emergence of photography, entertainers such as the dancer Cléo de Mérode, who became a cover girl, promoted everything from corsets to bicycles (Tétart-Vittu 1990: 98).

In the "Chronique" the actress was part of the more varied and arguably murky *belle époque* society that created the figure of the *Mondaine* as a leader of fashion. Although the *Mondaine* resided in Paris and was often French by birth, she became increasingly defined by the fashion media around the world as a leader of sartorial trends and the contemporary expression of *La Parisienne*.

In Britain, *The Queen*, in particular, followed its French counterparts in recording and celebrating actresses. In an issue of September 1880, we are given a detailed account of the costumes of Mrs. Florence in a play entitled *A Million*: "As in this play she is a leader of fashion, her toilettes must be examples of richness and style" (257). She wore two outfits by Worth and one from the Russian designer Muschowitz.

FIGURE 3.5 Two French Actresses. © De Agostini/The British Library Board/91016681.

The end of the nineteenth century saw an increasing focus on individuals who embodied the fashionable values of *mondainity* and chic. Many of these individuals came from the social elite or the aristocracy but many also came from the worlds of art and entertainment. They prefigured the significance of early Hollywood and later celebrity culture in promoting fashion and fashionable forms of femininity. At the same time, however, a war was approaching that would alter women's status and fashionable ideals in ways to which the supporters of "The New Woman" could only aspire.

Notes

1   See Ballaster et al. (1991), Beetham (1996), and Ferguson (1983).

2   See Wilson (2003 [1985]: 179–84), Williams (1982: 119–26), Breward (1995), and Gill (2009).

3   After the first Exhibition at Crystal Palace in 1851, there were Exhibitions in Paris in 1855, 1867, 1878, 1889, and 1900. The 1900 Exhibition spread over 550 acres and was visited by fifty million people. The French Exhibitions were much more commercial than the original British Exhibition, which had no selling prices: by 1855 articles had price tags and entry was chargeable (Williams 1982: 59).

4   See Steele (1998 [1988]) and Rocamora (2009a).

5   See Best (2007: Ch. 2) for a more detailed examination of this.

6   See Summers (2001: Ch. 3) and Beetham (1996: 75–9).

7   For a detailed examination of the development of the Gibson Girl see Patterson (2008: Ch. 1) and Kitch (2001: Ch. 2).

8   For more on Wilde's relationship with this group and his theories of consumer Modernism see McNeil and Miller (2014: Ch. 6) and Fortunato (2007: esp. Chs 3 and 4).

9   For more on "New Woman" themes in *Harper's Bazaar* at this time see White (2009) and Harris and Garvey (2004: 225–43).

4 PATRIOTISM AND COUTURE: FASHION JOURNALISM BETWEEN THE WARS

It would be a mistake to think that this horrible war had paralysed the creativity of French fashion [...] In America, in England, in Spain and in Italy we have continued to make our voice heard.

(*LA GAZETTE DU BON TON*, JUNE 1915: 15)

There is much talk of fashion leadership and of which country will gain it after the war is won. It is a vital question, for on it hangs great affairs of national and international trade, employment and standards of living.

(BRITISH *VOGUE*, MAY 1945: 34)

Introduction

The first half of the twentieth century was a period of unprecedented upheaval and social change, in part driven by the two world wars. The fashion press both mediated and promoted this "brave new world," engaging with wider social phenomena, while both conflicts were echoed by a war of words over control of the fashion industry, particularly French couture. During World War I (1914–18) the French and their allies perceived the continued promotion of French fashion as central to the war effort: "to support Paris fashion was now to uphold the principles of Western civilization" (Steele 1998 [1988]: 348). During World War

II (1939–45), control of the fashion industry was again at stake. The Germans used the occupation of France to censor the French fashion press between 1940 and 1945: *Vogue* and *Fémina*, among others, ceased publication. After Pearl Harbor, meanwhile, a parallel nationalism emerged in the fashion press in the U.S.

The fashion press also mediated social upheaval, particularly during the prosperity of the 1920s, after World War I had revolutionized women's economic and political status. Women over the age of thirty got the vote in Britain in 1918, American women in 1920. The first birth-control clinic opened in 1916. Fashion symbolized this new freedom, with shorter skirts, short hair, and the demise of the corset.[1] The "New Woman" or "Modern Woman" bought new magazines such as British *Eve* (1919), *Jardin des Modes* (1922), and *Mademoiselle* (1935). After the war, women increasingly appeared in the fields of couture, fashion journalism, and advertising. The press promoted the work of female couturiers, particularly Chanel, as symbolic of the new femininity.

This period also saw the advent of youth and celebrity in the fashion press, with the 1920s' "Bright Young Things" and the "Dames de Vogue." Slimness and sport became symbols of the new age. Many couturiers created sports clothing, and fashion editorials began to cover their creations and the fashionable ski and beach resorts where they were worn. From the 1930s onward, Hollywood stars provided a new fashion focus, and *Hollywood Patterns*, later *Glamour of Hollywood*, was launched by Condé Nast in 1932.

Fashion was closely associated with the Modernist movement in music, dance, and painting, and couture was promoted as one of the fine arts. Meanwhile, however, consumerism became more sophisticated, particularly in America, and an inherent tension emerged between fashion's artistic value and American mass manufacturing that reflected wider cultural conflicts between elite and popular culture.

As "being in fashion" increasingly covered lifestyle as well as clothing, new lifestyle magazines appeared for both men (*Adam* in 1925 and *Esquire* in 1933) and women (e.g., *Art, Goût, Beauté* in 1920), and society journals including *Tatler* and *Vogue* saw circulation rise. Coverage also increased in newspapers, particularly in America. *Women's Wear Daily* (*WWD*), launched in 1910, emerged as both a cultural and a trade oracle for the burgeoning American fashion industry.

Advertising became a professional industry. The Audit Bureau of Circulations (ABC) was created in 1914 in the U.S., and in 1931 in Britain. Given women's importance as shoppers, the economic significance of advertising revenues to fashion magazines, in particular, also increased. Fashion journalism also became more professional, with new college graduates entering the profession and the first courses for fashion journalism. Meanwhile, technological advances in printing meant that fashion photography started to replace illustration: *Vogue* spent $60,000 more on artwork than on photography in 1930 but by 1933 this figure was only $13,000 (Seebohm 1982: 187). *Vogue* published the first color cover in July 1932.

In the 1930s the Great Depression decimated couture sales. While new budget features appeared, a number of fashion magazines disappeared. In others, protectionism led to an increased focus on domestic design, particularly in the U.S. Both World Wars prompted Americans to develop both their fashion industry and their portfolio of magazines—notably those of Condé Nast and William Randolph Hearst—while imports from Paris were unavailable. Such developments were at the heart of a commercial conflict over the changing shape of the industry, particularly continued French hegemony. The growing importance of the U.S. as a clothing market, technological leader, the home of Hollywood, and publishing center was, perhaps, the most influential factor in this change.

World War I propaganda: A sartorial battle

The outbreak of war in 1914 saw a new style of reporting in the fashion press. *The Queen* covered military campaigns and featured a regular column entitled "The Country and the War," including photography (figure 4.1), as well as government recruitment for the newly formed WAAC (1916) and WRNS (1917). *Vogue* chronicled the war's effect on Europe: "The City Behind the Allies," for example, described media censorship in Paris and the disappearance of Americans belonging to the "smart set" (November 1914: 46). Charity formed an important part of magazines' war effort. American magazines focused on war relief, while in Britain *The Queen* and *Tatler* both reported on fundraising and became involved themselves—setting up dinner centers (*The Queen*) or collecting board games for servicemen (*Tatler*).

With coal and food shortages from 1916—rationing was introduced in 1918—the British press stressed the importance of economy. Paper shortages forced many fashion magazines to increase their prices, while others cut their coverage of international fashion in favor of patterns and home dressmaking. Mass-market weekly *Fashions For All* promoted this as a patriotic asset: "The woman who makes some of her own clothes, and thus saves money which can be invested in National War Bonds or War Savings Certificates, is economising in a most sensible way" (*Fashions For All*, June 1918: 3). After the U.S. entered the war in 1917, *Vogue* adapted "Smart Fashions for Limited Incomes" to "Fashions On A War Income."

Nonetheless, the appetite for fashion news remained strong. Fashion magazines provided diversion and American *Vogue*'s circulation in Britain quadrupled between 1914 and 1916. Its popularity in the trenches was said to be second only to that of the *Saturday Evening Post* (Chase and Chase 1954:

A REMINDER OF HOME.
A Little French Girl bringing the Christmas Dinner to a Sentry.

FIGURE 4.1 *The Queen*, cover, Saturday, January 2, 1915. © Victoria and Albert Museum, London/Hearst UK.

129). British *Vogue* was launched in 1916 as a response to bans on non-essential exports due to German submarine attacks. It was at first more bohemian than its American counterpart and had close links with the Bloomsbury Group. The founding editor, Dorothy Todd, eschewed fashion in favor of art and subcultural sexuality.[2] The publication was less successful than its American parent until it became more fashion focused and was published more frequently (Chase and Chase 1954: 137).

However, there was an inherent tension between the promotion of austerity and citizenship and the role of fashion magazines as shop windows for the industry:

> It is very hard on the conscientious fashion writer to feel perfectly wicked every time she spends a pound on adornment of her person! Advising other people is of course an easier matter; but it is by no means easy just now to give advice worth taking about clothes. (Mrs. Evan Nepeau, *The Queen*, April 10, 1915: 610)

The competitive threat and the promotion of French couture

Although Allied fashion magazines threw their support behind the French fashion industry, international competition over the industry and its cultural capital had started long before the war. By 1914, there were as many as seventy German and Austrian titles, many of which passed themselves off as French, such as *La Mode Parisienne* (1900–30) and *Le Chic Parisien* (1899–1938) (Gaudriault 1983: 122). These publications had been created to support the ready-to-wear industry in Berlin and Frankfurt. Meanwhile, in the U.S., *Ladies' Home Journal*, among others, was actively promoting American over Parisian fashion.[3] American magazines were already buying "Americanized" fashions created by amateur illustrators in New York and syndicated to the regional press (Schweitzer 2007: 135). By 1914, younger wealthy Americans were increasingly buying clothes from American designers and New York department stores rather than visiting the Parisian couture houses as had their mothers (Kelly 2005: 26–8); in 1913 the *New York Times* talked of "a real revolt" against Paris fashions.[4]

During that same year, *La Gazette du Bon Ton* examined the threat of foreign competition to the French industry. In March 1913, *Gazette du Bon Ton* editor Henri Bidou argued that: "Fashion is the only significant French industry in the US [...] and there are many couture houses that owe their prosperity to yankee spending sprees" (*Gazette du Bon Ton*: 177–8), but warned that German sales agents were "ensnaring" unsuspecting Americans with fake French fashion journals. The threat is already framed in warlike terms: the Germanic sales force "easily gain territory."

However, America itself does not escape criticism: "Parisian design is made more cheaply in Boston and Baltimore." Indeed, when Paul Poiret toured the U.S. during 1913, he was shocked at the number of copies of his dresses with spurious labels. On his return he founded Le Syndicat de Défense de la Grande Couture Française to counteract piracy.

With the outbreak of war, a number of French fashion magazines ceased publication (the elite *Le Journal des Dames et des Modes* and *Le Moniteur de la Mode*, as well as middle-class titles such as *La Mode Illustrée*). Many couturiers left Paris for the front—American retailer John Wanamaker found the Rue de la Paix deserted—although they soon returned. Other nations saw a chance to promote their own industries. In 1914 American *Vogue*, among others, promoted and reported the first American "fashion fête" held at the Ritz Carlton in New York in November,[5] apparently prompted by the fears of *Vogue* editor Edna Woolman Chase that French couture would not be available (Seebohm 1982: 91–2). (In fact, as early as 1912, the *New York Times* had launched a competition to design a dress and hat that would combine "patriotism, sentiment and business.") While the fête raised thousands of dollars for war relief, it upset French couturiers enough for Condé Nast to build bridges by organizing Poiret's San Francisco trip (see below) and a French fashion fête in November 1915, both of which were publicized extensively in *Vogue*.

In Germany, French terms were eliminated from the fashion discourse from July 1914 and magazines coined German replacements: *konfektion* for the French *confection* (ready-to-wear), for example. By August 1914 a committee had been formed to free women from foreign—especially French—fashion and by February 1916 there was a ban on luxury clothing and foreign cosmetics and perfumes. Various trade associations were formed to promote German design through the fashion press, and the first *Mode Woche* of German fashion in Berlin in August 1918 received extensive coverage.

As the war went on, the press named new fashions after German generals and drew inspiration from military uniforms (see *Die Elegante Welt* and *Die Dame* from 1915). The wider media depicted French fashion and its wearers as overly sexual or, more often, simply as prostitutes. Despite such propaganda, *Fashions For All* reported in January 1917 that German women had ignored government dictates and smuggled in French clothes and fashion magazines via Switzerland:

> Apparently their natural instinct overcame all patriotic feelings, or possibly Germany designs were too expressive of German "frightfulness" for sincere appreciation even by Germans. (*Fashions For All*, January 1917: 10)[6]

Meanwhile, in France, exports of couture nearly halved between 1913 and 1915, particularly to America and Britain (*Les Elégances Parisiennes*, June 1916: 40). The French government saw fashion and couture—France's largest export industry—as central to the war effort, and Paul Poiret and *La Gazette du Bon Ton* took a show to the San Francisco Exhibition in 1915 to promote French couture in America. Meanwhile French magazines explicitly linked couture and patriotism. In a special issue of *La Gazette du Bon Ton* to coincide with the 1915 Exhibition, a coquettish plate by Drian features a red, white, and blue costume entitled "La Marseilleise" (see plate 5), reinforcing the connection between fashion and French patriotism.

Two new journals were launched to promote French fashion around the world: the short-lived *Style Parisien* (July 1915 to February 1916) and *Les Elégances Parisiennes* (1916–24), which described itself as "la publication officielle des industries de la mode." Published by Hachette, it contained much of the usual material of a fashion magazine, and actively promoted the availability of the fabrics, patterns, and designs featured. Germaine Bongard, Paul Poiret's sister, also published ten issues of the journal *L'Élan* (April 1915 to December 1916), which sought to provide "propaganda for French art, French independence, in sum the true French spirit," including coverage of couture (Davis 2008 [2006]: 102).

For most of the war, the French fashion press concentrated on asserting the superiority of domestic haute couture. Although there is increasing editorial emphasis on simplicity and the replacement of lace and silk with linen and cotton, the real war is eerily absent. The annual flight to Deauville and the spas is reported on as usual. By 1916, however, there is a more direct call to arms from *Les Elégances Parisiennes*. In an editorial that asks "What should the French fashion industry do?" (June 1916: 37), the commercial conflict is couched in military terms: "All French industry must arm itself for the future conflict, a conflict which it sees will be as serious and as bitter as a real war."

While the magazine criticizes German and American copies of French designs, its main thrust is to assert the superiority of French aesthetics, particularly couture, "a superiority recognized by everyone" (June 1916: 37). According to *Les Elégances*, the Germans are furious at their inability to supplant the French dominance of fashion: "The capricious French genius will never be seen under the iron teutonic grip nor will the great couture houses succumb to the munitions of the Krupps factories" (June 1916: 37).

French taste and the unrivaled creativity of French couture were also the main theme of other magazines' propaganda. *La Gazette* justifies its return to print in July 1915 as following the lead of the "masters of fashion" who "affirmed their intention not to abdicate" but to "demonstrate to our friends on the other side of the Atlantic the persistence of our good taste." Drawing upon historical references to past conflicts, French heroism is defined by the defiant production of couture fashion: "The heroism of Paris has created a war of elegance, a permanent elegance."[7]

In spite of the fashion fête in New York, *Vogue* and *Harper's Bazaar* both embraced the fight for French couture. On October 1, 1914, *Vogue* ran an editorial entitled "Fashion Under Fire" (40–1), which argued that "the call to arms in France was veritably a Dies Irae for the dressmakers trade in Paris." Paris couture was regularly reported, and from 1917 the editorial support intensified. On November 15, 1918, the cover features a fashionable young woman holding up the saved "coeur de la France" (heart of France).

The British fashion press focused more broadly on home front propaganda rather than the domestic fashion industry. *The Queen* encouraged its readers to support British stores, but the notion of "acting in a patriotic manner" by buying domestic products was most overt in advertising rather than in editorial. However, the elite fashion press also promoted the purchase of French couture, arguing that to do otherwise would mean the death of some of France's best industries: "It is very nice for people to organise charities but charity is never so acceptable as well-paid work to the Frenchwoman" (*The Queen*, January 2, 1915: 27). After 1916, French couturiers' names featured more prominently in *The Queen*'s fashion plates, where designs had previously been anonymous, and color plates of French fashions were introduced.

The interwar years

Couture, art, and the magazine as cultural artifact

By the time of the Exposition Internationale des Arts Décoratifs et Industriels Modernes in 1925, Paris had re-established itself as the center of fashionable culture, despite fierce competition from both Berlin and New York, thanks to artists such as Picasso, writers such as F. Scott Fitzgerald, and entertainers such as Josephine Baker of the infamous Revue Nègre. Integral to the city's status was the emphasis elite magazines placed on couture designers, who from 1921 were protected by copyright as artistic creators: "I hear it said the art of dressing, nowadays, ranks among the fine arts. Some people talk of *Couture* [sic] as they would of painting and sculpture" (Baron Adolphe de Meyer, *Harper's Bazaar*, July 1928: 53).[8] Equally significant was the emergence of the elite fashion magazine as cultural artifact: "In both contexts—the high-end fashion journal and the elite maison de couture—[readers] were encouraged to appreciate the discursive construction of fashion as fine art" (Troy 2003: 79).

The first couturier to exploit the symbolism of haute couture as art commercially was Paul Poiret.[9] Poiret founded his business in 1903, at a time when Paris was a cosmopolitan cultural center of art, design, dance, and music as well as fashion, and when all these artistic milieux were creatively, socially, and commercially intertwined, as they would remain until World War II. From the outset, Poiret surrounded his couture house with artists and high culture: "I am an artist not a dress maker," he told the *New York Times* (September 21, 1913). In 1908,

Poiret became the first designer to produce his own house magazine or album: *Les Robes de Paul Poiret racontées par Paul Iribe* (Troy 2003: 162). More than catalogs, Poiret's "albums" were artistic works that showcased his designs as if they were artifacts: 300 signed and numbered copies of a second album, *Les Choses de Paul Poiret vues par Georges Lepape* (1911), were sold for 50 francs each (Troy 2003: 52–4). Prints from these albums were included in the art exhibition "Le Salon d'Automne" of 1909 and 1911, further enhancing the idea of couture as art.

While Poiret's publications added credibility to his artistic pretentions, it was the fashion press that cemented his status, particularly in the U.S. Arguably, this was the first time American fashion journalism had actively promoted a designer's work as art. The trade journal *Womens' Wear Daily*, among others, ran a feature in September 1912 entitled "Poiret Talks About His Art."

However, it was the magazine that Poiret himself established with the publisher of *Fémina*, Lucien Vogel—*La Gazette du Bon Ton* (figure 4.2)—that most clearly created a synonymy between couture and art, and established the fashion magazine as cultural artifact.

La Gazette du Bon Ton (1912–25)

Developed in part as a response to mass-market American copies, *La Gazette* was sponsored by and featured exclusive fashions from seven leading couturiers of the day: Poiret himself, Cheruit, Doeuillet, Doucet, Paquin, Redfern, and Worth. Members of Poiret's artistic coterie contributed to the journal, including luminaries of the École des Beaux-Arts such as Charles Martin, Georges Lepape, Georges Barbier, André Marty, Bernard Boutet de Monvel, and Pierre Brissaud (it was a chance encounter with the art of the latter two that prompted Vogel to create *La Gazette* in the first place).

The new journal was quite different from mainstream and middle-class magazines. Subtitled *Art, Modes & Frivolités*, it made artistic illustration its centerpiece, with ten fashion plates per monthly issue, seven of which featured the couturiers' work, the remainder being whimsical creations of the illustrators. Unashamedly elitist—an annual subscription cost 100 francs—*La Gazette du Bon Ton* "self-consciously mimicked the most elegant of its eighteenth- and early nineteenth-century predecessors" (Davis 2008 [2006]: 50). Like other such earlier magazines, *La Gazette* featured contributions on fashion from leading literary figures such as poet Henri de Régnier. It also covered art, decorative arts, society, music, and literary commentary, as well as discussions of fashion such as "In Praise of the Cape." It focused on the lifestyles of the elite and matters of taste, particularly in fashion.[10] Although there was advertising, there was no advertorial. The imagery moved fashion journalism from mere description to the evocation of mood, especially in the "creations" of the illustrators. The magazine

LE TOMBEAU DES SECRETS

ROBE D'INTÉRIEUR, DE WORTH

FIGURE 4.2 *La Gazette du Bon Ton*, "Barbier Illustration for Worth Dress," January 1, 1922. © Collection IM/Harbin-Tapador/British Library/kh190385.

explicitly configured couture as art: "The painters collaborate with the couturiers, women's clothing is a visual pleasure and certainly not inferior to the other arts" (November 1912: 3).

Its artistic ambitions were clear from the first issue: "When fashion becomes an art, a fashion gazette must itself become an arts magazine. Such a magazine is *La Gazette du Bon Ton* [...] The revue itself will be a work of art" (Editorial, Henri Bidou, November 12, 1912: 3). In positioning itself as an arts magazine and a cultural artifact, it was the hybrid precursor to today's niche fashion publications (the creators of *Visionnaire* cite it as a source of inspiration).

The idea of couture as art was echoed by the rest of the fashion press: American *Vogue* ran a piece on the artists turned fashion illustrators entitled "Beau Brummels of the Brush" (June 15, 1914: 35–7). After the war, the aesthetic values of *La Gazette du Bon Ton* began to influence others, including *Vogue* (see below), and fashion illustration achieved significant recognition as art (Barnes 1988: 16). As Seebohm points out, Vogel's artists closely reflected "more avant garde forms" and broke with the old-fashioned illustrations that Nast had also been trying to eliminate (1982: 171).

Nast's *Vogue* played a leading role in this new artistic vanguard. Its early covers, featuring the work of illustrators such as Helen Dryden and George Wolfe Plank, were arbiters of taste in America's fashionable world (Seebohm 1982: 164–5). Illustrators were credited on the contents page and reproductions of their work decorated the walls of fashionable New York restaurants, and in 1918 were also featured on paper bags sold to benefit the Red Cross (Derrick and Muir 2007: 6). During World War I Nast himself began to employ the "Beau Brummels of the Brush" and to appropriate their "avant-garde" forms as symbols of *Vogue's* modernity and, crucially, artistic integrity. The first Lepape cover appeared on October 15, 1916 in America and Britain; he went on to produce more than 100. In 1926 Nast outlined "*Vogue's* desire to promote all that is new in art" as long as it had "the intangible quality of chic" (Seebohm 1982: 180) and British *Vogue* produced a "Primer of Art" in 1938 (July 20). When Nast attempted to use Vogel's artists for fashion reportage, he found that their work was not accurate enough to appeal to his readers (ibid.: 178); but their cover art nevertheless defined *Vogue's* artistic sensibilities and brought fashion and art into the commercial mainstream.

Not to be outdone, in January 1915 *Harper's Bazaar* hired the Russian emigré Erté (Romain de Tirtoff), who had trained as a designer under Poiret, to create its covers (see plate 6). The following year, it signed an exclusive contract with him that would last for twenty-three years. Other prominent luxury magazines that were as much objects of beauty as providers of information included *Fémina, Les Feuillets D'Art* (1919–22),[11] and *Der Styl* (1920–2).

The overlapping of couture and art continued during the 1930s with the links between the Surrealist movement and designers such as Schiaparelli (see esp. Blum 2003; Baudot 2001; Martin 1989, Schiaparelli 2007 [1954]). Prominent among the

PARIS FROM

the foliated ramp of a grand staircase. Should this be considered an offence or commended as a sign of familiar love? A subtle race such as ours is capable—as has just been seen and in what an astonishing way—of defending with violence what it usually ill-treats, as certain surly lovers show little regard for those they love until the day a rival appears on the scene. . . .

Thus we, the citizens of the Palais-Royal, seem indifferent to our ornate dwellings that usage and the centuries have nibbled in all their parts. Given over to its obstinately permanent tenants and to the children and dogs of the neighborhood, our Garden, lined with its beautiful buildings, encloses only the most modest-scale rentals and lodgers. The Banque de France owns large properties hereabouts and its employees have slyly encroached upon us, but we defend ourselves in spite of our limited resources.

Above many a handsome salon, with only a ceiling between, are garrets filled with the romantic miseries of the heroes of Balzac. The hotel next door to me felt itself obliged to partition a large room with a painted ceiling which was crowded with nymphs and cupids. But it did not destroy this fresco. Thus the abundant bosoms and welcoming arms of a nude allegorical figure hang over the slumbering traveler while the remainder of her opulent anatomy terminates, hip and thigh, beyond the wall, into the next room. . . . With simplicity, we have remained among these beautiful reminders of the past. Four years of occupation have left us obstinately determined to live, turned us into the sort of community proposed by communal-minded Fourier of the last century, and never brought us, that I know of, any illicit fortune.

We were willing neither to escape nor to despair. We lived the slow life of a conquered population, determined to accord to the invader a minimum of obedience. We saw the food grow scarcer. Our quarter was near the Central Markets, a place of splendid delicacies, an inex-

• Situated in the very center of Paris, we are a sort of large poetic village that once was royal. At one of the corners of its quadrilateral enclosure, the little Théâtre de la Montpensier attempts to make us laugh. At the next corner, the actors of the Théâtre Français have the honor sometimes to make us weep.

We are a Palace. We are a Garden. Like sparrows that make their nests familiarly in the sculptured tresses of the statues, we find it altogether natural to dwell behind façades such as these.

One of the privileges of the Parisians is to feel intimate with the architectural remains of centuries of aristocracy. Even in the ancient, exhausted and durable heart of Paris —the Palais-Royal, the Cité, the Île Saint-Louis—we are still discovering, in the rear of a courtyard or behind the gape of folding doors, endless treasures of olden times adaptable to our modern life. The curls that have dropped from a carpenter's plane in some backyard may have fallen upon a statue to adorn the head of a gracious goddess, a torn bit of linen is laid to dry upon a carved stone garland, wild troops of Paris brats come sliding down

FIGURE 4.3 Colette, "Paris From My Window"," *Harper's Bazaar*, November 1944. © ADAGP, Paris and DACS, London 2016. Image courtesy of Fashion Institute of Technology/SUNY, Gladys Marcus Library, Department of Special Collections.

Colette stayed in Paris. . . . This is her first message
to America since the liberation of her beloved city.

MY WINDOW

by Colette

(Translated by Janet Flanner)

haustible source of meats, fresh vegetables, mounds of fruit—a clamorous market, as colorful as a fair of southern France, with its small wine bars where cool Beaujolais and golden Muscadet did not belie their names. We saw all the riches of our gifted soil diminish, grow dearer, then disappear. Before they vanished, substitute foods made their appearance. The time came when the weeds of the meadows took the place of our tender lettuce, white as a gardenia. Then the whiting, least savory of our sea foods, began to replace a cutlet of veal, the dogfish became edible, the toughest horned denizens of the deep passed as fish, the last butter melted away. . . . But what is to be gained by sifting such memories which are fixed forever in our minds?

One day I was reading aloud—sadistic diversion!—from a cookbook in which the old recipes streamed with butter, crackled with frying fat, emptied for the least of omelets the egg cart and the churn. "You take eight or ten eggs. . . ."

"From whom?" asked a little girl.

She was one of the children of these times, a hard and reasonable product of the war, who in her eleven years had laughed a little but never wept; a child who knew how to queue up in the food line, cook potatoes, steep a soup that contained only illusions; and who knew, like a veteran, how to manipulate the family ration card. But she could not imagine that eight or ten eggs could ever be a question of commerce, and so she gave to the verb "take" its boldest meaning.

Modesty aside, I do not hesitate to declare that we, the citizens of the Palais-Royal, conducted ourselves well all through this war that is not yet at an end. We have not whined; we have not blamed. Lacking staples and the power of purchase, we have been ingenious at "inventing" food as well as heat, for in our handsome houses one freezes beneath decorations of sculptured stone and between the great drafty windows constructed by the Revolutionary royalist , Philippe-Egalité. My hungry neighbors

have never failed to rescue and feed a lost cat or an emaciated dog. I learned all about making an economical dish called "*flognarde*" which is concocted out of three times nothing. (The first time was a failure, probably because I used only one times nothing.) My companions in misery also taught me how to contrive logs for the hearth out of old wrappings and newspapers. These, rolled very tightly and bound with wire, burn slowly, almost without flame and almost without warmth.

Above all, I learned in this noble place that a garret, in all its state of model misery, can be a crown; I learned how enforced sociability can be managed tactfully and what infinite gifts may be bestowed by nearly empty hands. No one need pity me for having lived four years between these walls without one day, one night, one hour of diversion. I chose to live the life of war. The lack of transportation, my age, an arthritis of the hip, tied me, less than my preference, to a window; it has been from there that the people of Paris, punctual in their goings and comings, dedicated to their work and privations, have set me an example.

And what a daily lesson I have had in reserve and lofty dissimulation! Wives without husbands, girls without brothers, children without fathers, thin little creatures without coats, running to workrooms without heat, to meals without meat, to a cup of coffee without sugar— and without coffee. Oh, all you "withouts" who pass by, how I know you all by heart. It would take a presence as constant as my own, an eye as sedulous as mine, to discover beneath your alert, dignified, and erect bearing any trace of disintegration, of the workings of that erosion you would be the first to deny; nor would you confess to a privation, added to all the others—today a little less bread than yesterday, tomorrow the rare ration of meat weighed by the gram, the ever-present menace to the children's health, the biting cold, blankets replaced by newspapers spread between the sheets, socks unraveled and reknit, undergarments cut (Continued on page 144)

Surrealists were the painters Salvador Dalí and Man Ray (later a photographer); collectors and socialites Charles de Noailles and Peggy Guggenheim; fashion illustrator Valentine Gross (Jean Hugo); writer and artist Jean Cocteau; composers such as Igor Stravinsky; and the designers Chanel and Schiaparelli—the latter two, of course, bitter rivals.

As part of Chanel's entourage, both Colette and Cocteau wrote regularly for fashion magazines. Colette contributed to French *Vogue* from 1922 until 1926, including reviews and commentaries on catwalk presentations (Fortassier 1988: 176). She later wrote for *Harper's Bazaar*, contributing articles from occupied Paris, "Paris From My Window" (figure 4.3). Cocteau wrote for *Vogue*, *Fémina*, and *Harper's Bazaar*, among others, often reflecting critically and philosophically upon dress (see "From Worth to Alix" in *Harper's Bazaar* of March 1937: 142, for example) and also contributed artwork. Meanwhile Surrealism influenced the fashion photography of Man Ray, Hoyningen-Heuné, Cecil Beaton, Horst, and André Durst at *Vogue*.[12]

The new journalists

The symbiosis between couture and the press extended to the journalists themselves: the English couturier Lucille, Lady Duff-Gordon, wrote fashion columns for Hearst newspapers and *Harper's Bazaar*, and the first American couturier, Mainbocher, was a former editor of *Vogue Paris*. This symbiosis was not always smooth. Chanel chose what was featured and demanded that her models not be shown on the same spread as models from competing couturiers (Seebohm 1982: 137–8). Editors did not yet have the upper hand.

In the U.S., fashion journalism was becoming more organized. The New York Fashion Group began in 1928 (it was incorporated in 1931) and included Virginia Pope of the *New York Times* and *Vogue*'s Jessica Daves, Carmel Snow, and Edna Woolman Chase. Its first offices were in the *Women's Wear Daily* building. Meanwhile the first courses in fashion journalism appeared, including at the Ray-Vogue School (now the Illinois Institute of Art) and the Tobé-Coburn School for Fashion Careers, which opened in 1937.

Fashion consultants began to provide detailed reports on the industry, including from 1927 the paradigmatic Tobé Reports. Tobé Coller Davis herself wrote seasonal syndicated fashion reports for the *New York Times* while another consultant, Amos Parrish, wrote a daily fashion column for the *New York Evening Journal* during 1929 (Pouillard 2013: 725–6).

Many of the growing number of female college graduates entered the profession. Vassar-educated Lois Long became fashion editor of the *New Yorker* in 1927 and created a wittier, more critical form of fashion reportage. A member of the New York social set, Long typified the "smart" young women who populated fashion journalism.

Fashion coverage also increased in newspapers: in 1920 a short-lived *Times Women's Supplement* appeared in Britain (Grant 1988: 8), while American newspapers appointed fashion correspondents and sent 100 reporters to the couture shows. *Vogue, Harper's Bazaar,* and American newspapers also introduced Paris correspondents, while the *New York Times'* fashion editor Virginia Pope introduced fashion photographs to American newspapers.

A new type of format emerged in fashion editorial that sought to define rather than describe the fashions from the couture houses. *Fémina* introduced interviews with leading couturiers to ascertain "the mode" for the season. As couture shows adopted a fixed format, with mannequins,[13] fashion journalists became "trend setters rather than trend followers" (White 1970: 113) (figure 4.4) and fashion magazines arbiters of all things fashionable: "We saw, we chose and we plucked the cream and only the cream of French dressmaking at its height," said *Harper's Bazaar* (September 15, 1937: 58).

In the rapid change of the new "Machine Age," fashion editorial emphasized the transitory nature of fashionable looks and magazines became anxious to identify "the new line" (*Fémina*, February 2, 1926: 7). As it had done for over a century, the fashion press capitalized on the fear that things would quickly become obsolete with the "smart set."

"The New Woman" and couture

The women who wore couture were an essential component in designers' marketing success: "Tell me what the famous forty have chosen and I will tell you what the Mode is" (*Harper's Bazaar*, June 1928: 65). This emphasis on celebrity clientele mediated broader cultural changes. A new post-war elite had emerged that combined money with youth, beauty, and the hedonistic lifestyle captured in Fitzgerald's *The Great Gatsby.* They frequented the café society and artistic milieu of Paris but also the Cote D'Azur, Deauville, and New York. The youthful elite became an object of media fascination for both society columnists and fashion magazines (Gundle 2008: 157–60). Personality also became a key part of the fashionable ideal as a means of maintaining the social distinction of couture and the elite: "You can see that it would take a personality with a capital 'P' to wear the Callot gown on the opposite page" (*Harper's Bazaar*, July 1928: 65).

This new society included the Duchesse de Noailles, the Duchess of Marlborough, Nancy Cunard, the Prince of Wales, and later Wallace Simpson, adventurers such as the aviator Amelia Earhart (the latter created her own fashion line with Molyneux), and their chronicler Cecil Beaton, who by 1930 was the official court photographer. Fashion reports focused on what such figures were wearing and which couturiers they frequented. Photography disseminated their chosen looks, often as part of their glamorous lifestyle: *Fémina* devotes several

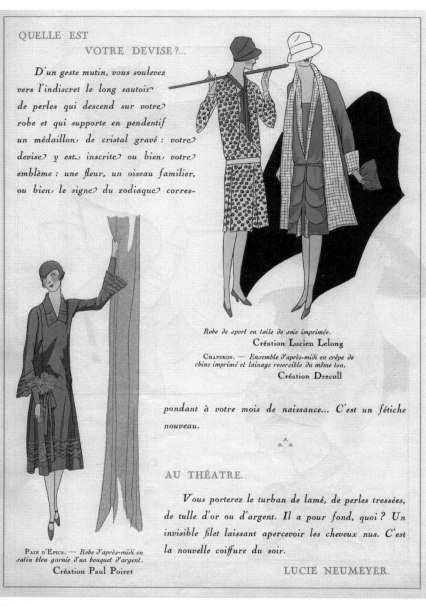

QUELLE EST
VOTRE DEVISE ?...

D'un geste mutin, vous soulevez vers l'indiscret le long sautoir de perles qui descend sur votre robe et qui supporte en pendentif un médaillon de cristal gravé : votre devise y est inscrite ou bien votre emblème : une fleur, un oiseau familier, ou bien le signe du zodiaque corres-

Robe de sport en toile de soie imprimée.
Création Lucien Lelong
CHAPERON. — Ensemble d'après-midi en crêpe de chine imprimé et lainage reversible du même ton.
Création Drecoll

pondant à votre mois de naissance... C'est un fétiche nouveau.

***

AU THÉATRE..

Vous porterez le turban de lamé, de perles tressées, de tulle d'or ou d'argent. Il a pour fond, quoi ? Un invisible filet laissant apercevoir les cheveux nus. C'est la nouvelle coiffure du soir.

PAIN D'EPICE. — Robe d'après-midi en satin bleu garnie d'un bouquet d'argent.
Création Paul Poiret

LUCIE NEUMEYER.

FIGURE 4.4 Fashion editorial from *Art, Goût, Beauté*, 1920s. © Florilegius/British Library Board. (The copy talks about the new craze for signature medallions and evening turbans at the theater.)

pages to the "Elégance Sportive at St Moritz" and the couturiers who have clothed the likes of La Comtesse de Santaferra for après ski (February 1926: 3–5). Fashion journalists were at the center of this new elite, including *Women's Wear Daily's* Paris correspondents Bertram and Alice Russell. Chanel was also part of the glamorous set for whom she designed, and the fashion discourse focused on her fashionable lifestyle: her home was featured in *Harper's Bazaar* in September 1937, for example. For members of this elite—aristocrats and actors alike—it became "a mark of elegance" to have a de Meyer portrait in *Vogue* (Gundle 2008: 158), and those pictured within its covers became known as the "Dames de Vogue."

Young women were at the forefront of what the British called "Bright Young Things" and the Americans "The Smart Set." As Catherine Keyser points out, fashion magazines linked "smart" to appearance, fashion, and intellect (2011: 14) and fashion copy "which does not contain either of these terms [*smart* or *smartness*] is indeed rare" (Carl Naether, *Advertising to Women*, cited in Keyser 2011: 14). Many of the new fashion journalists were themselves women—as well as those cited above, key figures included Martine Rénier of *Fémina* and Alison Settle, editor of British *Vogue*—as were the new generation of couturiers, including Coco Chanel, Madeleine Vionnet, Jeanne Lanvin, and later Elsa Schiaparelli. The fashion discourse sought to promote these designers and their work as part of the spirit of the new age, although designers such Lanvin, whose mother–daughter outfits jarred with this aesthetic, received less attention (Stewart 2008: 18–19). The elite French press was more circumspect in promoting the new femininity, retaining notions of distinction embodied in chic and elegance: "The readers of *Vogue* have taste and do not burden themselves with pretentiously modern ideas" (*Vogue Paris*, March 1925: 20).

Youth became a marketable commodity and slimness the new ideal. "It's not a question of taste or opinion, you must be slim […] because it's the very definition of modern beauty," argued French *Vogue* in November 1928 (16). Illustration, which remained dominant until the 1930s and longer in France, mediated this new femininity in boyish, elongated figures that were flat chested, stylized, and de-sexualized (Stewart 2008: 39–40).

Sport and clothing for sport—enthusiastically adopted and reinterpreted by Chanel, for example—also reinforced this youthful ideal. The British magazine *Eve* had a column entitled "Eve Plays The Game," covering skiing, golf, athletics, and tennis. American *Vogue* started a regular golfing column and pioneered motor racing with its "Motoring Notes," while *Fémina* promoted its own motor races and awards, and often featured the French female racing driver Hellé Nice and her couture wardrobe. New magazines espoused the free spirit of the age. The British publication *Eve* announced in its inaugural issue in 1919: "We are determined to let in the air—to ventilate every corner of our mansion."[14]

The influence of America

At the end of World War I, French couturiers facing rising costs needed to increase demand in the American market, by now the most important in the Western world. This meant adapting to the American consumer.[15] However, America's own fashion industry was also developing, first on Seventh Avenue and later, thanks to Hollywood, on the West Coast. The Los Angeles women's fashion industry was worth $1,205,000 in 1914; by 1935 it was worth $28,104,000 (Gundle 2008: 195).

Meanwhile Europe, and Paris in particular, came increasingly under the influence of America. A post-war influx of expatriates introduced cocktails, dances, jazz, sportswear, and cinemas. If the Europeans added fashionable style to these transatlantic fads, the U.S. was definitively the center of machine-age innovation and manufacture: aeroplanes, cars, radios, and later television.

Along with transportation and communications, the U.S. led the way in another key modernizing influence: the growth of advertising and its increasing presence in fashion magazines. National advertising revenues multiplied thirteenfold from 1900 to 1930—from $200 million to $2.6 billion (Scanlon 1995: 198). Fashion magazines benefitted, with advertising for cars and travel as well as fabrics, fashion, and beauty. Consumer spending on cosmetics in America increased from $17 million in 1914 to $141 million by 1925 (Scanlon 1995: 206). *Vogue* introduced a beauty supplement—*Vogue's Beauty Book*—to take advantage. New types of beauty columns appeared that invoked problems and gave tips to avoid them, often with advertorial for cosmetic brands. Meanwhile couture accessories became staples of both advertising and editorial: *Harper's Bazaar* had three pages of couture accessories in its January 1938 issue, for example.

The growth in advertising revenue was not without its drawbacks. It brought a new conflict between the editorial and publishing sides of the business. The Janus-head of fashion publishing was born. *Vogue* editor Edna Woolman Chase, when reminded by the advertising department that it paid her salary and that she was therefore beholden, retorted: "And you remember that what I make is all you have to sell and if it is not right both you and I will shortly be out of jobs" (Chase and Chase 1954: 90–1).

At the vanguard of this new, overtly commercial—but still glamorous—fashion press were the American publishers Condé Montrose Nast and William Randolph Hearst. US *Vogue*'s advertising revenues during the interwar period grew to $3.5 million; meanwhile those of *Harper's Bazaar* grew to $2.5 million (Zuckerman 1998: 162).

Condé Nast and *Vogue*

Condé Nast's advertising background led to his innovative focus on an elite audience in order to gain advertising from luxury brands. Nast acquired *Vogue* in

1909 and set out to make it "the consulting specialist to the woman of fashion in the matter of her clothes and personal adornment" (Seebohm 1982: 76). Sensing the advertising possibilities of a definition of fashion broader than dress alone, he moved *Vogue*'s focus beyond the Astor "four hundred" to a wider concept of the social elite—including Nast himself, whose Park Avenue dinner parties mixed showgirls with business tycoons, countesses, and jazz musicians (Angeletti and Oliva 2006: 123), and whose offices were filled with young society women. Under the editorship of Edna Woolman Chase (1914–51), Nast made *Vogue* bimonthly, increased its cover price (from 10 to 15 cents), and, although he retained patterns, introduced a number of new departments, including a Shopping Service in 1911 and a "Sale and Exchange" column, as well as specialized issues to target advertisers, including interior design and children's clothing.

Chase herself was a pragmatic Quaker who decried the inaccuracy of Nast's European "Beau Brummels of the Brush" and introduced detailed fashion writing, rigorous reporting, and specialist fashion departments. She nurtured relationships with the industry and persuaded retailers, fearful of plagiarism, to allow store credits to be included in the fashion pages. She was also responsible for the decision to publish Lee Miller's harrowing pictures of the concentration camps after World War II.[16]

Vogue's position as fashion arbiter extended beyond the elite. By the 1930s it already functioned as a trade journal and Macy's bought 100 copies a month for its employees (Seebohm 1982: 120). In a poll conducted for Mass Observation in 1939, British *Vogue* was cited by the majority as their magazine mentor in matters of fashion (Horwood 2005: 16).[17] Nast pioneered international publishing in America. With the launch of British *Vogue* (1916), *Vogue Paris* (1920), and short-lived forays into Germany (1928–9) and Spain (1918–23), *Vogue* became a bible in Europe, although both Brogue and Frogue, as they were termed at headquarters, struggled to find an initial editorial direction.[18]

Although Nast had originally eschewed fiction as too mass market, in 1935 *Vogue* merged with *Vanity Fair* and started to publish serious writing. In 1935 Nast introduced the Prix de Paris, a competition that offered young women writers a job at *Vogue Paris*: early recipients included the French novelist Colette and Jacqueline Lee Bouvier, later Kennedy.

However, it was in Nast's repackaging of the fashion magazine "as a desirable object in its own right" (Breward 2003: 123) and, in particular, his nurturing of the fashion photograph as art that his legacy is most visible. Nast scouted and signed exclusive contracts with numerous photographers and created his own *Vogue* studio in Paris in the 1920s which became a rendezvous for new artists and art photographers who would "want to see and be seen there" (Seebohm 1982: 204). The fluid boundaries between fine art and fashion in contemporary photography owe much to the magpie approach of the *Vogue* photographers of the 1920s and 1930s, themselves influenced by the Parisian avant-garde.

Early photographic pioneers nurtured by Nast included Man Ray, Baron Adolphe de Meyer, Edward Steichen, Beaton, and George Hoyningen-Heuné. While Surrealist Man Ray deliberately "decided to combine fashion and art" (Harsthorn and Foresta 1990: 14) (figure 4.5) on his first fashion assignment in 1922, it was painterly de Meyer who, arguably, created the modern fashion photograph by blending women and clothing into a desirable image of femininity. Meanwhile, Steichen's style was clean and direct, exploring fashion photography as a Modernist medium (Hall-Duncan 1979: 44). He created *Vogue*'s first colored photographic cover, in July 1932, drawing upon Modernist sensibilities.

By the late 1930s both *Vogue* and *Harper's Bazaar* were increasingly using photography to establish their respective artistic credentials and fashionable modernity. Nast obsessively monitored the success of illustrated versus photographic covers. This new experimentalism put fashion photography—and therefore the fashion press—in the vanguard of artistic Modernism, where it has largely remained.

FIGURE 4.5 Man Ray, "Model Wearing Vionnet Evening Gown with 'Brouette' by Oscar Dominguez." © Man Ray Trust/ADAGP, Paris and DACS, London 2016/Victoria and Albert Museum, London. (Man Ray often used Surrealist objects in his photographs and developed solarization, a technique that reversed the exposure to create dramatic effects of black and white.)

Hearst and *Harper's Bazaar*

Harper's Bazar was acquired by William Randolph Hearst in 1913 and added an extra "a" to its name in 1929. Hearst was a newspaper publisher but saw the commercial possibilities of an elite fashion publication. In 1929 he launched a British edition of the magazine and later took over the mass-market fashion magazines *Pictorial Review* and *Delineator*. Hearst also ventured into international publishing, acquiring The National Magazine Company in Britain in 1911. While Hearst continued to publish fiction, including Dorothy Parker[19] and Anita Loos, whose novel *Gentleman Prefer Blondes* "became a cultural sensation" (Keyser 2011: 63), he also sought to enhance *Bazaar*'s fashion credentials. In 1922 Hearst seduced *Vogue*'s first fashion photographer, Baron Adolphe de Meyer, to work for *Harper's Bazaar* in Paris. De Meyer also wrote a regular fashion column. In 1932 Hearst poached *Vogue*'s fashion editor Carmel Snow and made her editor-in-chief of *Bazaar*. Her departure was a major personal blow to Nast (Chase and Chase 1954: 226). In 1937 Hearst and Snow hired Alexey Brodovitch as art director. Brodovitch, whose design dictum was "surprise me," enhanced the graphic qualities and the artwork of the magazine, including publishing the iconic first action photographs by Robert Munkácsi in 1933 and creating a new sporty all-American fashion ideal in the process.

The Great Depression, Hollywood, and Nationalism

During the early years of the Depression (1929–33) couture sales faltered and fashion magazines, including *Vogue*, were badly affected by loss of advertising revenue (Chase and Chase 1954: 218). Nast lost his personal fortune on the stock market and the company was taken over in 1933 by Blue Ridge Investments. Some magazines folded, including couture-dependent British *Eve*, and others merged. For others, paradoxically, readership grew: *Harper's Bazaar* doubled its circulation between 1930 and 1940 (Sumner 2010: 75) and *Fémina* reached its peak circulation in the mid-1930s (Stewart 2008: 60). Fashion magazines, arguably, offered a diversion from economic woes, as epitomized by Snow's new fashion editor Diana Vreeland's whimsical fantasies in her "Why Don't You" column in *Harper's Bazaar*.

While elite magazines continued to promote French couture, new protectionist measures led to increased nationalism. French couturiers accused *Vogue* of promoting foreign designers and at a meeting of the Syndicat in 1938, Chanel viciously attacked the magazine (Seebohm 1982: 138). There was, undoubtedly, an increased focus on domestic design. In 1931 British *Vogue* urged its readers to "Buy British" and the London Fashion Group was created in 1932. *Harper's Bazaar* ran editions devoted to American fashion in the 1930s that were red, white, and blue, while *Vogue*'s first *Americana* edition was launched in 1938. It also inaugurated a special label—a blue-and-white celluloid tab with silver seal—for ready-to-wear American dresses that met *Vogue* standards (Mulvagh 1989: 124).

New magazines also emerged to support domestic industry. Created from *Apparel Arts*, the first trade fashion magazine in America, by two advertising men David Smart and William Weintraub, *Esquire* (1933–) sought from the first to be an elite lifestyle magazine, covering "what to eat, what to drink, what to wear, how to play, what to read" (Sumner 2010: 82). It had to work hard to promote consumerism as masculine.[20] Its styling features promoted American men's ready-to-wear (English 2013: 69–70). Circulation grew rapidly and by 1937 it stood at 675,000, largely at the expense of Nast's *Vanity Fair*. The success of a male lifestyle magazine may in part be explained by the rise of Hollywood and its leading men. Film was becoming a significant arbiter of fashion.

Early cinema had been dominated by Europeans, but the focus had moved to the West Coast after the war. In rural locations and poorer communities, Hollywood movies of the 1930s were arguably more influential than fashion magazines in determining the fashionable look. Equally influential were the fashion newsreels developed by Pathé and Gaumont, especially the *Pathé Animated Gazette*, which from 1911 showcased forthcoming fashions, frequently in color, and by the 1920s featured haute couturiers including Poiret and Lanvin (Evans 2013: 66). The feature films shown after the newsreels often showcased the same designs in a narrative context, which were given added appeal by association with the emerging stars of the Hollywood system.

While Hollywood was particularly influential in disseminating mass-market fashion (see Chapter 5), elite magazines soon capitalized on its popularity. Fashion editorials focused on which stars couturiers dressed, and photographs featured the stars in couture.[21] In the 1930s it was Hollywood stars who increasingly promoted everything from dresses to orthodontics: "Stars have Teeth Veneers," proclaimed *Harper's Bazaar* in April 1938 (122). Under the influence of Hollywood, the language of the fashion press also changed. Even elite French magazines started to employ Anglicisms to bring their copy up to date.

Glamour (1939–)

Recognizing the growing influence of the movies, in 1932 Condé Nast launched the mass-market *Hollywood Patterns* to capitalize on consumer demand for fashion and beauty information about the stars, and to support his ailing *Vogue Pattern* business. The new publication claimed to serve "the average woman's daily needs" by reinterpreting Hollywood's "fashion, beauty, and charm." It was extremely successful, and in 1939 was reborn as *Glamour of Hollywood* under the editorship of Alice Thompson. A monthly, it cost 15 cents and most covers featured a Hollywood starlet.

The inaugural issue ran to 134 pages and centered almost entirely on Hollywood. Its features included stars Joan Crawford and Rosalind Russell answering the question "What is Glamour?" (40–1). "Double Features" showed how to imitate the stars' looks (46–7), while "Do's And Don'ts" advised on avoiding "the pitfalls in borrowing from the stars" (48–51). It also had two pages of black-and-white photographs of American fashions with prices and stockists (54–5). By the end of its first year it had achieved newsstand sales of 200,000 (Sumner 2010: 93).

However, the pervasive influence of Hollywood was not enthusiastically received everywhere. As World War II approached, a new kind of aggressive nationalism found its way into the pages of the fashion press, particularly in Germany and Italy.

After World War I, the German fashion press had continued its resistance to French influence but also produced negative commentary directed at America, the source of "The New Woman" and "The Flapper", both of whom were reviled by the Fascist leaders.[22] There was also renewed support for the domestic fashion industry. In its first editorial as mouthpiece for the German fashion industry, *Der Styl* conflated nationalist ideology and fashion: "We take clothing as that which it has always been, as a mirror to the character and a testimonial to the style of the nation. To cultivate it is in serious times a right and a duty" (January 1922: 1).

As early as 1922 the magazine decries the negative influence of American morals on German women, as well its mass-market consumerism, in a lengthy polemic on the decadence of Berlin society (March 1922: 91). As Nazi ideology became more prevalent, the link between corrupting foreign fashion and America, especially Hollywood, became more pronounced.

World War II propaganda

Following the declaration of war in September 1939, things continued as normal in Paris and the Paris collections were shown in spring 1940. Couture, as during World War I, was a vital source of foreign currency and a key employer: 2,000 women and 500 men worked in Paris couture (Veillon 2002: 169). The fashion press, as elsewhere, encouraged purchasing as a patriotic duty (see plate 7). According to Lucien François, editor of *Votre Beauté*, the main role of *La Parisienne* in wartime was to remain a coquette. On May 14, 1940, however, the Germans broke through the Maginot Line and a mass exodus from Paris ensued. Woolman Chase describes how the staff of *Vogue Paris* left for Bordeaux, where the editor, Michel de Brunhoff, had presciently set up an office (Chase and Chase 1954: 281–2).

The German occupation of Paris in June brought many changes to the fashion industry and press. The Germans were anxious to appropriate the prestigious couture business, but Lelong resisted their attempts to move haute couture to Berlin. Many designers such as Chanel, shut their houses, others like Lanvin relocated to Biarritz or, like Molyneux, moved elsewhere.[23] For those who remained in Paris, it was a constant battle to maintain sales. In spring 1941, the couture collections were publicized in subsidized articles in the fashion press and newspapers both at home and abroad.

The Nazi occupiers meanwhile saw the fashion press as a means to gain control of the industry. As in World War I, the Germans published ersatz French fashion publications such as *La Femme Elégante* and *Mode Idéale*, which were printed in Vienna but distributed in France and featured German fashion or plagiarized French designs.

Meanwhile the Germans also created as many obstacles as possible for the French fashion journals. They limited the number of publications, and magazines had to be approved by the censor. Many refused—*Vogue Paris* rejected demands for pro-Nazi propaganda and editorial control, and ceased publication (Chase and Chase 1954: 284–5)—or resisted. The first permit was obtained by the long-established *L'Art et La Mode*, on condition of printing captions in German. The editor argued that they should also appear in French and English, due to her large overseas readership (Veillon 2004: 95). Meanwhile, *Marie Claire* relocated in 1940 to Lyons in Vichy France.[24]

The Nazi occupiers also tried taking a financial stake in French publications as a way to both control and profit from fashion publishing. The largest circulation fashion magazines—*Modes et Travaux* and *Le Petit Echo de la Mode*—were able to resist. In February 1943 Lelong was told that haute couture could no longer publicize itself; later that year, further restrictions forced many more magazines to close.

Throughout the war, many fashion journalists felt it incumbent to promote patriotic purchasing of luxury fashion and couture. From October 1940, after a grand gala at the Opéra, life in the upper echelons of Parisian society resumed much of its normal rhythm, albeit with German attendance, and the clothes of society personalities were recorded and promoted in the elite fashion press: *L'Officiel de la Couture et de la Mode* ran the column "As Seen at The Races" throughout 1941 and 1942.

Meanwhile in Vichy France, the fashion press promoted a new, more domesticated model of femininity (Veillon 2004 Ch.8). New vehicles appeared such as *La Plus Belle Femme du Monde*, another offshoot of *Votre Beauté*. These magazines were more mass market than the elite Paris-focused journals but also more subservient to Nazi ideology. They often adopted an aggressively nationalistic and anti-American tone that praised simplicity, modesty, and France's agricultural heritage in a discourse that echoed the German fashion press: *La Femme Chic* praised new, less flesh-revealing styles as "truly French" and for "not trying to emulate trans-Atlantic style," for example (July 1941).

Fascism and Fatherland: Germany and Italy

Die Dame (1911–43) and *Elegante Welt* (1912–62) were part of the new fashion press that grew up in Germany after 1918: by 1933 there were more than ninety periodicals in Berlin alone (Ganeva 2011 [2008]: 51). The Ullstein publishing empire, which owned nineteen newspapers and periodicals including *Die Dame*, as well as publishing patterns, was particularly focused on promoting a cosmopolitan view of fashion and society with sophisticated graphics, photography, and writing.

As Fascism took hold in Germany, the state-sponsored press portrayed all foreign influences as negative. A Nazi-sponsored textile magazine decries the "wrong-thinking of fashion magazines" and their promotion of "this crazy mixture of races" that are not "normal, European and German" (*Reichsbetriebgemeinschaft Textil*, July 1935, cited in Guenther 2004: 151). Increasingly, the rhetoric focused on the corrupting influence of the Jews who dominated fashion. Many prominent female fashion journalists were blacklisted after the Nazis came to power in 1933: Helen Grund, of *Die Dame*, was attacked for being "totally foreign." Her career, along with those of many other Jewish fashion reporters, ended following the Jewish purge of Kristallnacht in 1938.[25] Anti-Semitism meant that the clothing industry and fashion publishing lost their major source of talent. Ullstein was Aryanized by the Nazis in 1934, for example.[26]

As well as undermining foreign influence, the fashion press promoted the superiority of German clothing and the desired ideals of femininity. The Nazi regime again purged the fashion world of its foreign vocabulary, including "haute couture," and promoted new terms such as "SA-uniform brown." Magazines aggressively promoted nationalism in fashion: *Die Dame* advertised that its *Vogue* patterns were German creations, for example (Guenther 2004: 204). German fashion was linked closely to Nazi gender ideology, and magazines promoted the maternal ideal through a fashionable figure who espoused the traditional country dirndl. Patterns for the uniforms of the BdM, or the League of German girls (figure 4.6), were also promoted in magazines and newspapers (Guenther 2004: 121). By January 1943 fashion magazines were banned in Germany due to war shortages (American *Vogue*, May 1, 1944: 125).

The Italian press began promoting the domestic fashion industry after World War I. In 1919 *Lidel* (figure 4.7) was founded to promote a sense of Italian nationhood through fashion. Its founder, Lydia D'Osio de Liguoro, promoted the idea that imported luxury goods, specifically French couture, should be banned in the economic downturn after the war. With the coming of the Fascists, this nationalism took a more aggressive, sinister turn, and in the early 1930s Mussolini created Ente Nationale della Moda (National Fashion Body) to promote Italian fashion.[27] In 1936 the ENM published a dictionary that also aimed to purge fashion discourse of any foreign terminology and to create a "uniform social body and appearance in dress" (Paulicelli 2004: 24).

Periodical, front cover from *Schritte zu schonen schreiten, Germany,*
1938. © Victoria and Albert Museum, London.

LIDEL

LETTVRE ~ ILLVSTRAZIONI ~ DISEGNI ~ ÉLEGANZE ~ LAVORO

FIGURE 4.7 *Lidel*, November 1919. De Agostini/A. Dagli Orti/Getty Images.

As in Germany, peasant costumes were promoted as fashionable in Fascist-leaning magazines such as *Bellezza*. Later pro-regime fashion magazines, including *Bellezza* and *Per Voi Signora* (previously *Moda*), argued that patronage of Italian fashion provided important revenues to support the war effort. Meanwhile, they argued that French fashions promoted unhealthy bodily ideals that damaged women's reproductive functions. Later magazines promoted Mussolini's Renaissance ideal of the "bella figura," linking it to the idea of sport and healthy reproductive bodies. As with the Nazis, athleticism and modernity vied with domesticity and maternity as the dominant feminine ideal.

Patriotism and austerity: Britain and America

The fashion press of Britain and America also engaged with the war effort and government propaganda, and the American Office of War Information created a specific magazine bureau in June 1942 (Zuckerman 1998: 193). Surprisingly, advertising expenditure grew during the war as brands sought to ally themselves with the war effort, and sales of elite magazines, in particular, also flourished, even though restrictions on paper in both Britain and America affected the fashion press. *Vogue* patterns were integrated into the magazine itself, as was the Beauty Book, but while British *Vogue* moved to monthly publication, American *Vogue* continued to publish fortnightly.

Before the U.S. entered the war in December 1941, the American fashion press made a special effort to support both Parisian couture and British resistance to Germany. *Harper's Bazaar* reported on its efforts to reach the couture shows in January 1940 and Jean Morval's photographs show couture models posing against a backdrop of sandbags. Both British and American *Vogue* reported on the capital of couture under the rubric "Paris Now," focusing somewhat incongruously on the elite in the bowels of the Ritz in silk pyjamas by Molyneux (British *Vogue*, December 1939: 38–9).

From December 1941, however, the focus of the American fashion media was primarily on the home front and domestic industry. *Vogue's* fifth *Americana* edition was the first issue following the declaration of war, its cover emblazoned with the American Eagle. Inside, the magazine promised to "help you to live and dress with taste and beauty, in spite of low-ceiling, multiple duty lives" (January 15, 1942: 95). It also included "Free Voice Of Free People," a photographic essay by Edward Steichen on American ideals, as well as "American Original Designs" and a portfolio of American landscapes (January 15, 1942). Indeed, *Vogue* was at the forefront of the new nationalistic fervor, "showing how patriotism can be smart and smartness patriotic," as Nast's obituary in *Time* magazine remarked (September 28, 1942). In December 1941, Woolman Chase spoke to the Fashion Group of New York—a speech reprinted in British *Vogue* in May 1942—arguing that the war made *Vogue* more significant than ever in enhancing women's lives.

For magazines and manufacturers alike, buying American goods was couched within the rhetoric of nationalism and the economic importance of the fashion industry: "It pays taxes, pays workers, maintains morale, and can flourish on materials the fighting forces do not need. Refusal to buy only helps to dislocate the public economy" (*Vogue*, February 1, 1942: 50).

The most significant contribution of the fashion press in both America and Britain was in making a virtue of austerity—turning necessity into fashion. Although America did not suffer the same shortages and rationing as its European allies, there were restrictions on fabric, shoes, and later corsets, girdles, and bras. As well as promoting domestic designers, the press encouraged women to embrace the new restrictions, as in *Vogue*'s "Our Ration-al Lives" issue of April 15, 1942, for example, and chastised those who used the black market to break them. Prices were introduced into fashion features and a practical column appeared, "How to Buy What You Can Buy." Even restrictions were turned into a positive in "The Fashion That L-85 Built" (L-85 was a rationing law) (*Vogue*, February 1, 1944: 59). There was, however, a paradox in this as magazines also had to support their advertisers by promoting purchasing: *Vogue*'s advertorial column, Shophound, continued throughout the war.

Fashion magazines also supported women's war work, running features on women in the services, the Red Cross, and factories. At British *Vogue*, Lesley Blanche wrote a series on "Women at War," focusing on women in the forces, which lasted the full six years of the conflict. This was another source of tension as magazines sought to reassert the importance of feminine appearance, both as an antidote to the feared masculinization by the workplace and to support their advertisers' products. Both *Vogue* and *Harper's Bazaar* showed initial resistance to trousers—"Men returning from the front would hate it," *Bazaar* declared (January 1940: 3)—and short hair.[28]

British fashion magazines had to adjust to war more quickly than their American counterparts. *Vogue*'s first cover after the declaration of war, on September 20, 1939, was red, white, and blue with the royal crest (the September 8 edition had been printed before war was declared). Inside, *Vogue* promised to "make shillings do the work of pounds in dress, personal grooming, household management, cooking and gardening" and to be a "tonic to the eye and spirit" (26).

In spite of this, the press initially resisted calls for economy and austerity in fashion. When the Chancellor asked women to spend less on clothing, the fashion press rushed to protect the industry. *Harper's Bazaar* defended:

> our individual efforts at the ultimate "Front Line"—the shop doors of this country. It is our prosaic but urgent duty to keep those shop doors swinging. There is no excuse that your uniform and "some plain clothes" are enough. (January 1940: 66–7)[29]

Nevertheless, clothing rationing was introduced on June 1, 1941. *Vogue* reassured readers that it would be "summing up elegance to 66"—the number of clothing coupons initially allowed for each citizen. The fashion press showed women how to make the most of their coupons. British *Vogue* gave clear information in its Pattern Book on the amount of fabric and therefore coupons required for each garment, for example. It also introduced the prices of items into "Smart Fashions for Limited Incomes" and other fashion editorials. By 1942 both *Vogue* and *Harper's Bazaar* were promoting a simpler, informal style of dressing as the height of fashion.

The Utility scheme, which was first introduced into Britain in November 1941, placed restrictions on the types of garments to be produced in order to make decent clothing affordable for everyone. The fashion press supported the scheme enthusiastically and promoted practical items as smart: "Utility clothes aren't standard clothes. They are standard price clothes" ("Sign of the Times," British *Vogue*, January 1942: 52–3).[30]

In order to support the industry, much fashion editorial encouraged women to continue to make an effort with their appearance. This was represented as a patriotic imperative: "We shall not forgo the basic standards of beauty care we have come to regard as more of a duty than a luxury" (British *Vogue*, August 1943: 23). As the war progressed, the editorial focus shifted to looking attractive for returning servicemen.[31]

Vogue, in particular, embraced the wartime spirit. It remained undaunted when its Pattern Office was destroyed in the Blitz in July 1941, merely announcing that its Pattern Book was temporarily suspended. As well as photographing "Britain at War" for the Ministry of Information, Cecil Beaton produced a series of articles for *Vogue* entitled "Outlook" that examined the effects of the war on the country. (In a personal demonstration of patriotic duty, Beaton donated his photographic archive to be pulped for paper.)

When the Allies arrived in Paris in 1944, they were shocked by the seeming extravagance of Frenchwomen's dress compared to the austerity at home. The fashion press was the first to justify extravagant Parisian clothing as a symbol of resistance: "frivolity" was the only way in which a French woman showed that her spirit was not broken, argued Lee Miller in *Vogue* (January 1, 1945: 71).

However, many things had changed as a result of Paris's wartime isolation. As in World War I, other countries began to assert their fashion credentials on the world stage. By February 1944, American *Vogue* was already praising American fashion as "the earmark of democracy" in contrast to the elitism of couture (54). The emergence of new centers of fashion and the growth of their fashion press would be a defining characteristic of the second half of the twentieth century. Meanwhile, the emergence of a new mass-market fashion press in the interwar period would also present new challenges to the fashion system.

Notes

1   Although as Steele points out, these changes had been proposed before the war (Steele 1998 [1988]: 247–56).

2   For more on Dorothy Todd's editorship see Reed (2006).

3   See Schweitzer (2007) for more on the campaign by Edward Bok, *Ladies' Home Journal* editor, for American fashion.

4   Caroline Evans sees similar tensions in her book on fashion shows, *The Mechanical Smile* (2013).

5   For more on this see Matthews David (2006).

6   For a detailed examination of German fashion propaganda both before and during World War I see Guenther (2004: Ch. 2).

7   For more on French fashion and propaganda during the war see Steele (1998 [1988]: Ch. 11).

8   As scholars have pointed out (Evans 2005; Troy 2003), beneath this façade was the altogether more industrialized financial backbone of couture, which revolved around the mass-market copy produced on Seventh Avenue.

9   For a detailed examination of Poiret's contribution to this symbolism and Modernism see Troy (2003: 18–80).

10 See "La Mode et Le Bon Ton" (December 1912: 91) and "La Mode et Le Bon Goût" (February 1913: 125).

11 *Les Feuillets D'Art*, which was published in French and English, was another collaboration between Nast and Vogel. Published intermittently, it covered literature and art but also included fashion illustration.

12 See Hall-Duncan (1979).

13 See Evans (2013) for a detailed examination of this phenomenon.

14 For more on *Eve* see White (1970: 93, 113, 118).

15 For more on this see Evans (2005) and Troy (2003).

16 See Chase and Chase (1954) and Seebohm (1982).

17 For more on *Vogue* during this time see Seebohm (1982), Angeletti and Oliva (2006), and Chase and Chase (1954).

18 See Seebohm (1982: Ch. 8) for a detailed discussion of this.

19 Parker was originally a caption writer for *Vogue*.

20 See Breazeale (2000).

21 The fashion influence of Hollywood was especially powerful in rural Italy, where high rates of illiteracy still existed and fashion magazines were too expensive. Costumes that appeared in *Mannequin* were reproduced for the Italian mass market and sold in department stores, for example (Paulicelli 2004: 87–9).

22 For more on the interwar German fashion press see Sharp (2004) and Ganeva (2008).

23 For more on this see Veillon (2002) and Steele (1998 [1988]: 263–74).

24 For more on this see Veillon (2002).

25   For more on Grund's fashion writing career see Ganeva 2008: 84–102).

26   For more details on this see Guenther (2004: 143–65).

27   For a detailed examination of Fascism and Italian fashion see Eugenia Paulicelli (2004).

28   For more on the masculinization of women through war work see Gordon (2005).

29   For more on this see Howell (2012: Ch. 6).

30   For a more detailed account of fashion and clothing restrictions in Britain during the war and fashion magazine propaganda see Howell (2012) and McDowell (1997).

31   For more on this see Kirkham (2005).

5 DEMOCRATIZATION: POST-WAR SEGMENTATION IN FASHION MAGAZINES

A rhetoric of fashion as democracy, as an inherent right or manufacturer's guarantee, has swept over the style world and created a new fashion public, a new fashion prose, and a whole new hierarchy of new fashion magazines.

(MARY MCCARTHY, "UP THE LADDER FROM CHARM TO VOGUE," 1980 [1950]: 177)

Introduction

If World War I produced a new fashion landscape in which Paris was increasingly threatened by other clothing centers, the growing dominance of American publishers in fashion publishing had an equally significant impact. As writer and journalist Mary McCarthy notes in the quotation opening this chapter, the new journalistic order was characterized by the "democratization" of the culture of fashion and fashion commentary. Even in France, the early post-war period saw the launch of populist weeklies or bimonthlies, such as *Dimanches de la Femme* in 1922 and *Modes et Travaux* in 1919. Together with pre-existing titles such as *Le Petit Echo de la Mode* and *La Mode Pratique*, such publications disseminated not only images of couture and its associated lifestyles but also the practical means—patterns—to imitate them.[1] Meanwhile, the fashion newsreels of Pathé and Gaumont and later couturiers such as Poiret, as well as American department store shows and to a lesser extent couturiers' mannequin tours, introduced couture to a mass public.[2]

As Cynthia White has noted, during the interwar period *Vogue* "transformed the simple desire to be well dressed into an exorbitantly expensive and time consuming profession, beyond the reach of all but the most affluent" (White 1970: 94). Meanwhile, a new type of more mass-market fashion magazine brought together fashion and "service" in the glossy packaging typical of elite magazines: *Mademoiselle, Glamour, Seventeen,* and *Charm*[3] in the U.S., and *Marie Claire* and later *Elle* in France. Beneath an aspirational veneer, these magazines provided pragmatic fashion advice on a budget:

> Taste was the real "reason why" of GLAMOUR. Because this magazine was started with the very definite idea that there should be no price tag on good taste. It has grown and flourished on the principle of bringing fundamental good taste in clothes, decoration, in reading, writing, *living* to people whose incomes may be limited, but whose taste is strictly *un*limited. (January 1949: 57)

Meanwhile, there was a blurring of the distinction between fashion and service in the monolithic "service" magazines in America, further spreading the culture of fashion. *Ladies' Home Journal* substantially increased its fashion focus and included more couture fashion in the 1930s, for example (Walker 2000: 64). It also adopted the iconography of fashion magazines, using a Steichen color photograph on its cover in July 1936 and the work of Man Ray in November 1938. At the same time, a new type of more middle- and lower-middle-class journal also began to dominate in Britain, including *Woman's Journal* (1927) (figure 5.1), *Woman and Beauty* (1930), and populist weeklies including *Woman's Own* (1931) and *Woman* (1937), which borrowed heavily from the service ethos of what Zuckerman terms the "Big Six": *Ladies' Home Journal, Pictorial Review, Good Housekeeping, Woman's Home Companion, Delineator,* and *McCall's*. While *Woman's Own* and *Woman* were not, strictly speaking, fashion magazines, fashion was a significant part of their appeal and they extended the discourse of fashion into suburbia.[4]

The new publications made an impact through their quality and sheer scale: *Seventeen* sold 400,000 copies in its first issue (Massoni 2010: 45) and by 1939 *Marie Claire* had a circulation of 900,000 (Stewart 2008: 58). Advances in printing techniques, including machine-coated paper and Goss and Hoe presses that turned out completed magazines, meant that higher quality graphic effects could be produced at lower cost. *Woman*, the first British magazine to be printed by color gravure, had a circulation of 750,000 by 1939 and was selling 3.5 million copies by the late 1950s (White 1970: 97).

Graphic effects signaled luxury as well as modernity. The new fashion magazines adopted many of the visual cues of their elite counterparts: color photographs for covers, fashion shot "on location" rather than in the studio, black-and-white photography for fashion stories rather than just illustration, clear contents pages,

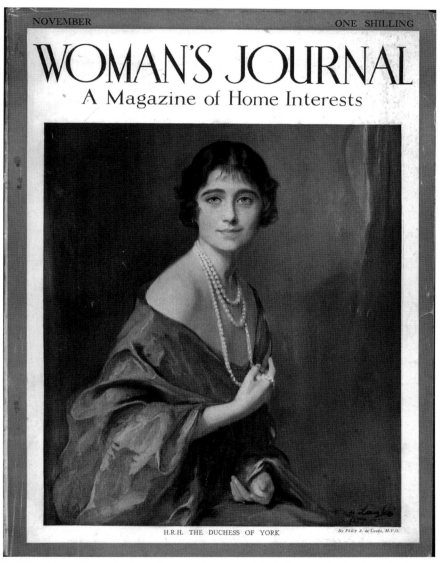

and more white space. The use of cover photographs rather than illustration led some to call *Marie Claire* "the poor woman's *Vogue*," while Nast viewed the elite *Vogue* pedigree as a crucial element in the appeal of the relaunched *Glamour*: "I believe style is as important in less expensive clothes as it is in those in the higher price level." *Glamour* itself boasted, "Published by Condé Nast publications. Publishers of *Vogue*" (Seebohm 1982: 335, 339).

The new magazines were aimed at the ever-increasing middle class, who were becoming not only better-off but also increasingly literate and well educated. Participation in higher education had quadrupled in the U.S. by the 1930s and in Britain between 1920 and 1950. There were also increased levels of employment among women, particularly in clerical and managerial positions: by 1945 18 million women worked outside the home in the U.S. (Walker 2000: 81). Editorial and advertising in the new American fashion press reflected these new working women and their symbolic modernity: *Mademoiselle* had an early careers column called "I Don't Want To Play the Harp!," while *Glamour* was relaunched in May 1941 to target "career girls."

Much of working women's newfound wealth was spent on clothing.[5] Expenditure on personal clothing more than doubled in the U.S. between 1940 and 1950, although clothes prices were falling, and by 1949 fashion was the second most important retail sector, beaten only by food (*Glamour*, January 1949: 72). Meanwhile, technological advances in clothing manufacture and the wartime development of a wide range of synthetic fabrics increased the availability of affordable clothing and created important advertising opportunities for magazines.

As noted earlier, advertising revenues had been increasingly steadily since the beginning of the twentieth century and by 1946 women's periodicals in America earned $381 million (Zuckerman 1998: 203), while agencies, including Benton and Bowles and Young and Rubicam, opened during the interwar period. Industry organizations such as the Audit Bureau of Circulation allowed advertisers and magazines to track circulation and readership more effectively, and targeting became more sophisticated.

Advertising was central to the new generation of magazines. Indeed, *Seventeen* had come into being specifically to take advantage of surplus fashion advertising during the paper rationing of World War II (Massoni 2010: 45). Using advertising to fund up to 50 percent of their publication costs, the magazines kept their cover or subscription price lower than the likes of *Vogue*—by the end of its first year *Seventeen* had an editorial-to-advertising ratio of 45/55 (Massoni 2010: 109)[6]—and promoted a growing array of consumer products. In July 1937, *Mademoiselle* included thirty-three pages of advertising in an issue of seventy-four pages but by 1948 it included 299 pages of advertising in an issue of 394. Magazines took an almost exclusively consumerist approach to their editorial, promoting branded products to solve readers' dilemmas: an article about DIY beauty treatments in *Mademoiselle*—"Elected on Looks" by Bernice Peck—was, in fact, an advertorial for courses at Richard Hudnut salons (September 1948: 203), for example.

Accessories also became increasingly significant in terms of both advertising and editorial, as they allowed women with more limited means access to the magic of couture. A dramatic increase in the number of designer perfumes was part of this trend. The first example was Chanel's No. 5, but by the mid-1930s *Fémina* contained ten advertisements for couturier perfumes, from Shocking by Schiaparelli through to Joy by Patou.

This all-pervasive "sell" characterized the new American magazines in particular, for which advertising was an ideological component of service culture. In 1929, *Ladies' Home Journal* had acknowledged the importance of advertising to the magazine and promoted its usefulness to the reader: "The advertising pages greatly enhance the value of the magazine to you. We call your attention to the helpful messages they bring to you, many of which rival even the editorial pages in 'information' and 'news'" (October 1929: 36). The new fashion magazines embraced a similar philosophy: the inaugural issue of *Marie Claire* (March 3, 1937) contains a note that the names and addresses of suppliers are given not as advertising but as useful information for the reader.

The U.S. led this new, democratized fashion press, and the publishing model and editorial format of the new magazines was shaped by the "Big Six" service journals. In particular, the new fashion titles adopted their range of editorial content, the use of experts, the interactive and intimate relationship with readers, the practical advice, and the emphasis on personal relationships in their treatment of fashion.

The democratization of the fashion press had inevitable implications for the symbolic value of fashion, which it threatened to undermine. The exuberant consumer discourse was underpinned by a desire to uphold social class. Taste re-emerged as a signifier to maintain social boundaries and the "distinction" of fashion culture. Meanwhile, the expansion of the new magazines and their influence over women provoked criticism. In the U.S. in particular, Mary McCarthy was just one of many critics who took issue with their consumerist content and regulatory discourse.

Mademoiselle (1935–2001)

Arguably, the new fashion magazine that set the blueprint for the others was Smith and Street's *Mademoiselle* (figure 5.2). Launched in 1935 as "the magazine for smart young women," it was aimed at college students and working female graduates. Known to its staff as Millie, its primary focus was fashion, but it also covered cookery, interiors, careers, relationships, entertainment, and restaurants, and published a wide range of high-quality fiction and nonfiction by

FIGURE 5.2 *Mademoiselle*, May 1,1938. Cynthia Hope, a *Mademoiselle* Cover
Contest Winner, wearing twin print ensemble in chiffon and crepe, and rough
straw Breton. Illustration by Paul D'Ome, originally published in *Mademoiselle*.
© Condé Nast.

writers, including Truman Capote, Katherine Anne Porter, and W. H. Auden. From the outset *Mademoiselle*'s approach to fashion was more prosaic than the proselytizing of its elite peers. It argued, "It's the fashion writers who cause all the trouble. They're not practical, that's what. They never stop to think that no girl likes particularly looking like a statue, nor an old-fashioned painting, nor an Abyssinian native" (October 1935: 10). *Glamour* was relaunched to compete with it and *Charm*,[7] while *Seventeen*, launched in 1944, was essentially its teenage incarnation.

The service legacy

Expertise

Service was central to the new American fashion magazines. One of the key features they borrowed from the "Big Six" was the use of experts to dispense editorial advice: *Ladies' Home Journal*'s beauty counsel came from "Hollywood's master make-up man," Percy Westmore, as did *Glamour*'s in its first issue, for example. However, Nancy Walker has detected a shift in the expertise of contributors after World War II, "from experienced homemakers and university professors to more consumerist representatives of various bureaus" (Walker 2000: 145). Specialist editors increasingly replaced the "experts": by September 1948, *Mademoiselle*'s fashion department had a fashion editor, six fashion assistants, two fashion "executaries", and a fashion copy editor. As the authority of the magazines with their readers increased, the legitimacy of the opinions of "The Fashion Editor" was assured. Other committees of so-called experts were formed from the magazines' readership, such as *Mademoiselle*'s College Board or *Glamour*'s Career Counselors, who provided market research insights for editors and advertisers alike.

As part of this expertise, magazines began to offer more targeted guides for readers' lives, such as *Mademoiselle*'s "Handbook for the Girl with a Job and a Future," which argued that "It helps you plan your job goals as well as wardrobes, budgets as well as your private life. Check your own attitudes and assets, give that phone a chance to ring" (September 1948: 277).[8] *Mademoiselle* also published a supplement on homes, "Mademoiselle's Living." Such guides, of course, also offered targeted opportunities for advertising revenues.

The custodians of magazines' expertise and cultural capital were the editors, who emerged from anonymity to become what Marjorie Ferguson describes as "high priestesses to the cult of femininity" (1983: 119).[9] The Editor's Letter became an essential feature that covered both the editorial contents and the viewpoint of the magazine, making it the key to reader identification within a publication. Elizabeth Penrose, editor of *Glamour*, took her readers to task over work ethic, for example (January 1949: 49), and in her first letter Helen Valentine, editor of *Seventeen*, proclaimed: "SEVENTEEN is interested in **how you dress.** We're not much on the tricky stuff, but we believe clothes must be right for you and the time, place and occasion for which you'll wear them" (Massoni 2010: 49).

The editors' authority came in part from their elite magazine pedigree. Elizabeth Penrose of *Glamour* had been editor of British *Vogue* from 1936 to 1939, for example, while *Woman*'s first issue argued that its fashion editor, Alison Settle, "knows her subject from every angle" and "has a flair for picking out the style points each season and helping every woman to look her best" due to her illustrious CV, including seven years as editor and director at *Vogue* and her roles as England's first fashion advisor and consultant, chairman of the Fashion Group in 1936, and so on. Helen Valentine herself had worked in the promotions department at *Mademoiselle* and *Vogue*, and later as editor of the latter's Pattern Book.

The magazines' expertise became part of their democratizing effect. Positing themselves as fashion insiders, they sought to extend the aspirational allure of the fashion world to their readers. *Glamour* and *Mademoiselle* both ran career features on the fashion industry. "How Fashion became Big Business," a twelve-page section in *Glamour* about jobs in the fashion field and the history of the industry, included a note that the author, Ruth Hawthorne Fay,

> began a long and successful career in fashion when she took a job in 1917. It was on *Vogue* under Edna Woolman Chase. No one is, therefore, more qualified to speak of the early days and of the influence *Vogue* has exerted on the fashion industry from its infancy to the present time. (*Glamour*, January 1949: 72)

Glamour also ran a biannual retail edition. *Elle* reported extensively on the new phenomenon of cover girls and the requirements and rewards of the profession (e.g., October 1946) and fashion careers in America. The magazines even offered direct access through competitions to become a designer or to visit Paris couturiers—from 1948, *Glamour* ran "Ten Girls with Taste," which afforded the lucky winner a trip to Paris and London. The trips were extensively reported in the magazines.

As Breward has pointed out in relation to British mass-market publications, such articles provided a vicarious spectacle akin to cinema and far removed from readers' real lives (1995: 208–10). But they also enhanced the glamorous veneer of the magazines and, on the surface at least, broadened the opportunity to participate in elite fashion.

Advertising and choice

Advertising was part of the service culture and the new fashion press actively embraced this fresh source of information. No longer consigned to the front and back of magazines, advertising was increasingly mixed with editorial, often framing a related article: *Mademoiselle* favored a half-page split, with advertising running down the outside of the editorial. Articles started to run continuations that drew the reader to the back part of the magazine, where the classified advertisements were still located.

Editorially, magazines became aspirational handbooks of consumer desirables, and there was a pioneering spirit in the way they sought actively to introduce their readers to all sorts of products. Where *Ladies' Home Journal* had offered a series of housing designs by renowned architect Frank Lloyd Wright in the early part of the century, after World War II *Mademoiselle* offered readers its own branded homes. Helen Valentine's initial vision for *Seventeen* was much more educational and cultural (Massoni 2010: 40), but after the war the magazine became much more consumerist in focus (ibid.: 151).

Pages began to be filled rather haphazardly with diverse merchandise (figure 5.3), and the democratizing rhetoric of choice stretched to fashion: "These magazines are here to give information—they are service magazines—if you give a woman five hats to choose from she is not going to be as satisfied as if she had twenty hats to pick from," argued Nast (Seebohm 1982: 336).

Purchasing advice provided opportunities for advertising and advertorial. Shopping columns proliferated with advertorial, including *Mademoiselle's* Mlle Wearybones' "Just Looking, Thanks," which covered everything from clothing to gadgets. *Glamour* adopted a more targeted approach with "Open House" which covered homewares, and the more extensive "Glamour Aisle" covering fashion, and "Beauty Aisle."

Themed issues emerged as a new way to enhance advertising appeal. In January 1946 *Mademoiselle* ran a "What's New Number" that featured the new fashion silhouette, the new Pan-Am plane, and a new car—Raymond Loewy Associates' Lightweight model; it produced a Latin American number (March 1946) and an annual College number each September. Meanwhile *Glamour* launched a biannual Advance Retail Edition exclusively for subscribing manufacturers and retailers, which offered copy quotes "plus other promotions aids" (November 1949: 1). Such a specialist edition helped enhance the magazine's fashion credentials among its general readership.

In the same way, the magazines themselves were actively promoted as commodities. They were positioned with distinctive slogans and readership profiles—*Mademoiselle* was "the magazine for smart young women" while *Glamour* was "the magazine for the girl with a job" and *Charm* "the magazine for the BG * Business Girl"—and covers that seduced potential readers with lists

FIGURE 5.3 Woman surrounded by accessories, 1930s. Courtesy of Advertising Archives.

of the contents inside. There was also a new emphasis on protecting magazines' features: *Mademoiselle* registered patents on all its regular departments, including "Just Looking, Thanks" and "Food for Fun and Fitness."

Critics of the consumerist culture noted the magazines' new, more insistent and even threatening warnings to women, whether general admonitions about appearance—"You are in a beauty contest every day of your life"—or specific needs, such as Mum deodorant because "this hateful, penetrating odour does cling to clothes." Horwood notes a similar tendency in Britain between the wars

(2005: 66–7). Mary McCarthy sees the specter of class origins at the root of this regulatory agenda, as they were in the nineteenth century: "Social failure is ascribed to a lack of 'fastidiousness,'" a lower-middle-class fear that first reveals itself in *Mademoiselle* (1980 [1950]: 191). *Mademoiselle*'s supplement on homes warned, "Walls may not have ears but they do talk about you, and so do the rest of your home furnishings! They'll blab if you're drab, if you're haphazard, if you're stuck in a rut" (September 1948: 243). As we will see, the regulatory tone and the specter of class also invaded fashion and beauty editorial.

Diversity of editorial

Allied to the new magazines' consumerism and service remit was an increase in editorial eclecticism in comparison with the traditional fashion press. The "Big Six" had been characterized by their breadth of editorial coverage, and *Ladies' Home Journal* was known as "the monthly Bible of the middle class" (Scanlon 1995: 4). Frequently their subjects would be mixed in an apparently haphazard way, with campaigning articles such as "Explaining the Facts of Life" opposite a fashion feature on home dressmaking (*LHJ*, June 1945: 38–9). The new fashion magazines adopted this broad range of content as a way to both attract advertisers and appeal to a wider readership. If domestic features predominated in the new mass-circulation British press, cookery and fiction were common on both sides of the Atlantic. Indeed, Nast identified fiction as an essential component of the new breed of mass-market fashion magazines (Seebohm 1982: 336). It accounted for one-third of the editorial in *Glamour* and *Mademoiselle*, and around 20 percent in *Seventeen*. As they were for the service journals, personal relationships were a cornerstone of the new publications: *Glamour* ran psychological features such as "Party Plague: Self-Consciousness" (October 1949: 100–1).

The new fashion press also mixed disparate subject matter: the first edition of *Elle* placed a piece on jealousy opposite a fashion spread, "Verdict on Elegance." An editorial from *Glamour* "celebrating a few of the people to whom the topsy turvy world owes gratitude" gave equal significance to Picasso, Palestinian peace, the musical *South Pacific*, Alexander Fleming, and Christian Dior (November 1949: 90). The magazines presented culture as a form of social currency—*Mademoiselle*'s arts column was tellingly entitled "Something to Talk About."

Fashion was also presented as a form of social currency, with Paris as its apotheosis. The copy linked fashion knowledge to social capital:

Study the new French clothes photographed in this issue, together with this digest, because you *femmes fatales* should be developing a definite clothes philosophy of your own. It's the year of the *individual you*, and unless you know your Alix, Chanel, Rochas or Molyneux, you are going to be baffled about how to dress to your type. (*Mademoiselle*, October 1937: 28)

Reader identification and the magazine community

At the heart of the "service" magazine was its interaction with its readers. In the early days of *Ladies' Home Journal*, readers were invited to visit the magazine's offices in Philadelphia, to send in tips for economizing in fashion, offer ideas for improving the fashion pages, and to write to the magazine with their views and queries.[10] As Mary Grieve, editor of British weekly *Woman*, later pointed out: "It no longer seemed appropriate that *Woman* should be speaking with quite such an authoritative, remote voice. The time of the monologue was ending; what we needed now was a place where a genuine dialogue could develop" (Grieve, *Millions Made My Story*, cited in White 1970: 153). For the mainstream fashion magazines, a similar mirroring of their readers and encouragement of a magazine "community" also became crucial (see *Marie Claire* below).

As noted earlier, the new fashion press created readers' committees and encouraged readers to participate in the content of the magazine. Reader identification and loyalty were also encouraged through competitions: those in *Mademoiselle* included photographic scholarships, fiction prizes, design prizes, and even the opportunity to be a cover girl:

> We stand ready to play fairy godmother to some perfectly gorgeous girl—a lovely who typifies the Ideal American Beauty that furriers rave about. She must have EVERYTHING, and photograph like five-hundred thousand dollars. CAN THIS BE YOU?. ("Calling Miss Mademoiselle," August 1937)

The new fashion magazines developed a more convivial tone: "And now having parted with the very last of our success-secrets, we'll have no sympathy for anyone who suffers from another of those ohmypoorbrain won't work, whereshallwegotonight moments" (*Mademoiselle*, February 1937). The readership were addressed directly as "you" and encouraged to identify with the magazine's persona through "synthetic personalization":[11] "Fiction will find first favour with us when its principal characters are smart, intelligent young women like yourself who compromise *Mademoiselle*'s readers" (July 1937: 61). The imagery of these magazines reflected this tone, with covers featuring smiling models, some of them readers.

Readers' letters and, later, the problem page were essential features of magazines such as *Seventeen*, *Marie Claire*, and *Elle* and the new British journals, whether in relation to clothing, beauty, cooking, home decoration, or personal relationships and employment.

Pragmatic fashion

As the fashion press adopted the educational, pragmatic approach of the service magazines, magazines became like sartorial primers for readers. As part of this education, readers were given such direct advice as to have a manicure once a week and a facial at least once a month. Fashion coverage was equally direct: "Shirtwaisters are dead." The "How To" feature emerged as a regular editorial component, giving readers clear rules about how to solve "wardrobe dilemmas." Fashion advice was delivered in the form of aphorisms, as in *Glamour*'s "Do's and Don'ts" and *Elle*'s "You will be fashionable if [...]"; "You will not be fashionable if [...]."

Economy was also central to the new fashion discourse. As well as patterns, magazines featured clothing that was generally affordable and local rather than the couture of *Vogue* and *Harper's Bazaar*, and provided prices and stockist information. Wardrobe planning was promoted as essential for a modern woman, and features that exploited the value of a garment became the norm, such as "One Dress and Ten Ways to Wear It." Separates—a new term—cropped up often as an economic way to stretch clothing budgets:

> Six mornings out of every seven you hie yourself to the office. Almost again as many evenings as you brush up against the bright lights. What shall you wear? We can answer your question in $200 or less: separates [...] The wardrobe on these two pages—and we hardly indicate the possibilities—has been built exclusively with separates, eleven all told. The total outlay, $181.55, and everything can be located at Lord and Taylor. (*Glamour*, September 1948: 194–5)

Consumption and economy were brought together in the form of directed narcissism. The new magazines justified spending money on clothes in multiple ways, often simultaneously: fashion, comfort, practicality, and multi-purpose usage were all criteria for "Your Best Buy In A Coat" (*Glamour*, October 1949). Despite considerations of economy, the approach and tone of the new fashion editorial was in general much more upbeat than that of the Big Six or the elite fashion press. *Mademoiselle*, in particular, put emphasis on fun in all aspects of its readers' lives, including dress: "I've seen the Dior collection and I simply drooled" (August 1948: 342).

The new breed of magazines also began to sell clothing to their readers. *Mademoiselle* opened its own shopping areas in major department stores in August 1937, announcing proudly:

> *Mademoiselle* Shops have been installed in important stores. The purpose: to give to you in fact and fabric, the crisp lively and wearable fashions you admire on our pages; to be your little oasis equipped with a spring of clear fresh style

and new ideas; to advise you on your own fashion problems, and to give you tremendously smart things with modest violet price tags. Everybody ought to be very happy indeed, especially yourself. (57)

Elle followed suit after the war with its "Bon magique" offers.

Romance and fashion

As Cynthia White notes in relation to the British journals, while *Vogue* might counsel the reader to wear blue because "fashion decrees it," the new publications would advise wearing blue "because he likes it" (White 1970: 148). If romance formed the core of the new magazines' fictional content, the editorial also overtly linked fashion to both romantic and career success. *Mademoiselle* advises that the appropriate dress will win the job and the man:

> In the fast competitive business world, clothes are a little extra that can score in your favour. There are no dividends to being Miss Mousy Sturdydrab—it's the attractive girl who gets the job, the promotion, the man. (September 1946: 145)

Within a rhetoric of female empowerment, the magazines reinforced conservative notions of gender relations: fashion was ultimately arbitrated by the male gaze. In Horwood's study, British women themselves attest to "keeping up appearances" for their husbands (2005: 57–74).

Luxury and aspiration

The magazines' luxurious images, advertising, and editorial contents created what the sociologist Jean Baudrillard would later label "empty dreams." Aspiration was a key selling tool, with vicarious luxury—particularly Hollywood—represented as a core value. Editorial wove aspirational lifestyles and escapist fantasy around accessible products:

> If you are in town, you can be a refreshment in luscent satin to the embryo tycoon who has been struggling through the heat and selling-waves of Wall Street. Your type is a smooth-browed, gardenia-cheeked, scarlet-lipped classi-fication, a haven for someone who has endured those blasts of searing air so mysteriously given out by urban asphalt at noon. (*Mademoiselle*, July 1937: 27)

While American magazines such as *Ladies' Home Journal* focused their profiles on ordinary Americans and *Vogue* featured the lives of society's elite, magazines such as *Marie Claire* and *Woman's Journal* gave readers vicarious access to the glamorous lives of Hollywood starlets, including features on their homes and fashion choices, in a way that prefigured contemporary magazines such as *Hello!* Paris was equally significant as a dreamscape, and was regularly invoked as the source of featured fashions: "There is an aura about Paris—a creative atmosphere, difficult to maintain in our commercial order of things" (*Mademoiselle*, October 1937: 28).

Meanwhile, the impulse toward democratization was tempered by more elitist notions of individualization and dressing to type, a more mainstream version of what the luxury journals termed "personality." Readers were encouraged to think of dress as a means to shape themselves while still adhering to group norms. In an article on hairstyles, for example, *Elle* readers are encouraged to choose between "The Busy Woman," "The Innocent," and "The Apprentice Vamp."

Creating women's insecurities in order to exploit them was not a new phenomenon in the fashion press. The mass-market dissemination of the desire to be fashionable, however—together with the increasing number of products and, by implication, of potential pitfalls—created a new type of rhetoric, and the fashion press became more insistent and dogmatic. The same was true in Europe, where European fashion magazines, seeing the success of the American publications, adopted many characteristics of the "democratic" American press.

Les amies de Marie Claire

Marie Claire was launched in France on March 3, 1937 as a weekly fashion magazine that combined the luxurious appearance of the elite fashion press with the more affordable price (1.50 francs) of the popular magazines (see plate 8). Its publisher, a successful textile and wool manufacturer named Jean Prouvost, was influenced by the glamorous art direction of fashion magazines such as *Vogue*. The new magazine's avowed mission was to teach women about fashion rather than dictating to them. By March 1938, like *Mademoiselle* before it, *Marie Claire* was advertising its own courses on beauty, fashion, and running a business (March 4, 1938: 63). By 1939 it was providing a mail order shopping service.

Marie Claire was distinctive from the outset. Its first issue argues that it wants to bring every Frenchwoman everything that might be interesting or useful to her in a magazine that is both "luxurious and practical." It was proudly nationalistic: "*Marie Claire* is resolutely French and it is above all with the other Marie Claires of France that it wishes to converse" (March 3, 1937: 20). While nationalism, as we have seen, was common in fashion commentary, *Marie Claire* transferred it from the clothing to the magazine itself. This was no doubt a marketing counterpoint to the strength of the American fashion press, exploiting underlying anxiety over U.S. influence in France after World War I.

Like its American counterparts, the new magazine provided specialist information from "expert" editors on beauty (Marcelle Auclair) and fashion (Olga

Volker). In the launch issue, *Marie Claire* promises that its beauty section will be low cost and speedy, and its beauty features regularly included home therapies or massage techniques. Although fashion and beauty formed the lion's share of editorial, the magazine reflected the diversity of the American press, with fiction, including photo stories, cookery, and entertainment news. Aspiration lay behind the travel column of Louise de Vilmorin, which transported readers to cities around the world and provided vicarious participation in Vilmorin's elite social world of aristocracy and celebrity.

Fiction and high-quality writing were particularly important to *Marie Claire*: Colette was a regular contributor, and the magazine published fiction by Irène Némirovsky (May 3, 1940), who was already a successful author. Given the growing anti-Semitism in France at the time, with the Germans on the verge of invading, this was a bold editorial decision. Later *Marie Claire* supported and published works by Françoise Sagan and Simone de Beauvoir.

Prouvost recognized the importance of Hollywood and celebrities to the success of his magazine. Borrowing from American fan magazines and Condé Nast's *Glamour* in particular, *Marie Claire* from the outset contained several pages on stars of stage and screen and later used them regularly in fashion features. This provided one of the elements of luxury that differentiated the new magazine from the popular women's press. In July 1939, *Marie Claire* carried a four-page photo montage story on Hollywood star Myrna Loy's trip to Paris, including her visits to Hermès, Balenciaga, and the races at Longchamps (July 7, 1939: 16–19).

In a new type of article—"Behind the Scenes"—*Marie Claire* often revealed the myths and secrets of Hollywood starlets. In "Every Woman Can Be Pretty," Auclair discussed and illustrated with photographs the studio transformation of stars such as Joan Crawford, Greta Garbo, and Marlene Dietrich (April 23, 1937: 14–19). Elsewhere it featured a *Heat*-style exposé of unflattering "Pictures they Hide" (August 26, 1939: 40–1). This type of feature helped demystify the stars, creating an equivalence between them and the readers, underlined by an element of intimacy and gossip. When it relaunched after World War II, *Marie Claire* adopted a similar approach to the world of couture and fashion, showing off-duty models outside Jacques Fath's studio in 1955, for example.

Marie Claire's initial fashion coverage stretched from "the models of the great couturiers" through to what it calls "practical models that even the least sophisticated can copy and make", accompanied by patterns. As with the American magazines, fashion advice was pragmatic and identified key trends or looks for the reader. *Marie Claire*'s innovation lay in the simplicity with which trends were articulated and illustrated: "The Important Points of Summer Fashion" listed five looks for daytime—"lots of boleros" and "clashing bright colours" and for evening "full skirts" and "draped busts" (March 3, 1937). Economy also featured in other new fashion articles, such as advice on how to use accessories to update outfits, how to use fabric offcuts, or how to use eight elements to make twelve outfits.

Ultimately, again, it was reader intimacy that distinguished the new magazine. The inaugural mission statement was inclusive and democratic, claiming that "Each and every one of you is a bit Marie Claire." Readers were encouraged to become "*amies de Marie Claire*"(friends of *Marie Claire*) and the first issue promised dowries of 100 francs for babies born between February 24 and March 3 whose weight was closest to the ideal, and "useful gifts" for all others from "fairy godmother" *Marie Claire*. Later issues continued the amicable relationship, with competitions and free prizes for readers seen carrying the magazine in provincial towns. The first *Grand Concours* (Big Competition) took place on May 13, 1937 in Paris, Caen, and Lisieux. Thirty subscribers who were photographed with the latest issue could receive a 100 franc prize. While these tactics were clearly commercial drives to boost readership and encourage advertising, they also contributed to the magazine's pervasive sense of camaraderie. Indeed, the competitions proved so popular that the police were asked to keep order at newsstands. By April 1938 there was a daily service bureau for *les amies de Marie Claire* (April 22, 1938: 51), which dispensed free beauty, fashion, and legal advice, and organized excursions and trips to exhibitions.

The problem page had proved key to the new generation of women's magazines in Britain and elsewhere. Uniquely, *Marie Claire* was able to combine this more homely content with high fashion and glamor. From the outset, Marcelle Auclair continued a dialogue with her readers through her weekly correspondence column, in which she answered readers' letters and advised them on aspects of love, marriage, careers, and points of law, or moralized on the dangers of dieting for young women (July 2, 1937: 4). She also made a biweekly radio broadcast on Radio City, "la minute de la beauté" (March 4, 1938: 4). Even after *Marie Claire*'s post-war relaunch in 1954, when it repositioned itself as a fashion specialist, Auclair, by then editor, continued with her problem page.

The magazine also adopted a more supportive approach toward women's social position than was traditional in either France or the fashion press, focusing, for example, on the enlightened employment policies of the couturier Madeleine Vionnet. Unlike its American counterparts, *Marie Claire* was not afraid to confront contentious issues such as sex or domestic violence. In common with the new breed of British journals, however, it favored motherhood as the feminine ideal. Many covers before and during the war featured children, and the magazine included sections on family life. It was another instance of magazines reinforcing conservative gender norms within an apparently more modern and empowering discourse. In "You have an Obligation to be Elegant," for example, *Marie Claire* argued that women needed to perfume and decorate the world (March 4, 1938: 4).

Marie Claire closed after the war and relaunched itself as a fashion monthly in October 1954. However, it still retained its correspondence column and more down-to-earth tone, as reflected in contemporary rubrics such as "100 idées de Marie Claire."

Elle and the "Bon magique" (1945–)

On November 21, 1945, Hélène Gordon Lazareff, a former editor of *Marie Claire* who had contributed to *Harper's Bazaar* during the war, launched *Elle* as a "woman's weekly" (issue 2 onward), published by Editions Défense de la France. From the outset *Elle* was targeted at the younger, reasonably affluent modern reader (figure 5.4). It included an "Elle Works" section and played an active role in political debates. It was the first French fashion magazine to discuss contraception and campaigned for birth control. Later editions analyzed the reasons for the postwar rise in the divorce rate, the need for adoption, inactive thyroids and other health issues, and the UN Conference (October 19, 1948).

Although its readership was more educated and cosmopolitan than that of *Marie Claire*, and its cover price was higher,[12] *Elle* adopted many of the practices of the more service-oriented publications. Its tone was relaxed and upbeat: the third edition (December 5, 1945) featured a laughing woman on the cover, for example, in contrast to the stern countenance usually presented by the elite press. Following American templates, the contents were detailed on the cover by October 1946, and by 1950 the magazine's sassy editorial standpoint had spread to the cover. The issue for March 6, 1950, featuring a glamorous young woman smoking, challenged the reader to dare to cry, to adopt the new color, and to become beautiful and slim in the magazine's company.

While fashion was its key content, *Elle* again adopted an eclectic editorial and advertising mix. Early editions carried publicity for everything from nose correctors to household cleaning products and, like its American counterparts, *Elle* often juxtaposed different types of article, including fiction, cookery, a problem page, and a weekly horoscope. Early editions had a pen-friend section— "Elles à Elles"—that sought to put readers in touch with one another, but by 1950 this had been replaced with a "Courier de Coeur" ("personal letters"), dealing with emotional issues, and "*Elle* Résout vos problèmes" ("*Elle* solves your problems"), a section unique to *Elle* that dealt with more practical legal and employment issues. By the 1950s *Elle* had followed its American rivals into supplements. It also began to publish glossy special editions—the *Cahiers de Elle*—which were more expansive and expensive than regular editions but offered more advertising potential.

Following the example of the American press and *Marie Claire*, *Elle* encouraged reader interaction. Early history quizzes soon gave way to more serious reader surveys on subjects such as depression (March 6, 1950: 10–11). While these surveys provided interesting editorial subject matter, they also offered information about the magazine's readership profile to share with advertisers, as American magazines had done.

Unlike *Marie Claire*, *Elle* concentrated as much on French acting talent, writers, or prominent working women as on the glamor of the Hollywood stars

FIGURE 5.4 *Elle*. First Cover, November 21, 1945. © Victoria and Albert Museum, London.

who were frequently used to support the Paris fashion industry: "Nowadays no international star can afford to dress themselves anywhere but Paris without losing their prestige" (October 1, 1948: 3). In 1949, the magazine inaugurated a women's cinema prize ("Prix Féminin du Cinema") to recognize the best-dressed actress.

Like the other new fashion magazines, *Elle* emphasized the expertise of its editors, whom it encouraged readers to address with their problems:

> Those who form the editorial team at Elle and put together your magazine every week are not infallible or exceptionally lucid but each of them has studied their subject matter in depth, each of them devotes their time and their experience to specific aspects or problems in women's demanding lives. So it's understandable that they can find solutions to these individual problems more easily than you who are dealing with all of them. (January 1, 1948: 4–5)

These early editors included Monique Danon (fashion) and Alice Chavane (beauty). By 1952, Françoise Giroud had been dispatched to America as a special correspondent, the fashion department had five members of staff, and *Elle* had its own commercial radio show, *Radio-Elle*.

Like *Marie Claire*, the magazine featured fiction and high-quality writing, particularly by women. It published Marguerite Duras and Marcel Pagnol, and the first version of Saint-Exupery's *Le Petit Prince*, as well as Sagan and Colette, whose memoirs "Souvenirs de Colette" appeared as a long-running series. It also had a weekly culture section.

Elle's fashion ideas were more avant-garde than those of the elite glossies, the new American magazines, or *Marie Claire*. It has been claimed that *Elle* launched "The New Look" in 1947 (Gay-Fragneaud and Vallet 2004b: 67); a decade later, on December 16, 1957, it predicted the success of the young Yves Saint Laurent. The magazine was an early advocate of color photography in shoots and supported fledgling fashion photographers such as Helmut Newton, Jeanloup Sieff, and Oliviero Toscani as well as its legendary art director and photographer of the 1950s and 1960s, Peter Knapp.

But *Elle* also made fashion innovation less intimidating by encouraging its readers to adopt an individual response to fashions rather than follow trends: "Choose what suits you, don't follow the dictates of fashion slavishly like a blind man does his dog, this is what we call the new elegance" (November 21, 1945: 16). As part of the process, *Elle* adopted the same educative stance as its American counterparts and *Marie Claire*. A two-page spread in the first issue on "La Silhouette Nouvelle" is divided into looks for Morning, Afternoon, and Evening, but with suggestions on how to adapt and adopt the looks depending on one's height and weight. Fashion advice was direct ("Get rid of your platforms"). As already mentioned, *Elle* also adopted the fashion aphorism as a mechanism for dispensing advice, like *Glamour*'s "Do's and Don'ts."

Economy was another element which *Elle's* fashion coverage shared with its counterparts, such as encouraging women to create several outfits from one or two new pieces. Equally significant were its patterns, especially for a wide range of knitted garments, which were often derived from those of the stars, such as Marlene Dietrich's cape (October 8, 1946). It provided hints for transforming old garments into fashionable ones or for creating an evening hairstyle using bits and pieces lying around the bedroom (December 5, 1945: 8) in a manner that was prescient of the DIY styling of *Nova* in the 1960s and the style magazines of the 1980s. As Nast had done, *Elle* offered its readers lots of choice as part of its service remit: "50 ideas for girls who work" (October 8, 1946).

At the same time, *Elle* also championed the importance of the elite French fashion industry in the postwar period. It argued that haute couture was the country's third largest export industry, and that the 522 foreign buyers who came to the shows brought money for wheat and milk (October 1, 1948: 3). French readers were urged to sort out their appearance—"The whole world is watching you" (September 10, 1946: 3)—and the *Parisienne* returned as a key fashion figure in its editorial to reflect the chic and the superiority of Paris fashion. As part of its editorial support for couture, *Elle* treated the shows as major news items: the cover for October 1, 1946 showed a girl with a *France-Soir* newspaper headlined "Elle reveals the secrets of the new fashions"—a message also plastered all over the background. Such a cover also enhanced Elle's fashion credentials.

Like its American counterparts, *Elle* positioned itself as a fashion insider, photographing those who attended couture shows from September 1946 onward and describing what went on behind the scenes. It also addressed the cost of couture, justifying the price of a 300,000-franc "Eugenie" dress by Dior, for example, by stressing that it includes the workmanship of 689 individuals. The magazine also reported extensively on the new phenomenon of "cover girls," providing on October 8, 1946 the vital statistics of model Monique Arnaud (1.63 m, 50 kg, waist 63 cm). *Elle* explains that a cover girl who is young, pretty, and has a perfect complexion could earn between 750 and 1,000 francs for an initial photo and 300 for reproductions. A later issue shows young models off duty outside the atelier of Jacques Fath—an *Elle* favorite—as part of the "Elle Travaille" section. By 1952, Françoise Giroud was reporting on the lives of a Fifth Avenue saleswoman (November 24, 1942: 58) and American "careerwomen" (December 1, 1952: 56–9), including Dorothy Shaver of Lord and Taylor and the fashion publicist Eleanor Lambert, the creator of New York Fashion Week. While these articles positioned *Elle* as being international and of the moment, they also gave both consumers and trade readers insights into American business practices.

Elle formed a successful reciprocal relationship with the fashion world. Following *Mademoiselle's* lead, the magazine created design competitions in collaboration with couture houses, especially Jacques Fath. It also offered its readers special promotions such as a Schiaparelli hat (April 26, 1947) or a free roll of fabric (January 1, 1948).

Elle also extended the link between journalism and retail. Its most influential innovation came in October 1948 with the launch of its "Bon magique" coupons. Designed to "struggle for quality over expense," these discount coupons were issued each week in the magazine. They could be sent off to the *Elle* Special Service Bureau for weekly offers or taken directly to suppliers, retailers, or *Elle* offices to earn discounts. Early examples focused on fashion, including Corot fabrics for 595 francs instead of 850 and a Simone Simon dress for 5,250 francs (around £5), but by 1949 the weekly offers also included items such as a breadboard (January 10). In November 1952, *Elle* launched its own ski holidays to France and Italy (November 17: 13, 46). Unsurprisingly, the sources of such offers were often the magazine's regular advertisers, although some, like an Easter blouse (March 26, 1950: 39), were unbranded. The new coupons fulfilled *Elle*'s goal of making high fashion more accessible to its readers but also created an innovative loyalty mechanism. Today, *Elle* still offers its readers exclusive products and a discount card in conjunction with retailers.

The illusion of democracy

In *Adorned in Dreams* Elizabeth Wilson refers to the "pseudo democracy" of fashionable appearances in the interwar years (2003 [1985]: 111). A similar phenomenon is evident in the fashion journals of the time. While the new magazines disseminated and popularized fashion culture, the rhetoric of choice and democratization was undermined by a more insidious regulatory discourse. This discourse, reinforced even by the fiction published in the magazines, suggested that a failure to comply with the magazines' dictums, particularly about fashion, would result in social failure or a lack of "cultural intelligibility."[13]

Underlying such insidious commentary was the specter of social class and a fear of revealing a lack of cultural knowledge.[14] In her aptly titled *Keeping Up Appearances* (2005), Catherine Horwood sees this social anxiety as being central to paradigms of dress in interwar Britain. Reader makeover articles started to appear, promoting the idea of physical self-improvement as a means of social betterment: "A body isn't necessarily a figure. A body is what you've been given, a figure is what you make of it" ("Accessory after the Body," *Mademoiselle*, October 1952: 87, cited in Walker 1998: 223).[15] *Mademoiselle* also published "Make the Most of Yourself," a column promoting the services of Renée Long, director of the Franklin Simons Personal Analysis Bureau. One unfortunate candidate was Jael Wells, a twenty-four-year-old graduate of the University of Minnesota working in the library department of a large fashion organization:

Jael had more than a measure of good looks, but she hid her light under a bushel—and what a bushel! Heavily rimmed glasses, an impossible hairdo, lack-lustre clothes, and a general impression of "signing off" rather than "taking off." (October 1937: 38–9, 54)

The magazines positioned themselves as central to this Cinderella transformation; for example, *Marie Claire* referred to itself as a "fairy godmother."

The moral imperative to make the most of oneself underpinned the magazines' fashion aphorisms and Foucauldian imperatives to fashionable display. *Marie Claire* warned: "You Have an Obligation to be Elegant" with a lengthy editorial that proposed cleanliness, harmony, and elegance as the cornerstones of social acceptability (March 4, 1938: 4). *Mademoiselle* argued that a hairdresser's appointment was more important than a lunch date:

Effort counts. Extra pains—the care with which you choose your clothes and put yourself together—result in that smooth coordinated effect. **Time** pays off like a lucky slot machine. Don't buy in a rush. Don't dress in a rush. Put your face on calmly and take ten minutes to change it whenever necessary. Make your hairdresser appointment instead of a lunch date. Take the time to plan your wardrobe *in advance*; take the time to keep it in tip top running order by checking regularly: cleaning? mending? altering? **Money** matters only incidentally in looking your best. But don't be a tightwad. (June 1948: 145)

As in earlier periods, "taste" was acknowledged as a key social discriminator. While the magazines implied that taste could be acquired by following their advice and purchasing their suggested products, they nevertheless acknowledged that some people were intuitively more tasteful than others. Despite the clear contradiction of their apparent rhetoric of democracy, they admitted that taste was as exclusive as Paris fashion: "There are several requisites to being well-turned out. **Taste** is the little bell that rings 'yes' or 'no'. Frankly, it's as indispensable as conscience. If you aren't sure of your taste, study those who are" (*Mademoiselle*, June 1946: 145).

In America, as we have seen, suspicions of their underlying regulatory discourse earned the new magazines numerous critics. Betty Friedan's major polemic against women's magazines, *The Feminine Mystique*, was published in 1963, but long before this, female journalists such as Joan Didion had criticized the new publications' obsession with perfection, their focus on fashion, their pseudo-psychology, and their overarching consumerism (Walker 1998: 228–61). Others parodied the axiomatic style of the fashion advice, as the English writer Marganita Laski did in "Choose the Clothes that Suit You" (*Atlantic Monthly*, May 1950: 90), while the magazines even took an ironic approach to their own tone, as in *Mademoiselle*'s pastiche of Diana Vreeland in its discussion of fashion editors (September 1948: 164–5).

One of the most biting and lengthy pieces of criticism of the new fashion press was the two-part article penned by Mary McCarthy in *The Reporter* in 1950, "Up the Ladder from *Charm* to *Vogue*" (1980 [1950]: 174–92), with which this chapter opened. McCarthy objected to the magazines' discursive style, their advice, and their quest for perfection, with its implication that readers were currently imperfect. Her most vicious critique is aimed at *Charm*, which McCarthy sees as being entirely premised upon failure: "addressed to the insecure and maladroit, [it] echoes in a national hollowness of social failure and fear" (ibid.: 190).

Flair (1950–1)

A further target of McCarthy's invective was *Flair*, which was resolutely elitist and, arguably, appeared as an antidote to this apparent democratization (figure 5.5). The brain-child of editor Fleur Cowles, whose circle included writers such as Tennessee Williams, artists like Dalí, Hollywood star Douglas Fairbanks, and U.S. presidents, *Flair* described itself as a "magazine for the moderns" and the "aristocrats of taste"; more significantly, it "aimed to give direction and depth" according to Cowles' editorial letter in the advertising prototype, penned in gold ink. This same prototype contained a "Letter to Americans" from Jean Cocteau, foregrounding the magazine's links to European culture.

Boasting an impressive editorial team—including Arnold Gingrich, former editor of *Esquire*, as general manager and George Davis, former fiction editor of *Harper's Bazaar*, as managing editor—the first issue featured a cut-out keyhole-style cover, short stories from Williams and Angus Wilson, the latter's on specially textured paper, the first American reproductions of Lucien Freud's art, a feature including photographs of the Duke and Duchess of Windsor's home on the French Riviera, fashion drawings by Gruau, and colored fashion images by painter Sylvia Braverman.

Each of the subsequent issues was themed, including April's Paris Fashion issue (1951), which contained a pop-up of the center of fashion, the Place Vendome, and fiction from Simone de Beauvoir and Colette. This issue, according to Cowles, coined the term "cool" as a signifier of all things fashionable. Other regular contents of the magazine included art criticism, travel, interiors, politics, literature, and "It's About Time," a social page.

Flair organized its coverage from the collections into key stories: hemlines, panels, waists, sleevelessness. It was, however, in its privileging of image over text—a feature decried by Mary McCarthy—that it was truly modern: "It [*Flair*] is a leap into the Orwellian future, a magazine without content or point of view beyond its proclamation of itself, one hundred and twenty pages of sheer presentation, a journalistic mirage" (1980 [1950]: 187). With its innovative use of cut-outs, fashion illustration, and photography, as well as its 3-D pop-ups, *Flair*

FIGURE 5.5 *Flair*, February 1950. © *The New York Times*. Courtesy of Vinmag Archive Ltd.

anticipated the shift toward the dominance of the image in fashion journalism that occurred from the 1960s onward.

Although it was popular among the fashion fraternity of Seventh Avenue, *Flair* failed to attract advertising and folded after a year.[16] If Cowles' attempt at elitism was ill-fated, however—and even *Vogue* became more populist following World War II in both design and content[17]—the resurgence of haute couture and the advent of Christian Dior gave the industry and the elite press an opportunity to reassert the distinction and mystery of the original fashion object and its own position within the fashion media hierarchy in the face of the tide of democratization.

Meanwhile, *Seventeen*'s "teena" market was rapidly expanding: it would influence the fortunes and face of the fashion industry in the late 1950s and 1960s and beyond.

Notes

1 For more on this see Pouillard (2013).

2 For more on this see Evans (2013, esp. Chs 3 and 4).

3 *Charm* was absorbed into *Glamour* by Condé Nast when it purchased Street and Smith in 1959.

4 For more on the impact of these journals in Britain see White (1970: Chs 3 and 4) and Breward (1995: 195–213).

5 See Crane (2000: Ch. 3).

6 Even by 1919 two-thirds of *Ladies' Home Journal*'s revenue came from advertising (Scanlon 2000: 202).

7 Seebohm doesn't mention *Charm* as a source of competition or inspiration for *Glamour* as it was considered more downscale, but after its relaunch in 1950 by Helen Valentine as "The Magazine For Women Who Work" at an increased price of 25 cents, it certainly became a competitor. When Condé Nast acquired the title in 1959, its circulation was only 15,000 less than that of *Glamour* (Endres and Lueck 1995: 109).

8 These guides were also a feature of the "Big Six"—*Ladies' Home Journal* offered "Patch Box leaflets on Beauty," for example.

9 See Ferguson (1983: Ch. 5) and White (1970: Chs 3 and 4) for more on this.

10 Editor Edward Bok devoted two days a week to answering readers' letters, which were guaranteed an individual reply (Scanlon 1995: 50).

11 See McLoughlin (2000: 68–73).

12 From December 1947 it was obliged, along with other weekly glossies, to increase its price to 20 francs per issue (*Elle*, December 16, 1947: 10).

13 Butler (1993: 110).

14 See Bourdieu (2010 [1984]).

15 A feature adopted successfully by *Brigitte* in 1957.

16 See Cowles and Dunne (2014) for more on *Flair*.

17 It adopted a bold, busy format, collage-type layouts, and a tabloid sans serif typeface, and started to include more mass-market fashion (Holgate 1994: 57, 67).

6 THE GOLDEN AGE: FASHION JOURNALISM AND HAUTE COUTURE IN THE 1950s

Introduction

It is our role to recognize fashions when they are still only the seeds of the future. The designers create, but without magazines their creations would never be recognized or accepted.
(CARMEL SNOW, CITED IN "THE STYLOCRATS," *TIME*, AUGUST 18, 1947)

The period after World War II witnessed renewed optimism, prosperity, and a consumer boom. As British Prime Minister Harold Macmillan boasted in July 1957, "most of our people have never had it so good." Fashion was again swept up in the optimistic desire for the new, as championed by an editorial from *L'Officiel de la Couture et de la Mode* in spring 1947: "What are known as the whims of fashion, they are the spirit of discovery, the use of science and its marriage with tradition. It is a sign that humanity is not exhausted in spite of everything" (49).

Paris haute couture reasserted itself at the summit of fashion immediately after the war, a period widely recognized as a golden age[1] in which fashion journalism was again instrumental in promoting couture as "a specialized power that exercised its own separate authority" (Lipovetsky 1994: 76). As Carmel Snow attests (see above), journalists assumed a greater authority and critical function and this was, therefore, a golden age for fashion journalism too, especially in New York. An influx of emigrés from Europe, including Alex Liberman at *Vogue*, brought new Modernist perspectives to what has been hailed as "the golden age of American magazine design" (Owen 1991: 56) and New York "replaced Paris as the mecca of fashion photography by the early Fifties" (Hall-Duncan 1979: 136).

News reporting and propaganda during the war had underlined the power of the visual, leading to the increasing privileging of image over text in fashion magazines. The *Art Directors Club Annual* in 1955 identified "a transition from word thinking to visual thinking" (cited in Holgate 1994: 52). At the same time, wartime technological developments meant that the expanding band of fashion photographers had access to the Hasselblad, developed from the aerial camera, which allowed more varied perspective and wider-angled shots in fashion images and greater opportunities for catwalk reporting. Meanwhile, the introduction of Kodak's Ektachrome in 1946 allowed photographers to process their own film, leading to faster turnarounds to meet copy deadlines and affording more opportunity for visual freedom (Carter 1974: 142).

Although the Fashion Group had been in existence since 1930 and formal fashion journalism training had begun before the war, it was during the late 1940s and 1950s that fashion journalism became perceived as a serious profession. As Holgate notes: "A profession is shaped by the recognition that it is a profession, that it offers specialized knowledge and definitive attributes" (1994: 46) and for journalists these skills were centered on the ability to identify new trends, as summed up in Carmel Snow's comments to *Time* magazine above. A *Vogue* promotional leaflet boasted:

> *Vogue*'s editors are women trained in fashion analysis and selection, in trend forecasting and clothes psychology; they are in constant touch with the creative minds and merchandise sources in the women's field; sensitive to every new trend, expert in analyzing, appraising, selecting, discarding. (Cited in Holgate 1994: 20)

Powerful new fashion groups emerged during the period, including the New York Couture Group (1943), the forerunner of the CFDA, which was started in 1962, as well as the Fashion Group itself. The Fashion Institute of Technology (FIT), founded as the MIT for fashion industries, opened in 1944 and by 1952 Parson's School of Design in New York was offering a BSC in Fashion in conjunction with New York University (NYU).

Thanks in large part to Dior's "New Look", fashion became front-page news and media coverage increased. In 1938, some ninety journalists covered the Balenciaga presentation; by 1949, more than 300 journalists from all over the world were covering the Paris Couture shows (*L'Officiel*, Hiver 1949: 108). By 1957 there were 500 press and more than 800 buyers (*Time*, August 12, 1957). As well as *Harper's* Snow and Bettina Ballard, fashion editor of American *Vogue*, those attending included the other new doyennes of the profession such as Sally Kirkland of *Life*, Eugenia Sheppard of the *New York Herald Tribune*, and Virginia

Pope and later Carrie Donovan of the *New York Times*, as well as Alison Settle of the *Observer*, Alison Adburgham of the *Guardian*, Ernestine Carter of the *Sunday Times*, and Alice Chavane of *Le Figaro*, Françoise Giroud of *L'Express*, and Andrée Castanié of *L'Officiel* in France.

In Britain, lauded journalists such as Alison Settle had their columns syndicated in the regional press, as did Eugenia Sheppard in America. The increase in the availability of cheaper air travel also improved the ability of the press and buyers to cover the shows. Furthermore, while journalists still had to work through the night to photograph the collections—the clothes had to be returned to the couturiers the following morning to show to buyers—reports could be telephoned and photographs wired around the globe.

The enhanced status of the profession was due in part to the efforts of the first serious fashion PR, Eleanor Lambert. When Lambert launched the first Press Week in New York in 1943, reporters were, for the first time, able to cover an organized schedule of American shows. Prior to this there had been no formalized period of presentation, and regional American journalists had no direct access to the designer collections.

The U.S. remained the most significant fashion market and the relationship between the American press, buyers, and manufacturers and the Paris designers was the backbone of both couture's renaissance and fashion's newsworthy status. The American press were also instrumental in the promotion of new fashion centers, particularly Italy, as both journalists and buyers sought to discover the next new designer or fashion look.

As fashion became news, so the discourse surrounding it became more urgent in tone, and more self-important. The newsworthiness of fashion was due in part to Dior's savvy marketing but also to the secrecy of Parisian couture at a time when "a new hemline was as closely guarded as a barrel of plutonium in the U.S." ("A Hectic Week of Paris Showings," *Life*, March 1951: 101). The publishing of a new collection was not permitted before a specific date in order to avoid plagiarism and protect magazine editors, although there were a number of rebellious infringements of these "rules." In 1949, *Time* reported Carmel Snow's fury at *Vogue* having published details of the new Paris collections a full three weeks early ("A Gentleman's Disagreement," September 12, 1949), and both Eugenia Sheppard and Elizabeth Penrose of the *New York Times* defied the Press Week rules on the American collections in 1955 and 1959, respectively ("It's Ridiculous," *Time*, November 16, 1959).

At the same time, a split emerged between magazines and newspapers and their fashion coverage in the face of increased commercial and journalistic pressures. The growing clout of fashion industry advertising—particularly that of retailers and manufacturers in America—as well as the enhanced status of the couturiers as fashion's originators increasingly challenged press impartiality, especially in magazines. As we have seen, magazines had acquired their Janus-head before the war, but now new channels of influence were opening and budgets were growing. According to Peterson, advertising revenues for magazines more than doubled between 1945 and 1955, from $286.3 million to $622 million (1956: 25).

Editors such as *Harper's Bazaar*'s Carmel Snow and the *Herald Tribune*'s Sheppard were powerful enough to withstand commercial pressures, according to Marc Bohan, erstwhile designer at Patou and Dior: "[Snow would] take me out to lunch and explain exactly what worked and what didn't. Eugenia Sheppard did the same sort of thing. There were no flowers or compliments" (Bohan, quoted in Rowlands 2005: 401–2).

Snow and Sheppard were exceptions, however. For others, it was increasingly difficult to adopt any approach other than *copinage* (unerring support). The situation grew worse following the explosive and much-fêted arrival of Christian Dior and "The New Look": there was pressure on journalists to discover new talents or gossip—to which they were more likely to gain access through support rather than criticism.

Meanwhile, new international fashion centers opened up—for the British and Italians, as well as for the French, fashion could provide much-needed foreign currency—and the domestic press became cheerleaders for their national center's bid for buyers and international profile. Initially, British *Vogue* did not cover the American collections, while London designer showings were noticeably absent from its American counterpart, for example. Influential trade journals, such as *Linea Italiana*, also championed their domestic industries.

The post-war rhetoric of fashion also renewed its emphasis on glamor, and notions of "grooming" and "elegance" again became central to definitions of femininity: *Harper's Bazaar* was aimed at the reader "who thinks of herself as a woman every minute" (Mackenzie Stuart 2013: 168). Sartorial regulation was strongly enforced, with "After Five Fabrics" and a differentiation between married and unmarried women which mirrored that of the nineteenth century: strapless gowns were permitted for the former but not for the latter (Le Bourhis 1989: 17). A woman's life turned on social success or failure, as mediated by the male gaze; for example, *L'Officiel* encouraged its readers to be "aimable" (lovable) (Hiver 1949: 142). Photography of the period reflected this renewed elegance and glamor in models such as Dovima and the works of Dahl-Wolfe, Irving Penn, and Richard Avedon, in particular. Indeed, Devlin argues that much of the early postwar photography "perpetuated an enshrined pre-war image of the untouchable lady" (1979: 135) (figure 6.1).

However, by the late 1950s things were changing, in both the rising hemlines and the new emphasis on youth. In September 1954 *Harper's Bazaar* introduced a new feature entitled "At My Age" for the forty-year-old woman: "This we believe is the age of elegance, the age of many of our readers." But by 1958, the emphasis in British *Bazaar* was on "Young Outlook" and the value feature "The Well Spent Pound." This, together with the growth of television and its domination of advertising budgets, was to create new challenges for the fashion press.

FIGURE 6.1 American *Harper's Bazaar*, 1950. Photographer Lillian Bassman (b. 1917). Dress by Omar Kiam for Ben Reig. © Estate of Lillian Bassman/Victoria and Albert Museum, London/Hearst Magazines UK, the dots were handpainted after photographic development.

A mythic love affair: Dior and the American press[2]

As far as Ernestine Carter is concerned, the renaissance of Paris as fashion capital was firmly linked to the advent of Dior's couture house in February 1947 and the efforts of the American fashion press:

> The Paris Couture had picked itself up after the trauma of the Occupation, led by the loyal stalwarts, American *Harper's Bazaar*'s Carmel Snow and American *Vogue*'s Bettina Ballard, the press of the world re-gathered, most of them smelling deliciously of Rochas' latest scent, Femme. With the dazzling success of Dior, the buyers once more zero-ed in. It didn't really matter that air travel had widened the fashion horizon. (Carter 1977: 50)

The link was not serendipitous. Christian Dior's Head of House, Suzanne Luling, "knew well that the fate of new fashion houses rested in the hands of the American press" (Pochna 2008: 119). Prior to the war, fashion journalism had been created and directed in the Parisian salons of society women such as Marie-Louise Bousquet, who was hired by Carmel Snow in 1946 as fashion editor of *Harper's Bazaar*. In 1947, however, the French press was still recovering from the conflict: *Elle* magazine was still in its infancy, *Marie Claire* had not yet returned, and magazines such as *L'Officiel de la Couture et de la Mode* and *Jardin des Modes* were closely linked to the established couture houses and lacked either the circulations of the American press or its production values, due to paper rationing and shortages. According to Pochna, Luling "leaked" the news about Dior to Mrs. Perkins, the Paris editor of *Women's Wear Daily*. It made headlines on November 17, 1946 (120), before *Life* took up the news. By the summer collections of 1946, Dior was, according to Ballard, "much talked about," particularly in French press circles (1960: 228).

Meanwhile, both Carmel Snow and Bettina Ballard had spotted Dior's talents while he was working at Lelong. Indeed, Snow had him photographed by Henri Cartier Bresson for *Harper's Bazaar* in 1946 and told The Fashion Group that year that the new designer at Lelong was "full of ideas" (Rowlands 2005: 361).

In 1947 Carmel Snow tried to persuade wealthy American retail buyers to stay in Paris for the opening of this prodigious talent—"This new Christian Dior will produce some extraordinary things"—but many returned home after the main fortnight, so only eighteen turned up for the first collection (Pochna 2008: 154). Those who left missed a seminal moment not only in the clothing but also in its presentation, as Dior sprayed his attendees with his new perfume, Miss Dior: "We were given a polished theatrical performance. We were witness to a revolution in fashion and to a revolution in showing fashion as well" (Ballard 1960: 231). Afterwards, Snow recognized the shift in fashion and coined the best descriptor for a collection that had produced standing ovations: "God help the buyers who bought before they saw Dior. This changes everything." Later, or maybe at the time, she told the designer, "It's quite a revolution, dear Christian. Your dresses have such a new look" (Rowlands 2005: 365).

The hierarchical protocol of the show circuit was established even at the first Dior show, with Snow being given pride of place on a gray sofa, other important editors and later American buyers on gilt fauteuils, and the rest in armchairs, the front-row seats being, as ever, the most prestigious. By the 1950s the couture shows themselves had become news, and newspapers and news magazines, such as *Life*, reported who attended and printed photographs and descriptions of the backstage preparations.

For Dior's second collection on August 6, 1947, the salon on the Avenue Montaigne was full to bursting: no American buyer was going to miss the new fashion sensation a second time. The fashion press was intrinsic to perceptions of Dior's brilliance. American *Vogue* had an illustrated cover showing Dior's "market-woman skirt" and hailed "a new house, with a new vigour and new ideas." It called Dior "the talk of the town," as important to Paris as "current political and economic news," and included ten pages of Dior's ideas in its sixteen-page "Paris Fashions" feature (April 1947). In France, meanwhile, *L'Officiel*'s response was more measured, describing merely "a collection full of new lines" (April 1947: 73)—suggesting that Suzanne Luling's instincts about the French press were not wrong.[3]

The Dior legend grew, encouraged in particular by Snow, who noted, "Everyday and every place I go, I get criticized for the amount of publicity I am giving him" (Rowlands 2005: 367). Dior's shows became the cornerstone of the journalists' schedule and the hottest ticket on the Paris circuit: "Drenched in champagne, bruised by swinging cameras, one's hat knocked off, one's clothes smouldering with cigarette burns, one didn't so much emerge as become extruded" (Carter 1974: 75–6).

Helped by Dior's success, Paris regained its status of the mid-nineteenth century and the Roaring Twenties: it was again the fashion capital of the world. Once more the Americans brought their dollars and technology in exchange for French culture and, more particularly, couture. As with the boom in couture in the 1920s, the American press were key:

> The post-war dominance of European couture as the model for fashion design in North America was fuelled by the fashion press and the retailers. Merchants not only placed advertisements in fashion publications but also gained free advertising when magazines photographed couture models and mentioned where they were available for purchase in North America. (Palmer 2001: 95)

Although the rebirth of Parisian couture did not rely entirely on Dior, by the mid-1950s he accounted for the lion's share of couture exports to the U.S.:

Lipovetsky claims 50 percent (1994 [1991]: 58). Like Poiret before him, Dior himself took his goods to the U.S. when in September 1947 he became the first Frenchman to be invited by Dallas department store Neiman Marcus to receive its "Oscar" for services to couture. Like Poiret on his first U.S. trip, Dior was eagerly followed by both specialist magazines and the general press: Cecil Beaton claimed that Dior had as much press coverage as Winston Churchill on his first visit to America (1954: 299). Although "The New Look" had not been unanimously well received in the U.S.—there were protests from feminists who objected to its impracticality and from men who objected to its covering of women's legs—the controversy only increased the publicity. Indeed, the whole American *Vogue* team joined Dior on the transatlantic crossing, 3,000 people greeted him in Dallas, and even the *Wall Street Journal* ran a survey on its readers' opinions of "The New Look" (Pochna 2008: 196–9).

"The New Look" made fashion, and more particularly hemlines, news. Dior continued to change the "line"—a key word in the fashion journalist's lexicon—creating new names for each (the "Ovale," the "Tulip") (figure 6.2), and thus giving journalists ready-made headlines. The Maison Dior also provided press packs that included official photos and advice on styling, including hats, umbrellas, handbags, and shoes (Pochna 2008: 266–7). Dior was, in turn, rewarded with extensive press coverage. In 1953, *Women's Wear Daily* ran a seven-day feature, "The Dior Story," and by 1957 he had made the cover of both *Time* magazine and *Paris Match* and numerous covers of *Vogue*, *Harper's Bazaar*, and *Elle*. *Le Figaro's* fashion editor, Alice Chavane, had so many interviews with Dior that she later published them as a monograph, *Je suis Couturier*. In 1956 Dior featured in a CBS documentary.

Dior opened a New York branch in 1948 and launched a special collection of ready-to-wear for the U.S. market and later bonded copies and patterns. There was also plenty of copying on Seventh Avenue, bringing couture design to the mass market. It was this involvement of the vast swathes of America "on a buying spree" that placed fashion—particularly Dior fashion—at the heart of the mainstream media. *Life* magazine described this effect in relation to the popular Margrave-style dress of 1947: "In wholesale houses of all price brackets, enterprising scouts were busy adapting Margrave to their particular medium." In a matter of months, mass-market retailers Orbach's in New York were "proud to feature their Margrave at $8.95" ("Dior," *Life*, March 1, 1948: 88).

Other Parisian couturiers objected to Dior's apparent collusion with copyists and cozy relationship with the American press and buyers. Balenciaga, in particular, disliked the press and, together with Jacques Fath, had been deliberately delaying his shows to disrupt their print schedules and avoid cheap Seventh Avenue copies. In 1956 he and Hubert de Givenchy banned journalists altogether due to their perceived influence on American buyers. *L'Officiel* also took up the case in winter 1949 in an article entitled "L'Amérique et Nous," objecting

FIGURE 6.2 Fromenti Sketch of Dior. © Victoria and Albert Museum, London/with kind permission of *The Lady*. (Sketches were still the most popular way to record couturiers' silhouettes at this stage.)

to American manufacturers' appropriation of couturiers' models and names in tones redolent of *La Gazette du Bon Ton* in 1913: "The publicity value of Parisian couturiers is frequently used by American firms on the pages of the daily papers and the specialist fashion magazines" (180). But the rise of American fashion also reflected the influence of the industry's first public relations doyenne, Eleanor Lambert.

Eleanor Lambert and the advent of fashion PR

Originally an art publicist, Eleanor Lambert was asked by the U.S. designer Annette Simpson to represent her in 1932. Lambert spent the next seventy years advancing the cause of fashion—American fashion in particular—and was a powerful force in organizing the industry into a profession. Hired by the newly formed New York Dress Institute in 1940, Lambert shifted the focus from manufacturer to designer. Her first contribution was to reinstate Mainbocher's defunct best-dressed list as "The International Best Dressed List," providing publicity for designers and news material for fashion journalists and others for years to come. As well as designers such as Valentina and the design staff of Bergdorf Goodman, the first ballots were cast by Ballard, Snow, and Vreeland, as well as the fashion editors of news syndicates and the New York newspapers. *The New York Times* of December 27, 1940 announced that the award was "taken over this winter for the first time by the key designers, fashion authorities and members of the fashion press in New York, as the world's new design centre." Lambert's office sent exclusive preview photographs of the winners to the newspapers: The *New York Times* got the first pick, the *Daily News* the last (Fine Collins 2004). By the 1960s the judging committee comprised only of journalists: Vreeland, Eugenia Sheppard of the *New York Herald Tribune* (see below), Margaret Case (*Vogue*), Nancy White (Snow's niece and replacement at *Harper's Bazaar*), and Sally Kirkland of *Life*.

A more original contribution to the fashion industry was Lambert's creation of Fashion Press Week at the Plaza Hotel in New York in 1943. Lifestyle or fashion editors were offered all-expenses-paid trips to see clothes in a single week. Their subsequent reportage was designed to get stockists to place advertising in their respective publications. For the first time, a wide body of journalists were able to preview clothes before their arrival in the stores. There was a pressroom on site, and journalists were given press releases and unique photographs. According to Lambert's biographer, John Tiffany, the experience transformed many general lifestyle editors on regional papers into fashion specialists (2011: 23). The template was so successful that other countries followed suit under Lambert's guidance.

Inspired by Hollywood's Academy Awards, in 1943 Lambert launched the "American Fashion Critics Awards" in association with Coty, which provided further impetus to the fashion press. The primary committee was made up of thirty-four prominent editors from New York publications, including Carmel Snow, Edna Woolman Chase, and the *New York Times*' Virginia Pope, whose recommendations were circulated to a further 500 regional editors. Winners received a bronze female statue known as a "Winnie," designed by the sculptor Marina Hoffman, and a $1,000 war bond. Nominees included Hattie Carnegie, Mainbocher, Claire McCardell, and Valentina. While the award gave designers recognition, it also generated "news" for journalists. "The Cotys", as they became known, were a huge success, and in 1956 Lambert introduced a Hall of Fame for designers who had won more than three times. The Council of Fashion Designers of America (CFDA), inaugurated in 1962, was another Lambert brain-child. By 1981 the CFDA had its own awards, which rapidly replaced "The Cotys".

Having been among the first observers to recognize the connection between designer and celebrity brand, Lambert had a virtual monopoly on couture and designer fashion. During the 1950s, she was publicist for Bill Blass, Halston, Norman Norell (the first recipient of "The Cotys"), Claire McCardell, Hattie Carnegie, Pauline Trigère, Mainbocher, and the milliner Lily Dachas, as well as French couturiers such as Jacques Fath and Christian Dior, and emerging Italian designers like Simonetta. Lambert aggressively pursued the fashion press to get coverage for her designers:

> Nothing would stop Miss Lambert. If editors didn't bite, she would simply find an alternative method for getting her clients' names and work into newspapers and magazines. She would write spirited biographies, and send out detailed press releases and photographs with the hope of getting them published. (Tiffany 2011: 231)

By the late 1960s, the biannual schedule of shows was well established, and American fashion was on the world map. Ironically, many designers now left Lambert and hired their own in-house publicists. As the archetypal fashion PR, however, it was Lambert who had created a publicity system that generated fashion as news with the designer at its heart.[4]

Fashion as news

"The New Look," Dior's manipulation of the press, Lambert's organization of press schedules, and the mythical secrecy of the shows had made fashion news. It also turned fashion journalists into reporters—sleuths looking for a story:

From the moment I boarded a plane to cross the Atlantic my nose started to twitch like a hunting dog in anticipation of what new talents I might uncover, what new faces I could produce for *Vogue*, what fashion trends I could find. It was a search not only for fashion news but for gossip, for titbits that could be used in "People are Talking About". (Ballard 1960: 243)

Mainstream magazines such as *Life* and *Time* regularly reported fashion, and even buying trips to Paris by major department stores made news stories (de Pietri and Leventon 1989: 27). Advances in technology also meant that Europe was becoming more accessible to fashion reporting; where reports and photographs had once been sent by courier and boat, now they were sent by telephone, air, and cable. Although Ernestine Carter still took six days to travel by train from Florence to Paris in the winter of 1963, now advances in air travel made such journeys far easier (Carter 1970: 110).

The emphasis on news meant that journalists were always in search of it: "Fashion editors see it as a news story and if there isn't a headline in it, the hell with it" (Eugenia Sheppard cited in Ballard 1960: 308). In her autobiography, Ballard notes how Carmel Snow would fish for information on what looks *Vogue* would be featuring, although Ballard never revealed her exclusives (1960: 264). Meanwhile Snow, who herself remained stony-faced during couturiers' presentations, would guard her own insights, instructing an assistant to mark down the key models by digging her in the ribs (Rowlands 2005: 356).

The widespread journalistic interest reflected fashion's position at the nexus of the shifting cultural values of the postwar world. Once again, fashion embraced and explained everything: "Virtually every industry in America today is vitally concerned with the fashion appeal of its products and services," announced a *Vogue* publicity leaflet in 1959 (Holgate 1994: 116). In April 1956, BOAC sponsored an edition of *Harper's Bazaar* entitled "British Flight of Fashion" (see plate 9) and advertised itself as the airline for "fashionable people all over the world." This type of cross-promotion and cultural appropriation became more and more prevalent, with advertising for fabric manufacturers often featuring designers' clothes and listing retail stockists. This not only defrayed costs and created publicity for the designers, retailers, and fabric houses and their merchandise, but also allowed manufacturers to benefit from association with the prestige of couture and the modernity of the latest "look" (see plate 10). This type of publicity was particularly important in Italy, where the fabric manufacturers supported the development of Italian fashion after the war by sponsoring the couture and boutique shows in 1951 and beyond.

As aspirational lifestyles rather than actual needs became more significant in generating consumer appeal, the emphasis on "new" became a leitmotif of all discourse, including fashion journalism. Fashionable clothing was framed within the context of other innovations, such as modern art. British *Harper's Bazaar* shot a Dior dress against the backdrop of a painting by Anthony Crosthwaite (September 1954) while its American counterpart shot a Givenchy dress against a Fernand Léger painting (April 1956) and the latest car models ("The News is Portable," American *Harper's Bazaar*, June 1954). Again, this type of fashion spread allowed manufacturers such as Packard to benefit from an association with modernity and fashionability.

Fashion editorial also began to combine travel and fashion features, using exotic locations to signify glamor and modernity. Tourism was particularly employed in service of the Italian look, including a *Vogue* feature on Capri in which the photographer John Coffin "couldn't resist recording Italian fashion" on his holiday (July 1947: 30–3). As Valerie Steele has noted, such an approach often relied on "stereotypical touristic anthropological digressions" (1994: 498).

In the early 1950s fashion was configured as a unified and universal "look" in a way that is unthinkable today, such as when *Harper's Bazaar* announced "The 1954 Look" in March. Magazines emphasized the "new" in relation to "line," reflecting the bold silhouettes of Dior and Balenciaga, who benefitted from arresting headlines. Front covers announced "News From Paris," while British *Harper's Bazaar* in April 1950 used a telegram-style layout, supposedly from Snow, to highlight the immediacy of its information: "Dior's horseshoe neckline is the most conspicuous single fashion of the season" (April 1950: 42). Meanwhile British *Vogue* reported on "news in pockets" and "news in brooches" (April 1949: 56–7).

Underlining the emphasis on "line," the fashion press promoted the fear of being out of fashion: "You can't be a last year girl," admonishes *Harper's Bazaar* in 1947 (cited in Rowlands 2005: 147). Even Hollywood was afraid of releasing a film with an out-of-date hemline.

Newspaper journalism

Although Ballard argues that not much "fashion sense" is needed to report on the couture shows "if you accept news as news," she goes on: "Being able to weigh the relative values of various silhouettes, to distinguish design from sensationalism, and to maintain some relation between fashion and women does demand a certain amount of fashion judgment and discernment" (1960: 262). The late 1940s and 1950s saw the emergence of a new professionalism in fashion criticism and an increase in the power of newspaper journalists.

The journalists were almost exclusively female, with the notable exception of John Fairchild, head of *Women's Wear Daily* Paris bureau: "No aspect of the news is further from the comprehension of the average male editor than fashion," remarked the American Press Institute in 1951 (Garret D. Byrnes, *Newspapers in Fashion*, cited in Voss and Speere 2013: 3). Unfettered by the advertising pressures of the glossy magazines but more limited in what they could convey visually, these women created a new standard of critique and prose: "The by-lined fashion editor, reporting from the couture shows and commenting on trends, was a post-war development. Through the 1940s and 1950s, however, hers was a mature voice of authority addressing a middle class readership" (Polan 2006: 162).

As examples, Brenda Polan cites the British newspaper sorority of Alison Settle, Winefride Jackson of the *Daily Telegraph*, Ailsa Garland of the *Daily Mirror*, Iris Ashley of the *Daily Mail*, Alison Adburgham, and Ernestine Carter. Even more influential, however—at least in terms of numbers of readers—were the American newspapers. Fashion coverage and advertising revenue in the *New York Times* both increased under the fashion editorship of Elizabeth Penrose, formerly of British *Vogue* and later editor of *Glamour*, who joined the newspaper in 1955. Penrose introduced a daily column of fashion news and encouraged her journalists to critique rather than merely report. One of her hires in 1955 was a young erstwhile Parsons design student, Carrie Donovan, who went on to become a legend in American fashion journalism, working at *Harper's Bazaar* and *Vogue,* before returning to the *New York Times* in 1977 as style editor.

Eugenia Sheppard

If Penrose encouraged her protégés at the *Times* to critique the collections, it was another American journalist, Eugenia Sheppard of the *New York Herald Tribune*, whose style of fashion reporting epitomized critical appraisal. Ballard calls her "the most important woman to emerge as a newspaper authority in the 1950s" (1960: 299). Sheppard had become a reporter at the *Tribune* in 1940 and quickly outshone the newspaper's existing fashion reporter, Lucy Noel, whom she replaced in 1947, with her witty and slightly acerbic style. On couturier Jean Dessès' "Dovetail look," she commented, "Dessès has always been inspired by birds. But I think it's time somebody came right out and told this nice guy to switch to biology or some other ology. Anything but birds." Or on the buttons and bows of Paris Couture in 1957: "It's all terribly cute, but like giving a girl candy when she craves steak" (cited in "The Press Hemlines of the Week," *Time*, August 12, 1957). Sheppard's forthright commentary frequently saw her banned from shows, but she simply got buyers to sketch the season's looks for her (ibid.). In 1956 Sheppard started her column "Inside Fashion," which covered both the clothes and the characters of fashion and was syndicated throughout the country; by 1966 it appeared in 100 newspapers around the world. According to Geraldine Stutz, former president of New York department store Henri Bendel, "Inside Fashion" was "the beginning of modern reportage" (cited in Schiro 1984). By focusing on the people who made and wore the clothes, Sheppard brought a broader human interest to fashion journalism and expanded its editorial appeal. Sheppard's erstwhile colleague Richard Kluger also notes her revolutionary style, which prefigured the focus on "beautiful people" that was to characterize fashion commentary in the 1960s:

With the introduction in 1956 of her thrice-weekly column, "Inside Fashion," Sheppard revolutionized the journalism of style by adjusting its focus from inanimate fabric to the people who designed and wore it. By deciding whom and what to write about she could create a whole new pattern of social commentary. (1986: 625)

In her twenty-year tenure, Sheppard arguably made herself fashion's most powerful arbiter and critic: shows would not start without her (Schiro 1984). Sheppard won four front-page awards for her fashion coverage from the New York Newspaper Women's Club and today is honored by the CFDA media award inaugurated in her name in 1987.

A recognized profession

As fashion became news, fashion journalism came of age. The impact of Dior and "The New Look" turned designers into household names, while the New York schedules also helped former amateurs become professional reporters. There was an explosion in journalism and allied metiers such as publicists, photographers, and models. In 1949 *Glamour* compared the contemporary fashion world with that of 1914:

> Where were all the girls who now plan the fashion shows, write sparkling advertisements, map out publicity campaigns and the myriad co-ordinated tie-ins between store and manufacturer, fabric maker and the press, which today spread before the customer each new season's fashion story? Where were the stylists, the name designers, the fashion consultants, the high-powered executives who get their pictures in the papers? There weren't any in that era. (January 1949: 113–14)

Journalists were expected to be extremely knowledgeable, and Grace Mirabella recounts the extensive market and manufacturer knowledge required of *Vogue*'s specialist departments (1995: 96–101). As new fashion centers opened up and the schedule became more grueling, the pressures on journalists increased. However, there were elements of glamor in the social whirl of parties and champagne:

> For the fashion critic, the *sturm und drang* of the Paris Openings follow on from the openings in Rome, Florence and London. Already she has an overdraft of fatigue from travelling, typing and long-distance telephoning, from parties and interminable talking, photographic sessions at six o'clock in the morning and dress shows morning, evening and late night. ("The Weather in the Salons," first published in *Harper's Bazaar* June 1960, cited in Adburgham 1966: 16)

The life of the fashion editor or reporter became a subject of fascination and scrutiny, from Paramount Pictures' *Funny Face* (1957), starring Fred Astaire, Audrey Hepburn, and Kay Thompson as fashion magazine editor Maggie Prescott (based on Diana Vreeland and *Harper's Bazaar*) to *Life's* photographic feature in March 1951 on "Bettina's Busy Day," which covered the hectic schedule of the *Vogue* editor in Paris for the shows (see front cover). Ballard largely staged the photo-story herself, but its inclusion in a mass-market, non-specialist publication—albeit that *Life's* fashion editor was Sally Kirkland, a *Vogue* alumnus whom Carter calls "a significant force in fashion"—reflects the wider interest in what was increasingly recognized as a serious profession.

The fashion journalist was expected to be able to distill the message from the couturiers, pronounce on the significant trends, and make judgments on key looks for both readers and buyers. The role, as vividly described by British journalist Alison Adburgham, remains essentially that of the professional fashion media today:

> Now comes the Paris week, with the fighting on the stairways, the multi-lingual shrieking in the salons; a week of over-heating, under-eating, little sleeping; a week of vitiation and dehydration, ineffectively compensated by indifferent champagne. And yet she survives. She brings herself sufficiently alive to turn a confusion of impressions into a fusion of trends, from which she can distil the essential essence of the coming season, assess the position and prestige of individual *couturiers* and from a matter of some two thousand models she must pick out the distinctive dozen of most significance. ("The Weather in the Salons," first published in *Harper's Bazaar* June 1960, cited in Adburgham 1966: 16)

As the journalist was required to be decisive in her view of fashion, so fashion commentary became both more dogmatic in tone—*L'Officiel* announced "les commandments de la mode"—but also more informative. It told the reader not only what was in fashion, but why it was in fashion and how to wear it: "Dior has an utterly new summer coat which he calls a 'dustcoat'. These coats are worn with complete casualness, buttons unfastened, your hands in your pockets, just as a man would wear a raincoat" (British *Harper's Bazaar*, April 1950: 50).

Further recognition of the growing profession of fashion journalism came with the emergence of a number of new trade organizations. In 1959 Carter, Alisa Garland, and Winefride Jackson formed a group to represent the fashion editors of the leading national newspapers and magazines in Britain (Carter 1974: 128–9). In America, The Fashion Group grew in numbers and influence in the 1940s and 1950s. In addition, the New York Newspaper Women's Club, founded in 1922, started to recognize the profession with its prestigious Front Page Awards, handed to fashion writers and editors. Other awards to acknowledge the expertise of the profession included the Neiman Marcus Awards, started in 1938 for distinguished service in the field of fashion, which honored journalists including Sally Kirkland of *Life* in 1955 and Marie-Louise Bousquet, Paris editor of *Harper's Bazaar*, in 1956.

The profession's growing confidence was reflected in self-exposure. In April 1944 American *Vogue* introduced eight members of its fashion staff, and a spread in *Harper's Bazaar* from February 1958 featured pictures of the photographer Richard Dormer and a shot of his assistant Roy McArthur and the fashion editor Josephine Easton playing cards (72).

That said, fashion journalism was still relatively poorly paid and therefore still largely the prerogative of the monied. While Lord and Taylor's Dorothy Shaver, the first female president of a department store, was paid $100,000 per annum, Carmel Snow received $20,000 as editor of *Harper's Bazaar*. Babs Simpson, a fashion editor at *Vogue*, earned $35 a week ($1,820 per annum) in the 1950s (Rowlands 2005: 196).

Carmel Snow and Bettina Ballard

The rise of fashion journalism as a profession owed much to the power and prestige of the editors and fashion editors of *Harper's Bazaar* and *Vogue* and, perhaps most significantly, the redoubtable Carmel Snow and Bettina Ballard, a view supported by Carter among others (1974: 152).

Although Edna Woolman Chase at *Vogue* had been a potent force in fashion before the war (she was replaced by Jessica Daves in 1952), it was Snow who dominated the international fashion scene after it. She was the first fashion editor to visit Paris in 1944 and made it her mission to save couture. It was she, rather than Vreeland, who covered international collections, leaving the latter to cover American fashion and Seventh Avenue. Meanwhile at *Vogue*, the Paris collections, which had been managed by French *Vogue* before the war, came under the remit of the U.S. fashion editor Bettina Ballard. This was partly because the Paris editor did not want to feature prêt-à-porter or ready-to-wear clothes but also reflected the power of America in terms of both buyers and press (Ballard 1960: 222). It was Ballard rather than Daves who soon came to rival Snow in journalistic clout, both with the couturiers and the buyers. Hired on the basis of a pastiche of Cecil Beaton in *The New Yorker*, Ballard was sent to Paris by Woolman Chase after only a year (ibid.: 13). She returned to New York in 1939 and after a brief return to Paris in 1945 was made fashion editor of American *Vogue*.

Vogue's circulation topped that of *Bazaar* in both America and Britain—although for a period in the mid-1940s the publications were equal in terms of circulation and advertising revenues (Mackenzie Stuart 2013: 156)—but *Bazaar* was seen as the more cutting-edge of the two, as reflected in photographer Richard Avedon's decision to turn down *Vogue* in favor of its rival. Snow was a hands-on editor and worked closely with art director Alexey Brodovitch and fashion editor Vreeland on every aspect of the magazine, laying out photostats of every page: "I adopted the custom I used throughout my life at the *Bazaar* of putting my book on the floor" (Rowlands 2005: 149).

For both Snow and Ballard, the show circuit was a grueling process, shooting through the night at their respective studios in Paris and rising early to review the work before it was sent out. Snow famously arrived at the Maison at 6 o'clock one morning to capture a Balenciaga model before the buyers.

Snow was awarded the Légion d'Honneur in April 1949 for her services to French couture and is widely credited, including by Ballard, for recognizing and promoting the talent of Balenciaga and Dior and for launching the careers of several other designers. They included Hubert de Givenchy, whom Snow noted in March 1952 as "The New Name To Know":

Paris has a new young man—Hubert de Givenchy. His boutique clothes have won the world. They are modern (many separates), fresh and sagacious. He knows—to the last ruffle—exactly how far to go. Everyone is crazy about his white shirtings—his upcut beach pants—huge chic bags—his new approach to colour—his blanchisserie. (152–3)

When Snow announced that she was visiting Italy in July 1951, the buyers followed: in 1951 there were eight at the Florence Collections, but by 1952 there were 300 (Rowlands 2005: 430). The American press also took notice. Although Italian fashion had been covered by *Women's Wear Daily* since the late 1940s, and British *Vogue* had run a feature on "The Fine Italian Hand" (September 1946: 45–9, 81), *Life* only focused on Italy after Snow's endorsement: "Italy Gets Dressed Up" (August 20, 1951: 104–12). Snow was also credited with raising the profile of Emilio Pucci by asking Saks to copy a skirt, and with leading the world to Ireland and the Irish designer Sybil Connolly. Snow single-handedly championed the return of Coco Chanel in 1954, when the French press ignored her because of her alleged links to the Nazis. She commissioned a piece from Chanel's friend Jean Cocteau in the March issue: "Her return to the Parisian scene represents far more than the reopening of a great maison de couture. She arrives as a sign that we must vanquish the inflation of mediocrity" (Cocteau, American *Harper's Bazaar*, March 1954: 168).

Snow's pronouncements on couture were always clear-cut: "Fath has the most brilliant collection of his career. All his clothes show every curve of a woman's body, and are intensely pretty; suits and dresses look magically fitted to the body skintight' (March 1954: 132). This did not always win favor with the designers however, and despite her close relationship with Balenciaga (Rowlands 2005:

392–401), Snow managed to get herself and the whole of *Bazaar* banned for a season (402).

Most importantly, perhaps, Snow believed passionately in the knowledge and judgment of the fashion editors and the need for them to lead where others dared not. She was never afraid to take risks in her views on fashion and in the look and feel of the magazine:

> Sometimes the reporters miss the prophetic dress—the biggest fashion is not always the most obvious. Often a buyer will see it and then deliberately skip it, knowing that her customers would find it too extreme. A magazine can and should take chances that a merchant can't. If I think that a dress is important I don't care if it has been bought or not. I mark down the number in my little red book and give to Avedon or Louise Dahl-Wolfe. The photograph usually evokes both praise and criticism. But I just sit back and wait. For I know that in six months, maybe a year later the public will be ready for it. (Snow, cited in Rowlands 2005: 355–6)

Snow was also not afraid to take risks with hiring staff—or firing some, like Erté, when necessary. Her hand-picked team included Brodovitch; the photographers Louise Dahl-Wolfe and Richard Avedon; Marie-Louise Bouquet; Irene Brin, who worked as a columnist at *Corriere della Sera* and wrote for *Bellezza* as Italian editor; and, of course, Diana Vreeland as fashion editor, of whom more in Chapter 7. Snow's only real misjudgment came with the prescient creation of *Junior Bazaar* in November 1945; previously a section of the main magazine, it faded after three years in May 1948 due to a lack of advertising revenues.

Ultimately Snow was unceremoniously replaced by her niece, Nancy White Paine, in 1957 (Rowlands 2005: 464), undone by her editorial integrity as the women's press faced growing pressure for circulation and advertising in the face of increased competition from television, economic downturns—the American post-war boom was fading by the mid-1950s—her age in an industry focused increasingly on youth and, perhaps, her legendary drinking. Ironically, Snow embraced her technological nemesis when she televised *Bazaar's* fashion reports on the couture shows on *The Wide Wide World* on March 31, 1957 (Rowlands 2005: 460).[5]

The work of femininity

While *L'Officiel* argued that the spring collections of 1947 brought a new feminine line to fashion—"We are increasingly moving towards a fundamentally feminine line" (52)—"The New Look" was criticized by some women for bringing back both corsets and the regulatory rituals of dressing, which they associated with the concerted post-war effort to return women to the home and to prioritize the notion of "grooming" as the essence of womanhood. "At last the Parisienne has become a woman again," enthused *L'Officiel* of the new fashions. "Grace and charm, enticing gestures are enough to convince even the most hostile" (*L'Officiel*, Christmas 1947: 101).

The fashion magazines once again foregrounded both dress and the allied arts of beauty as a woman's main preoccupation. In a feature entitled "Take A Week for Beauty" in January 1950, British *Harper's Bazaar* instructs its readers: "During this week, make no late evening dates, get a maximum of sleep and do a minimum of jobs, apart from the main business of getting yourself into shape" (48–9). While the leisured lifestyle which such a regime requires reflects the readership of the magazine, similar notions of women's aesthetic responsibility appeared elsewhere. Being "well groomed" became part of the fashion lexicon in both editorial and advertising copy.

Fashion commentary renewed the notions of "elegance," "femininity," and "taste" as the defining parameters of womanhood. Once again the pages of the fashion press were filled with the threat of social exclusion or embarrassment for fashion faux pas ranging from wearing silk during daylight hours to having the wrong length of skirt. Even *Elle* ran an article entitled "From Negligence to Refinement" in April 1957. Fashion rules that had relaxed during the war were now rigorously upheld: "Clothing was about looking stylish and appropriate according to the very set demands of different settings and different times of day" (Mirabella 1995: 101). In 1956 British *Harper's Bazaar* ran an article on fabric etiquette entitled "The Material Difference Between Day and Night" (January 1956: 48–9).

Magazines promoted an idea of glamorous femininity based on the competitive art of sartorial superiority. Elegance was particularly important for the French magazines, as was the appetite for fashion. More than seventeen new fashion publications were launched in France after the war and circulation for fashion weeklies grew to over 7 million in the early 1950s, more than twice that of weekly news magazines (Cline 2008: 50, 53). As well as fashion magazines, a number of etiquette manuals re-emerged to guide women, particularly in grooming and elegance. In 1949 *Marie France* ran an article giving the views of five experts—two of whom were magazine editors—on what constituted elegance, "Cinq Experts en Elégance ont decidé" (December 12, 1949: 22–3).

Along with the cult of grooming came a renewed emphasis on domesticity. Advertising in particular focused on women as wives and mothers, while businesses in the U.S. reinstated policies against hiring married women, especially those of child-bearing years (Dellis Hill 2004: 77). This focus on the home was also prevalent in the fashion press. There were twice as many articles on home-making in *Vogue* in 1950 compared with 1940, for example, and the cover for December 1950 features a woman holding a baby (Dellis Hill 2004: 78). In France, even political magazines such as *Femme Françaises*, which had been founded during the resistance, had a post-war makeover to incorporate recipes, patterns, stories, fashion spreads, and a large photo cover (Cline 2008: 52–3).

Allied to the emphasis on domesticity was a new passivity in the way fashion magazines mediated femininity. Women were once more primarily a spectacle in the male gaze. *L'Officiel* advocates that women should aim to "please the viewer rather than frighten, surprise, or astonish." Equally, women's moods should be placid and their face "undisfigured by bad temper—so unattractive to men." "They should be lovable by supporting their men folk—listening, understanding and consoling" (*L'Officiel*, autumn 1949: 140).[6]

Photography reflected this elegant, spectacular woman, as Hall-Duncan notes in relation to Penn's iconic "Twelve Beauties" (American *Vogue*, May 1, 1947): "The graceful poses in which Penn places his models form a beautiful pattern of shape and line but also give an accurate vision of the impeccable grace of 1950s' clothing and the woman for whom they were designed" (1979: 157).

The new hybrid trade press

The role of *Women's Wear Daily* in the initial success of Dior reflected the growing influence of the trade publication in international fashion. However, *Women's Wear Daily* also reflected the growing influence of segments of the trade press on the consumer market. As consumer magazines such as *Vogue* increasingly functioned as trade oracles on fashion trends, a number of hybrid trade publications emerged that appealed to professionals and laity alike. Like the consumer magazines, these publications carried many advertisements for fabric houses that promoted designers' clothing.

Women's Wear Daily

Begun in 1910 as a quarterly publication at 50 cents a year, *Women's Wear*, as *Women's Wear Daily* was first known, announced that it would be a purveyor of knowledge for those in the industry: "It will be the aim of the publishers to present its subscribers a succinct epitomization of the most important happenings and events occurring in the women's wear industry" (June 1910: vol. 1, no. 1).

From the first, *Women's Wear* covered important fashion news. In 1914 it reports on Chanel's "extremely interesting sweaters which embrace new features" (July 27, 1914), while a cover from October 1917 has five sketches of "Poiret's Ideas for 1917" which are "Sketched in Paris Especially for *Women's Wear*." The quarterly also reported on retail news and major world events, such as the sinking of the *Titanic* in 1912. Arguably, it pioneered the idea of fashion as news. By the next decade it was already using "Daily" in its title and calling itself "The Retailers' Newspaper." However, it also commented and reported on the world of "The Smart Set" in its copyrighted feature "They Are Wearing," which began to blur its function between trade and consumer press.

After World War II, the magazine became increasingly international in coverage and influence. As well as Dior, it was also instrumental in the promotion of Italian fashion, supporting boutique lines with particular enthusiasm. This in large part reflected the efforts of Elisa Massai, who was an economic journalist on the Milan daily *24 ore*, but who from 1949 to 1983 reported on Italian fashion for *Women's Wear Daily* (White 2000: nn. 41, 34). *Women's Wear Daily* was particularly powerful in corralling the interest of the American media, as couturier Micol Fontana remarked: "Once you have been in *Women's Wear Daily*, they all want an interview" (quoted in White 2000: 162).

L'Officiel de la Couture et de la Mode

In Europe, meanwhile, much of the trade press remained fiercely nationalistic and had strong links with both fabric manufacturers and makers of clothing. In France, *L'Officiel* had since its launch in 1921 promoted itself as an organ of the French industry (see plate 11). It was a powerful voice for both the couture industry and the fabric manufacturers who supported it through advertising, which, unusually, was separated from the editorial. It gave details of the designer, the model, the fabric, and where to buy them. However, it also had a consumer readership as well as an international trade audience, and its editorial content included the arts, interiors, and recipes. It even had an English translation of its key fashion contents in the back section of the magazine. Published every two months from the end of the 1940s, the magazine primarily covered the couture collections but also promoted other aspects of French culture, such as music, as emblems of French creativity and artistry. In a 1947 editorial, Jacques de Lacretelle of the Académie Française makes an explicit link between fashion and French culture:

> In countries which create fashion, there is generally a versatility and ready enthusiasm. But it must be grounded firmly in good taste. A bit of fighting spirit does no harm. All of these things are united in the French temperament. (*Printemps* 1947: 49)

As American brands became increasingly visible in Europe and couture copies abounded across the Atlantic and elsewhere, and as Italian fashion started to pose a real threat to French predominance, *L'Officiel* became more defiantly nationalistic, as in the editorial "L'Amérique et Nous" cited above.

Pl. I.

PLATE 1 *Le Cabinet des Modes*, January 1, 1786. © Bibliothèque nationale de France. (The *Cabinet*'s plates pioneered very detailed and high-quality engravings.)

(1214.)

Pelisse Turque, Garnie de Martre.

PLATE 2 Pelisse Turque Garnie de Martre. *Journal des Dames et des Modes*. Paris, France, 1812. © Victoria and Albert Museum, London. (Note that the illustration is still not branded at this stage.)

PLATE 3 *La Mode Illustrée*, June 14, 1868. Two Women in a Carriage. © Victoria and Albert Museum, London. (The figures' luxurious shiny fabrics, extravagant costumes and presence at Le Bois suggest the aspirational lifestyle of *La Parisienne*. By now, the plate is branded.)

LE FOLLET

Boulevart St Martin, 61.

Toilettes pour Longchamps.

Robes de Camille - Chapeaux de Mᵐᵉ Baudry, r. Richelieu, 87.

Plumes de Chagot ainé, r. Richelieu, 81.

PLATE 4 *Le Follet, Journal du Grand Monde.19th Century.* Jules David. © Victoria and Albert Museum, London. (The mother's dark fabrics, modest style, and demeanor mediate her function as moral custodian. The yellow bonnet is uncharacteristically bright, suggesting artistic license.)

LA MARSEILLAISE

PLATE 5 "La Marseillaise." Etienne Drian. *La Gazette du Bon Ton*, July 1914.
© Victoria and Albert Museum, London. (The title and the use of Tricolor colors
suggest nationalism, but the whimsical artistry denotes it as a fashion plate, imbricating
patriotism with the creativity of French fashion.)

PLATE 6 Erté cover for *Harper's Bazaar*, January 1923. © Sevenarts Ltd/DACS 2016. Image courtesy of the Advertising Archives/Harper's Bazaar/Hearst Magazines UK. (Like others of the period—*Vogue* and *Fémina*, for example—Erté's covers function as artifacts, conveying mood rather than clothing.)

PLATE 7 *Vogue Paris*, December 1939. Christian Bérard. © ADAGP, Paris and DACS, London 2016/
Vogue Paris. (Christian Bébé Bérard was a regular contributor to *Vogue*. As in Drian's plate, fashion is
imbricated with patriotism.)

PLATE 8 *Marie Claire*. First Cover, March 1937. Courtesy of Marie Claire Group, France.

HARPER'S Bazaar

British
Flight
of
Fashion

April 1956

Three Shillings and Sixpence

PLATE 9 British *Harper's Bazaar*, April 1956. © British Library Board HIU. LON. A309/
Harper's Bazaar/Hearst Magazines UK.

PLATE 10 "Les Couturiers ont choisi." *Fémina*. 1948. © Victoria and Albert Museum, London. (The significance of the fabric manufacturers to haute couture is reflected in this plate linking them to the couturiers' creativity.)

PLATE 11 Les Editions Jalou, *L'Officiel*, winter 1947. Collections issue 37–8. © René Gruau. Courtesy of Les Editions Jalou. (Gruau was a frequent contributor to elite magazines and his cover illustration suggests the creativity and desirability of haute couture in the manner of the consumer press.)

NOVA

MARCH 3s

A NEW KIND OF MAGAZINE FOR THE NEW KIND OF WOMAN

Mr Sofa the Psychiatrist

This is No. 1 of the British monthly with the 1965 approach. What's the isometric system? Mary Rand figures it out. What does Christopher Booker say about Miss Cardinale? (That's her above.) Who's Mr. Blond? Pages & pages of answers, plus Jill Butterfield, Robert Robinson, Elizabeth David, Irwin Shaw— and Paris fashion. And where's 'Terra Nova'? Explore inside

PLATE 12 *Nova*, March 1965. © www.timeincuk.content.com.

PLATE 13 "Hungry?" *Dazed and Confused*, Issue 15, 1994. © Rankin. Photograph courtesy of the photographer. (*Dazed and Confused* often used irreverent humor to highlight issues surrounding the mainstream commercial discourse, such as the extreme body ideals expected of high fashion models.)

THE FACE

No 22/JULY 1990 £1.50 • US $4.75
ITALY L5500 GERMANY 9.50M SPAIN 435PTAS BELG. 105 BFR

THE 3RD SUMMER OF LOVE

Stone Roses on Spike Island, an A-Z of the new bands, Daisy Age fashion, Hendrix and psychedelia

'Kiss my butt!' Sandra on Madonna

Prince in Minneapolis: tour preview

Indian summe
photograp
Corinne Da

JOHN WATERS / MICKEY ROURKE / MARSHALL JEFFERSON / TIM ROTH

07

0 74470 72689 0

PLATE 14 *The Face*, July 1990. Photograph © Corinne Day/Trunk Archive, Kate Moss @ Storm/Bauer Consumer Media/Courtesy of Vinmag Archive Ltd.

PLATE 15 Ana, London, September 30, 1998. From "Go Sees" SHOWStudio
2001. © Juergen Teller. Courtesy of Juergen Teller. ("Go Sees" spanned nearly a year.
Teller photographed every aspiring model sent to his studio by agencies framed by the
doorway.)

the gentlewoman

Fabulous women's magazine, issue nº 6
Autumn and Winter 2012

Angela Lansbury

UK £6.00

USA $14.99

PLATE 16 *The Gentlewoman*, autumn/winter 2012. © Terry Richardson. Courtesy of
The Gentlewoman.

Linea Italiana[7]

The Italian fashion industry used its postwar Marshall Aid—economic assistance from the U.S.—to build its fashion textile industry (White 2000: 21) and by 1951 the French press were talking warily of the "Florence Bomb."[8] Italy had its own powerful trade organ, *Linea Italiana*, which emerged after the war with a subtitle of "I Tessili Nuovi" ("new textiles"). It initially appeared biannually, covering both fashion and textiles, and attracted a consumer readership (ibid.: 26). The magazine focused on Paris as the center of design, regularly reporting Paris fashions but also featuring Italian designs next to their Parisian source of inspiration (ibid.: 78). It also placed Italian fashion in the context of broader Italian culture, especially architecture. However, by winter 1949 *Linea Italia* was promoting boutique wear and emphasizing the advantages of Italian over foreign fashion: lower prices combined with craftsmanship, fabric and finish, color and practicality. A similar emphasis appeared in other Italian magazines, including the consumer glossy *Bellezza* and the knitwear trade magazine *Linea Maglia*. In 1950 a new consumer magazine, *Novita*, appeared to support the emerging fashion market; it merged with *Vogue* to become *Vogue Italia* in 1965 (Puccinelli 2014: 245).

As Nicola White has pointed out, the American press also emphasized boutique as the core appeal of Italian fashion, especially *Vogue*, where Ballard recognized the style's potential appeal to the American market. By 1961 Italian fashion had created such a strong identity that *Life* ran a feature entitled "The Bold Italian Look that Changed Fashion" (Steele 1994: 502).

The Ambassador

In Britain, culture was also used to promote the domestic fashion industry in *The Ambassador*. As Claire Wilcox observes, *The Ambassador* was not strictly speaking a fashion magazine, but "with its heavy glossy pages and colour reproduction, the magazine had the 'feel' of fashion" (Breward and Wilcox 2012: 174).

After the war, the Incorporated Society of London Fashion Designers set out to promote British designers as well as fabrics and manufacturers. Its principal ally, the trade magazine *International Textiles*, was relaunched in 1946 by editor and proprietor Hans Juda as *The Ambassador*, a "British export journal." A unique and influential trade paper, at the height of its success it had subscribers in ninety countries. *The Ambassador* covered Paris Couture as well as publishing supplements on textiles and fashions, and even had a section on historical fashions written by James Laver, costume curator at the Victoria and Albert Museum.

Juda's wife Elsbeth, known as Jay, art-directed, photographed, and styled the magazine in ways that were innovative even for the consumer press. Having met Carmel Snow, Elsbeth was influenced by the avant-garde graphics and fashion

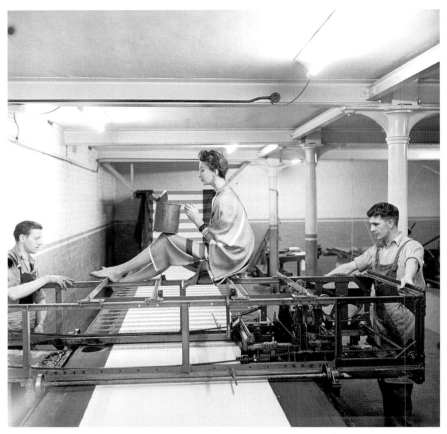

FIGURE 6.3 Barbara Goalen on a screen printer. Photo by Elsbeth Juda, Lancashire, England, 1952. © Elsbeth Juda Estate/Victoria and Albert Museum, London.

presentation of *Harper's Bazaar*. Leading contemporary artists such as Graham Sutherland and John Piper provided artwork for covers and collaborated on designs for British fabric houses in 1953. Hans Juda wanted to promote British culture in its broadest sense, so the magazine's editorial remit was broad and innovative. Fashion shoots often featured prominent British industries, such as the Lancashire textile mills (figure 6.3) or the Esso oil refinery at Fawley, both of which were used as backdrops for clothing (Breward and Wilcox 2012: 60–1).

 The Ambassador was fiercely nationalistic in its support for, and promotion of, British design. To develop exports, the Judas formed partnerships with prominent American retailers, notably Stanley Marcus of Neiman Marcus and Dorothy Shaver of Lord and Taylor, and from 1949 initiated "British Weeks" with Shaver at her New York store. In 1951, meanwhile, *The Ambassador* argued that London fashion deserved a higher ranking in world fashion ("London Looks Up," 1951, no. 9: 76). The claim would prove prescient as London rose to international fashion prominence in the 1960s.[9]

A new era was dawning. The end of the 1950s saw print advertising revenues increasingly pressurized by television, as well as an economic downturn. A new mood and a new, younger fashion consumer took center stage, having been identified by *Seventeen* at the close of the war. A new type of fashion—and a new type of journalism—was needed for this changing audience.

Notes

1   See Wilcox (2008), Palmer (2001), de Pietri and Leventon (1989), and Steele (1998 [1988]: Ch. 13), among others, for a detailed examination of the resurgence of Haute Couture after World War II.

2   For the most detailed examination of this phenomenon see Pochna (2008).

3   *Elle*, however, was enthusiastic: "The collection that knocked out the entire world" and "Everything that shines is Dior" (March 1947).

4   See Tiffany (2011) for more on Lambert.

5   For more on Snow see Rowlands' biography (2005). For more on Ballard, see her autobiography (1960).

6   For more on this see Walker (1998) and Cline (2008).

7   This is not the same magazine as *Linea Italiana*, launched in 1965.

8   For more on postwar Italian reconstruction see White (2000) and Stanfill (2014).

9   For more on *The Ambassador* see Breward and Wilcox (2012).

7 THE RISE OF INDIVIDUALISM: THE 1960s AND 1970s

Introduction

Now, although the old attitude prevails, it disguises itself under the mercurial cloaks of old money versus new money; fashion versus vulgarity; the old aristocracy versus the new; the with-it opposed to the unwith-it. The new social attitudes rely on a shifting perspective. As fast as the unwith-it discover the with-it, the with-it scurry frantically on to the super-with-it. One never quite becomes the other. And since the old hard and fast rule no longer applies generally, certain modern desperations are set up.
("SOCIETY: THE INDEX," *THE QUEEN*, JULY 14, 1965: 49)

The 1960s were, as *Queen* points out, a period of "shifting perspective" and "new social attitudes" that witnessed the advent of modern pop culture; the Beatles; space travel; Western defeat in Vietnam; the widespread availability of the contraceptive pill; a consumer and baby boom in Europe; and in fashion prêt-à-porter, street fashion, and the notion of individual style: "The style of the 1960s was also about style—about style as a way of life, style as the self and yet also style as fun" (Wilson 2003 [1985]: 178). Fashion became a transient and disposable commodity that expressed an unconventional new world order dictated as much by the street as by couture. The alliance between fashion and pop culture—particularly popular music[1]—brought male fashion to the fore and made London's Kings Road and Carnaby Street important centers of fashion innovation. More importantly, "the look" replaced "elegance" as the key fashion discriminator: "A dress or a suit isn't fashion, a look is" (Foale and Tuffin, *Daily Mirror*, 1962, cited in Webb 2009).

Fashion editorial used words like "cool," "with-it," "kooky," "clobber," and "gear," and fashion became aimed firmly at the young.

British *Vogue* revitalized "A Young Idea" in 1961, begun in 1953, and *Queen* soon introduced "About 20." Impudence replaced respect in clothing, fashion photography, and copy, while editors like *Queen's* Anne Trehearne pronounced Paris boring and refused to visit. In the new cult of youth and disposability, being "in the know" replaced social position as the marker of distinction (Lipovetsky 1994: 101) and cultural capital shifted to those at the center of the new pop art culture. Older society fashion editors—what photographer William Klein called "All those women in thick glasses and hats" (Harrison 1991: 98)—found themselves replaced by younger women who were part of the fashionable set such as Marit Allen, who worked at *Queen* and *Vogue,* and Grace Coddington.[2]

A new icon of femininity emerged: the single girl who was financially and, by implication, sexually independent. Fashion photography both created and reflected her changing status and freedom: shots became much more active and the single girl jumped, ran, and looked real. She had "attitude." A Lolita-like prepubescent figure, the single girl, like the *Jeune Fille* before her, signaled eroticism held in abeyance.

But sex was moving center stage, from bikini-clad girls on the pages of the *Daily Mirror* to the features and problem pages. An increased emphasis on the body in the dress brought with it new parameters of femininity. It was not coincidental that *Slimming* magazine, launched in 1969, was phenomenally successful. As John Berger noted, women increasingly surveyed their bodies and judged their own femininity (Berger 1972: 63).

Paris reacted to the shifting international landscape with limited success, and its prominence was challenged by both London and Italy. Meanwhile the first televised couture shows in 1962—Dior and Balmain—changed the restrictions on the release of visual material, and newspapers were subsequently permitted to have professional sketchers in the shows. With some of the mystique of couture removed, however, *Queen* pronounced Balenciaga and Givenchy dead on October 6, 1965 in a report entitled "The End" (102–5)—Balenciaga did indeed close his couture house in 1968.

A new type of designer clothing emerged in Paris and elsewhere: prêt-à-porter. Yves Saint Laurent launched Rive Gauche in 1966, the first stand-alone prêt-à-porter label from a couturier with its own boutique. Ready-to-wear, manufactured clothing was no longer the poor relation of haute couture. Instead, it "came to embody the spirit of fashion in its most vital expression" (Lipovetsky 1994: 94). For ordinary women, new synthetic fabrics such as nylon, standard Americanized sizing, and new forms of retail such as credit-friendly mail order all made stylish fashion more accessible.[3] The fashion press began to offer their own exclusive mail order to readers, frequently by emerging new designers: Biba's first fashion success was a pink gingham dress and scarf at 25 shillings (£2.50), that appeared as an exclusive in the *Daily Mirror* in May 1964 (Hulanicki and Pel 2014: 32–3).

Women's purchases of clothes, footwear, and cosmetics exploded—in Britain, expenditure increased 78 percent between 1956 and 1965 (White 1970: 179)—and advertising revenues boomed. Together with advances in color reproduction and cheaper printing (White 1970: 208), such a lucrative market brought the creation of a new type of fashion publication. The *Sunday Times* launched the first Sunday supplement in February 1962, with Ernestine Carter as women's editor and Mark Boxer, formerly of *Queen*, as editor and art director. Eager to benefit from expanding fashion revenues, the *Telegraph* followed suit in 1964 and the *Observer* in 1965. The Sunday supplement made fashion commentary far more widespread: "These 'free' magazines brought fashion, previously the preserve of the wealthy or initiated, into every home in the country, and fashion became an increasingly valuable indicator of status" (Hulanicki and Pel 2014: 38). Both the color supplements and the newspapers themselves hired specialist fashion photographers: "They began to give newspaper fashion a reputation it had never had before" (Felicity Green, cited in Webb 2009: 148).

The fashion press expanded to exploit new consumers and the new disposable culture. Among the British launches was *Petticoat* (1966), which targeted the fifteen- to eighteen-year-old market who the magazine's marketing folder identified as having £250 million a year of uncommitted spending money (White 1970: 188). Other new magazines included *Honey* (1960), *Rave* (1964), and *19* (1968) in Britain, while in the U.S. *Cosmopolitan* was relaunched in July 1965 by Helen Gurley Brown, author of *Sex and the Single Girl* (1962). Meanwhile, as the fashionable male emerged as an identifiable figure, magazines such as *Town* in Britain and *GQ* in America set out to attract the new readership.

Meanwhile, power was increasingly concentrated in a limited number of publishing houses. In Britain this saw the advent of the monopolistic International Publishing Corporation (IPC), which by 1961 owned Fleetway, Odhams, and Newnes (White 1970: 179–81). In the U.S., Condé Nast continued to expand, purchasing Street and Smith in 1959 and therefore rivals *Seventeen* and *Mademoiselle*; the latter was merged with *Glamour* in the same year.

The end of the 1960s brought a reaction against the optimism of the earlier part of the decade. The counter-culture movement born of the civil unrest in America over Vietnam, civil rights, the assassinations of Kennedy and Martin Luther King, the rise of Black Power, and the student riots in Paris of 1968, as well as other protests across Europe, created a new mood of cynicism. The 1970s would present a more challenging environment for fashion and fashion publishing.

In September 1968 *Nova* announced: "Fashion is Dead." It was not, of course, but the traditional model of fashion in which Paris told the world what to wear was overturned by what Valerie Steele terms "anti-fashion." In *Nova*, fashion editor Caroline Baker clarified the assertion: "Ten years ago fashion writers could still command: hems will be shorter; waists are out. Now we hardly dare predict past the middle of next week. Fashion in its strictest sense is dead" (*Nova*, September 1968: 55).

Fashion was subject to a kind of schizophrenia that challenged journalists: "The myriad styles in Paris created a mood of enormous confusion. Even the shrewdest fashion veterans were asking questions rather than making pronouncements," observed *Time* in 1971 ("Short and Shorter," February 8, 1971: 52). Multiple influences appeared at once and music was still influential as fashion became increasingly tribal and divided into subcultures (see Hebdige 1988 [1979]: Part Two). The nihilism of punk and its associated deconstructed clothing vied with the sometimes seedy excesses of glam rock or the hedonism of Andy Warhol's Factory, the nightclub Studio 54 in New York, the rise of disco, and the "black is beautiful" culture.

Meanwhile, in the U.S. the feminist movement became increasingly vocal. One of its cornerstones, Betty Friedan's *The Feminine Mystique* (1963), had been highly critical of the role of women's magazines in promoting limiting definitions of femininity. In 1970 militant feminists occupied the offices of both *Ladies' Home Journal* and *Cosmopolitan* (Scanlon 2009: 178–9; Zuckerman 1998: 208–9). Feminism was equally widespread in Europe. The icon of sixties' consumerism—the girl—was rejected by all but the youngest of publications and *Cosmopolitan*, which still focused on "The Cosmo Girl." The teenage boom was over and women, particularly "working women," became the new focus for the fashion media.

Toward the end of the 1970s a new cultural optimism emerged, particularly in the U.S., where *Vogue* heralded "Success '76" (August 1976). This new optimism focused on the dynamic career woman, a new type of comfortable sportswear, and an emphasis on health and well-being. More specialist publications targeted the career woman or the health-conscious, such as *Working Woman* in the U.S. (1976) and *Santé* in France (1977), respectively. While these magazines did not specialize in fashion, their arrival and the growth of consumer interest in health and fitness impacted upon the fashion press.

Overall, a new type of fashion—and of fashion writing—emerged during the 1970s that was centered on self-styling. Enabling rather than dictatorial, it was based on the touchstone ideas of "freedom" and "choice." As subcultural influence bubbled up, the street began to feature in fashion editorial. *Nova* led the way, but *Elle* also ran a photo-led feature on fashion in the streets of Saint-Germain-des-Près in July 1977 (46–7) and Bill Cunningham inaugurated his street fashion shots for the *New York Times* in 1978. Individualism emerged as a key cultural signifier, as epitomized by Condé Nast's 1979 launch *Self*.

Swinging London

Like Paris in the 1920s, London in the mid-1960s became the center of the "youthquake," a term coined by Diana Vreeland in American *Vogue* in January 1965. *Women's Wear Daily* dubbed the city "Swinging London," and the appellation was picked up by *Time* magazine in a famed editorial on April 16, 1966 that marked the apotheosis of mythical London chic. (The industry was a step ahead of the press: British designers, including Mary Quant and Tuffin and Foale, had been invited to New York to present their wares in a "Youthquake" fashion show the previous year.) Fashionable photographers such as John Cowan used London as a backdrop to denote modern sensibilities (Martin 2002: 180), while British pop television shows such as *Ready Steady Go* generated fashion stories through its young presenter Cathy McGowan, and rising stars such as Cilla Black and the Rolling Stones became the subject of fashion editorial.

London's fashionable set congregated in the new cafés and boutiques on the King's Road and Carnaby Street, or the flats of "Chelsea Set" designers such as Quant, including young journalists Marit Allen, Brigid Keenan, Caroline Baker, and Molly Parkin. Fashion, as Saint Laurent observed, was increasingly happening on the streets (Lipovetsky 1994: 92). The London fashion scene was a close-knit world, in which designers and fashion editors were friends and were sometimes interchangeable: Parkin went from making hats for Biba to being *Nova*'s first fashion editor, and Hulanicki from being a renowned fashion illustrator who illustrated "Shophound" for *Vogue* to the creator of Biba, for example.

London's "swinging" permissive status was largely a mythological media construction (Breward 2004: 151). The British fashion press both promoted and exploited this newfound fashion and cultural leadership. As the fashion emphasis shifted away from Paris couture shows to young designers in London, fashion editors in the British capital found themselves increasingly influential in discovering the latest new label. The British fashion press was instrumental in supporting new designers (Wilson 2003 [1985]: 174–5) and promoting the myth of London's cultural and creative leadership (figure 7.1). In 1963 the *Sunday Times* inaugurated its International Fashion Awards with the aim of establishing London as a world fashion center (Carter 1974: 149–53).

Magazines from *Vogue* to *Rave* mediated London's fashion creativity and youthful modernity in photography and discourse. At *Nova*, first Molly Parkin and later Caroline Baker were supportive of friends in the London fashion scene:

> How you will be dressing depends mainly on the influence of our own designers. They are Biba, Foale and Tuffin, Jean Muir, and Ossie Clark and Alice Pollock. Each season they produce the best and most wearable clothes of all. No exclusiveness about them either. Theirs is the mass-market world. (*Nova*, September 1969: 55)

FIGURE 7.1 Jean Shrimpton in a Mary Quant cardigan shift and long-sleeved shirt. Photo by John French for *The Sunday Times*, 1963. © John French/Victoria and Albert Museum, London.

Fashion journalists and designers often mixed at nightclubs such as Ad Lib, but journalists were also expected to do the rounds of boutiques and workshops to find new and interesting designers: "We would know when they had a new collection ready and would have a girl who was one of their friends who would put the clothes on" (Allen 2005).

Fashion exclusives became a selling point of newspapers: an article by Barbara Griggs in the *Evening Standard*, "Let Me be the First to Tell You," is flagged by the newspaper as "Another Gold for Griggs" (October 26, 1962) while on December 22, 1964, Felicity Green got the front and back pages of the *Mirror* to promote fashion and the new world order (Green 2014: 92–3). Featuring in a newspaper could change retail fortunes, according to Vanessa Denza, creative director of the 21 shop at Woolands department store:

> The press used to come to me for stories, because you were doing new things all the time. There were very good writers like Barbara Briggs and Ernestine Carter. Veronica Papworth at the *Sunday Express* was great. If you got a dress in there you sold hundreds and hundreds of the same style. (Webb 2009: 53)

If the new Sunday supplements brought color to newspaper fashion—along with new younger shoppers and advertising revenues—they also placed fashion within a broader cultural context. At populist titles like the *Mirror*, Green aimed to "make it fun" (2014: 45) and of unisex appeal through popular culture, such as by using the QPR football team as models. Hedonistic fun was at the heart of the "Swinging London" myth, along with other cultural signifiers that placed the city at the nexus of the Modern Age.

The modern age

Fashion found itself at the forefront of what future British Prime Minister Harold Wilson called in 1963 a "white hot technical revolution." Designers, including Paco Rabanne and Courrèges, created space-age looks to engage with the new spirit of modernity and fashion journalism also created new signifiers to suggest modernity and futurism, including the space race itself. Art director Peter Knapp created a moon backdrop for the cover and an evening-wear feature for French *Elle* as early as October 1959. In America, where Avedon used the rockets of Cape Canaveral as a backdrop in *Harper's Bazaar* in February 1961, space also projected a new kind of nationalism based on U.S. technological superiority and vision in the Cold War.[4] As Djurdja Bartlett has shown, fashion and the fashion press were equally important in promoting communist ideology in Eastern Europe (2013: 46–57).

The cross-over among the worlds of fashion, art, architecture, and music provided more means for magazines to suggest youth, change, and innovation. Terence Donovan's photographs for *Town* incorporated "a broad sweep of contemporary cultural references" (Harrison 1991: 202). The new Modernist architecture of London provided the backdrop for fashion shoots in British *Vogue* (February 15, 1961)—"London Revisited"—and in 1965 Georgina Howell used settings such as the Birmingham Bull Ring for an *Observer* fashion shoot: "Our fashion editor has been finding new clothes to keep pace with the new architecture" (Webb 2009: 11–12).

As a result of such cultural fusion, the fashion press of the 1960s came to represent modernity for a new generation of literary figures. Kingsley Amis, for example, wrote a commentary on the social aspects of beauty in British *Vogue* entitled "Off Beat Beauty, or why Henrietta Maria kept her eyes Open." The article—Amis references de Beauvoir as well as Bacon, Brigitte Bardot as well as Keats and Van Dyck's portrait of Henrietta Maria—purports itself in favor of "the two-tone hairdos and outlandish lipsticks by which the modern woman deliberately distorts herself out of the china doll image" (British *Vogue*, February 15, 1961: 77). Meanwhile Henry Miller wrote on "Woman throughout the Ages" for *Harper's Bazaar* in October 1962 and a young Tom Wolfe opined on "The New Art Gallery Society" in November 1964.

"The beautiful people"

As in the 1920s, of which the decade was in many ways a sartorial pastiche (Wilson 2003 [1985]: 172), a new social hierarchy developed on both sides of the Atlantic (although it was particularly associated with "Swinging London"). Based on style rather than on money or class, it included everyone from young musicians, such as The Beatles and the Rolling Stones, to models such as Twiggy and Jean Shrimpton, who became household names rather than anonymous clothes horses, and young artists such Peter Blake and David Hockney. Fashion photographers became celebrities, reflecting the growth in their influence as the primary vectors for communicating fashion's new mood: they included the Earls Lichfield and Snowdon as well as David Bailey, Terence Donovan, and Brian Duffy. Even hairdressers became fashionable figures, including the ultimate sixties icon Vidal Sassoon.

In the U.S. the list included socialites such as Babe Paley and Jackie O (a name coined by *Women's Wear Daily*), and later Andy Warhol and his Factory set, and regulars at Studio 54 such as David Bowie and Bianca Jagger: "Régines, Café Reginette and Studio 54 are the best places to catch a glimpse of New York's nightcrawlers, fashion claques (*sic*) and young arbiters in their new night-time looks"

FIGURE 7.2 *Interview*, Bianca Jagger, September 1975. Cover photograph by Chris von Wangenheim. Courtesy BMP Media Holdings, LLC. 30.

(*WWD*, September 12, 1977 cited in Foley 2011: 28). A leading light was John Fairchild, who returned from Paris to become editor-in-chief of *Women's Wear Daily*. Fairchild introduced a new section, "The Eye," to cover the international world of what he dubbed "the beautiful people" and it became the bible of the social set. Circulation soared. In 1972 Fairchild launched *W*, a magazine exclusively devoted to this society.

Meanwhile, Warhol himself launched *Interview* magazine (1969–), a key mediator of the modern cultural fusion and its participants: "We were reaching people in all parts of town, all different types of people. The groups were getting all mixed up with one another—dance, music, art, fashion and media" (Warhol and Hackett 1981 [1980]: 162). (Warhol began his career as a fashion illustrator.) Initially based on interviews with emerging "celebrities" of film, under Rosemary Kent's editorship (1973) the magazine extended its reach to broader contemporary culture, including Warhol's own "artistic" circle (figure 7.2). *Interview* magazine adopted an unconventional artistic style. Its covers were illustrated and its layouts had the feel of Warhol's own screen prints (Gundle 2008: 323).

The beautiful people became ubiquitous in fashion editorial from *Honey* to *Vogue*, where George Melly posed with Shrimpton in "How to be a Hit when you're a Miss," shot by Bailey (September 15, 1961: 108–21). In London, the bible was *Queen,* "emblematic in its day of a swinging Britain where the old and new orders were beginning to collide and collude" (Haden-Guest 2006), It drew together pop culture, fashion, and the beautiful society, epitomizing "the new spirit" of Colin McInnes' novel *Absolute Beginners* (1959).

Queen and the new irreverence

Jocelyn Stevens had bought the ailing *Queen* magazine ("the" was dropped from the title in 1962) as a birthday present for himself in 1957 (figure 7.3). He staffed it with young up-and-coming journalists, including Beatrix Miller from American *Vogue*, Francis Wyndham from *Harper's Bazaar* as theater critic, novelist Elizabeth Jane Howard as book reviewer, Quentin Crewe and Clement Freud as restaurant critics, Betty Kenward from *Tatler* as social editor, and Norman Parkinson, along with existing editor Anne Trehearne, for fashion. Stevens hired Mark Boxer as art director; when Boxer left to launch the *Sunday Times* color supplement in 1962, Stevens replaced him with Dennis Hackett, who went on to edit *Nova*. In 1962 two young journalists, Caterine Milinaire and Marit Allen, were hired to set up the "About 20" fashion column. Allen was, according to Harrison, "probably the most influential fashion editor of the 1960s" (1991: 208) and by 1963 she and Milinaire had moved to *Vogue*. Quickly *Queen* journalists became "beautiful people" in their own right.

The Queen
September 13th 1961
2/6

Autumn Fashion
Number
Clothes you
can't live without

FIGURE 7.3 *The Queen*, September 13, 1961. Courtesy of Vinmag Archive Ltd/ Hearst UK.

Queen was not strictly speaking a fashion magazine, but its irreverent approach to fashion was an essential part of its transformation into what Haden Guest calls a stylish "cult": "We were trying to take the pomp out of fashion and bring it back to earth" (Allen 2005). Stevens describes the fashion department he took over as "a little primitive":

> The clothes, hats, jewellery, shoes, etc were brought back to the office where they were packed into suitcases and sent off to the LNA studios, which were somewhere near Fleet Street. A day or two later the suitcases would return accompanied by one print of each outfit, with or without the right hat, and a bill for £5 for each print, which included the model fee and all expenses. (Coleridge and Quinn 1987: 8)

Queen later created its own studio in the basement, although in fact the situation Stevens describes would have been the norm for most magazines, except for *Vogue* and *Harper's*, which had their own studios and extensive budgets.

Queen's editorial approach would nowadays be considered self-indulgent. In 1960 Parkinson shot thirteen pages of the Paris collections in a helicopter over the city in order to circumvent the couture houses' restrictions ("Take Off for Paris," August 31, 1960: 20–37). Along with *Town*, *Queen* pioneered and showcased the raw, often documentary-style photography of Donovan, Brian Duffy, David Bailey, and Jeanloup Sieff, along with the likes of street photographer Saul Leiter and Helmut Newton. The photographers all loved working with a magazine at the forefront of fashion (Harrison 1991: 202). In 1963 Diana Vreeland called *Queen's* "Colouring Book" fashion story (February 27: 53–76), printed in expensive gravure, the most beautiful she had ever seen (Coleridge and Quinn 1987: 14).

In 1964 Beatrix Miller left to become editor of British *Vogue*. Meanwhile Trehearne was replaced as fashion editor by Lady Clare Rendlesham, formerly editor of *Vogue's* "Young Idea" pages. Rendlesham continued her enthusiastic support of British designers, and *Queen* continued to adopt a bold approach to fashion. In 1964, *Queen* published a Norman Parkinson fashion story that epitomized the new era showing the Rolling Stones and a model: "How to Kill Five Stones with One Bird." The story featured clothes by Quant's Ginger Group, promoted in *Queen's* typically ironic but individualistic style:

> The Ginger Group (in case you're just back from an incommunicado jungle) gives you every season (with extra spicing at half-time) clothes that all go together, so that you can dash out and do a bit of mad compulsive buying when your mood drives you on, without fatal effect. (22 April 1964: 71)

In 1964 Rendlesham was the only fashion editor to stay in Paris for the inaugural Courrèges collection. She had the clothes photographed by Helmut Newton, flown in from New York, and used the images for sixteen color pages and the cover. No other magazine had a single picture:

> You *must* take Courrèges. He's the most terrific phenomenon to hit fashion for years, the heaven of Paris personified. We went to the collections. We saw. *He* conquered. We came out dancing in the streets and resolved to bring you for the first time a complete advance coverage of his sensational clothes—and only his—a week before anybody else can see photographs of the Paris Collections. Because you must take Courrèges and now. He's too good to keep. (August 26, 1964: 37–51)

(In a shift from the elite to the populist typical of *Queen*, Rendlesham goes on to advise that Courrèges-type fabrics may be available at the likes of Woolands, Wallis shops, Fortnum and Mason, and Harrods.) Such was *Queen*'s influence that when Rendelsham published her black-bordered couture obituary, *Women's Wear Daily* reported: "*Queen* kills off Balenciaga."

Queen was not alone in challenging fashion orthodoxy. A new irreverence became widespread in both text and iconography, though it was not universal. Ernestine Carter's "Fashion Choice" in the *Sunday Times* remained reverent and cultivated, assuming a certain level of education: "The new prints are the antithesis of this conventional prettiness. Their clamorous color contrasts and bold flower patterns recall the Polynesian prettiness of Gauguin's Tahitian paintings" (*Sunday Times Magazine*, January 13, 1963: 22–3). At the populist *Mirror*, meanwhile, fashion editor Felicity Green adopted an altogether more cheeky tone to report on the advent of culottes: "The message, in a word, from Paris is KNICKERS" (February 25, 1967: 14–15).

Meanwhile a new apostate stance also emerged in fashion photography, arguably pioneered by William Klein in the late 1950s with his photographs of the collections for *Vogue*, such as elegant close-ups of couture with models smoking (Harrison 1991: 98). As the photographer himself admitted, the clothes were secondary to the concept and "there was always sarcasm in my fashion pictures" (ibid.). Meanwhile, Armstrong-Jones' early photographs for *Vogue* brought humor to the fashion pages (ibid.: 202). As photographers became increasingly powerful arbiters of fashion—"more and more fashion is fashion photography" (Sontag, British *Vogue*, December 1978, cited in Harrison 1991: 14)—and beautiful people, tensions grew with the fashion industry over their distorted presentation of the clothes themselves. In 1965 *Time* ran an editorial entitled "The Furore over Fashions: Far Out Photography" (March 3: 42), claiming designers were furious that "their clothes were being downgraded to props." Despite Fairchild's complaints in 1966 that Avedon's deformations discouraged women from buying clothes (Harrison 1991: 16), the genie was not easily put back in the bottle, thanks in part to the encouragement of one Diana Vreeland: "I've never heard of any criticism and never heard of any argument," she told *Time* in relation to "Furore over Fashions."

The empress of fashion: The influence of Diana Vreeland

Time profiled Vreeland soon after she had taken over the editorship of *Vogue,* but already noted a more youthful and daring approach, including a fully nude model lying supine on the beach. It explained, "She is, in fact probably the single most fabled, venerated and respected backstage force in fashion today" ("The Vreeland Vogue," *Time,* May 10, 1963). When Alexander Liberman put Vreeland in charge, *Vogue* had become under Jessica Daves a rather staid—albeit commercially sound—magazine. Vreeland turned it into the lightning rod of sixties' fashion and an innovator in how fashion was represented. As Liberman himself said, "She was the most talented editor of her period because she was able to stamp an era on the reader's mind" (Angelotti and Oliva 2006: 173). Vreeland's enthusiasm for sixties' London, for example, was central to the mythical status of the city and its designers.

Vreeland became an iconic figure, her dogmatic editorial style and sometimes excessive fashion fantasies parodied in photographer William Klein's film *Qui êtes-vous Polly Maggoo?* (1966). She was the decisive journalistic presence at the shows, where many other journalists were invisible and anonymous. According to Grace Coddington, "It would be like the sea parting as she swept in" (2012: 100). Her influence in many ways pre-empted the more conceptual and fantastical representation of fashion that emerged later in the 1980s and 1990s.

Vreeland believed that fashion was more about dreams than clothes: "A dress doesn't matter, it's the life you're living in that dress" (*The Eye Has to Travel,* 2006). A stylist before the term was invented, she thought conceptually about fashion features and created narratives around themes, most famously sending German model Veruschka to Japan to partner a Japanese Samurai in a story shot by Richard Avedon entitled "The Great Fur Caravan" (October 15, 1966), loosely based on an erotic Japanese love story called *The Tale of Genji* which, according to fashion editor Polly Mellen, Vreeland had only heard about and never read (Vreeland and Mellen 2013: 200). It was allegedly the most expensive shoot in *Vogue*'s history, involving eighteen hat boxes and fifteen hearses (black trunks) filled with clothes (ibid.)—this at a time when it was usually the fashion photographer who created the concept for photographs: "In those early days a photographer like Helmut Newton or Guy Bourdin was very strong and came up with all the ideas for a *Vogue* photo shoot. I merely brought along things to dress them" (Coddington 2012: 96). As Hubert de Givenchy observes in the documentary *The Eye Has to Travel*, Vreeland did not just report—"She created fashion."

Vreeland also understood that fashion was part of wider culture. Laird Borelli notes that her "Vogue's Eye View" contains many broader cultural references (1997: 251), and her office walls were covered with all sorts of images. She intuitively grasped the significance of youth and music for sixties' fashion. She coined the term "Youthquake" in January 1965 in a poetic editorial that captures her vision of the decade and crystallizes its significance for the reader:

> Gone is the once upon a dream world. The dreams still there, break into action: writing, singing, acting, designing. Youth, warm and gay as a kitten, yet self-sufficient as James Bond, is surprising countries East and West with a sense of assurance, serene beyond all years [...]
>
> The year's in its youth, the youth in its year. Under 24 and over 90,000,000 strong in the U.S. alone. More dreamers. More doers. Now. Youthquake 1965. (*Vogue* 1965: 112)

Vreeland chronicled "The Beautiful Young People: Who's Next"—and then peopled *Vogue* with them. She took the first picture of Mick Jagger in 1964; discovered and promoted models such as Penelope Tree, Veruschka, and Lauren Hutton—and published their names; vociferously championed young photographers like David Bailey; and published covers of and features on the stars of stage, screen, and music, including Catherine Deneuve and Shirley MacLaine, that mirrored what was happening in the London fashion scene (but not elsewhere).

Above all, Vreeland was brave. She ignored deadlines and guidelines and followed her own instincts. This was particularly true of color—a key component of 1960s' fashion—which she often used thematically. Vreeland saw color conceptually but also viewed it as part of her editor's mission: "We must try and really help people with colour because most people are colour ignorant" (Memo to Mrs. Ingersoll, December 27, 1967, Vreeland and Mellen 2013: 218). Vreeland's colored visions influenced fashion in the real world, as Mellen notes:

> She wasn't afraid to dedicate twenty pages to pink—and when she did advertisers would grab the colour and there would be pink lipstick and nail polishes all over the ad pages. Before you knew it you were seeing pink on every street corner. Her influence went far beyond the editorial pages of the magazine. (Vreeland and Mellen 2013: 10)

Youth, the dolly bird and *Honey*

This dolly dress cut out and ready to sew.

(*HONEY*, JUNE 1964, COVER)

If Vreeland was a significant force in popularizing London's youth fashion and new feminine ideals, so too were the dolly bird and new British youth magazines such as *Honey*. The dolly bird was a peculiarly British take on the single girl as a feminine icon. Hilary Radner argues that the figure of the single girl was an artificial construction based around "the look," and attitude (2000: 130). Indeed, the dolly bird herself was reduced by young British fashion photographers to a commodity: "[Jean Shrimpton's] imitators [...] were almost interchangeable. All had long clean hair, preferably blonde, interchangeable pretty faces, inter-changeable long legs" (George Melly, cited in Breward 2004: 170).

Radner suggests that the single girl placed consumerism rather than maternity at the heart of being feminine (Radner 2000: 128). As many scholars have pointed out about the dolly bird, however (Craik 2003 [1994] and Breward [2004], among others), this apparent icon of sexual emancipation contained a number of contra-dictions. Not least, her identity was based on a commodified eroticism that was linked to consumer goods and the pleasure of men. Although *Honey* reflected the spirit of youthful consumerism and the importance of achieving "the look," it also reflected the tension between the dolly bird's dual status as both consumer and product. It actively promoted careers for women, for example, such as "How to be Your Own Tycoon," which featured boutique owners and jewelry designers (March 1966: 68–70)—but the same issue also contained a "Bride of The Month" feature.

Launched in 1961, *Honey* was, unlike its other teenage counterparts, a monthly glossy. It borrowed from the young, inclusive magazines like *Mademoiselle* in openly engaging with its readers, and its upbeat, youthful tone was new to the British fashion press. Its content reflected its readership's interests: fashion, beauty, music, film and television, and package holidays, as well as horoscopes, romance, and fiction. Like other magazines, it focused on service and friendship, but with a fun 1960s spirit:

> Ever felt a bit shy, meeting new folk? Yes? Then you'll know exactly how we're feeling now, meeting you for the very first time. What fun lies ahead of us! Discs and dancing. Old friends and new. Adventure. In fact, all manner of exciting and, interesting, simply shattering things. (*Honey*, launch editorial)

However, *Honey*'s real innovation was to combine service with pop culture. Readers became groupies or "Honeys," and a *Honey* bus toured the country

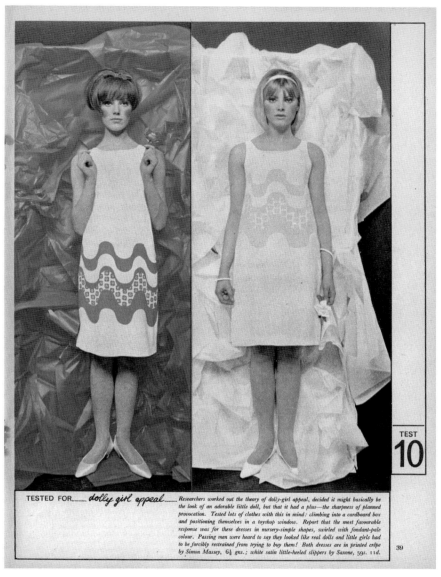

TESTED FOR....... *dolly girl appeal*......

Researchers worked out the theory of dolly-girl appeal, decided it might basically be the look of an adorable little doll, but that it had a plus—the sharpness of planned provocation. Tested lots of clothes with this in mind: climbing into a cardboard box and positioning themselves in a toyshop window. Report that the most favourable response was for these dresses in nursery-simple shapes, swirled with fondant-pale colour. Passing men were heard to say they looked like real dolls and little girls had to be forcibly restrained from trying to buy them! Both dresses are in printed crêpe by Simon Massey, 6½ gns.; white satin little-heeled slippers by Saxone, 59s. 11d.

39

TEST
10

FIGURE 7.4 "Tested for Dolly Appeal", *Honey*, January 1966. © www.timeinccontent. com. Courtesy of Vinmag Archive Ltd.

giving beauty advice in department stores—stores that soon had a hundred *Honey* boutiques, which sold clothing and accessories featured in the magazine. At one stage there were even *Honey* hairdressers. July 1967 brought a *Honey Book of Pin-Ups*, a key feature of pop magazines, including iconic dollies such as Sandie Shaw and Twiggy.

The launch issue, edited by Audrey Slaughter, who later worked on *Over 21* and launched *Working Woman*, included a *Date Book* by Cliff Richard and the first fashion feature, on raincoats, was entitled "How to Catch a Rain Beau." It also included a feature on "How to Become A Model." It initially described itself as "the lovely young magazine," but by 1963 its masthead proclaimed "Young, Gay and Get Ahead," reflecting the more proactive attitude of the dolly bird.

Increasingly, "the dolly" became synonymous with the "Honeys" and a common figure in the magazine. In January 1966, for example, it ran a "Tested for Dolly Girl Appeal" fashion feature that promoted designer Simon Massey's dresses through live modeling in a toyshop window (figure 7.4). Meanwhile, make-up features showed how to alter the shape of the face or create new looks, often based on an iconic dolly bird—"The Cathy McGowan look"—complete with appropriate products.

Honey's main fashion feature often focused on replicating a look, such as "Viva Maria And You" (April 1966: 104–6), which featured the looks of Jeanne Moreau and Bardot in the film of the same name. The rest of the fashion editorial, however, was practical. As well as *McCall's* patterns, the magazine included something "all ready to sew", such as a fun-fur coat in October 1966—"yours for well under £7"—and a budget feature, "Capable Kate." Increasingly, the latter was used to promote a more individualistic style, and in June 1966 the magazine ran "Ideas for the Individualist" (42–3). Illustrated by Biba's Barbara Hulanicki, the piece argued:

> The age of the individualist is sadly waning under the weight of mass production and type-cast clothes [...] We went out on a limb, took a top from that famous "Second-hand Rose" Barbara Streisand. Rummaged through cobwebby attics, chased through street markets and sale rooms. Even the local junk shops had a look in. If we can do it, so can you! So quick-quick step out-of-line Individualist.

Although in March 1966 *Honey* announced "Dolly Girl to be an MP," by 1968 it had become more campaigning, dealing with racism and the anti-Vietnam protests in Grosvenor Square. By the mid-1970s, a serious woman had replaced the smiling dolly bird: "The youth cult is over and the teenage market has disappeared—the cohesiveness of the group has gone" (IPC representative, cited in White 1970: 37).

By the late 1960s a new mood prevailed. Fashion iconography came to reject "Modernism" (Harrison 1991: 211). Instead, it adopted the ethnic imbued with a spirit of hippy romanticism and new fashion pages manipulated "foreign" places to give cultural depth to Western fashion (Cheang 2013).[5] But if fashion photography was reaching outside the studio for signifiers of cultural mood, new discourses were needed to mediate it.

The enabling discourse and *Nova* (1965–75)

Fashion needs re-thinking: start here.

(*NOVA*, COVER, FEBRUARY 1970)

Established magazines struggled to react to the cynicism that emerged in the late 1960s toward fashion and consumerism. It was left to *Nova* to launch a new type of fashion journalism (see plate 12). It changed the tone, showing its readers rather than telling them, enabling rather than lecturing. In this way, *Nova* prefigured the hybrid "style" magazines of the 1980s by mixing culture, politics, and fashion in often controversial ways.

Originally launched by Newness in response to psychologist Ernest Dichter's research on "the New Woman" (White 1970: 223), *Nova* was not strictly speaking a fashion magazine. Like *Queen*—whose deputy editor Dennis Hackett became *Nova*'s editor in September 1965—it was more of a lifestyle publication, defined by its irreverent and pioneering attitude toward everything from homosexuality and domestic violence to Prince Charles, the royal family, and Paris fashion. Although it launched as "A new kind of magazine for a new kind of woman," it had, like *Queen*, a fairly unisex readership.

The launch issue expressed the new kind of practical realism that was to characterize the magazine's approach to fashion in particular:

> This is a magazine for women who make up their own minds. It is dedicated to the startling proposition that women have more to think about than what to do about dinner. Our theme is that a woman's life in 1965 is more interesting and more exciting that any escapism, so let's sit out the fantasy and make entertainment out of reality. (*Nova*, launch issue, March 1965)

Nova looked different. It was graphically innovative, mixing small photographic formats, especially in fashion features, and turning pages upside down (September 1967). Art director Harri Peccinotti had worked for *Twen* in Germany, which, along with *Elle* in France, had taken the lead in graphic design from New York magazines as the U.S. became more insular and conservative in reaction to the Cold War. The European magazines created new styles of art direction and layout, including text as a graphic element with bold and colorful typefaces.

Nova also ran provocative photography, including Bob Richardson's "suicide" of Angelica Huston in Clobber clothes in 1972.[6] It ran lengthy articles of 4,000 to 5,000 words by illustrious names such as AS Byatt ("On the Agony of the Middle Class Liberal," June 1969), but equally it had a regular horoscope, a problem page, and in the 1970s financial advice and a "Nova How to Service," giving advice such as how to change a plug (August 1970). In 1968 it was bought by IPC.

The *Nova* approach to fashion was as innovative and irreverent as the rest of the magazine. According to Peccinotti, the fashion pages "were almost an insult to fashion at times" (cited in Beard 2002: 27). The first fashion editor was Molly Parkin, an artist, while Penny Vincenzi, formerly of *Queen* and later of *Cosmopolitan*, wrote features. David Hillman, who joined *Nova* in June 1969 from the *Sunday Times* magazine, recalled that Parkin was "unfettered by the accepted view of the fashion system" (Hillman and Peccinotti 1993: 39). Parkin's editorials reflected her fierce belief in the British fashion scene, as well as a more individualistic and pragmatic approach to dressing. In a feature tellingly entitled "Far From Paris and All The Better for It" featuring clothes from mid-market retailer Wallis (August 1967: 40–5), Parkin argued, "At last in Britain some of the best young designers are getting together with the best manufacturers; an important move for both them and the buying public." She lambasts those "who continue blindly to take their lead from Paris and ignore the abundance of creative talent in this country," and praises the Wallis clothes for combining a contemporary look "with solid seams and inbuilt wear resistance."

By the end of 1967, Parkin was gone. Her provocative approach—including a September spread on a python with naked men hidden behind styled pop-ups—proved unpopular with advertisers (Parkin 1993: 180–2). She re-emerged as fashion editor of *Harper's Bazaar* (1968) and shortly after of the *Sunday Times* (1969).

Parkin's replacement at *Nova*, Caroline Baker, was no less impudent: she pronounced fashion dead in September 1968, as we have seen. However, that very pronouncement introduced an innovative street-style fashion spread of random people in London and Brighton "wearing what they please." Baker pioneered the "straight-up" fashion shot, beloved of the 1980s' style press and now a staple of bloggers and fashion magazines everywhere (Beard 2013). She, along with deputy Brigid Keenan (who went on to be "Young Fashion" editor at the *Sunday Times*), also promoted the individual and the street as the key influences in fashion:

Their clothes have nothing to do with Paris, fashion pages or anything but the personal feelings of their wearers—ideas filter from them to the fashion world, instead of the other way round. Trends are no longer set, they just happen. ("Fashion is Dead," *Nova*, September 1968: 55)

In September 1969, *Nova* ran a feature on the Paris collections that focused not on what was being shown but on what the fashion journalists were wearing. Baker herself is photographed wearing an army surplus belt, a self-dyed T-shirt, a scarf from Kensington Antique Market, and a custom-made pair of white shorts. She brought the same *bricolage* style to *Nova*'s fashion pages: "Fashion depends more upon the way an outfit is put together than upon the clothes themselves. The bits and pieces added make the look" ("Adding up to Something Good," *Nova*, March 1973: 88–91).

Baker saw her more open-ended style and enabling tone as reflecting changes in women's perceptions of themselves; she saw her role as fashion editor as being to encourage women to experiment and dress as they pleased (Beard 2013: 32). In August 1974 she ran a feature on the versatility of "any piece of cloth big enough to be wrapped around the body to take the place of clothes," complete with instructions on how to turn it into a dress, a dressing-gown, a beach wrap, or a skirt (32).

As the tone of other magazines also became less dogmatic, the very notion of fashion was turned on its head. Baker's enabling discourse was echoed elsewhere. Among others, *Elle* argued that a new fashion climate had appeared:

I don't understand, Sonia Rykiel often says, why a woman needs someone to tell her the length of the skirt she should be wearing: she only needs to look in the mirror. We agree. In matters of fashion, there haven't been any dictates for a long time. (March 1974: 70)

New challenges

Despite the promise offered by *Nova*, the early 1970s were a dark time for fashion journalism. Feminist suspicion combined with a severe economic downturn, increased costs of production—especially paper—reduced advertising budgets, and ongoing competition from other media caused declining circulations for women's magazines in general. Fashion magazines were not immune, even those with a more liberal agenda such as *Elle*: Bonvoisin and Maignien report a decline of around 40,000 between 1966 and 1971, and argue that French upmarket fashion titles were particularly badly hit by the recession (1986: 28). Similar declines were experienced elsewhere. In the U.S., newsstand sales dropped dramatically and advertising sales on *Vogue* fell by 40 percent in the first quarter of 1971 (Angeletti and Oliva 2006: 207). The face of fashion journalism changed forever as magazines shifted from full-time staff to freelancers. Many publications, including French *Elle* and *Harper's Bazaar*, reformulated their contents as well as their look, and *Harper's Bazaar* and *Queen* were merged in 1970 (White 1970: 36–7). Diana Vreeland found her extravagant, fantasy vision of fashion replaced in 1971 by the more pragmatic one of her deputy Grace Mirabella, who argued: "We must change our focus. From dress-up fantasy to real life" (Mirabella 1995: 153).

FIGURE 7.5 "Jump/1970." Photograph by Jim Lee. All Rights Reserved/As seen in the Historic Archives at the Victoria and Albert Museum. Courtesy of Jim Lee. (Lee drew upon those escaping from Communist Eastern Europe for this image.)

Everywhere covers got busier as magazines attempted to arrest and woo readers— *Elle*'s cover of September 1974 lists six content items and then ironically "Etc […] etc […] etc […]." Inspired by the same purpose, the free cover offer, frequently cosmetics, made its appearance.

Given the economic downturn, magazines were at pains to empathize with the budgetary constraints of their readers. New rubrics focused on value clothing and thrift shopping. *Elle* and *Marie Claire* introduced features on DIY fashion in 1974: "Les idees d'Elle" and "Les Cent Idees de Marie Claire."

Fashion journalism's dialogue with the "outside world" was thrust into sharper focus (Harrison 1991: 124) (figure 7.5) as contemporary issues of politics, gender, and race emerged from subcultural ghettos.

Race and *Essence*

Although Mirabella made Beverley Knight American *Vogue*'s first black cover girl in 1974, the ideal of femininity in *Vogue* and, indeed, most fashion magazines did not often include women of color. Black models had started to appear in Paris, but race still haunted fashion journalism. Nancy White, by then editor of *Harper's Bazaar*, championed the first black cover girl, Donyale Luna, in 1965 and gave

Avedon a one-year contract to shoot Luna for spreads within the magazine. His photographs caused advertisers from the South to withdraw their support for the magazine and Hearst himself objected, ending Luna's U.S. modeling career. In 1968 protestors picketed the offices of *Harper's Bazaar* to demand a greater presence of black models. Attitudes were more liberal in Europe, where British *Vogue* successfully put Luna on its cover in 1966, shot by David Bailey.

In 1970, however, *Essence* was launched in America as the first fashion magazine aimed at middle-class black women. It covered fashion and beauty but also social and political subjects and fiction. The magazine's second editor, Marcia Ann Gillespie, forced advertisers to use black models in their publicity in the magazine. By 1976, advertising revenues were $3.7 million and circulation 500,000 (Zuckerman 1998: 230). A more widespread use of black models did not come until much later and, with the exception of Naomi Campbell, only recently on covers.

Meanwhile, the fashion photography of Helmut Newton, Guy Bourdin, Sarah Moon, and Deborah Turbeville, among others, reflected the darker side of contemporary debates and fashion's new subcultures, as well as the developing porn industry—dystopia rather than 1960s' utopia (O'Neill 2013 [2000]: 150). Despite objections from some fashion journalists, including Ernestine Carter, the decadent aesthetic was to prove seminal in later decades, influencing, for example, Carine Roitfeld and Tom Ford in their collaboration at Gucci in the 1990s.

Francine Crescent, editor of French *Vogue*, promoted the work of Bourdin and Newton, in particular, which foregrounded issues of sex and gender (although even the French complained over a fetishistic portrayal of Jenny Capitain as a cripple) (Steele 1997: 291). However, the questioning of gender norms was becoming widespread in fashion journalism.

Magazines for men

In part, *Nova*'s appeal to a unisex readership—like *Queen*—was a corollary of the blurring of gender boundaries in clothing and hairstyles in the early 1970s.[7] The fashion press had been targeting male readers since the early 1960s, but men's new importance was largely the result of the link between music and fashion in popular culture. Heralded by the 1950s' Beatniks in America and the Teddy Boy, a new dandy—"the Mod"—was born in Britain.[8] New shops and designers supplied menswear. Paco Rabanne had started menswear in 1959; now Biba as well as more fashionable tailors such as Tommy Nutter followed suit.[9] The hedonistic "playboy" aesthetic, which had developed in America in the 1950s (see Ogersby 2003), became widespread. New magazines appeared to appeal to the new market. *Man about Town* (1952) was relaunched as *Town* in 1962; *Playboy* arrived in Britain, as did its British compatriot *Penthouse* (1965); and in America *GQ* began as a

FIGURE 7.6 *Esquire*, January 1958. Courtesy of VinMag Archive Ltd/Hearst Magazines International. (This cover epitomizes the new "cool" attitude that *Esquire* adopted in the 1960s, along with the irreverent "new journalism" from the likes of Gore Vidal and Tom Wolfe.)

quarterly fashion supplement for *Esquire* subscribers in 1957. Like *Town*, *Esquire* itself pioneered a new graphic style (figure 7.6) and new journalism from the likes of Tom Wolfe. Male fashion also appeared in women's fashion magazines such as *Honey* and in "lifestyle" magazines such as *Queen* and *Nova*.

In the 1970s, the rise of the Gay Rights movement provided a new impetus to the fashion-conscious male. Expenditure on male clothing rose, as reflected in *L'Uomo Vogue*. Originally launched in 1968 as a biannual trade magazine to support the burgeoning Italian menswear industry; it became a monthly in 1975. Cultured and urbane, and published in Italian and English, with photography by Oliviero Toscani, *L'Uomo* became a bible of international style in the 1970s, supported by the expanding Italian menswear industry. From shoots in Ireland, "the green country of Swift, Shaw, Joyce and Beckett" (December/January 1973: 146) to photo-stories from nightclubs—Castell's in Paris and Max's Kansas City in New York, "where the most adventurous and colourful parts of American culture express themselves"—*L'Uomo* disseminated the subculture of the new (homosexual) dandy. *Men's Vogue* was launched in 1971 as a supplement to the main magazine in the U.S. and *Vogue Hommes* as a biannual (1979) in Paris.

Fashion as feminist freedom and *Cosmopolitan*

Meanwhile, feminism was examining the relationship between fashion and femininity:

> In the early years of the women's liberation movement, feminists condemned the entire package of fashion. Liberation meant breaking out of the strait jacket of controlled femininity. Dress, fashion, and cosmetics were seen as trivialities that functioned ideologically to construct a false femininity. (Evans and Thornton 1989: 1)

The feminism of the 1970s did not emerge in a vacuum. Gender roles were changing everywhere as women became more economically active. Divorce rates increased dramatically and abortion became legal, even in Catholic countries such as France (Loi Veil in 1975). Many feminists saw fashion as part of the patriarchal apparatus of female oppression, and fashion and writing about fashion were reviled and undermined.

One response was the launch of new women's magazines to mediate new attitudes. *F* magazine, launched in France in 1978, refused to show women as sex objects or consumers, and contained no fashion or beauty editorial. Its launch circulation of 400,000 was not much smaller than *Elle*; even in 1981 it had 200,000 readers (Bonvoisin and Maignien 1986: 84). In America, *MS* was launched in 1971 and *Spare Rib* appeared in Britain in 1972.

Another response was for established magazines to change the emphasis of their editorial: *Honey* became more political under the editorship of Carol Sarler, for example, and fashion content was reduced. In the late 1970s, French *Marie Claire* added "Femmes," a supplement with a feminist stance that denounced sex in advertising campaigns, profiled leading female figures, and reported on local feminist issues. Highly popular, it revived the magazine's fortunes (Bonvoisin and Maignien 1986: 31). In January 1979, *Marie Claire* extended its feminist positioning by hiring a lawyer to advise readers on civil rights. It also started to include the "enquêtes," or investigations into controversial topics such as Sweden's ban on smacking, that still form an essential part of the magazine's positioning today. However, fashion still accounted for most of the main magazine's content and the couture and prêt-à-porter shows continued to be covered in great detail.

Meanwhile, Helen Gurley Brown at *Cosmopolitan* adopted a different approach, bringing together female emancipation with fashion, beauty, and sexual freedom: "They say they can't stand the girls we photograph—that they look sexy. I say if looking pretty makes a girl feel better, she ought to do it" (Gurley Brown, cited in "Liberating Magazines," *Newsweek*, February 8, 1971: 36–7).

Gurley Brown created *Cosmopolitan* with her publisher husband David. After the success of *Sex and the Single Girl* (1962), she developed a prototype of a new magazine called *Femme* aimed at working women in their twenties and thirties. Focusing on "the woman on her own," Gurley Brown sensed that such women were "swept under the editorial rug" and were "often patronised and treated as objects of pity" (*Femme* proposal, cited in Landers 2010: 223). She argued that women needed a new editorial approach to match their new aspirations. This prototype formed the basis of the relaunched *Cosmopolitan* in 1965. From the outset, the magazine's agenda was about female empowerment not only through work and sex but also through beauty and fashion. Gurley Brown added beauty and health features to the existing *Cosmopolitan* mix (Scanlon 2009: 154), and fashion and beauty took up more of the magazine than articles on sex in the first seven years (7.6 percent compared to 5.2 percent; Landers 2010: 234).

Gurley Brown's frank approach to sexual matters and treating women as sexual beings defined *Cosmopolitan* publicly and, arguably, politically. It also had a dramatic impact on other magazines: by the late 1960s, even the well-bred *Mademoiselle* had begun to feature articles on sexuality and Mirabella comments on the preponderance of sex in 1970s' *Vogue* (1995: 160–1). Nonetheless, *Cosmopolitan* approached sex with an irreverence and boldness that distinguished it from the more genteel voices of the women's press: Burt Reynolds featured as a male centerfold in American *Cosmopolitan* in April 1972, and Mr Germaine Greer, aka Paul de Feu, in British *Cosmopolitan*.

Cosmopolitan's focus on work and finance made it the bible of the "working woman" before such a type had been defined. Successful women were integral to this project and celebrity profiles were an important part of the early content: Jane Fonda featured in the first issue, while female movie stars, such as Charlotte Rampling and Isabelle Adjani, starred in fashion shoots.

Gurley Brown set out to match the aesthetic standards of *Vogue* and *Harper's Bazaar* but with content that addressed the wider concerns of the modern woman's life (Scanlon 2009: 144). From the outset the cover presented the Cosmo Girl—the image was created by fashion photographer Francesco Scavullo—as groomed, glamorous, and beautiful. The cover always had the same format, though the background color, clothes, hair, and make-up changed, and the girl was always sexy but "never moody, sad, dirty or lewd" (Scanlon 2009: 158). *Cosmopolitan*'s cover girl arguably defined the look of fashion magazines in the 1970s and beyond, as publications all sought to project the idealized face of the reader on the cover: Close-cropped faces became the norm.

The Cosmo Girl became about making the most of yourself independently in all aspects of your life:

You are that Cosmopolitan girl aren't you? You're very interested in men, naturally, but you think too much of yourself to live your life entirely through him. That means you're going to make the most of yourself—your body, your face, your clothes, your hair, your job and your mind. How can you fail to be more interesting after that? (First issue of British *Cosmopolitan*, March 1972)

Gurley Brown featured fashion appropriate for the budgets of her readers: "Don't sell her down the river with a $5,000 Armani evening gown" (Scanlon 2009: 161). Erotic allure was a defining feature of *Cosmopolitan* fashion spreads however, and titles reflected this: "Swimsuits He'll love you In" or "Clothes to get you Back in His Arms." The tone of the narrative stories, however, suggested feminist empowerment:

Getting back to basics [...] Barbara, far left, cuddles up to Gary on the kind of patchwork quilt her great grandmother might have stitched. But there's nothing remotely old fashioned about this cotton "house dress". Seamed to fit better than a slip, who will ask a girl in a halter neckline dress to do the washing up? Dress by Early Bird £7. (British *Cosmopolitan*, February 1972)

Gurley Brown saw beauty and fashion as essential to workplace success and self-esteem, putting her at odds with those feminists who saw any kind of sartorial or beauty regime as undermining the authentic self. A former advertising executive, she also recognized the importance of fashion and beauty advertising to the bottom line. She managed to marry feminism with fashion and beauty to create empowering freedom of choice: "What we have always wanted are options—be they something as trivial as the mini or as profound as legal abortion" (Gurley Brown cited in Scanlon 2009: 176).

The relaunch of *Cosmopolitan* was hugely successful. Average monthly circulation increased from 782,000 to 1.05 million copies between 1965 and 1968, and versions were launched in Britain in 1972 and France in 1973. In 2012 *Cosmopolitan* had sixty-four international editions and in 2015 it remained the largest-selling monthly in America (Zimmerman 2012).

An all-American ideal and American *Vogue*

Influenced by *Cosmopolitan*, other fashion magazines started to focus on fashion as empowerment. Nowhere was the shift from 1960s' optimism and fashion fantasy to 1970s' realism and the demands of "the working woman" more apparent than at American *Vogue* under the editorship of Grace Mirabella. When she took the helm in July 1971, Mirabella asserted that the focus of the magazine would be "fashion for real life" (Angeletti and Oliva 2006: 213). Her editorial "Point of View" set out to be a guide to "shopping, buying and wearing" (Borelli 1997: 252).

Everything about the magazine changed, from the new emphasis on fashion information—what was available, where and what for; guides to shoes, coats, and evening dressing—to the look of the cover, which began to feature Arthur Elgort's healthy, smiling, all-American girls. These new icons of femininity mediated the focus on well-being of body and mind that emerged in the 1970s. Vogue created an enhanced beauty section to encompass health, with as many as ten features per month by 1976.

Mirabella also wanted the reader "to learn things about fashion, politics, personalities, travel and the arts that she never knew before" and to put "more of a demand on the intelligence of the magazine" (1995: 145). Current affairs and coverage of successful women increased—the September 1973 issue features a discussion of the Equal Rights Amendment by Susan Sontag (100) and a profile of Diane von Furstenburg and her $90 million fashion, accessories and cosmetics business.

Vogue's fashion editorial showed women wearing clothes in real-life situations—"clothes to enjoy your life in" (Fall Forecast, July 1971)—although Mirabella also published the controversial work of more avant-garde photographers such as Helmut Newton and Deborah Turbeville in May 1975, resulting in canceled subscriptions in the Bible Belt (Mirabella 1995: 161). While Mirabella still covered European fashion, a new nationalism focused increasingly on the U.S. and sportswear from the likes of Halston and Geoffrey Beene. This was particularly evident in 1976, the bicentennial of the U.S.: "American Beauty Now"; "American

Style '76—the Word is Ease" (February 1976: 144–51, 125); "Help Keep America Beautiful" (cover, August 1976); and "Success '76: the look American women invented" (August 1976: 65).[10]

The copy accompanying the "Ease" spread exhorted readers to use this nationalism as a reflection of their own:

> There is a way of dressing—a way of looking—that to American women is like a way of life. It has to do with a certain freewheeling casualness and dash that goes through and through and up and down. It's hair that moves, it's make-up that lets skin show through. It's clothes that are so easy in and of themselves and give such a feeling of ease they relax every gesture.

Toward the end of the decade a new type of commentary emerged in the fashion press, particularly in France. It focused on the creativity and quality of couture ready-to-wear. A lengthy editorial from *Marie Claire* in January 1979 entitled "La griffe qui rassure" (84–5), for example, underlined both the exclusivity of the work—how a couturier who dresses Sylvie Vartan or la Baronne de Rothschild is necessarily an expert and properly trained—and how many of the techniques and fabrics used in prêt-à-porter are the same as in haute couture. Similar promotion of the desirability of the designer label was to characterize the next decade of fashion journalism throughout the Western world.

Notes

1   Journalist Lesley Ebbetts worked on fashion at *Rave* magazine and also at Radio 1 (Webb 2009: 184).

2   Salaries were low—Allen got paid an extra £2 a week to write the *Vogue* fashion copy and Coddington started on £1,100 a year, plus luncheon vouchers (Coddington 2012: 89).

3   Catalogs such as Freemans, Littlewoods, and Grattan offered credit, often on weekly terms that favored all classes of consumers. They soon outstripped other forms of retail in Britain (Hulanicki and Pel 2014: 24).

4   See Baldaia (2005) and Harrison (1991: 129–30).

5   Supported by the airlines, shoots often took a "leisurely three weeks" (Coddington 2012: 104)

6   For more on *Nova*'s photography see Harrison (1991: 228–31).

7   See, e.g., Lipovestky (1994: 107–17).

8   For more on this see Breward (2004: 125–50).

9   See Breward (2004) and Webb (2009) and Hulanicki, and Pel (2014), in particular on these shops and designers.

10   The French press started to report on American fashion in the 1970s.

8 COMMERCIALISM VERSUS CREATIVITY: THE 1980s AND 1990s

THE BIG DIVIDE: two completely different sorts of women are catered for now by the top designers. It's nothing to do with money or age—just a completely different life-style. On one side is the SUPER SOCIAL SOAP OPERA woman—she shops at Valentino or Ungaro and faints with delight at each new perky outfit she is determined to carry into middle age. On the other side is the woman who is prepared to spend £500 on a simple serge frock from Comme des Garçons, who buys from Armani and Gaultier, and house-hops in Italy, rather than embassy hopping in Paris: hers is a mega-career between New York, London and Paris.

(*HARPER'S AND QUEEN*, JANUARY 1985: 73)

London is ruling. After a grim few years when all was quiet and glum, a bubble of energy burst on the capital, unleashing a wave of angry young talent. Out came Alexander McQueen, Copperwheat Blundell and Hussein Chalayan: the new rude school of design. Out came Suede, Elastica and Sleeper—the noise of Britpop. Damian Hirst, the Chapman Brothers and Mark Wallinger cut through the arty fart. The dirty realism of photographers Juergen Teller, David Simms, Corinne Day and Craig McDean ripped up the humourless artifice of high fashion.

(QUICK, "CAPITAL, WHY IS LONDON CALLING AGAIN,"
***i-D*, SEPTEMBER 1996)**

Introduction

The last two decades of the twentieth century were characterized by what *Harper's and Queen* termed a "big divide." The spirit of consumer-driven optimism that prevailed in the 1980s was washed away by the mid-1990s by a new *fin-de-siècle* anxiety, reflected in grunge fashions and collections by the likes of Alexander McQueen (see Arnold 2001; Evans 2003) and a less genial fashion discourse, as reflected in Quick's comments above, in comparison to *Harper's*. These tensions were more broadly reflected in the pages of the fashion press: "Where the 1980s were euphoric, the 1990s set out to be critical [...] The 1990s gave a counter image of fashion that was located within an aesthetic of imperfection" (Montfort 2004: 167).

An equally important division emerged between established international designers and avant-garde style driven by local subcultural street fashion. Tribalism became more important in fashion as pop culture, particularly music, continued to play a pivotal role in how young people used dress to define their identity. In the fractured postmodern and free market world, fashion offered an anchor for identity, as epitomized in the style culture of London's Camden Market. This tribalism was examined by the journalist Peter York in *Style Wars* (1980), which also traced the rise of the Yuppie—an affluent new professional tribe dedicated to consumerism that crossed the divide.

The different approaches to dress were reflected in the fashion press. The glossy fashion magazine underwent increasing conglomeration and international expansion. The 1980s saw the launch of the first non-francophone *Marie Claire* in Japan (1982) and the dramatic globalization of *Elle*. The 1990s saw further expansion from *Elle*, *Marie Claire*, and *Vogue* into the emerging fashion markets of Asia, Eastern Europe, and Latin America.

Meanwhile, a new type of hybrid unisex magazine—self-defined as the "style press"—emerged in Britain to cover the music, club scene, and street style of the New Romantic era: *i-D*, *The Face*, and *Blitz* (figure 8.1) were all launched within six months of each other in 1980. As Christopher Breward (2004: 193) noted in relation to Camden Market, the style press could be seen as both a symptom of and an antidote to free market philosophies and globalization. As technology made independent publishing more viable in the 1990s, their "slash and paste style" (Tungate 2012 [2005]: 91) paved the way for a range of independent hybrid titles, such as *Dazed and Confused*, *Purple*, and *Tank*.

The "style" magazines fundamentally reshaped fashion journalism. As mainstream media sought to appropriate their capital among youth subcultures, older journalists were again eased out in favor of younger ones: the fashion editor of the *New York Times*, Carrie Donovan, found herself replaced by a journalist in her twenties, Amy Spindler, in 1993 (Callahan 2014: 79). "Style" had a class

FIGURE 8.1 *Blitz*, No. 45, September 1986. Photo: Mark Lewis. Courtesy of Professor Iain R. Webb. (This editorial reflects the anti-commercial stance the "style press" first adopted.)

aspect—it related to a new working class rather than to a patrician or authoritarian persona—and its tone was ironic and knowing.

Both the fashion glossies and the style press mediated broader cultural shifts. The glossies in particular benefited from the beginnings of globalization spurred by the end of the Cold War, the creation of the European Union, and widespread financial deregulation. Both were aided by technological advances in communications from fax machines and satellite TV to personal computers and the advent of the World Wide Web in 1989: British *Vogue* launched its internet site in 1996.

Meanwhile, global opportunities led to the proliferation of the highly marketed "designer" brand: "Designer labels are groovy again, and there's nothing like a Chanel to gladden a girl's heart," argued *Elle* in October 1987 (186). As in the 1960s, economic prosperity in North America and Europe led to a consumer boom—but unlike the 1960s, spending was less about freedom and choice than about money, conspicuous consumption, and image. Shopping became a leisure pursuit—U.K. retail sales rose by 76 percent between 1980 and 1987 (Godfrey 1990: 178)—and the link between money and fashion became overt. *Marie Claire* announced: "The rich no longer need to slink about in the shadow of Presbyterian disapproval. They are welcomed. They are fashionable. They are role models" (September 1988: 54). The movie *Wall Street* (1987), the touchstone of conspicuous consumption, famously intoned a new mantra "Greed is Good." In such a climate fashion became as much about hubris as hemlines:

> We began to think that what defined a person was not so much *his* name, attitudes and background, but the names that labelled everything about him—his clothes, his watch, toiletries, form of transport—and the attitudes and background *they* brought to him. (McDowell 1994: 2)

Once again, fashion was in the vanguard of social change as designer labels fused identity and brand status with a desirable lifestyle, a link repeated in both advertising and editorial copy. Despite the global recession of the early 1990s and a brief shift to "dirty realism," designer labels continued to market idealized lifestyles, driven in large part by Tom Ford at Gucci. Brands and their licensed perfumes and accessories were more about capital than creativity: "Fashion was first and foremost about big business and only secondarily about design" (Mirabella 1995: 188). While this had consequences for the industry—designers became expendable even from their own labels (see McDowell 1994: Ch. 4)—it also had profound consequences for fashion journalism.

Image became the dominant driver in fashion, thanks not only to the proliferation of fashion advertising but also to the advent of the music video and MTV. In London, meanwhile, the so-called "Blitz Kids" who frequented the eponymous Covent Garden nightclub took their image so seriously that admission was based on appearance. In the U.S., the "right" designer jeans could be a passport to New York's fashionable nightlife (Dellis Hill 2004: 113).

Branding was not new. Its power had been recognized by Poiret, Chanel, and Dior among others. What was new was the scale. In the 1980s, "designer" brands became ubiquitous—and big business. The change was led in the late 1970s by the Americans and Italians.[1] By the middle of the decade *Time* estimated the value of Giorgio Armani's empire at $1 billion. By 1999, sales of Polo Ralph Lauren alone were worth $1.7 billion (Agins 2001 [1999]: 83). It seemed that everyone wanted to get involved. As the 1980s progressed, designer diffusion lines and mid-market chains from Benetton to Next brought labels to the high street. On the other side of the coin, fakes appeared on market stalls around the world (English 2013 [2007]: 147).

As fashion became more international—the press referred increasingly to "The International Collections"—it also became increasingly decentralized and polymorphous. A new couturier, Christian Lacroix, who had been lionized by the international fashion press since his first collection at Patou in 1985, put Paris back at the center of media attention. Even in Paris, however, catwalks reflected multiple sources of creation, from the Italians and Americans to the Japanese. By the 1990s Paris was in crisis. *Le Monde* bemoaned the undermining effect on French design houses, and haute couture in particular, of lucrative licensing deals (Benaïm 1996). It perceived this weakening as part of a broader crisis in French culture.[2]

Meanwhile, Britain had also become a focus of attention in the 1980s thanks to designers such as Body Map, Katherine Hamnett, and Betty Jackson. The first London Fashion Week debuted in 1984. As Paris declined, London's reputation grew, inspired by pop culture and a whirl of creativity in many fields: the hybrid magazines, the growing reputation of St. Martin's alumni in all fashion disciplines, the rise of Britpop, the YBAs, and designers such as Galliano and McQueen (see Quick, above). In 1996, *Newsweek* ran a cover entitled "London Rules" and in 1997 there was a "Cool Britannia" insert in *Vanity Fair* (Callahan 2014: 122). In June 1998 *Vogue* ran a "Best of British" edition that even included England's soccer team.

A new wave of nationalism appeared as countries sought to promote their own designers. The Italian press grew larger and more influential, and *L'Uomo Vogue* and *Vogue Italia* were key authorities in fashion publishing in the 1980s.

Alongside the rise of designer empires, the business story of fashion in the 1980s and 1990s was increasing conglomeration. In 1987 Bernard Arnaud, who financed Lacroix's rise, created the powerful LVMH conglomerate, which now owns brands such as Dior and Céline, as well as the eponymous Louis Vuitton. Richemont, formed in 1988, owns Chloé along with luxury watch and jewelry brands. In 1999 François Pinault, who owns Kering (formerly known as Pinault, Printemps, Redoute), acquired shares in the Gucci Group and now owns Yves Saint Laurent, Stella McCartney, and Alexander McQueen, among others.

The international expansion of fashion brands and increasingly global television and print media saw the balance of power between the fashion industry and the fashion media shift further toward the advertisers, due to increased advertising budgets and the growing influence of public relations. In 1999, the *Wall Street Journal* reporter Teri Agins published *The End of Fashion: How Marketing Changed the Business of Fashion Forever*. Marketing had also changed the face of fashion journalism forever.[3]

A media explosion

The explosion in media coverage of fashion in the 1980s reflected the opportunity for increased advertising revenue from ever-more powerful brands. In addition, the overt link between designer fashion and the rich and powerful made fashion both the ultimate signifier of affluence and status and also more generally culturally significant: "In the 1980s fashion became a star like those who engendered it. The market for magazines full of images expanded enormously" (Montfort 2004: 167). By the 1990s fashion had become a key cultural discourse in society.

Magazines grew physically bigger to include all of their advertising. By 1988 the biannual collections issues of *Vogue Italia* and *L'Uomo Vogue* were thicker than the New York phone directory, largely funded by designer advertising (Coleridge 1988: 211). Technological advances and the advent of more cost-efficient printing processes also contributed to growth.

As designer menswear grew, so did the male fashion press promoting "the new man." Alongside the increasingly powerful *L'Uomo Vogue*, new titles engaged with the style-conscious male, including *For Him* (later *FHM*, 1984), *Arena* (1987), *GQ* (1988), and *Esquire* (1991) in Britain; *Details* (1984) in America; and *Vogue Hommes International* (1984). Such titles were followed in the 1990s by reactionary and more populist "new lad" magazines, such as *loaded* (1994).

As a response to the increasingly crowded market, fashion magazines emulated the designer labels and became "brands" marketed on lifestyle. The mass-market magazine continued to decline, to be replaced by niche titles aimed at the growing band of affluent working women, including *Options* (1982), *Lear's* (1988), *Red* (1998), and the short-lived *Frank* (1997) and *Mirabella* (1989). More youthful and practical mass-market titles included *Prima* (1986) and *Best* (1988), from German publishers Gruner and Jahr and Bauer, respectively. New launches were in general carefully managed, only taking place after extensive testing and numerous prototypes.

Like the industry itself, the fashion press underwent a process of international expansion and conglomeration (Gough-Yates 2003: Ch. 3). In 1988 Thomsons sold their consumer magazines to IPC (International Publishing Corporation) (Gough-Yates 2003: 52). Hachette, meanwhile, was bought in 1980 by Japanese car manufacturer Matra as a platform for multinational media expansion (ibid.: 100). Led by COMAG, a joint venture between The National Magazine Company and Condé Nast, publishers took control of their own distribution.

Meanwhile fashion coverage increased in newspapers, which launched new supplements. In France, *Madame Figaro* appeared in 1980, aimed at the sophisticated, affluent reader and championing traditional morals and ethics in its coverage of fashion and beauty along with the arts, decoration, and careers. Initially published six times a year, it became weekly in 1984 and is credited with doubling the circulation of *Le Figaro* (Bonvoisin 1986: 48–9). Advances in color printing meanwhile saw fashion appear regularly on the front page of the main sections of newspapers, particularly pretty girls in erotic "Sun dresses" (McDowell 1994: 146; Polan 2006: 166).

The Italian fashion press and Anna Piaggi

New weekly supplements were also launched in Italy—including *Io-Donna* (*Corriere de la Sera*) and *D* (*La Republica*) in the 1990s—but they were overshadowed by the general growth in Italian media powered by the exponential growth of Italian fashion, the emergence of Milan as a fashion center, and the rise of superstar designers such as Armani, Versace, and Dolce & Gabbana. Largely funded by indigenous manufacturers and textile houses, Italian designers advertised heavily in the domestic and international fashion press (Puccinelli 2014: 240). In 1985 the value of fashion exceeded the value of foodstuffs in the Italian balance of payments (Coleridge 1988: 173–281).

The Italian menswear industry was championed by *L'Uomo Vogue*, which under the editorship of Cristina Brigidini had by the 1980s become the international authority on menswear (Puccinelli 2014: 245). The womenswear industry was supported by existing magazines such as *Amica* (1962–) and the relaunched trade journal *Linea Italiana* (1965–) and by new magazines, including *Donna* (1980–), created by Flavio Lucchini, who was also responsible for the success of *L'Uomo Vogue*. In its launch edition, *Donna*'s editor Gisella Borioli outlined a more cultural approach to fashion, although in fact the magazine became most renowned for its interviews with Italian ready-to-wear designers:

> Fashion has never been as relevant as it is in 1980; and the magazine has been created to understand our times and bear witness to them […] *Donna* will speak of fashion but not that alone: clothes and cultural trends, design and economics, beauty and politics, health and modes of behavior, entertainment and sociology, music and literature. (Cited in Frisa 2014: 148)

One of the more remarkable individuals to emerge from Italian journalism in the late twentieth century was the editor and stylist Anna Piaggi (1931–2012), who used both her collaborations with Italian *Vogue* and her own appearance to promote Italian fashion. With no formal fashion training, and a career including the women's magazine *Arianna* (1957–) and her own illustrated avant-garde fashion magazine *Vanity* (1981–3), she was hired in 1988 as a consultant by the new editor of Italian *Vogue*, Franca Sozzani. For the next twenty years Piaggi created her legendary *doppie pagine* (double pages)—collage-style moodboards of text and images that placed fashion in a broader cultural context by including food, art, and furniture as well as clothing. Piaggi's own eccentric style—accessorized with a white powdered face, brightly rouged cheeks, and often blue hair—became a front-row fixture of the international shows, and she joined what Nicholas Coleridge calls the fashion "First Name Few" (1988: 243). Piaggi was also a long-term muse and friend of Lagerfeld and milliner Stephen Jones, and arguably pioneered the idea of the journalist as sartorial spectacle.[4] Her fashion styling was the subject of a 2006 exhibition at the Victoria and Albert Museum in London entitled "Anna Piaggi Fashion-ology."

Global magazine brands and *Elle*

Gérald de Roquemaurel believes there are clear reasons why fashion magazines are easily exported: "What their readers have in common is consumption, along with the fact that they buy the same kinds of cultural and material products" (Joist 2004: 171). The expansion of fashion magazines into new markets such as Asia and Eastern Europe mirrored the increasingly global franchises of the fashion brands themselves—and the West's global cultural colonization. As the brands grew, so too did their advertising vehicles. L'Oréal owned a 49 percent stake in Lagardère Media, publisher of *Marie Claire*, for example, and the magazine's expansion was largely driven by L'Oréal's need for a vehicle in new markets (Moeran 2008: 271). The expansion gathered pace in the 1990s.

By 1990, *Vogue* already had seven international editions but it expanded into emerging markets in Asia, Russia (1996), and Mexico (1999) in the late 1990s, adding seven new editions. Even this expansion was more restrained than that of *Marie Claire* and *Elle*. *Marie Claire* added eighteen new editions of its main title as it expanded into Western Europe and Asia,[5] and added an accessories title, *Marie Claire 2*, and a separate magazine, *Idées* (1991). By 1999 *Elle* had added twenty-seven new editions,[6] starting in the U.K. and the U.S. in 1985 and expanding to Latin America, Asia, and especially Europe.

International expansion brought numerous advantages. It allowed for economies of scale, as Goubaud's had in the nineteenth century. The launch issues of U.K. and U.S. *Elle* both featured Yasmin Parveneh (later Le Bon) from the same Gilles Bensimon shoot, for example (figure 8.2), while *Elle* Europe

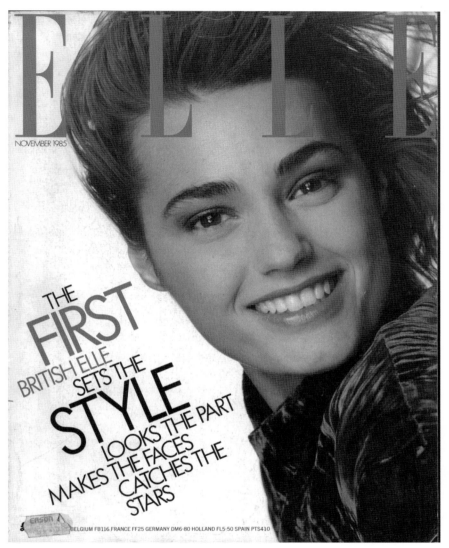

FIGURE 8.2 British *Elle*. First Cover, November 1985. © Victoria and Albert Museum, London/Hearst Magazines UK.

circulated photographic and editorial material from a central pool. Expansion allowed magazines to share an insight into the newly fashionable in different cities, giving the brand "insider" capital. Advertising was also duplicated: by the end of the 1980s, 30 percent of the advertising in European editions was the same (Gough-Yates 2003: 101).

Media companies adopted different strategies to position their brands, either broadly presenting themselves as symbolic of Western cultural sophistication or engaging more actively with the local market. One of the most monolithic expansions was that of *Elle*. Hachette brought staff from new magazines to Paris for two or three months to learn the culture of the magazine (Gough-Yates 2003: 100). The British magazine—a monthly, like all international editions—was somewhat different from its parent but clearly related to it: a "cousin" not a "clone." Hugely successful—by September 1986 it had a monthly circulation of 217,342 (Gough-Yates 2003: 103)—British *Elle* reflected the new way of researching and launching a new magazine (see Gough-Yates 2003: 99–106).

British *Elle* (1985–)

Elle launched in November 1985, targeted at young urban career girls: "*Elle* at that point was THE magazine. It had just launched when I joined, I think about six months earlier, and it was THE cool magazine" (Armstrong 2014). Its launch had been preceded by a prototype in Britain and America—*Elle International*—created in partnership with News International and a September 1985 insert in the *Sunday Times*.[7] *Elle International* had two editions—one in the spring of 1984 and a second a year later—which are much more fashion and beauty oriented than the French original. They heavily promote the French heritage and consequent fashion expertise of the brand: the first cover star was Isabelle Adjani, and "Elle Style" (Spring 1985: 80–97) contains an "indispensable French touch of insouciance and seduction," for example. The use of exported cultural values to define a magazine was adopted by other global brands, most notably *Vogue* for its launch in Russia, where its positioning relied heavily on importing American glamor (see Bartlett 2006).

By the time *Elle* proper launched in October on British newsstands, however, the magazine had a distinctly British feel. Edited by Sally Brampton, who had been involved with *The Face* as well as with *Vogue*, the magazine combined the youthful irreverence, urban bias, and graphic feel of the British style press with traditional glossy production values: "THE FIRST BRITISH ELLE SETS THE STYLE, LOOKS THE PART, MAKES THE FACES, CATCHES THE STARS."

Brampton retained elements of French *Elle*, including "Actu-elle," "Bon magique," recipe cards, horoscopes, travel, social issues, and "Idées Elle"—one jacket, six looks—along with its emphasis on practicality, with sewing and knitting patterns. However, Brampton's first article "Stamp Out Sloanes," co-authored with Tony Parsons (14–16), clearly aligns the magazine with the avant-garde subculture rather than with the establishment. She followed the French parent by mixing designers—a profile of newcomer Azzedine Alïa—with more accessible offerings. A shoot by fashion editor Lucinda Chambers is inspired by the Japanese designers but is created from customized high street items, positioning Chambers as a style arbiter on a par with the designers themselves (120–3).

Even as British *Elle* broadened to cover politics, money, and motoring, the irreverent postmodern stance remained, shifting the voice of the fashion press away from straightforward cheerleading: "Ungaro girls look like carefully upholstered wing-back chairs and will have to have their doors widened to accommodate his increasingly enormous shoulder lines and triplicated frilled peplums" ("Frocking," November 1987: 81–2).

Elle may be seen as profoundly changing the cultural references of the fashion discourse, acting as what Grant McCracken calls a radical opinion leader (1986: 76–7). In Brampton's words, "We almost ran down the street dragging our readers with us" (cited in Jones 1995).

Meanwhile the American edition, described by publisher Mary Beth Russell as a "style publication" rather than a fashion magazine (Endres and Lueck 1995: 77), was equally successful in adopting an innovative approach—"*Elle*'s content and layout were typical of the MTV mode that was taking over everything in that time: it had snappy cover lines, flashy photos, and trendy clothing on teenage models" (Mirabella 1995: 14)—and prompted Anna Wintour's appointment at *Vogue* (ibid.: 15). The first edition in October 1985 featured fur-lined parkas, but shared similarly graphic layouts and energetically posed models with its British counterpart. The magazine also pioneered the regular use of ethnic cover girls (Endres and Lueck 1995: 77).

Although its early success faded during the recession of the early 1990s, *Elle*'s ability to constantly re-invent itself has meant its survival. The *Elle* brand had forty-five international editions in 2015.

New vectors and producers of fashion

As fashion brands and magazines expanded their reach, so new avenues also appeared to bring fashion on to the international cultural scene, including the blockbuster fashion exhibition—pioneered by Diana Vreeland at the Metropolitan Museum of Art, when she inaugurated a series of exhibitions sponsored by the fashion world—and the now infamous Met Galas and music award ceremonies. Above all, however, it was television's embrace that made fashion a more universal cultural discourse.

The impact of television on the coverage of fashion took two forms. The first was programs about clothes and designers, linked particularly to the rise of daytime television. The second was the advent of what is now called "fashion programming" (Warner 2014: 1). The police series *Miami Vice* (1984–9), for example, was as widely discussed for showcasing the menswear of Armani and Gianni Versace as for its actual plots. Indeed, the series inspired American *GQ* to run a fashion spread in 1985 of real New York policemen wearing *Miami Vice*-style clothing (Cunningham et al. 2005: 213). Meanwhile the soap opera *Dynasty*, which premiered in January 1981, became an arbiter of fashion: "*Dynasty* was seen like a fashion authority like *Vogue*, where women got new fashion ideas and learned ways to dress" (Cunningham et al. 2005: 224).

Another avenue for fashion programming was the rise of the music video, particularly following the launch of MTV in August 1981. Designers such as Versace, Dolce & Gabbana, and Jean Paul Gaultier provided clothes for VJs (video jockeys) in return for a credit (McDowell 1994: 98). Soon the influence of the VJs was being rivaled by that of new fashion-aware music icons, particularly Madonna. The CFDA awarded both MTV and *Miami Vice* awards for their contributions to fashion in the 1980s (Cunningham et al. 2005: 219).

Alongside simply portraying fashion, TV also became a style arbiter through shows that discussed and promoted looks and brands. *House of Style*—hosted by supermodel Cindy Crawford in 1990—cemented MTV's influence over fashion. By 1994, the show had an estimated audience of 4.8 million (McDowell 1994: 98). *Style with Elsa Klensch* debuted on CNN in 1981. Klensch, a former journalist for *Women's Wear Daily*, *Vogue*, and *Harper's Bazaar*, focused on the older woman and could have a positive effect on sales for the brands she promoted, according to Betty Jackson (2015). By 1994, Klensch had 3.1 million viewers (McDowell 1994: 98).

In Britain, October 1986 saw the launch of the BBC's *Clothes Show*, a magazine-style format with production values influenced by MTV. The initial presenters, designer Jeff Banks and breakfast TV presenter Selina Scott, were soon joined by Caryn Franklin of *i-D*. Of the show's features—including catwalk reports and "get the look" advice—it was the makeovers that proved most popular with viewers (Polan 2006: 156). In spring 1988, the BBC launched *Clothes Show Magazine*, aimed like the television programme at presenting high fashion as part of mainstream popular culture (the first issue had a feature on "Soap Couture", for example). In 1989 the first *Clothes Show Live* event was launched at the NEC in Birmingham. Meanwhile, features-led daytime shows included daily fashion reports and makeovers.

Two of the most successful early fashion TV shows were Canadian. *Fashion Television* (1985–2012) and *Fashion File* (1989–2009). The latter, launched by CBC (Canadian Broadcasting Company), covered all aspects of the fashion industry. For seventeen years it was presented by Tim Blanks, later editor-at-large at Style.com, and was syndicated in 120 countries. By 1997, fashion had its own cable channel, Fashion TV; founded in France by Michel Adam Lisowski, it sought to bring a magazine format to a global audience.

Shifting power relations

If the fashion press faced growing competition from increasingly global vectors of fashion dissemination, the designer brands also challenged its authority. The brands' huge advertising budgets changed the balance of power as the growing quantity of advertising increasingly undermined editors' traditional role as gatekeepers: "Nowadays the mightiest of fashion brands, by virtue of their heavy duty advertising, take their message directly of the public—unfiltered by the subjectivity of editors" (Agins 2001 [1999]: 15). Designers also used their financial clout to try to gain a measure of editorial control and "the prestige that a positive mention in *Vogue* could confer" (Mirabella 1995: 187).

Brands increasingly paid for advertising on an understanding that it would also buy a reciprocal quantity of editorial coverage. Coleridge ascribes this development to the Milanese and the Italian publishing arm of Condé Nast, who agreed a ratio of 50 percent: in return for eighty pages of advertising, a designer's clothes—featured only as a complete look—would be featured forty times in editorial (Coleridge 1988: 211). The practice was widely adopted, particularly in the U.S. Coleridge later denied that such understandings are common (Tungate 2012 [2005]: 115), but it is noticeable that contemporary editorial pages do indeed often resort to featuring complete looks from one designer.

Some designers sought further control, and even provided editorial material themselves (McDowell 1994: 52). Although magazines might still criticize a designer's work by simply ignoring it, the growing power of the major advertisers led to increasing uniformity in both editorial coverage and imagery (Harrison 1991: 273). An attempt by new editor Carla Sozzani of Italian *Elle* in 1987 to create a more avant-garde, inspirational magazine in contrast to *Vogue Italia* ended after only three issues due to Italian advertisers' refusal to endorse her international, as opposed to Italian editorial coverage (Cullen 2014: 263).

Paradoxically, meanwhile, the power of certain fashion editors grew. As McDowell remarked, "Designers are only as good as fashion arbiters believe they are" (1994: 160). While journalists had always had the power to make a designer, the stakes became much higher. Figures such as Suzy Menkes and Anna Wintour now emerged as power brokers of the industry. The size of the American market placed huge value on positive coverage by American *Vogue* or newspaper editors such as Bernadine Morris, fashion critic at the *New York Times* (Jackson 2015).

Suzy Menkes

It was Suzy Menkes at the *International Herald Tribune* (now *The International New York Times*) whose views became most widely respected and feared by the industry. A newspaper journalist who began her fashion career under Charles Wintour (Anna's father) at the *Evening Standard* in London, Menkes joined the *Tribune* in 1988 as style editor and remained there for twenty-five years. Prior to Cambridge University she had however spent a gap year at the haute couture school (Ecole de la chambre syndicale de la haute couture) in Paris. Like Piaggi, she was, and is, one of the "First Name Few" and was assiduously courted by designers (McDowell 1994: 143). Menkes perceived her role as being a critic: "I think of myself as a fashion critic, like a theatre critic—one must have an absolute standard, an international standard" (Coleridge 1988: 128). This frequently got her banned from shows, but the rigor of her criticism also earned respect—an accolade had real gravitas. In 2014 Menkes joined Condé Nast as International Vogue Editor online; moving with the times, she has also become a powerful commentator on Instagram.[8]

The growth of PR

Managing the image of the fashion brands meant not only a proliferation of public relations but also a change in the relationship between PR and fashion editors. PR originally provided access to clothing for shoots and purveyed valuable information, but as their numbers and influence grew, the relationship became less collaborative: "The era of sustained, close working relationships between editors and designers was over" (Mirabella 1995: 188).

Sociologist Angela McRobbie suggests that the growth of PR brought a more cynical and manipulative dimension to the relationship between the fashion industry and the media (McRobbie 1998: 151–75), a view echoed by Polan (2006: 162, 170) and lampooned in the television series *Absolutely Fabulous*. Press officers increasingly controlled access to the seasonal catwalk shows that were now not only fundamental to the job of the fashion journalist but also spectacular showcases for a designer's brand image, and thus for potentially lucrative licensing sales and sales of secondary lines.

By the early 1990s, all the fashion centers had centralized their fashion shows: Paris at the Espace du Louvre, Milan at the Fieri, New York at Bryant Park, and London at the Natural History Museum. Catwalk shows for haute couture and, increasingly, prêt-à-porter became the heart of the fashion calendar. Everyone fought for access, from the press to fashion students. *Le Monde* reported in March 1996 that 2,000 journalists attended the Dior show, compared to 950 in 1981. Seating was rigorously hierarchical, based on the status of the fashion journalist. Pride of place in the front row went to the arch barometers of style, such as John

Fairchild, Hebe Dorsey of the *International Herald Tribune* and her successor Suzy Menkes, and Anna Wintour, who in 1988 became editor of American *Vogue*. Newspaper journalists, less subject to advertising managers than their magazine counterparts, could be more outspoken in their views and many were banned from a show for a season or two if their reviews offended (they included Dorsey, who famously wrote about what she did instead of going to the Dior show). Designers had long had tiffs with the media, of course, such as Balenciaga's falling out with Carmel Snow, but there was a new autocracy to the dynamic between designer and press. Even the magisterial John Fairchild found himself at odds with Saint Laurent after supporting Christian Lacroix's debut on the front page of *Women's Wear Daily* (Coleridge 1988: 52).

Promoting the designers

The designers were now the very heart of the fashionable elite, as both business managers and media celebrities. Designers' image became less about their clothes and more about their lifestyle as it was exploited in service of the brand. Once again *W* was in the vanguard of promoting American designers as fashionable icons, but the designer profile became a staple of all forms of fashion journalism, particularly in specialist magazines. As Lisa Armstrong recalls, "These were lengthy four thousand word articles: It was *Vogue* and it had to have an article or profile on a major serious designer each month" (2014).

Designers also promoted themselves through their own magazines, which were usually visually driven and functioned as glorified catalogs to promote a brand image and lifestyle. The first magazines were created by avant-garde brands such as Katherine Hamnett, which launched *Tomorrow* in 1985 (it refused to take advertising and only lasted for two issues). Comme des Garçons created *Six* (1988–91), a biannual that coincided with the launch of the seasonal collections. It lasted for eight issues. Comme's designer Rei Kawakubo told the *New York Times*: "High fashion has to have a mystery about it. This is the next step: visual representation of the collection, purely for image." The A3-size magazine—mostly shot in black and white—was largely a mixture of cutting-edge art and design rather than the brand's clothing. Although it showcased the work of leading fashion photographers such as Steven Meisel, Peter Lindberg, and Juergen Teller, by issue 4, fashion accounted for less than 20 percent of its 212 pages (Harrison 1991: 292).[9]

By the 1990s the big designer brands were producing glossy "magalogs" at vast expense. McDowell reports that *Le Magazine de Chanel* cost $300,000 to produce, for example (1994: 50). These catalogs often provided greater creative freedom for innovative photography than the mainstream press (Harrison 1991: 273). However, the style press was also rewriting the fashion discourse.

The style press and its legacies

I think in terms of style culture you can look at 1980 as being year zero because in the three months between May and August, i-D, The Face and Blitz launched. Three very different magazines but they came quite quickly to define something that was style culture or the style decade.

(JONES 2014)

As noted by Dylan Jones, 1980 produced three independent chronicles of "style culture." All were "hybrid" magazines that followed in the footsteps of *La Gazette Du Bon Ton* and Warhol's *Interview* by placing fashion in a broader cultural context, inspired largely by the creative spirit of London's fashion, music, and nightclub scene. They had limited circulations and remained at the margins of mainstream fashion, but they epitomized McCracken's norm-violating opinion leaders (1986: 76–7) and their radical approach changed the fashion press in influential ways that a decade later had been absorbed into the commercial mainstream.

i-D (1980–)

Although fashion was important to all three publications, only *i-D* originally proclaimed itself "A Fashion Magazine":

> I-D is a Fashion/Style Magazine. Style isn't what but how you wear clothes. Fashion is the way you walk, talk, dance, and prance. Through i-D ideas travel fast and free of the mainstream—so join us on the run!. (*Smile i-D*: Issue 1, 10)

Founded by Terry Jones, a former *Vogue* art director, *i-D* set out to capture what it called "mode" on the street in the now ubiquitous "straight-up" shot:

> STRAIGHT UP: Every issue includes a report, from your open-air catwalk the street. We snap and chat to you the Model. This issue visits: Kensington M'kt, The King's R'd, Blackbull R'd, Euston Road and Camden Lock M'kt. (Issue 2: 2–13)

As discussed in Chapter 7 the "straight-up" had been used in French *Elle* and *Nova* during the previous decade—Caroline Baker was, perhaps unsurprisingly, an early contributor to *i-D*—but *i-D* put it in the foreground. The promotion of the legitimacy of street fashion as an inspirational and aspirational paradigm defined *i-D*'s unique "vision" or visual signature (Rocamora and O'Neill 2010 [2008]: 186).

FIGURE 8.3 Sade. First trademark winking cover of *i-D*, No.13, April 1983. © Nick Knight/Trunk Archive. Image courtesy of The Advertising Archives. (A wink had been used as early as issue 7, but this cover marks the shift to portrait and the trademark winking style.)

i-D was in other ways a natural successor to *Nova*, championing "Dress Hire" from costumiers (issue 2) and "How to make a poncho" (issue 3). Graphically, however, it was unique: it was initially a landscape format held together by staples, with distorted headlines and a typewriter—later computer—font that prefigured the style of *Dazed and Confused* and *Wired* in the 1990s.

The magazine soon made an impact. By 1984 its cover price had doubled (to £1), it defined itself as a "Worldwide Manual of Style," and it had been invested in by *Time Out*'s publisher Tony Eliot, who chose it over *Blitz*. The "All Stars Issue" in 1983 pioneered the trademark winking cover—the i-D logo tipped on its side looks like a smiley wink—with Sade, then a young singer who had studied at St. Martins (see figure 8.3). Like *The Face* and *Blitz*, *i-D* covers chronicled the emerging stars of music and screen. The magazine also launched the careers of many key figures of fashion journalism and photography, including Dylan Jones (editor 1986–8), Caryn Franklin (fashion editor 1986–8, editor 1988–9), Avril Mair, more recently fashion director of British *Harper's Bazaar* (1994–2005), and photographers Corinne Day, Juergen Teller, Craig McDean, and Nick Knight.

As *i-D* developed, its subcultural stance moved increasingly close to the mainstream as it shifted to a more global view of trends in fashion, clubs, music, and culture. It cemented its image as the creative world's "style bible" by embarking on an *i-D* World Tour in 1989 which visited ten countries with an event that included DJs, dance acts, and fashion (Godfrey 1990: 118). In the 1990s it became more lifestyle focused and incorporated trends in interiors, furniture, art, and even beauty (March 1997 had a beauty special, for example). In 2004 Terry Jones took back full control of the magazine, and in 2012 he sold the company to online youth publisher Vice.[10]

The Face (1980–2004)

The Face, launched in May 1980, was originally devised as a music magazine. Its founder, Nick Logan, was a former editor of *Smash Hits* and *New Musical Express*:

> This is THE FACE, issue numero uno, licensed to thrill. The first new rock magazine of the Eighties, a totally new slant on the modern dance. Tell a friend THE FACE is here. (*Face* 1, May 1980)

By the end of the year *The Face* was proclaiming itself "The World's Best Dressed Magazine" (*Face*, 8) and although music remained central to its coverage and provided much of its early advertising revenue, its core subject became fashion as it related to both music and, increasingly, culture in general. The narrative style of its fashion images was influential, as were its alumni: stylist Amanda Grieve, later Amanda Harlech, creative muse to Karl Lagerfeld; writer Sally Brampton, later founding editor of British *Elle*; and art director Robin Derrick, later creative director of *Vogue*, among others. According to Jobling (1999), *The Face* originated the concept of stylists and photographers working as teams, including Simon Foxton and Nick Knight (1986), Melanie Ward and Corinne Day (1990–3), and Inez van Lamsweerde and Vinoodh Matadin (1994–9). Printed on glossy paper, it sought to emulate the production values of *Vogue* without its focus on haute couture.

The graphic originality of art director Neville Brody (1981–6) led the professional journal *Design and Art Direction* to hail *The Face* as "probably the most influential design journal of the 1980s" (Jobling 1999: 36). Its style, like that of *i-D*, was adopted by the increasingly influential British advertising agencies as they co-opted the attitudes of Britain's subcultures, again absorbing them into the mainstream. Journalists from *The Face*—Dylan Jones, Julie Burchill, Tony Parsons, Jon Savage—became the dominant voices of cultural commentary in the mainstream press. Meanwhile, as a shorthand for chronicling shifting trends in fashion, art, design, clubs, and other contemporary phenomena, *The Face* adopted the "in" and "out" column first pioneered by *W* in 1972, which soon became a pervasive feature of fashion journalism.

By 1985, *The Face* had a circulation of over 60,000 (January 1985). In 1986, buoyed by response to its male fashion, it launched the male style magazine, *Arena*. *The Face* continued to flourish into the 1990s, selling 100,000 copies a month at its peak. After Logan sold the magazine in 1999, however, its new owners, Emap, "didn't know what to do with it" (Jones 2014) and *The Face* lost its way in an increasingly competitive market.

Blitz (1980–91)

Blitz, founded by the Oxford graduates Carey Labowitz (publisher) and Simon Tesler (editor), was a general arts journal that featured literature, film, and art as much as music and the club scene. It even had an advertising column. By the third issue the magazine had national distribution through WH Smith and had won *The Guardian* Student Media Award for Best New Magazine.

Fashion also featured, especially while Iain R. Webb—later fashion editor of the *Evening Standard*, *The Times*, *Harper's Bazaar*, and *Elle*—was in charge of fashion from 1983 until 1987. According to photographer Mark Lewis, the fashion pages under Webb were as much a "social document" as "beautiful clothes and bodies" (Webb 2013: 243). Webb himself argued that his pages were meant to inspire rather than dictate, stressing the importance of individual style and treating clothing as an adjunct to creative expression:

> I WOULD HOPE that the pictures are seen as a reflection of the multi-faceted society in which we live. They are intended to INSPIRE, DELIGHT, or even at times, ANGER. They are essentially photographs which just happen to have

clothes within their boundaries. These pictures should be used as a spring-board for creativity on the part of the reader. (Webb 2013: 003)

Webb introduced an end-of-year fashion round-up and a more open question-and-answer format for detailed interviews or conversations with designers. One of his most renowned features asked twenty leading designers—including Galliano, Jean Muir, Jasper Conran, and Vivienne Westwood—to customize Levi jackets. The jackets were presented in a show at the Albery Theatre in June 1986, then auctioned in aid of the Prince's Trust.

The stylist Kim Bowen, a former St. Martin's student who had been fashion editor of *Harper's Bazaar* in Australia, replaced Webb in 1987. She became infamous for her acerbic catwalk reviews (see, for example, "Fashion's a Disease But What's the Cure?" [January 1990]). After Bowen's departure in 1989, *Blitz* used freelance fashion stylists and writers, including Susannah Frankel. Resolutely independent, it refused big company finance and disappeared in the recession of 1991 (Webb 2013: 013).

Meanwhile an equally spirited magazine emerged in France when *Jill* was launched in 1983. Founded by Elisabeth Djian, it promoted a more feminine and romantic look and has been cited as an inspiration by Marc Jacobs and Hedi Slimane.

Stylists and auteurship

All three of the British "style" magazines claimed with some justification that they had collectively defined the 1980s. Just as importantly, they also redefined the boundaries and tone of fashion journalism in ways whose effects are still being felt. The structure of traditional journalism also changed, particularly as a new division opened up between writers and the stylists who created the image.

Stylists were both a legacy of the style press and a product of newspaper editors' anxiety over the cost of photographs (Polan 2006: 168). The rise of fashion styling was also an antidote to advertising imagery that showed clothes in a way that traditional editorial spreads had done (McDowell 2014). The new stylists bore little resemblance to the fashion editors of the past. Even their appearance challenged fashion orthodoxy:

Fashion people used to look polished and pristine [...] But those dictating fashion now not only don't look smart, half the time they don't look washed. Most of all, they don't look important. They have turned the received language of clothes on its head. Theirs is a very different vocabulary, one that the rest of us are only beginning to understand. Smart and shiny doesn't mean power. (Hume 1993: 44)

Like Vreeland, the stylists at the new magazines sought to capture the fashion mood and created a new type of thematic fashion narrative: similar work was surfacing from Liz Tilberis and Grace Coddington at British *Vogue* (McDowell 2014; Jobling 1999: 19–33). However, the style press, which operated on shoestring budgets, provided a showcase for these emerging professionals alongside photographers, hairstylists, and make-up artists (another burgeoning profession). The magazines gave editorial credits in lieu of payment, shifting the image creators to center stage. Mainstream magazines followed suit, highlighting their own contributors. Image creators, particularly stylists, became branded auteurs who were also sought-after in fields such as advertising and music video. Meanwhile, make-up artists such as Bobby Brown and François Nars went on to create their own brands of cosmetics, which later became part of the mainstream—Estée Lauder bought Bobby Brown in 1995 (Eldridge 2015: 203).

Fashion narratives

Creating a narrative theme to capture the mood of clothing for a fashion spread was not exclusive to the style press. The approach had been championed by Vreeland, and it reappeared at British *Vogue* in the 1980s, particularly in the collaboration between Grace Coddington and photographer Bruce Weber. The clothes themselves were frequently subservient to the overall concept, to the chagrin of figures such as *Vogue* editorial director Alexander Liberman (Harrison 1991: 280). When Coddington—already a recognized force in fashion—moved to America, "the style essay" became a defining feature of *Vogue* there too (Angelotti and Olivia 2006: 262–71).

The Face pushed boundaries with its narrative fashion spreads by exploring the cultural subtexts surrounding clothing, including gender, race, fetishism, and Surrealism (Jobling 1999: 39), placing fashion at the heart of the cultural discourse and the real world. The baton was taken up in the 1990s by *Dazed and Confused* where photographer Rankin, founding editor along with journalist Jefferson Hack, and stylist Katie Grand further blurred the boundaries between conceptual and fashion photography. Rankin looked to take the fashion medium and "twist it a little each time" to interrogate the system, including its models in "Hunger" (see plate 13) and "Big Girls Blouse" using oversized models (Rankin in Shinkle 2010 [2008]: 95). In 1998, in an edition art directed by Alexander McQueen, a cover story by Nick Knight used models with a range of disabilities ("Fashion-Able," no. 46), further challenging fashion's paradigms.

Narrative work was also being explored at *Tatler* and later at the *Sunday Times* by Isabella Blow, like Piaggi a distinctive and spectacular fashion figure. A particular champion of milliner Philip Treacy and Alexander McQueen, Blow created "outré spectacles" both on the page and in person (Fury 2013: 153).

New discourses

With the ubiquity of fashion in popular culture and the energizing of the fashion media by the style magazines, the quantity and importance of fashion writing both increased. A new type of writer emerged: the "style" journalist who wrote about clothing in a broader cultural context, such as Dylan Jones and Robert Elms. The link between fashion and lifestyle also provided a new focus for fashion journalism generally, as writers began to talk about fashion in sociological and anthropological terms. A new breed of writers followed Tom Wolfe's "new journalism" and used opinion, wit, and new types of narrative to bring fashion to life, including Tamsin Blanchard and Mimi Spencer. Colin McDowell at the *Sunday Times* introduced a column of "Fashion Moments" that commented on fashion history, designers, and cultural trends, often with waspish irony (Polan 2006: 168). British *Vogue* introduced a fashion features department that included the industry's leading writers, such as Sarah Mower, and Lisa Armstrong.

As designer brands became increasingly accessible, a new signifier emerged—the nebulous concept of "style"—that sought to uphold fashion's role as a discriminator of taste:

> They construct style and fashion as insider knowledge, possessed by young urban taste makers whose seemingly innate sense of "what's going on" sets them apart from the masses and puts them in the lead in terms of subcultural capital. (McRobbie 1998: 154)

A new discourse emerged—influenced by Wolfe, Fairchild's *W*, and especially by the British style press—that used irony to exclude those not party to the sartorial knowingness of the fashion cognoscenti, such as when *i-D* declared itself a "Trendy fashion magazine" in its fiftieth issue (August 1987). The "in" and "out" column—pioneered by Fairchild in 1972—became a defining feature of 1980s fashion discourse. Even British *Elle* was not immune, opining in December 1985 on "Trash Presents," including Hermès mink jogging suits. Fairchild had also coined the term "fashion victims," but in the new knowingness of the style press the real victims were those outside the fashionable world. A similar, albeit more gentle, knowingness permeated more mainstream journalism, from *Details* to Lisa Armstrong and later Marion Hume at the *Independent* and Menkes at the *International Herald Tribune*. The idea of "style" shifted. Eventually it would become synonymous with fashion.

In the 1990s, irony became cynicism as existing and new subcultural magazines like *Dazed and Confused* began to question the commercialized fashion system and rework its paradigms. Photography increasingly featured gritty settings, unkempt models, and real people together with degenerate narratives giving rise to the term "heroin chic."[11]

Dazed and Confused and British creativity

From the outset the style press was supportive of the British fashion industry, including London's first Fashion Week in 1984: "We were the toast of the world and the Americans called us *darling* and *brave* and *fabulous* and *fierce* and paid homage with the Yankee dollar" (Brampton, *The Face*, January 1985: 85). After all, many of its emerging talents had studied with the designers at St. Martins and were influenced by the same musical and club culture.

In the 1990s British creativity was foregrounded in a new interaction between fashion and art led by the Young British Artists (YBAs) and *Dazed and Confused* (1991–), itself inspired by Warhol's *Interview* (Rankin in Shinkle 2010 [2008]: 91). Launched as a niche fanzine of "urban ideas for creative people," *Dazed* sought to explore the links between art, music, film, and fashion. As arts editor Mark Saunders put it, "We wanted the magazine to be proactive culturally—as opposed to being a passive observer of culture" (Hack and Furniss 2001: 168). *Dazed and Confused* worked with artists such as Damian Hirst and Sam Taylor Wood on specially commissioned projects that fused fashion and art, making British visual art fashionable as much as making fashion visual art. The hybrid style press became an integral part of the myth of British creativity and innovation— together with fashion, art, music, and advertising—summed up in what Tony Blair identified as "Cool Britannia."

Mainstream fashion and media brands sought to bring the dynamic style subcultures into the system and, by the late 1990s, British designers were running established Paris fashion houses and British journalists and stylists were sought-after, particularly in America: Anna Wintour became editor of American *Vogue* in 1988; Liz Tilberis became editor of *Harper's Bazaar* in the U.S., with Hamish Bowles as style director; Glenda Bailey, former editor of *Honey* and launch editor of British *Marie Claire*, became editor of American *Marie Claire*; Grace Coddington and writer Sarah Mower joined the staff of American *Vogue*; while stylists Debbi Mason and Anna Cockburn became fashion director and fashion editor, respectively, of a revamped *Mademoiselle*.

Gender and the advent of the male fashion magazine

The style press was also responsible, in part, for the growth in male fashion media in Britain and the emergence of the "new man."[12] The men's lifestyle magazines familiar from America and other parts of Europe had no long-term equivalents in Britain (see Ogersby 2003: 57–87). Aimed at both sexes, the style press— especially *The Face*, whose readership was more than 60 percent male—began

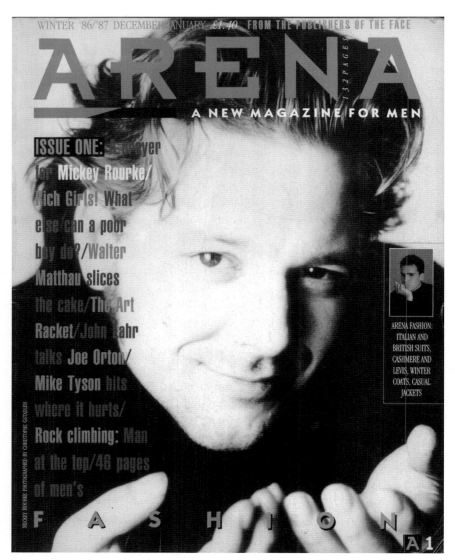

WINTER '86/'87 DECEMBER JANUARY £1.40 FROM THE PUBLISHERS OF THE FACE

ARENA

32 PAGES

A NEW MAGAZINE FOR MEN

ISSUE ONE: A cover for Mickey Rourke/ Rich Girls! What else can a poor boy do?/Walter Matthau slices the cake/The Art Racket/John Lahr talks Joe Orton/ Mike Tyson hits where it hurts/ Rock climbing: Man at the top/46 pages of men's

F A S H I O N

A1

ARENA FASHION: ITALIAN AND BRITISH SUITS, CASHMERE AND LEVIS, WINTER COATS, CASUAL JACKETS

MICKEY ROURKE PHOTOGRAPHED BY CHRISTOPHE GSTALDER

FIGURE 8.4 *Arena*. First Cover, December/January 1986. © Bauer Consumer Media. Image Courtesy of Vinmag Archive Ltd.

to explore gender through the figure of the new romantic dandy and the idea that clothing was an important expression of identity for both sexes. Arguably, Ray Petri's "Buffalo styling" in *The Face* and later *Arena*, which drew upon gay and body-building iconography (Jobling 1999: 143) and disruptively coded accessories (see Mort 1996: 56), was central to the imagery of the "new man" in advertising, as adopted, for example, by Levi 501s.

The Face presented fashion as part of the broader consumption of the urban unisexual style cognoscenti (see Edwards 2003). The embrace of "style" to encompass every area of culture and consumption from restaurants to reading material allowed for a less gendered identity to consumption. *The Face*'s popularity with male readers, particularly the work of stylist Ray Petri, and the growing demand for advertising vehicles to reach the "new man" led Nick Logan to launch *Arena* in November 1986 (figure 8.4). *Arena* was a bimonthly, 132-page glossy aimed at slightly older men (twenty-five- to thirty-four-year-olds) which, although heavily biased toward fashion and grooming, also covered other "current emblems of fashionability," such as interior design, gourmet foods, and sports such as windsurfing. As in *The Face*, it peddled shared knowledge for the cognoscenti, including the benefits of Katherine Hamnett peg trousers, where to shop, or how to manage skincare (*Arena* No. 4). Fashion was mostly designer and was covered in both "Vanity" fashion spreads and "Avanti" retail and brand guides. Visually *Arena* was both stylish and avant-garde, but its tone retained much of the irony of *The Face*, whose editors Dylan Jones (1988–92) and Kathryn Flett (1992–6) both worked there. By 1994 Flett had launched a twice-yearly collections special, *Arena Homme Plus*. As noted earlier, the arrival of *Arena* then led to further male launches and fashion supplements—such as *FHM Collections* (Edwards 2003: 132).

A new figure arose to challenge the fashion-conscious new man in the 1990s: the "lad": younger, brasher, determinedly heterosexual. The "lad's mag" placed men firmly back in the realm of sport, drinking, and heterosexual sex. Initially, *loaded* (1994–2015), the pioneer of the genre, only included fashion under pressure from IPC executives, as James Brown, the founding editor, thought that grooming was for "horses" (Crewe 2003: 47), but by 1996, in a search for lucrative advertising revenues, it carried a high street fashion insert. By the end of the decade, there was a *loaded* Fashion spin-off and even branded *loaded* hair products. In Britain, the link between masculinity and fashionable consumption had been made.

The fashionable personality

In many ways, the most significant shift in the fashion media in the 1980s and 1990s was a new focus on the "fashionable personality," a forerunner of today's celebrity icon. From the Nancy Reagan "power gang"[13] and Princess Diana—with her personal stylist, *Vogue* editor Anna Harvey—to the new stars of independent cinema ("the Brat Pack") and music icons like Madonna, fashion coverage became less about clothes than about the people who wore them and the designers who created them. Fashion and social distinction have always been linked, but the designer era was marked by the widespread commodification of individuals and their lifestyles, as epitomized in television programs such as *Lifestyles of the Rich and Famous* or magazines such as *People* in the U.S., or *Hello!*, launched in Britain in 1988. As Lynn Hirschberg has noted, it was the perceived accessibility of the aspirational icons, the intersection of mass and class, that characterized the appeal of the "designer personality" (Hirschberg, cited in Tonchi 2012: 11).

A new addition to the fashionable elite emerged in the late 1980s: the super-model. The status of the new supermodels was about economic as much as esthetic capital: they were the designer-branded and commodified incarnation of the "Dress for Success" ethos championed in Mirabella's American *Vogue* in the 1970s and an antidote to the androgynous woman who dominated editorial and advertising in the 1980s.[14] As Dellis Hall points out, the supermodels signified a new eroticism and body-conscious American glamor (2004: 130). On British *Vogue*'s cover of January 1990, Peter Lindberg photographed Linda Evangelista, Christy Turlington, Cindy Crawford, Tatjana Patowitz, and Naomi Campbell as icons of the new decade. They became much sought-after as popular arbiters of style and celebrities in their own right: Turlington recalls that her personal appearances for Calvin Klein underwear prompted "all kinds of craziness—people asking me to sign their underwear, you name it" (Derrick and Muir 2007: 192). There was even a magazine, *Supermodel*, that reported on their lives, fashion choices, and beauty secrets (Church Gibson 2012: 199).

The supermodel phenomenon mediated a feminine ideal focused primarily on esthetics. The focus of the fashion discourse had moved away from careers and "real life" toward an increasingly narrow focus on appearance as the sole definition of feminine power,[15] prompting criticism from feminists such as Naomi Wolf (*The Beauty Myth*) and Susan Faludi (*Backlash*).

In July 1990 Kate Moss was photographed by Corinne Day for *The Face* (see plate 14). The "waif" look and its attendant "heroin chic" presented a challenge to the Amazonian supermodel and marked a turning point. The new type of gritty realism was to permeate beyond the style press: Moss was shot by American *Vogue* in March 1993.

Celebrities and *InStyle*

In the late 1980s *W* began to report on the lifestyles and clothing of Hollywood stars. In the following decade, Hollywood celebrities became the new representa-tives of the symbolic prestige of fashion, partly influenced by their inclusion on the covers of the style press.

Many actors and actresses initially eschewed fashion as damaging to their creative authenticity, and their clothes went unremarked even in *Vogue*'s social pages in the 1980s and early 1990s (Armstrong 2014). By 1995, however, *USA Today*'s fashion editor Elizabeth Snead had stopped covering the European shows and concentrated on Hollywood fashion instead (Agins 2001 [1999]: 39). Meanwhile Armani, having seen the benefit of selling clothing through *American Gigolo* and *Miami Vice*, had become the most visible designer at the Oscars: *Women's Wear Daily* dubbed the 1991 ceremony "the Armani Awards" (Agins 2001 [1999]: 137).

The link between celebrity and fashion was cemented—and exploited—in 1993 with the advent of *InStyle* in the U.S. Launched by Time Inc. as an offshoot of *People* magazine, *InStyle*'s first preview issue was already 106 pages long and carried thirty-five pages of advertising. The editor's letter linked style with celebrity and lifestyle:

> This is the preview issue of *InStyle*, developed by the editors of *People*. Like *People*, we will take you into the lives of the most fascinating men and women in the world today. But the name of our magazine signals *InStyle*'s distinctive approach. To us, style is not about fads or labels but the expression of personality. To be in style means to live with confidence and individuality, grace and spirit. (September 1993: 8)

The magazine focused on the homes of the rich and famous, including Prince Charles, Annette Bening, Halle Berry, and Ivana Trump. Other features included news on everyone from the Clintons to supermodels and celebrity fundraising. Fashion and beauty accounted for around a quarter of the editorial, including two pages of street style, although the interview with Annette Bening references Armani, Donna Karan, Jil Sander, and other designer labels that "reflect her minimalist aesthetic" (75).

By the launch issue of *InStyle* in June 1994—after three preview issues—Fashion and Beauty had become a separate section. "The Look" combined reportage with a designer profile, while the beauty section was starting to educate readers in how to achieve the aspirational celebrity look, in this case that of Michelle Pfeiffer.

This tutorial approach to celebrity looks came to define *InStyle*. By 1997 it was subtitled Celebrity+Lifestyle+Beauty+Fashion, defining trends as the clothes worn by the stars and introducing the "Steal This Look" beauty feature. In May 1997 it initiated readers into the designer handbag, explaining why it was an affordable passport to designer status:

> It may take clothes to make the man, but just a single accessory can make the woman: a status handbag. Carrying one can transform a T-shirt and jeans into a fashion statement or elevate a little black dress to a party stopper. Status purses, while not inexpensive, are often a lot less costly than other designer items (Sharon Stone carries her $140 Louis Vuitton makeup case as an evening bag) and can sum up the wearer better than a résumé. ("Signature Style": 113)

The article goes on to highlight the cachet of the status purse in the context of Gucci handbags and who owns them, from Madonna to Princess Diana, restaurants where they can and should be seen, items they should be filled with, and clothes that match. As well as providing opportunities for brand advertorial, the *InStyle* approach places the celebrity at the nexus of symbolic value.

InStyle was phenomenally successful, particularly among more affluent consumers. It was already in profit by 1997 (Agins 2001 [1999]: 138). It was also popular with designers as a highly effective selling tool, as Friedman notes: "It sells off the page in a way that many fashion magazines do not. *Vogue* does not. And that's indicative of people's desire to dress like their celebrity" (Friedman 2014). In 2001 *InStyle* was launched in the U.K. by IPC.

In a sense, *InStyle* personified the shifts of the 1980s and 1990s, with its focus on lifestyle and personality as the defining symbolic capital of fashion, anchored, as it would be in the new millennium, to celebrity.

Notes

1   See Sonnet Stanfill (2014) for more on the Italian side of this development.

2   See Rocamora (2001) for a detailed examination of this crisis.

3   For detailed accounts of the development of designer branding in the 1980s and 1990s see: Agins (2001 [1999]), Coleridge (1988), McDowell (1994), and Tungate (2012 [2005]).

4   For more on Piaggi and her contribution to fashion see Piaggi (1998) and Clark (2006).

5   See website for details.

6   See website for details.

7   In fact the American version of the magazine was originally planned as a joint venture with *The New Yorker* but when Condé Nast bought the latter publication, publisher Si Newhouse had no interest in launching a competitor to *Vogue*, so Murdoch stepped in as partner.

8   For an examination of Menkes' work as a fashion critic see McNeil and Miller (2014: 125).

9   The magazine was relaunched as a moving app in 2014.

10 For more on the history of *i-D* see Godfrey (1990), Jones (2001), and Jones and Enninful (2010).

11 See Callahan (2014) for more on the heroin epidemic in fashion in the 1990s.

12 See Nixon (1996), Mort (1996), Jobling (1999), Crewe (2003), and Benwell (2003).

13 See Silverman (1986) for more on this.

14 For more on this see Church Gibson (2012 [2010]: 196–205).

15 See Cone and Marley (2010: 137–51) for an examination of this phenomenon in relation to *Marie Claire*.

9 A GLOBAL DISCOURSE: THE NEW MILLENNIUM

If fashion is for everyone, is it fashion? The answer goes far beyond the collections and relates to the speed of fast fashion. There is no longer a time gap between when a small segment of fashion-conscious people pick up a trend and when it is all over the sidewalks.

(MENKES, "THE CIRCUS OF FASHION," *NEW YORK TIMES*, FEBRUARY 10, 2013a)

Introduction

Interconnectivity has had profound implications for fashion and its media. The internet and the growth of global communication, with the advent of smart phones and tablets (the iPhone appeared in 2007, the iPad in 2010), have largely defined the twenty-first century along with the explosion of social media: Facebook launched in 2004, Twitter in 2006, and Instagram in 2010. As the hinge between the fashion industry and the public, traditional print journalism has, as Menkes points out above, found itself under attack by fast fashion and fast information: bloggers, streamed live catwalk shows, fashion film, direct marketing through social media, books, exhibitions, and television and "free" sponsored or e-tailer-based magazines, as well as other mobile forms of entertainment.

The new fashion millennium is fast and furious. "There is no longer a time gap between when a small segment of fashion conscious people pick up a trend and when it is all over sidewalks" (Menkes 2013a). The speed of communication has increased the speed of the fashion cycle. Designer brands now produce six collections a year and sometimes as many as ten, if one includes menswear and regional showcases in markets such as Dubai and China. Meanwhile mass-market retailers such as Zara refresh their catwalk-copy product on a twice-weekly basis (Tungate 2012 [2005]: 41). Arguably this "fast fashion" cycle is no longer a cycle but a constant fashion feed (Sherman 2015), epitomized in the recurrent signifier "now" of fashion editorial.

The advent of Instagram has further accelerated the demand for change, yet meeting this demand threatens to make fashion media as disposable as the fashion they report. As Suzy Menkes has argued, the rapidity of change creates a dislocation between media reporting and the consumer's wardrobe, circumventing the authority of traditional media:

> The story here is also about control, with the work of the big fashion houses increasingly unfiltered by journalistic critiques or magazine spreads. The clothes most worn by people are the clothes least commented on by the press. The images now go directly to customers via online shows with advertising campaigns as a backup. (Menkes 2013b)

The appetite for fashion has been further fueled by instant gratification. Internet retailing has become a global phenomenon, from the designer fashion of Net-a-Porter, launched in 2000 by former fashion journalist Natalie Massenet, to the mass-market clothes of ASOS, launched the same year. Net-a-Porter had a turnover of over £500 million by February 2014, with 6 million unique users a month (Leith 2014). ASOS, meanwhile, had 9.1 million active customers in December 2014, many in new international markets, and a turnover of nearly 770 million in 2013 (asosplc.com).

Fashion journalism had been closely linked to shopping since the earliest magazines featured service bureaus and mail order features. In the new millennium e-tailers blurred the distinction further through their online magazine format. In 2012 Net-a-Porter started *The Edit*, a weekly online magazine that foregrounded specific looks and key items being sold on the site. While online magazines are now ubiquitous among fashion e-tailers, many have latterly also adopted traditional print. *Asos magazine*, created in 2007, was in the second half of 2014 the most widely circulated fashion magazine in the U.K.—it sold 486,168 copies, according to ABC figures—and growing. Net-a-Porter's e-tailing print magazine, *Porter*, was launched in February 2014 and achieved a circulation of 152,000 in its first year, with distribution in sixty countries worldwide (Saner 2015). The digital edition or app offers readers the opportunity to purchase directly from the page.

As e-tailers encroached onto magazine territory, fashion magazines themselves have moved into shoppable content where readers use apps to click and buy. American *Vogue* worked with Rewardstyle and invested in e-tailers such as Farfetch, a global independent boutique network, and *Harper's Bazaar* began its own e-commerce arm, Shop Bazaar (Certo-Ware 2014). Magazines have faced issues with fulfillment for luxury brands, according to Masoud Golsorkhi, editor-in-chief of *Tank*, which abandoned its shopping platform: "If you're selling a Givenchy coat where there are only twelve of them in the UK, and ten have been pre-bought, by the time I take that, photograph it, put it in the video, put it on my website, and people see it, it's sold out" (Golsorkhi 2014).

The impact of instant information upon marketing and new forms of journalism has represented a new challenge. Although all the major German fashion titles were online by 2001, the fashion industry and its media were relatively slow to embrace new digital technologies. The film-based website SHOWstudio was still meeting industry resistance in 2006, for example, six years after its launch (Shinkle 2010 [2008]: 114–15). American *Vogue*, although linked to Condé Nast-owned Style.com, only launched its own website in 2010. As late as 2009 *Women's Wear Daily* declared, "For fashion companies, 2009 is turning out to be the year of social media" (Bartlett et al. 2013: 5).

Most traditional media brands and trade vehicles have begun operating multiple platforms, including tablet versions, and incorporated social media into their online mix. Some, like *Elle*, have adopted a 365-degree approach, incorporating digital into the magazine, with journalists working across print and other media (*BOF*, *Companies and Culture*, Spring 2014: 18), while others, such as *GQ* and *Vogue*, have separate digital teams. Nonetheless, most have struggled to monetize their online content. In 2015 some, like *The Times*, used paywalls, while others used affiliate pay-per-click models, where they were paid if the reader went on to buy advertised products. Still others followed the example of Business of Fashion (2007–) and use sponsorship or followed bloggers into sponsored content. This new form of advertorial has even been embraced by the niche press, according to Jefferson Hack, editorial director and publisher of Dazed Group, whose *Dazed* (formerly *Dazed and Confused*) included a six-page collaboration with Tods in October 2013: "It's become a hot issue now as media organizations look for new revenue streams in light of dwindling print advertising" (Sunyer 2014).

Much of the new fashion journalism is free, again shifting the model toward advertising sponsorship. Consumer expectations of free content have been exacerbated by the arrival of free magazines such as Britain's *Stylist* (2009), which by 2015 had a circulation of over 400,000 according to ABC, and the e-tailing magazines. Traditional publishers have entered the fray, with Hearst launching a free offshoot of *Marie Claire*, *Branché*, in the U.S. in March 2014. The launch issue—described on its masthead as "In the Know, On the Pulse, Plugged In," and featuring Alexa Chung as cover star—was distributed in key New York hotspots. It was entirely paid for by advertising, which occupied half of its forty pages. A summer New York issue was followed by a bi-coastal New York and LA issue in the fall. In a circulation drive reminiscent of the original French *Marie Claire* give-aways (see Chapter 5) 250 copies of the LA distribution included a limited edition Reese Hilton-designed canvas tote bag containing $650 worth of free beauty products, available at specific daily locations.

Media brands responded to challenges to their budgets and their authority by diversifying. Condé Nast has extended the Vogue brand into conferences and festivals, books on designers, cafés, and education. In April 2013, Condé Nast opened its own Condé Nast College of Fashion & Design, offering *Vogue* branded courses, and in November 2015 opened the Condé Nast Center of Fashion & Design in Shanghai.

Brands also introduced new formats to make magazines more portable, like their digital competitors: *Jalouse* introduced a mini-handbag version in 1999 inspired by Italian *Glamour* (Gay-Fragneaud and Vallet 2004b: 72), and when *Glamour* was introduced into the U.K. in 2001 it was in this now widely adopted format.

Digital technology and social media give advertisers direct access to their customer base, reducing the need for mediated marketing, as Dylan Jones notes: "Everyone's trying to circumvent media by talking directly to their customers" (Jones 2014). Fashion film, for example, has been co-opted by international brands, e-tailers, and fashion magazines as a primary form of publicity, including virally, as with Lanvin's Autumn/Winter Show in 2011. Indeed, some argue that the film has replaced the catwalk as the primary disseminator of fashion ideas (Bruzzi and Church Gibson 2013 [2000]: 1). The channels of diffusion continue to multiply: television, film, books and exhibitions, online content—"The concept of the branded museum show is now becoming a reality," observes Suzy Menkes (2011)—are all being used to market fashion, further challenging traditional media brands.

The celebrity remains a key fashion icon and marketing tool, cemented by magazines such as *Glamour, InStyle, Grazia*, and *Look*. The mythology is underlined by blogs, from celebrities' own social media accounts to "red-carpet fashion awards," street-style photography blogs, and, increasingly, the websites of mainstream media brands. Other sorts of "showbiz," such as the virally promoted Victoria's Secret show, flood the internet. Teenage girls and young women follow a brand's models with a fervor and idolization once reserved for boy bands. Digitally manipulated images of perfected celebrity bodies and faces are in perpetual circulation, normalizing and codifying these as dominant standards and creating disturbingly unattainable "identifactory fantasies," whilst vilifying less perfect ones. The fashionable body has always been an artifice,[1] but the individualization of this synthetic body through the prism of celebrity humanizes it as reality.

Perhaps the most significant impact of the new technologies and platforms was to shift the nature of the industry from a closed specialist universe to something more akin to mass entertainment. The advent of SHOWstudio's fashion film in 2001, live catwalk streaming in 2010, fashion blogs in around 2005, multi-layered websites, Facebook, and Instagram have created an interactive dialogue for those within and outside the industry, and have deconstructed the "expert paradigm." Both Caroline Evans and Gary Needham have remarked (2013 [2000]:

104), however, that the resulting apparent democratization of the fashion world reflected the ascendancy of the image of fashion as a consumable product (Evans 2013 [2000]: 80). Evans argues that real democratization has affected only the image rather than luxury clothing, but collaborations between high-fashion designers and high street retailers, most notably H&M, have arguably, increased the accessibility of the luxury designer for some consumers.

By 2014, however, things were changing. Commentators claimed that the blogging phenomenon was on the wane due to Instagram (Klein 2014), the mainstream media's reclaiming of blogging from 2009 onward (Titton 2013: 130; Givhan 2014), and the declining representation in street-style photography of "real" people in favor of industry insiders (Titton 2013: 136). At the same time, print circulations appeared to be stabilizing (Yi 2014), and the niche fashion magazines that appeared at the turn of the millennium have been joined by a seemingly endless supply of others, including Condé Nast's biannual *LOVE* (2009), *Fantastic Man* (2005), Penny Martin's *The Gentlewoman* (2010), and *Suitcase* (2012). Ane Lynge-Jorlén observes that readers value these titles for their expensive production values, their exclusive taste communities, and "their complex and rather elitist mediation of fashion" (2012: 7). Such magazines may thus function to counteract the democratizing influence of the blogger and the Internet. They protect the symbolic elitist value of fashion, with their emphasis on high-quality photography, philosophical debate, and concepts such as "artisanal" rather than the blander "luxury." Meanwhile street-style bloggers, in particular, present fashion insiders as the new celebrity fashion icons (Titton 2013: 130–5; Church Gibson 2012: 127). This reaction to the democratizing and demystifying effects of the global digitized media makes Suzy Menkes' question "If fashion is for everyone, is it fashion?" the fundamental question of the digital age.

Conglomeration and homogeneity

By 2012 fashion was a global industry worth over $1trillion (Tungate 2012 [2005]: 1), making it the second biggest global economic activity in terms of trade intensity (Corner 2014: 71). The expansion of the major fashion conglomerates has continued apace. The growth of global communication and the opportunities for increasingly dispersed production has resulted not in greater diffusion but in greater concentration (Gilbert 2013: 14), compounded by the effects of the global financial downturn of 2008. The industry continues to be dominated by Western global brands and oligopolies, from the luxury brands of LVMH, Kering and Richemont to the high street presence of Zara, H&M, and J Crew, resulting in increasingly homogeneous shopping districts:

It is sometimes difficult to remember whether one is in Oxford or Oxford Street, Stafford or Stanford, California Shopping Mall, for the same chain stores are everywhere to be seen, and for that matter Nanjing Road more closely resembles Bond Street or Fifth Avenue than it resembles Shanghai in the 1930s. (Wilson 2006: 37)

Internet retailing, which itself encouraged the homogenization of the global marketplace, has not been immune from global consolidation. In 2015 the Italian online retailer Yoox and Richemont's Net-a-Porter merged to create "the world's biggest luxury fashion store." According to Net-a-Porter's founder Natalie Massenet, "It is a store that never closes, a store without geographical borders, a store that connects with, inspires, serves and offers millions of style-conscious global consumers access to the finest designer labels in fashion" (Mulier 2015).

The global high street has been reflected in a global newsstand where Western brands such as *Vogue*, *Cosmopolitan*, and *Elle* have acted as partners for their global industry clients. By 2015 *Vogue* had twenty-one national editions, *Grazia* twenty-three, *Elle* forty-six, and *Cosmopolitan* sixty-four, with their worldwide reach increased by their websites. Financial power, however, has remained in the hands of the advertisers. Following the 2008 global recession, declining advertising budgets combined with falling circulations and competition from bloggers and social media to create an increasingly competitive market.

There has been further consolidation of the fashion media into fewer publishing houses. Time Inc. bought IPC U.K. publishers in 2001, while Hearst Corporation acquired Hachette Filippacci in 2011 from French media company Largardère and became the owner of *Elle* (outside France) and *Red*, among others, to add to its existing fashion stable of *Harper's Bazaar* and *Marie Claire*. Major international conglomerates also include the German publisher Bauer, the largest privately owned European publishing group, with brands such as *FHM* and *Grazia* in Britain, and Italian publisher Mondadori, which owns *Grazia* elsewhere. According to Hearst's president, David Carey, "All around the world I think you'll see a spike in consolidation. There are clear savings to be had" (cited in Jannarone 2014).

Some magazines disappeared, particularly those aimed at the youth and teenage market, including *Mademoiselle* (2001), *Teen* (2008), *Elle Girl* (2006), and *Cosmo Girl* (2008) in the U.S. Britain's *Company* magazine went online only in 2014, although it retained a street-style print edition. Despite growth in the menswear sector, male titles also vanished, including *Men's Vogue* (2008), *Arena* (2009), and *loaded* (2015). A number of new magazines established themselves, however: *Glamour* became the highest circulation fashion magazine in the U.K. and *Numéro*, launched in 1999, had both men's and international editions.

As David Gilbert notes, the international magazines, while they include local designers and events, constantly refer back to the established fashion centers.

Paris, Milan, New York, and London have continued to dominate, thanks to the might of the global fashion brands and publishers (Gilbert 2013: 11–12), bringing increasingly homogeneous Western ideals of beauty and fashion. While the dominant global brands—*Vogue*, *Elle*, *Cosmopolitan*, and *Glamour*—used non-Caucasian models in local fashion features, the models neither featured on front covers nor made their way back to the American or Western European editions (Yan and Bissell 2014: 194–214).

However, the decentralization of the industry has continued in the increasing importance of what Lise Skov terms "second-tier" fashion cities (2011: 152). New fashion weeks were created—Berlin and Oslo, Dubai and Lagos—but they have found it difficult to attract global media coverage (Skov 2011: 152). Global connectivity has also encouraged the development of "emerging" fashion markets in China, Brazil, Russia, and India, and latterly in Mexico and Indonesia, together with new media to support them.[2] In an issue devoted to Mexico, *Tank* noted that luxury brands were "salivating over new sources of cash, customers and tall tales" (Golsorkhi 2015: 20) (figure 9.1). China, in particular, has become key to the health of international fashion magazines: "The September issue of Chinese *GQ* is fatter than the American September issue of US *Vogue*. [China is] such a great market for us on a very old-fashioned business model" (Jones 2014).

Fashion blogs have also helped spread the geographical focus of fashion, "endlessly re-configuring the fashion map" (Rocamora 2013: 158). Bloggers, especially street photographers, have highlighted new markets, as Yvan Rodic of Face Hunter remarked:

> I celebrate individual style from all around the world with an emphasis on "unusual" places such as Kiev, Jakarta or Reykjavik, and don't only cover the four big fashion weeks. Everybody already knows about Paris or Milan; to me, posting an inspiring picture from Santiago de Chile or Helsinki has much more value. (Oliver 2012: 261)

Meanwhile, new media in China has begun to reconfigure the national fashion identity beyond Western colonial norms (Reinarch 2013: 144).

Unconstrained by global advertisers, bloggers have been able to showcase new and upcoming designers: "A platform can be given to designers whose lack of economic capital has excluded them from the media, a space crucial to success in the field of fashion" (Rocamora 2013: 157). This has also created space in the real world, as seen in the growing number of indigenous designers showing at Shanghai Fashion Week.

FIGURE 9.1 *Tank* Maxico, Volume 8, Issue 3, spring 2015. Courtesy of *Tank*.

Fashion: *The* cultural conversation

The growth of social media such as Facebook and Instagram has created a "camera culture" in which clothing choices are captured on a continuous, unregulated, and unfiltered basis. This created a sartorial self-consciousness and appetite for change that drove the rapid turnover of the fashion cycle. It has also, according to Vanessa Friedman, created a universal recognition of the power of fashion as a marker of identity:

> Fashion as a communications tool is ever more important with the rise of social media, especially the rise of visual platforms like Instagram, because people take a picture and they look at it and they make a judgment based on that and that goes round the world before they hear what anyone has to say. (2014)

First Lady Michelle Obama regularly updated her clothing preferences for a global audience on the blog Mrs O (mrs-o.com), and other celebrities and brands have been equally active in social media. Olivier Rousteing, the creative director of French couture house Balmain, had one million followers on Instagram in 2015. His global reach, however, is extended by that of his celebrity following, the "Balmain Army." Fans such as Kanye West, Kim Kardashian West, and model Rosie Huntingdon-Whitely themselves have a global network of followers in the millions.

It is thus unsurprising that fashion has become what Lisa Armstrong calls "part of the cultural conversation" (2014). Indeed, one might argue that it has become THE cultural conversation. Brenda Polan notes that it has "more coverage in the media than any other comparable area of human interest and endeavour," and brings subjects as diverse as food, hotels, music, film, and television under its umbrella (2006: 154). In this argument, knowledge of fashion has become the world's defining cultural capital.

Furthermore, what Rocamora calls the "permanent present" of fashion publicity (2012: 97) has created an environment "saturated with images of fashion." Fashion has itself become not only garments on racks but also, as Elizabeth Wilson observes, "a ritual spectacle, a regime of images celebrating a continual carnival of change" (2003 [1985]: 248).

The first significant change in the cultural conversation came in 2000 with the global dissemination of catwalk shows on Condé Nast-owned Style.com, the first public access website showing catwalk images, which had previously only been available online through subscription to trade sites such as WGSN. This was a key challenge to the exclusivity of the fashion conversation, in which only industry "gatekeepers" (Kawamura 2005: 79–82)—journalists, stylists, and buyers—had immediate and unlimited access to the information. *Vogue* editor Anna Wintour had some initial difficulty in persuading designers wary of plagiarism to allow their images to be shown on the site (Evans 2013 [2000]: 78).

The advent of fashion film and live streaming has increased the global reach of the conversation—and its marketing potential—still further. Burberry's Autumn/Winter 2010 Show on February 25, 2010 was marketed as the "world's truly global fashion show." Beamed live in 3-D to five key cities and worldwide via seventy-three websites, including *Vogue*, *Grazia*, and CNN, it reached an estimated global audience of 100 million and became a top-ten trending topic on Twitter. Burberry also sold sheepskin jackets featured in the show online for seventy-two hours (Amed 2010). The show changed the model for both the marketing of high fashion through instantaneous selling and for fashion journalism. If the catwalk was instantly globally accessible, the exclusive prerogative and specialist authority of the fashion media were lost. Today, all catwalk shows in the major fashion centers are streamed live via magazine websites such as Vogue.com, web-only platforms such as stylist.com, or the brand's own websites.

Meanwhile, television and film continued to play an important role in fashion marketing, bolstered by the continuing importance of the celebrity as a fashion icon. Films such as *The Devil Wears Prada* (2006) and more significantly television series such as *Sex and the City* (1998–2004) or *Gossip Girl* (2007–12) made designer brands household names, with stars such as Sarah Jessica Parker and Blake Lively presented as tastemakers in the fashion media.[3] Meanwhile the first shoppable film, *Kingsman*, appeared in 2014, orchestrated by director Mathew Vaughn and Natalie Massenet, whose menswear site, mrporter.com, was the e-tailer.

The fashion industry itself has become a popular subject for film. Biopics of designers included three about Yves Saint Laurent in 2014 alone, and *Christian Dior and I* (March 2015), charting the arrival of new designer Raf Simmons at Christian Dior. Documentaries about fashion journalism included *The September Issue* (2009), which charted the putting together of the eponymous edition of American *Vogue*; *Bill Cunningham New York* (2011), about the *New York Times* street fashion photographer; *The Eye Has to Travel* (2011), a biopic of Diana Vreeland; and *Mademoiselle C* (2013), about Carine Roitfeld—since 2012 International Fashion Director of *Harper's Bazaar*—and the launch of her independent fashion magazine *CR Fashionbook*. The films further exposed and demystified the culture of the fashion world. Penny Martin noticed that behind-the-scenes exposure was also important to users of SHOWstudio: "I think our audience is extremely fascinated with the culture of the industry itself" (Shinkle 2010 [2008]: 117). However, as marketing tools that raise the profile of the partici-pants and their products, the films paradoxically also uphold the symbolic value of fashion—the exposé of the rigors of haute couture in *Christian Dior and I* reasserts the importance of the original and artisanal, a paradigm that Lipovetsky had argued was irrelevant in the democracy of fashion.

As noted elsewhere (Bruzzi and Church Gibson 2013 [2000]: 6–7), the blockbuster fashion exhibition has grown dramatically in the early twenty-first century, with a growing number dedicated to living designers. Such exhibitions are another powerful promotional tool, extending fashion's reach as a cultural conversation. Indeed, the 2014 book *Vogue and The Metropolitan Museum of Art Costume Institute* reviews the "parties, exhibitions, people" at the center of this phenomenon. Arguably, such exhibitions and their catalogs serve to reposition fashion in the realm of high culture and art, thus perhaps redressing the balance of the internet's democratizing and demystifying impulses.

The new century, particularly since 2010, has also seen a dramatic rise in the number of fashion books published. They range from the mass-market *Fashion* (Dorling Kindersley 2012), a reflection of the cultural ascendancy of the subject matter, to more artistic niche titles, such as Juergen Teller and Nicholas Ghesquière's *The Flow* (Steidel 2015). Once again, the latter often function as promotional vehicles for designers and photographers. While the behind-the-scenes access of such books again seems to demystify the creative process, the books are also marketing vehicles that uphold the symbolic value of the luxury fashion object as art, working against the democratizing impulses of the internet.

SHOWstudio and fashion film

According to fashion photographer Nick Knight, founder of SHOWstudio: "The Internet's the world's most rapidly developing medium. It's where everything's being created. The site allows me to work with different creators of images, with people I really like" (Frankel 2004: 192).

Knight launched SHOWstudio in November 2000, recognizing the potential impact of the Internet upon global fashion communication and also the potential of the fashion film. Knight felt that the Web could better showcase clothes "designed to be seen in movement" than print (Amed 2010), but he also wanted to deconstruct the process of fashion image-making and open up a hidden world, pioneering the "behind the scenes at the shoot" (Martin 2010 [2008]: 113–15) (see plate 15). This exposé of the inner workings of the fashion industry is now a media staple, particularly in digital media and films such as *The September Issue*.

Knight also recognized the potential for democratization that digital offered the catwalk. His collaboration on designer Alexander McQueen's final show—"Plato's Atlantis" in 2009, which also featured Lady Gaga—first showcased the catwalk as global spectacle (a year before Burberry streamed their show). The website crashed but the industry took note. Suzy Menkes dubbed it a "techno-revolution" and Gucci Group's CEO called it the biggest game-changer in the business (Kansara 2010).

From the outset, SHOWstudio.com was interactive, inviting comment and collaboration from viewers, with downloadable garment projects that could be styled and re-posted on the site (Martin in Shinkle 2010 [2008]: 119), opportunities to submit film, and chatrooms, which Knight calls "essential." Meanwhile, *The Fashion Body*—a project of forty-two short films—was activated by the spectator clicking on various parts of a woman's body.[4]

SHOWstudio was highly experimental, and Knight's earliest projects explored the creative possibilities of technology. As an established fashion photographer, Knight was able to draw upon industry talent and his inaugural film was an animation shot in a 3-D scanner, *Sweet* (2000), which showcased stylist Jane How's sweet-wrapper reproductions of clothing from the likes of Comme des Garçons (see SHOWstudio.com's archive). In the accompanying commentary by Susannah Frankel, Knight argued that he wanted to show "how much effort, and even pain, goes into making a single dress. I wanted each garment to seem precious, like an art form." Knight's reassertion of the symbolic value of fashion as art, in opposition to the fast fashion of the digital age, has been bolstered by collaborations with architects, dancers, and musicians, again siting fashion in a broader cultural milieu.

Despite its early innovations and Knight's desire to deconstruct the system, SHOWstudio later accepted advertising and may, therefore, be seen as having entered the commercial mainstream. By 2015 the website was operating as an industry as well as consumer lookbook, in addition to offering a multi-layered magazine experience with profiles, industry parties, and live fashion showcasing.

SHOWstudio hosts industry discussion panels as well as "Analysis" of its themed projects. In 2014, for example, it created "Sans Couture," based around a shoot for *The Independent* by Knight himself, stylist Amanda Harlech, and the newspaper's fashion editor Alex Fury. The website's pages included a fashion film, the editorial photographs, a video of "behind the scenes at the shoot"—originally streamed live—and video commentary by Fury and Harlech about the couture designers featured, thus simultaneously demystifying the process and upholding the value of the clothing. The video analysis suggests that editorial insight is still relevant to the digital platform: that merely showcasing product and process leaves the viewer none the wiser (a view to which we will return).

By 2005, SHOWstudio had created a fashion film season and by 2009 it was the subject of a Somerset House exhibition—"Fashion Film, Fashion Revolution"— again placing fashion film and, by association, fashion itself in the realm of high culture. Around the same time, the mainstream media and fashion brands caught up (Menkes 2011; Uhlirova 2013: 122). Film and video quickly became a staple of fashion journalism for interviews, scene-setting, parties, and particularly for back-stage commentary. Magazines such as *GQ*, *Elle*, and even *Stylist* have introduced interactive apps to allow readers to activate video features, especially advertising film content. *Tank* magazine's highly sophisticated Fashion Scan has introduced new interactive technology into its print magazine to allow readers to activate multimedia features on every page or feature (Golsorkhi 2014). *Tank* editor Masoud Golsorkhi believes that such interactivity could measure user interest and involvement for marketing purposes in far more sophisticated ways than mere circulation figures or website hits: "We are now measuring the users' attraction to products in fine, fine detail, where they come, what they look at, what pictures actually trigger them to watch a movie, how long do they stay and watch" (Golsorkhi 2014).

Fashion film made by luxury brands does not depend on magazine websites or print editions for diffusion. Much of this content is spread directly from the brands' own websites or via Youtube. Although such dissemination again takes the fashion conversation outside the traditional media outlets, it also helps reinvest fashion with value beyond the simply commercial.

Fashion film soon developed different forms, including those made by famous directors such as David Lynch, whose narrative *Lady Blue Shanghai* (2010) promoted a Dior handbag (see Khan 2012: 236–8), or by artists such as Argentine avant-garde director Lucrecia Martel, who made *MUTA* (2011) for Miu Miu (Needham 2013: 106). The films blur lines "between what might have previously been termed art and what might have previously been termed media or lesser forms of culture with a commercial imperative" (Bartlett et al. 2013: 3).

Fashion blogs

Among the greatest demystifiers of the fashion process have been the fashion blogs. According to William Oliver and Susie Lau, blogs dismantled the apparatus of the fashion system:

> Brands are strictly managed and correct representation is key, with journalists, stylists, and editors often working under rigid guidelines. To some extent, blogging shattered this notion. As unmoderated, independent voices, bloggers had the freedom to say whatever they wanted about the style, equality and relevance of any fashion "product" they chose. They also had the ability to reach virtually anyone, anywhere. (Oliver 2012: 14)

The first significant fashion blogs appeared around 2005, including Diane Pernet's "Shaded View of Fashion" (credited by *BOF* as the first fashion blog), Scott Shuman's "The Sartorialist," Kevin Ma's "Hypebeast," and Bryan Yambao's "Bryanboy" (2004). According to blogger Susanna Lau of "Style Bubble" (2006), however, the real catalyst for the rise of fashion blogs was the creation in 2005 of the community forum "The Fashion Spot" (2012: 13). The fast-paced daily "posts" of the early blogs—whether street-style photography or the bloggers' own affordable outfits—soon fueled the fashion appetite and the speed of change.

By the second decade of the twenty-first century, some sources were claiming there were around two million fashion blogs (Rocamora 2011: 409) while others have placed the figure as "low" as 8,117 (Hahn and Lee 2014: 104). The answer clearly comes down to definition. In *Style Feed*, Lau and William Oliver listed forty top fashion blogs that reached 25,000 people a day (2012: 15), while the British Fashion Council included fifty-two approved blogs on its blog portal. Whatever the quantity of blogs, the most renowned include many of the "first generation" above, as well as Yvan Rodic's "Face Hunter" (2006), "Garance Doré" (2006), Tommy Ton's "Jak&Jil" (2008–14), and Tavi Gevinson's "Style Rookie" (2008–14), started when she was eleven years old. Meanwhile, 2009 saw the advent of Chiara Ferragni's "Blonde Salad" and 2010 Leandra Medine's "The Man Repeller" and *Vogue Nipon's* "Anna Della Russo".

Blogs assume a number of forms: personal, often diary-style formats; street style; product-specific: streetwear and menswear on "HypeBeast", for example; lifestyle blogs; or corporate blogs for brands or stores and, latterly, mainstream magazines.[5] There are also those like "The Business of Fashion" (2007–) which offer detailed analysis of the industry, and "Fashionista" (2007–), a humorous news commentator, that function like fully fledged websites and are well-respected sources of industry information (Oliver 2012: 10). Of the consumer blogs, the street-style format has been one of the most successful. Ton's Jak&Jil started as a lifestyle website about his native Toronto but he achieved more success with his landscape shots of the fashion world (Amed 2010),[6] while Garance Doré created her blog to publicize her fashion illustration work but turned to street-style camera work under the tutelage of one-time partner Schuman (La Ferla 2014).

By placing themselves outside the monolithic corporate and system, bloggers have presented themselves as "the voice of truth" (Armstrong 2014), and their unmediated outsiders' posts about their own affordable outfits, shopping preferences, or up-and-coming designers represented one of the most disruptive impacts of the first-generation fashion blogs. Their tone was and is more conversational, down-to-earth, and irreverent than that of traditional authoritative reporters: "I think that they're just a bit more personal; I want to call it the reality television equivalent of new media" (Medine 2014). Such reality included Medine sending herself up for her questionably stylish but weatherproof look during New York's freezing fashion week in 2015 ("WHY DID I WEAR THAT?", Man Repeller, February 24, 2015*)*.

Compared with the digitally—and surgically—enhanced celebrities of the mainstream fashion media, bloggers presented an alternative, more authentic idea of beauty and fashion that has created greater identification among their followers and further disrupted traditional means of fashion communication. Their original raison d'être was an unbridled enthusiasm for the fashionable world rather than any professional expertise, as reflected in, for example, the excitement of one of Susie Lau's early Style Bubble posts:

> Straight up, I shop A LOT! Most of the time, I'm not even buying anything but I just love the experience of browsing, picking things up, touching clothes. ("The Bubble Loves to Shop", Style Bubble, March 3, 2008)

For readers, the fashion blogs provided a less didactic idea of fashion than the traditional media (Bolter 2001: 42). Links enable them to click through to other blogs, websites, images, and films, while comments boxes created online communities where readers could hold their own conversations. Thus the blogs—like all social media—made readers participants rather than mere consumers, thus creating a fashion forum that was both more intimate and more democratic, without the top-down hierarchy associated with professional fashion journalism. Later bloggers—"vloggers"—have used video as a way to create a similar feeling of intimacy and authenticity: "When vloggers sit in their bedrooms and test make-up or pull their latest fashion purchases out of a shopping bag, it re-creates real-life experiences and turns the blogger into someone who is a friend" (Bradford 2015: 203).

This ersatz psychological closeness is central to followers' identification with blogs and bloggers. In the past, as we have seen, youth magazines created a similar effect with chummy references to "our ed," who in turn addressed her "Honeys." Now any remnant of matriarchal hierarchy has been replaced by a relationship based on amity. In a post on gold dresses, "Gold Copy" (Style Bubble 06/09/21), Lau acknowledges her followers' adverse reaction and even provides a hyperlink to it—"Now you guys had a pretty mixed reaction toward the gold but it's no use—I'm still feeling very magpie-ish"—while at the same time promoting an affordable example from Marks & Spencer. It is as if a fashion-conscious friend were filling in friends on her latest discovery, and the tone is gossipy and conspiratorial: "Get there before the eBaydevilspawn do."

And yet, as Agnes Rocamora has noted (2013 [2000]: 160–2), blogs are not entirely free from the paradigms of the traditional fashion discourse—their poses are reminiscent of classic fashion photography, for example. In a sense, their daily posts are a perpetual fashion "makeover" that confirm the transformative power of clothing espoused in the traditional fashion media. Lau's "Gold Copy" blog, for example, educates readers in the fashion system: "In the UK, there's always a 'hit' high street dress every season. It's usually a catwalk knock off that gets pimped out by all the glossies." It also manipulates the aspirations of the celebrity/fashion nexus: the M&S dress Lau promotes is "a combination of the YSL dress and the Burberry Prorsum dress that Sienna Miller wore to the Costume Gala in New York".

If the initial impact of the fashion blogs was to demystify and democratize the industry, the industry soon recuperated the bloggers into the fashion system. By September 2009 four of the first-generation bloggers—Garance Doré, Tommy Ton, Bryanboy, and Scott Schuman—had been invited to sit in the front row at the Dolce & Gabanna catwalk show (figure 9.2), complete with laptops and desks from which to blog (Titton 2013: 128). They were not alone. Lau herself and Tavi Gevinson of Style Rookie had become fixtures on the fashion circuit, often to the chagrin of established fashion journalists who saw their own status diminished by these upstarts. In some cases, even their actual view was diminished: in 2010 a *Grazia* journalist tweeted that Gevinson's Stephen Jones headgear was blocking her view of the Dior catwalk (Givhan 2014).

Many of the first-generation bloggers have been employed by established fashion titles searching for the irreverent subcultural capital they could bring: Lau became a regular contributor to *Dazed* and Garance Doré a columnist for French *Vogue*. In 2013 Leandra Medine of The Man Repeller made nine mini-series films for Style.com, while both Scott Schuman and Doré were recipients of the Eugenia Sheppard Award for Journalism in 2012. As established bloggers have become more fashion insiders than outsiders, the definition of the "establishment" has blurred. In 2015 Lau posted about a visit to the opening of the Balmain store in London (March 15). Although her tone remains in parts irreverent, Lau's presence at such an opening contrasts starkly with her early shopping recommendations, as do photos of her wearing expensive designer clothing at fashion weeks.

FIGURE 9.2 D&G show 2009/10 with bloggers on front row: Tommy Ton and Bryanboy. Image courtesy of Dennis Valle.

The mainstream media have not only employed leading bloggers. They also have integrated blog content—fashion blogs, street-style photography, interactive commentary, hyperlinks—to their own digital platforms. *Grazia*'s Stylehunter and Suzy Menkes' Instagram, *Elle* editor Lorraine Candy's blog, and the *Guardian*'s Jess Cartner Morley's weekly fashion modeling, for example, resemble independent blogs in their content.

Meanwhile bloggers' integrity and very raison d'être were called into question as they were co-opted by fashion brands (Mesure 2010; Menkes 2013a). Many blogs have banner publicity and pay-per-click advertising from which the bloggers derive revenue or a revenue share from web media networks such as Glam or defunct Now Manifest (see Bradford 2015: 209). Others have been directly sponsored by high street and high-fashion brands. When LibertyLondonGirl ran a story on Pringle, for example, in which the pieces were chosen and styled by blogger Saskia Wilkins in her own home, the sponsorship did not affect the piece's reception: "It was totally sponsored and it was incredibly popular" (Wilkins 2014). Some bloggers become brand spokespeople, as Lau did for Gap, while others pursue joint ventures: Anna Dello Russo collaborated on a range of accessories for H&M in 2013 (Titton 2013: 132), for example.

The most prevalent cooperation between bloggers and the industry takes the form of the basic advertorial, in which bloggers post about a brand's products in return for payment or free products. This type of sponsored content or advertorial is, of course, not new to fashion journalism. An established blogger such as Saskia Wilkins of LibertyLondonGirl argues that such links should be acknowledged:

> I became quite trenchant about the disclosure policy on LibertyLondonGirl, because I got fed up to the back teeth with younger bloggers. New bloggers were essentially lying to their readers, they weren't disclosing that they were gifted presents or comped a hotel or a review stay. I felt that was extremely dishonest for several reasons, because blogging is an intimate connection with your reader. You set yourself up having a certain life and people find that aspirational. It's dishonest to provide a life that doesn't actually exist. (Wilkins 2014)

Sponsorship of blogs, however, has inevitably raised questions about their credibility. It also threatens to undermine the authenticity of their "voice of truth," thus risking upsetting their readers: "We're getting to a tipping point. People are starting to push back. They want to be able to believe what [bloggers] are saying" (Schuman, quoted in Givhan 2014).

The most successful bloggers have been eager to expand their franchise, merchandising their brand across a range of media. Leandra Medine at Man Repeller—which in 2014 employed five people—observes: "I don't really consider us a personal style blog anymore at this point [...] I'd like to call it a media company, but also understand that we're not quite there yet" (Medine 2014). Medine, like other renowned bloggers such Zoe Suggs of Zoella, has published her own book (2013) and collaborated with mainstream media, including Style.com and *Harper's Bazaar*. She has also worked with retailer Barney's and clothing brands Michael Kors, Superga, and J Crew, among others (Wallace 2014).

This expansion of bloggers' activities mirrors that of the established media franchises, further blurring the distinction between the industry's "insiders" and "outsiders." Few mainstream magazines have remained content with a print edition: "Today we have to refer to a magazine's branded content across the entire eco system. That includes print, digital, Web and video—social media to a certain extent" (Mary Berner, President and CEO of the Association of Magazine Media, cited in Yi 2014). As well as the eponymous magazine, Dazed Group also encompasses *Another Magazine* and *Dazed Vision*, the advertising agency MAD, and Dazed White Label. Launched in 2013, White Label makes creative content for brands that want their publicity to resemble Dazed Group's products, including Armani, Chanel, and Nike (Sunyer 2014).

The celebrity fashion nexus and *Grazia*

If the success of bloggers stems in part from their personality-as-brand approach, such a strategy echoes the broader celebrity-as-brand approach that has characterized the first decades of the twenty-first century. As Bruzzi and Church Gibson note, "The desire for fast fashion has been exacerbated by the extraordinary influence of celebrity culture, one of the most notable features of the new millennium" (2013 [2000]: 2).

The relationship between fashion media and celebrity is complex. While individual celebrities can go directly to social media to cut out fashion journalism's traditional influence over trends, celebrities have also provided many editorial opportunities, particularly since *InStyle* inaugurated the celebrity as the dominant fashion icon in the U.S. (see Chapter 8). In February 2005 the arrival in Britain of the Italian magazine *Grazia* as a glossy fashion/celebrity weekly was symptomatic of a new appetite for celebrity fashions in which the marriage between fashion and celebrity has become a commodified spectacle: "Now you can't see an actress on the way to the gym without every single item which has been given to her itemized. There's a hunger out there for this kind of thing. It's become a kind of showbiz" (Armstrong 2014).

Grazia was launched by EMAP under license from Italian publishers Mondadori, with an editorial team of six experienced journalists, including Fiona McIntosh, a former editor of *Elle* and the *London Evening Standard*; Jane Bruton, editor, a former editor of *Eve*; and Paula Reed, style editor, who had held a similar position at the *Sunday Times*. The launch issue featured Kate Moss on the paparazzi-style cover. Backed by a £16-million marketing budget and an earlier taster of 650,000 free copies featuring Jennifer Aniston, it sold 155,157 copies. By 2007, *Grazia's* monthly aggregate circulation was over 700,000, outselling *Glamour*, Britain's bestselling monthly magazine. The magazine was the subject of a Sky television show and had readers who were "addicted" (France 2007). By 2008, *Grazia* had a greater advertising volume than *Vogue* (Gallagher 2008).

Grazia captured a cultural moment. Unique in the market, it was glossy and fashion-focused, unlike the plethora of weekly celebrity titles that had launched in the wake of *Hello!*, but it was weekly, unlike mainstream fashion glossies or even *InStyle*. Its weekly publication recognized the new millennium's desire for speed of fashion information and proved central to its appeal: "In today's culture where immediacy is at a premium, *Grazia* will be the most modern glossy magazine in Britain," announced editor-in-chief Fiona McIntosh (Day 2005). Its masthead proclaimed it "Britain's First Fashion Weekly," and the magazine's ability to reflect the industry's ever-shorter production schedules made it popular with retailers and consumers alike. McIntosh reported that readers would take the magazine into stores and demand the merchandise featured (Bradford 2015: 37). Items showcased in the magazine frequently sold out immediately—even woolly gray tights (France 2007).

The mix of celebrity and fashion was central to *Grazia's* appeal, as pre-launch focus groups suggested they were the only elements that interested the target audience (Church Gibson 2012: 127). Nevertheless, the breadth of editorial and newsy focus gave the magazine more intellectual status than other celebrity-dominated magazines, while still providing a celebrity fix for affluent women wanting to indulge a "guilty pleasure" (France 2007). Indeed, *Grazia* received more attention than any other magazine in Church Gibson's *Fashion and Celebrity Culture* (2012). It was particularly associated with the TV show *Sex and the City*, promoting its looks and its star "Carrie"/Sarah Jessica Parker as a fashion icon (see Church Gibson 2012: 113, 120, 127).

Grazia borrowed presciently from fashion blogs. From the start it included street style and featured paparazzi-style celebrity front covers: airbrushed, perfect covers had failed in research (France 2007). It often pegged fashion trends on street-style photographs rather than catwalk or celebrity pictures for increased accessibility (Bradford 2015: 155). This "no brow" approach was also reflected in the unique mixture of high-end and high street fashion: "Before *Grazia*, high end and high street fashion were always edited separately. Right from the start we had no problem showing them side by side" (Bruton 2014). In November 2008 it even created an issue in front of shoppers at London's newly opened Westfield shopping center, reflecting its accessible persona.

Grazia capitalized on its print success. It went online with Grazia Daily in 2008 (it later also hosted a bloggers' network) and in 2012 it launched an edition for i-Pad and i-Phone and a YouTube Channel, FashTag. The same year saw the hugely successful Grazia Fashion Issue Live, in conjunction with London Fashion Week. The magazine has been syndicated globally and in 2015 sold 8 million copies worldwide (bauer media.com), showing that the fashion celebrity nexus is a global phenomenon and merchandising tool.

New icons

Just as it seemed that new media might make journalists largely redundant, the opposite happened. Members of the fashion media themselves have become celebrities, thanks in large part to blogs: "Formerly anonymous fashion editors, stylists, and buyers whose names, faces and figures were only familiar to their colleagues and in their work environment, have become part of fashion media imagery" (Titton 2013: 134). This focus on the mediators of fashion arguably both re-establishes the symbolic value of fashion in the face of the democratization of the internet and social media, and also re-establishes the value of the insider or expert in fashion journalism. Celebrity is related both to professionals' position but also to the visual "authenticity" of their perceived leadership within fashion's collective narrative (ibid.: 131).

In her analysis of British *Vogue*, Anna König noted a growing emphasis on the insider aspects of the industry (2003: 211) and a shift away from talking about clothes to talking about the mediators themselves. The advent of the term "fashionista" and the increasing focus on "fashion insiders"—everyone from Business of Fashion (Autumn 2013) to *Vogue* (April 2015) published lists of key players in the field—emphasizes the cultural capital of those in the inner elite. Indeed, the fly-on-the-wall documentary, while apparently demystifying the world of fashion journalism, has, in fact, served to restate the professionalism of its practitioners. Despite the challenges, the authority of editorial opinion seems ever-more powerful. E-tailers, in particular, have noted that the validation of established journalists adds value and therefore sells clothes (Bradford 2015: 159): *Grazia*'s founding editor Fiona McIntosh joined MyWardrobe.com, for example.

In a sense, then, fashion journalists became part of the story. Each country has its local heroes (see Business of Fashion's 500, for example), but there are several global figures: critic and industry powerhouse Suzy Menkes of *Vogue*; creative doyennes Carine Roitfeld, editor-at-large for *Harper's Bazaar*, Franca Sozzani, the more than twenty-five-year editor of Italian *Vogue*, Elisabeth "Babeth" Djian, editor of *Numéro*, and Grace Coddington. The most globally recognized and symbolically—and financially—powerful figure, however, is probably Anna Wintour, editor-in-chief of American *Vogue* and creative director of Condé Nast, aptly configured as "Brand Anna" (Levine 2011).

Anna Wintour

In the *Wall Street Journal* in 2011, journalist Joshua Levine remarks that Anna Wintour's authority and network far exceed that of a magazine editor, making her a key industry power broker: it was she who advised LVMH's Bernard Arnault to hire Marc Jacobs as designer for Louis Vuitton, for example, and she has helped young designers get financial backing, both personally and through the CFDA/ Vogue Fashion Fund, which she founded following the 9/11 attacks (2001). Equally significantly, it was Wintour who inaugurated Fashion's Big Night Out in 2009 in an effort to resurrect the recession-struck industry. Modeled on Parisian all-night cultural festivals, the late-night shopping party was televised globally the following year, when it included 1,000 retailers and began with New York's largest ticketed public fashion show (Levine 2011).

Levine also suggests that Wintour recognized the growing cultural impact of fashion before others, a view endorsed by Si Newhouse, chairman and co-owner of Advance Publications, who argued that "Anna is ahead of the wave" (Angelotti and Oliva 2006: 282). Wintour certainly embraced—and helped legitimize—the fashion celebrity nexus, gradually replacing *Vogue*'s supermodel covers with celebrities from Hollywood, music, sport, politics, and fashion. By 2003, all twelve issues of Vogue featured a celebrity cover (ibid.: 275). Many of these celebrities, including Gwyneth Paltrow and Sarah Jessica Parker, belong to Wintour's global network and have become regular fixtures on the red carpet of the MET Costume Gala, of which Wintour became chairwoman in 1995. Thanks to its broadening beyond fashion, the Gala has come to rival the Oscars in terms of coverage, and in 2010 raised $9 million. In testament to Wintour's contribution, the Metropolitan's Costume Institute was renamed The Anna Wintour Costume Center in 2014.

From the start, Wintour's editorship was permeated by an engagement with popular culture, with references in both her Eye View and, later, the Editor's Letter (Borelli 1997: 254). Her first cover in November 1988 featured the body of smiling young Micheala Bercu, in contrast to the fixed head shots that had characterized Grace Mirabella's editorship, and mixed a couture Lacroix jacket with jeans in an echo of the British style press and street fashion (ibid.: 251, 256). In a bid to make the magazine more culturally relevant, Wintour also included more mass-market fashion (ibid.: 258). She has created key advertising issues around themes such as "Power" and "Age," as well as launching *Teen Vogue* (2002) and *Men's Vogue* (2005–8) and building the September issue into an industry bible.

The 2009 film *The September Issue* cemented Wintour's status as the most iconic global fashion editor (see Church Gibson 2012: 132–5), although it also showcased the talents of her colleagues, especially Grace Coddington, whose "style essays" define *Vogue* under Wintour (Angelotti and Olivia 2006: 262–71).

Wintour's influence over the fashion industry continued to grow when she oversaw the launch of Vogue.com and took editorial responsibility for the e-commerce development of Condé Nast's Style.com (Abnett 2015). Her presence at a catwalk show immediately bestows fashion status (Tungate 2012 [2005]: 123) and she was noticeable by her absence from Alexander McQueen's early shows (Callahan 2014: 107).[7] While Wintour has continued to encourage pioneering photography at *Vogue*,[8] editors such as Carine Roitfeld and Franca Sozzani may have stronger creative reputations, but Wintour's strength is business. She sees *Vogue* as a huge global brand to enhance, protect, and make "part of the conversation" (Levine 2011). Most of all, it has been Wintour's ability to create herself as a global brand that has enhanced the authority of *Vogue*.

Niche magazines and the symbolic value of fashion

In 2004 Rafal Niemojewski noted the advent of a new type of fashion publication: "They cannot be defined as fashion magazines, strictly speaking [...] With their avant-garde positioning, they take a fresh look at fashion, placing it in an interactive relationship with the plastic arts, music, the cinema and the 'celeb' world" (2004: 180).

The new millennium saw the launch of a multitude of niche fashion magazines, including *Tank* (1998); *Numéro* (founded 1998, launched 1999); *032c* (2001); *Nylon* (1999); *Exit* (2000); *Pop* (2000); *Another Magazine* (2001); *Dansk* (2002); *Purple Fashion* (2004: relaunch of *Purple*, 1992); *Sleaze* (2004); *A Magazine* (2004); *Fantastic Man* (2005); *Hunger* (2011); *Wonderland* (2004); *The Gentlewoman* (2010), and *Garage* (2011). They joined the second wave of style magazines launched in the 1990s, such as *Dazed and Confused* and *Visionnaire*.[9]

While many of these magazines are biannual, some are monthlies—*Nylon*, *Numéro*—or part of mainstream media organizations: *POP*, formerly *Pop*, is owned by Bauer, *LOVE* is part of Condé Nast, and many, including *The Gentlewoman*, are distributed by COMAG. A number originated in the U.K., but niche titles have increasingly appeared across the globe in both established and new fashion centers: *Nylon* is New York based; *A Magazine* is from Belgium; *Purple Fashion*, *Self Service* and *Numéro* are French; *032c* is from Berlin, *Dansk* from Denmark, and *Garage* from Moscow.

Despite their widespread geography, niche magazines share a number of defining characteristics: issues are themed and numbered, printed on high-quality paper, larger and more expensive than the average fashion magazine and closer to an art book, with limited or no contents on the cover. As Niemojewski notes above, they are also "hybrid," placing fashion in a broader cultural context. Although they can be bought at the newsstand, many are subscription based. It is precisely the limits of their schedules, their high production values, and their premium pricing that both create their attraction for their readers (Lynge-Jorlén 2012: 8–9) and reassert the elitist symbolic value of fashion: "I do think with the whole internet, people expect magazines to be more special" (Jop Van Bennekom, founder of *Fantastic Man*, quoted in Tzortzis 2007). It is perhaps not surprising in this context that *A Magazine* has issues "curated" by leading avant-garde designers.

As Lynge-Jorlén has observed, the niche hybrids operate at the cutting-edge of fashion. Many of their contributors are established creative professionals— *LOVE*'s founder and editor is stylist Katie Grand, who worked as a consultant for numerous brands including Marc Jacobs, for example—and they are widely read in the industry. They function as trendsetters in clothing, styling, photography, and design (Lynge-Jorlén 2009: 11), with fashion pages that frequently privilege mood over clothing and covers that capture an attitude rather than aspiration— Beth Ditto on *LOVE*, for example, or Angela Lansbury on *The Gentlewoman* (see plate 16). While Stéphane Wargnier has criticized such magazines as unmediated "playgrounds for their staff" (2004: 165), it is precisely their self-reflexive and closed perspective that has helped them counter the democratizing impulses of the internet. As Olivier Zahm, founder of *Purple*, argues:

As an independant [*sic*] magazine, it has maintained a commitment to artistic individuality, integrity and intelligence. So we also resist the drift towards the Internet, the future home of magazines and practical consumption, in preference for art's unpredictability and a sense of true fashion design. (*PurpleFashion*, issue 4, Fall/Winter 2005/6: 18)

As Masoud Golsorkhi of *Tank* puts it, they are an "antidote to the mainstream ubiquity of celebrity" (2014).

By mixing fashion with other arts and focusing on long-form journalism— *032c* featured a nine-page interview with a Berlin professor on the post-heroic age (Tzortzis 2007)—niche magazines represent fashion in a more intellectual vein than the fast fashion of the digital age.[10] Talking of his vision of fashion and artistic culture, Zahm turns to abstraction:

Purple's conceptual territory has been a chiaroscuro, double-edge, ambiguous, on the verge of abstraction. It refuses to explain itself or offer an apology. It's an artistic position still largely unexplored. (Zahm and Fleiss 2008: Preface)

In addition, many niche magazines, particularly those based in Britain, have adopted the ironic tone of the early style press. An ironic approach effectively distances those who are not "in the know" and reinforces the closed universe of fashion insiders. This impression is reinforced by the use of first names—"Cara on Kim" (*LOVE* 13, Spring/Summer 2015)—and assumed knowledge. *LOVE* contributors have no biographies. They are general leaders in their field, and the reader is expected to be familiar with them.

This tribal feel is another part of the magazines' attraction for readers, according to Lynge-Jorlén. Editor Penny Martin pointed out that in 2014 there were 25,000 members of *The Gentlewoman* club who participated in reader events: "I was aware that there was a growing community around the magazine, and there were women, and men, that wanted to get involved in what we were doing so we started to do real life, real world events" (Martin 2014).

This symbolic repositioning of fashion away from the disposable has paid dividends: *The Gentlewoman*'s circulation grew from 72,000 to 98,000 in five years (Martin 2014), *Tank* has returned to bimonthly publication, and *Numéro*, which added *Numéro Homme* (2007) and international editions (figure 9.3), generated $10.6 million in 2013 (Diderich 2014).

In praise of the experts

Despite blogs and niche magazines, journalistic expertise and mainstream print media have remained resilient. In 2014 and 2015, ABC figures suggested their circulations were stabilizing, while *Vogue*, *Harper's Bazaar*, and *InStyle*, among others, were growing (Durrani 2014b). Nicholas Coleridge, managing director of Condé Nast Britain and president of Condé Nast International, remarked, "This is a stellar time to be in branded magazine publishing" (Durrani 2014a). Meanwhile digital operators, including Business of Fashion, have introduced print publications.[11] In addition, there are signs that advertisers are still attached to the production values and authority of print:

> They (the luxury brands) all still want to be in print rather than online. They still think of print as more prestigious and I think it's to do with exclusivity and the idea that the Internet is infinite and the repository of everything from the brilliant to the banal and dreadful, whereas a newspaper or a magazine is, by definition, an edited summary of the people who work on its points of view. (Armstrong 2014)

It seems that, in a saturated virtual world, showing without telling may be losing its appeal—witness the move of e-tailers into editorialized print magazines with expert points of view. According to *Porter* editor Lucy Yeomans, Net-a-Porter's customers said "their most authoritative inspiration for fashion was still print, what they wanted was real curation and a point of view" (Saner 2015).

The new millennium has witnessed dramatic shifts in the mechanisms for the diffusion of fashion and the entry of new voices into the fashion media. Both

大都市 **Numéro**

1

KIRSTEN DUNST
不纯真年代

PHOEBE PHILO
清醒的简约主义

COUP DE COEUR
改写时装语言的设计新星

JEFF KOONS
充气娃娃与新消费主义

贾樟柯
私享日记本

SEPTEMBER 2010 人民币30元
ISSN 1007-8142

9 771007 814006   17>

New Era

FIGURE 9.3 *Numéro* China, first edition. *Numéro Chine*. Photo Tiziano Magni, Direction Aritistique Joseph Carle, model Liu Wen with Robe Dior Haute Couture. Image courtesy of *Numéro*.

developments have democratized the discourse of fashion. The pace of fashion change increased, bringing a seemingly insatiable appetite for news and information. While this has led to a global proliferation of fashion culture and imagery, the authority of established fashion magazines and critical voices has remained, albeit in changed channels of delivery. Furthermore, there are signs that a new symbolic elitism has emerged in fashion insiders, bespoke fashion product, and niche magazines.

Notes

1   See De Pertuis (2010 [2008]) for more on this.

2   For more on this see Breward and Gilbert (2006), Bruzzi and Church Gibson (2013: esp. Chs 1–4), Bartlett et al. (2013: Ch. 12), and Skov and Melchior (2011).

3   See Warner (2014: Ch. 7), and Church Gibson (2012, Ch. 4).

4   See Khan (2012).

5   See Rocamora (2009b and 2011) and Bradford (2015: 199).

6   Employed by Style.com and American *GQ* to cover fashion weeks, a post previously occupied by Scott Schuman of The Sartorialist, Ton shut down his blog to pursue his photographic career.

7   McQueen was so angry about Wintour's lack of endorsement that when American *Vogue* asked to shoot a "Highland Rape" dress he demanded that it be flown in its own seat with an escort: the magazine complied (Callahan 2014: 107).

8   Photographers such as the energetic Mario Testino, the documentarian Steven Meisel, and the artistic Steven Klein, among others, have found a showcase for their work in Wintour's *Vogue* (see Angelotti and Oliva 2006: 284–389).

9   For more on this and niche magazines in general see Lynge-Jorlén (2009, 2012).

10   See McNeil and Miller (2014: 128–31) for a detailed and astute discussion of this phenomenon in relation to *Acne Paper*.

11   Business of Fashion has produced biannual special editions covering various industry topics since 2013.

10 FACING THE FUTURE: THE EVOLVING FASHION MEDIA

In an age of endless bombardment of information, gossip, babble, white noise, many of us yearn for something different, something more sophisticated and thoughtful. Here's hoping you will find such treasures to cherish in Harper's Bazaar.

(JUSTINE PICARDIE, "THE NEW SPIRIT OF FASHION",
***HARPER'S BAZAAR*, APRIL 2015: 62)**

The symbiotic relationship: Uncertainty

No one knows what the future holds for fashion journalism, although *Harper's Bazaar* editor, Justine Picardie, suggested it offers a contemplative antidote to the noise of the global age. The status of the profession has been much debated of late in industry and academic circles: *Fashion Projects* dedicated a recent issue to "Fashion Criticism" (2013), with interviews among professionals, and there has been much discussion in *Vestoj*.[1] All the industry specialists with whom I spoke agreed that the industry is still in a state of flux: "It's a revolution, like the industrial revolution, and the world has changed and there will be winners and losers" (Jones 2014). They expected attrition in the numbers of both practitioners and publications: "I have no idea what it will look like in five years' time but I know it won't look like now' (Armstrong 2014). It seems probable, however, that multiple channels of fashion diffusion will remain and that brands will continue to communicate directly with consumers through fashion film and social media.

Meanwhile fashion media brands continue to diversify their franchises:

Draper's is now a brand which is applied to a number of activities: it's applied to a weekly magazine, it's applied to a website, it's applied to four national awards, it's applied to two big conferences. (Musgrave 2014)

Many see the blurring of editorial with sponsored brand content as an acceptable business compromise. As Jefferson Hack puts it, "If there is a degree of transparency about the brand's involvement, it's win–win for everyone. Accept it and move on" (Sunyer 2014). Jones and Armstrong emphasized the need to work with advertisers, and American *Vogue* editor Hamish Bowles argued that: "I'd say that advertising and editorial complement each other. Fashion is all about creating desire, and both advertisers and editors want to seduce the consumer; after all, that's our job" (Cronberg 2013a: viii). Meanwhile consumers seem accepting: "Some buy fashion magazines almost as much for ads as for the editorial," argues David Carey, president of Hearst (Jannarone 2014). There are others, however, such as former *Vogue Paris* editor Irene Silvagni, who believe that such relationships have eroded the credibility of fashion journalism itself: "Nobody trusts critics now. A critic should be fair and understand the history of fashion. But this often isn't the case anymore; we're trapped by the incestuous relationship between advertisers and publishers" (Cronberg 2013b). The brand consultancy of fashion journalists, likely to increase (Armstrong 2014), further muddies the waters. Even the redoubtable Menkes has been accused of playing to the crowd on Instagram (Aylmer 2016).

Perhaps that is why in summer 2015 Condé Nast appeared to be moving its electronic business away from its core print brands, announcing that Style.com would be its e-tailing platform and merging editorial under the Vogue brand (Abnett 2015). That said, the erosion of the boundaries between journalism and commerce seems likely to continue.

Cultural imperialism and global opportunities

Emerging markets such as the MINT countries (Mexico, Indonesia, Nigeria, and Turkey) seem ripe for development. Meanwhile *Vogue China*'s readership exceeded those of British and Italian *Vogue* in 2014 and *Business of Fashion* listed its editor Angelica Cheung as one of its "Game Changers" (Amed 2014: 23–5), but evidence suggests that maturing markets develop their own fashion industry and their own fashion media. In more established Asian fashion markets such as Singapore and Hong Kong, local independent magazines are more popular than imports, including *Her World*, *Teenage*, and *Bella Nuyon* (Singapore) and *Next Magazine* and *Jessica* (Hong Kong) (Tay 2009: 142).

In Russia and China, as we have seen, indigenous media brands are also emerging. In 2015 Business of Fashion reported on the launch of *Leaf*, a self-published magazine by former *Elle* editor Leaf Greener on the new Chinese mobile platform WeChat, which boasted 500 million users (Ying 2015). Global publishers were not far behind: *Vogue China* launched its smartphone app on WeChat (ibid.).

Gender identities and new demographics

The world's aging population, particularly in the West, also presents possible new opportunities for fashion media. In 2014, Marcus Rich, chief executive of IPC Media, commented: "Forty-plus women, or GenerationYnot! as IPC calls them, turn to our titles to inspire them and advise them in every aspect of their lives" (Durrani 2014b). Céline's decision to use celebrated eighty-year-old writer Joan Didion as the face of its brand in 2015 may reflect shifting consumer demographics—arguably it had as much to do with Didion's intellect as with her age—and suggested a new, more cultured kind of fashion icon for this group. Angela Lansbury was nearer ninety when *The Gentlewoman* put her on the cover, but editor Penny Martin noted that it was the most popular issue at that stage, among cover subjects as diverse as Vivienne Westwood, Beyoncé, Céline's creative director Phoebe Philo, and actress Olivia Williams. Martin believes her readership is defined as much by attitude as by age:

> Our readership is actually very, very diverse in age. It's a fashion audience, clearly and I'd say we have a very strong readership coming from the art world and business, so they tend to be culturally engaged people, but you can see when you meet them that they're extremely switched-on media consumers. (Martin 2014)

Porter magazine's first cover announced: "A Celebration of Incredible Women," again signaling a more authoritative feminine icon.

Meanwhile, the continued growth of the menswear market presents further media opportunities. *The New York Times*, for example, introduced a monthly Men's Style Friday section in April 2015 after a 30 percent increase in men's related advertising in the newspaper.

Democratization and distinction: Digital versus print

In the West, there were signs in 2015 that the blogging boom might be on the wane, particularly since established brands developed their own social media presence. Condé Nast announced in February 2015 that it was shutting down its blogging portal Now Manifest. Robin Givhan of the *Washington Post* notes the underlying reasons by which the mainstream media were able to resist the challenge from blogging:

> Newcomers are drawn to fashion, not because they are determined to change it, but because they are mesmerized by it. They want to be the next Anna Wintour—not make her existence obsolete. They love fashion. And fashion loves them back. Then swallows them whole. (Givhan 2014)

While digital continues to develop with the launch of digital-only brands such as Bauer Media's *The Debrief* in February 2014, it does not have universal appeal, and print seems a long way from dead. *Draper's* editor Eric Musgrave pointed out that only 25 percent of the magazine's subscribers visit the website (Musgrave 2014) and iPad magazine editions have performed disappointingly (Burrell 2014).

As noted earlier, advertisers still covet print recognition: "They like the online but there is not a PR who doesn't say, 'Oh yeah but we were hoping for a piece in the paper as well'" (Armstrong 2014). Unsurprisingly, therefore, Apple chose *Vogue* to launch the Apple watch, with supermodel Liu Wen wearing the watch on the November 2014 cover of *Vogue China*. The prestige of print even resonates with the younger generation, perhaps even more so as it is not their norm (anecdotally, my students are reluctant to tear up magazines and desecrate their editorial vision, and Eric Musgrave reported that his daughter respects her *Teen Vogue* more than her phone apps) (Musgrave 2014).

Some new entrants focused on print, including *Monocle*, launched by *Wallpaper* founder and former *Financial Times* columnist Tyler Brûlé in 2007. Although it has a website with video content, the magazine editorial is only available to subscribers: "It's just common sense. Why would we generate all of these stories and invest in editorial and annoy our core readership by giving it all away free?" (Brûlé cited in Spanier 2013). Published ten times a year, *Monocle* boasted 18,000 subscribers in 2015, each paying an annual $150 (monocle.com). Brûlé, who also runs shops for branded merchandise and difficult-to-find items featured in the magazine and an online radio station under the Monocle brand, deliberately eschewed social media and iPad versions of the magazine, arguing that constant communication exhausts and dilutes the essence of the brand (Spanier 2013).

Nonetheless, the multi-platform brand remains the modus operandi, with the varying strands performing different journalistic functions, as Emmanuelle Alt, editor of *Vogue Paris*, pointed out on the relaunch of the brand's website: "The print version will always remain a platform for the expression of creativity and inspiration while the site remains above all else a news and information outlet" (Chilvers 2012). Vanessa Friedman sees the challenge for fashion journalists as "thinking about how you tell a story in various different forms" (Friedman 2014). The limitation of popular platforms such as Twitter and Instagram is that they favor only easily digestible information rather than critical analysis—"If something is a column it should never be a tweet" (ibid.)—arguably ghettoizing serious fashion criticism (see Aylmer 2016). However, SHOWstudio's journalistic analysis, noted in Chapter 9, suggests that expert verbal commentary can illuminate apparently self-explanatory imagery. As Menkes says, "I like to think that I can be a conduit, analysing fashion as I see it" (Collins 2013: 69).

It is perhaps the expertise that is lacking. While some brands, such as British *Elle*, have adopted a 360-degree approach with journalists working across all forms of media, many media outlets—particularly magazines—do not have established journalists working across digital platforms, which has created inconsistencies between the print and digital editorial: "Initially fashion journalism online was for the B-team wasn't it? [...] They were never treated as seriously, there still is a legacy of that" (Martin 2014).

The Web's lack of spatial and editorial limits, including the perceived redundancy of editing, may be seen as being detrimental to both the quality and the authority of fashion journalism, as noted by Robin Givhan, Stefano Tonchi, and Guy Trebay (Goldenberg 2013). As Armstrong says bluntly, "There's infinite capacity for dross" (2014). Betty Jackson is just one designer to regret the loss of the expert and unbiased criticism of 1980s' commentators such as Brenda Polan at the *Guardian*: "I'm afraid that now quantity has taken the place of quality sometimes" (Jackson 2015; see also Menkes 2013a). Penny Martin notes the negative effect even on still images of the Web and YouTube: "It means we're prepared to look at images that are far less beautifully produced, and there's almost been a kind of lack of visual ambition" (Martin 2014). Nonetheless, as one critic commented, "fashion journalism has been hijacked by the visuals," which has again sidelined writing.

Observers, including McNeil and Miller, have also noted an emphasis on reporting rather than criticism or point of view (2014: 124). As Armstrong says, "Fashion criticism is morphing into something else on every publication [...] I think fashion criticism is becoming more like fashion reporting which is to say— here was a blue dress, here is a pink catsuit" (Armstrong 2014). She and others attribute this to commercial pressures and advertiser power. A critical review can mean not only a show ban but a ban on interviews and access to clothing for shoots: "As opposed to a music or film critic, a fashion journalist or editor banned from participating in industry affairs is, in effect, prevented from doing their job"

(Cronberg 2016).[2] Others, including Betty Jackson, believe it reflects the quality of the writers themselves: "Fashion commentary is only very interesting when the journalist is very knowledgeable, otherwise you do end up with this situation where they say 'Oh, they showed a blue jumper'" (Jackson 2015).

Although former *Grazia* editor-in-chief Jane Bruton sees catwalk trends as almost obsolete—"just a way of organizing the huge amount of product that is available" (Bruton 2014)—collections issues of fashion magazines remain enduringly popular. This suggests a clear consumer desire for a season overview that may be better met by objective, informed opinion than by the subjective preferences of bloggers, whom Friedman claims react to collections mostly on a visceral level (2014).

Betty Jackson, meanwhile, finds the often arbitrary groupings of the season's catwalk very unhelpful:

> It's really more confusing than anything because allegedly everybody's done all these things that perform in these tribal categories. But it's not giving you the essence of the look. It's skimming the surface of designers and what they are about rather than giving you an in depth collection. (Jackson 2015)

The return of the expert paradigm

Although some observers believed the Internet would threaten the role of the expert journalist (Jenkins 2006: 52), in fact the need for specialist knowledge in the fashion media has appeared to increase. Anna Wintour herself has argued that, "With all the new media outlets out there, with all the noise, a voice of authority and calm like *Vogue* becomes more important than ever" (Wintour, cited in Levine 2011). Eric Musgrave makes a similar point: "What people look to us for is some analysis of what it all means [...] *Drapers*, for example is very good at analyzing the news, putting it into context" (Musgrave 2014).

The renewed emphasis on "curation" suggests an acknowledgment of the importance of expertise, and point of view, evidenced in the continued success of *Glamour*'s infamous "Do's and Don'ts." According to Colin McDowell, the success of Condé Nast's *LOVE* is largely down to the expertise of stylist and editor-in-chief Katie Grand:

> *LOVE* is a hugely successful magazine because it has a strong point of view. It's Katie Grand, plus Condé Nast, so she gets the best photographers and she is good at discovering the very best photographers. The pictures are really very strong. (McDowell 2014)

Dylan Jones also believes that strong editorial opinions are key to *GQ*'s appeal: "We basically say that this is good and this is bad" (Jones 2014). Meanwhile Cathy Horyn was pursued by *New York Magazine*'s fashion site in 2015 because of her distinctive views, according to *The Cut*'s editorial director Stella Bugbee: "Cathy was always on our dream list for her unique authority and style" (Steigrad 2015).

That said, it seems unlikely that the citizens' voice will not be heard in some way and will continue to develop the fashion media. In 2012, for example, readers' complaints led *Seventeen* to abandon the use of photo-shopped models.

Ubiquity and loss of desirability

The ubiquity and proliferation of fashion in the digital age has had consequences for both the industry and its media: if fashion is no longer special it is no longer desirable. Even in the past, Betty Jackson argues, "You had to be niche and special. People were a little concerned if you were selling to all these department stores. You were a bit over exposed" (Jackson 2015).

Major conglomerates such as LVMH and Kering have recognized the danger by raising price points, limiting distribution and store expansion, and focusing on smaller rather than mega brands (Solca 2015). Meanwhile the rise of Etsy—a craft-based website—and the rise of customized products also suggests that the vanguard of the industry is moving away from mass production toward more limited or exclusive fashion.

There also seems to be a move toward making the shows more exclusive again. Although Tom Ford's attempts to present his collection to a limited press audience were undone through bloggers' protests (Amed 2013: 10), much of the real business of buying is done in discreet pre-show visits. Some observers, therefore, have suggested that the shows move to coincide with the arrival of the goods in store in order to promote the new season and shoppable merchandise (Lock 2013: 33). Journalists, like buyers, would preview the collections in advance, with the possibility of exclusive reporting.

The omnipresence of the celebrity–fashion link also seems to be on the wane in developed markets, according to Armstrong: "The very exclusive brands are peddling away from mass celebrity endorsement" (2014). Hermès' "Wanderland" exhibition at the Saatchi Gallery in 2015, for example, focused on the brand's craftsmanship rather than its wearers. Meanwhile editorial, at *Harper's* and *Vogue*, seem to have moved beyond the celebrity/fashion nexus to include more arts, careers, and intellectual discussion again.

Magazine as artifact

The dynamic market for niche magazines also seems to reflect a desire for what Betty Jackson calls the "magical"—something out of the ordinary: "I think it's a big part of our industry, selling a dream or an aspiration" (Jackson 2015). The language of the media has reinforced this special quality with its emphasis on "bespoke" and "artisanal," and Colin McDowell argues that fashion media play an important role in fantasy and escape: "Fashion is fantasy and in a way it should stay like fantasy; it shouldn't be like some terrific comic book" (2014). Silvagni argues that Grace Coddington, say, knows "how to make people dream without having advertising stand in the way," moving beyond designer-dictated total looks and featuring unknown designers (Cronberg 2013b: LIV).

Perhaps the future of the fashion print media will be closer to that of the niche fashion magazine, with less frequent publishing schedules and higher cover prices but more emphasis on high-quality production values and long-form journalism: the magazine as artifact rather than purely commercial vehicle. In *Fashion Criticism*, Peter McNeil and Sanda Miller highlight this quality in *Acne Paper*: "It is a fashion magazine but one that deliberately calls to attention the art and artifice that goes into the fashion industry" (2014: 131). For readers, Lynge-Jorlén argues, niche publications are more like collectors' items than magazines (2012: 21): they offer a moment of respite in an overloaded digital world.

Tribalism

Fashion journalism appears to be becoming ever more tribal. Both successful bloggers and niche magazines have loyal communities and shared values, and perceive communal identity as part of their appeal to readers. As mentioned earlier, magazines such as *The Gentlewoman* promote a readers' club and the same concept is at the heart of *Monocle*. The fashion media thus seem likely to fragment further into smaller, more defined communities, particularly for print, with only a few major players.

Plus ça change

In some senses, it feels as if the wheel has come full circle. The fashion media speak to closed communities with a shared sensibility, with print being collected like the early albums, media brands purveying branded goods, and a blurred line between advertorial and editorial. If the fashion media are to have a role, they will need to reassert their expertise, point of view, and capacity to make modern-day Emma Bovarys dream. Fashion writing needs to enlighten on the intricacies of the clothes and designers' creative vision. This requires knowledge of fashion history, and perhaps fashion journalists should, like Menkes, be educated in construction alongside their design colleagues. That said, as Elizabeth Wilson remarked in response to Barthes' underlying antagonism toward fashion, a world from which fashion was banished "would be a world without discourses, a world that is without culture or communication. Such a world cannot, of course, exist, or if it did it would not have human beings in it" (2003 [1985]: 58). And if fashion journalism is the purveyor of the symbolic value of fashion, then, to paraphrase Barthes, without fashion journalism there would, arguably, be no fashion at all.

Note

1 See, for example, "Fashion Writing: On Fighting the System; What's Wrong with the Fashion Industry" and *On Fashion and Power* (issue 4).

2 See Hadley Freeman "Torn off a Strip" (2008) for a discussion on this.

BIBLIOGRAPHY

Magazines

19 (1968–2004)
Adam (1925–73)
Aglaia: The Journal of the Healthy and Artistic Dress Union (1893–4)
Allgemeine Moden-Zeitung (1799–1903)
Allure (1991–)
Amica (1962–)
Another Magazine (2001–)
L'Aquarelle Mode (1865–90)
Arena (1987–2009)
L'Art d'être Jolie (1904–5)
L'Art et la Mode (1880–1975) (formerly *L'Art de la Mode* [1880–3])
Art, Goût, Beauté (1920–36)
Bella (1988–)
La Belle Assemblée (1806–32)
Bellezza (1941–)
Blitz (1980–91)
Brigitte (1886–)
Burda Moden (1950–)
Le Cabinet des Modes (1785–93)
Charis (1802–4)
Charm (1941–59)
Company (1978–)
Le Conseiller des Dames et des Demoisellles (1846–92)
Cosmopolitan (1965–)
Die Dame (1912–37)
Dazed and Confused (1991–)
Delineator (1873–1937)
Mme Demorest's Quarterly and Mirror of Fashion (1860–99)
La Dernière Mode (1874)
Details (1982–2015)
Donna (1980–)
Les Elégances Parisiennes (1916–24)
Die Elegante Welt (1921–37)
Elle (1945–)
The Englishwoman's Domestic Magazine (1852–79)

Esquire (1933–)
Essence (1970–)
Eve (1919–29)
The Face (1980–2004)
Fantastic Man (2005–)
Fashion Projects (2004–)
Fashions For All (1908–19)
Fémina (1901–38)
FHM (1992–)
Flair (1950–51)
Le Follet (1829–71)
Frank (1997–9)
La Gallerie des Modes (1778–87)
Gallery of Fashion (1794–1803)
Garage (2011–)
La Gazette du Bon Ton (1912–25)
The Gentlewoman (2010–)
Giornale Dedicato al Bel Sesso (1786–8)
Giornale delle Dame e delle Mode di Francia (1786–94)
Glamour (1939–)
Godey's Lady's Book (1830–98)
GQ (1957–)
Graham's Monthly Magazine of Literature, Art and Fashion (1826–58)
British *Grazia* (2005–)
Harper's Bazaar (1867–)
Honey (1960–86)
i-D (1980–)
InStyle (1994–)
Interview (1969–)
Jalouse (1997–)
Jardin des Modes (1922–96)
Jill (1983–5)
Le Journal des Dames et des Demoiselles (1841–1902)
Le Journal des Dames et des Modes (1797–1839)
Le Journal des Demoiselles (1833–1922)
Journal des Luxus und der Moden (1786–1827 [1808])
Ladies' Home Journal (1883–)
The Lady's Magazine (1759–63; 1770–1832)
Lear's (1988–94)
Lei (1933–8)
Life (1936–[1972] 2007)
Linea Italiana (1965–)
loaded (1994–2015)
LOVE (2009–)
Lucky (2000–15)
McCall's (1873–2002)
Madame (1952–)
Madame Figaro (1980–)
Mademoiselle (1935–2001)
Man About Town/Town (1952–1962)

Marie Claire (1937–)
Marie France (1944–)
Maxim (1995–)
Le Mercure Galant (1672–1832 [1724])
Mirabella (1989–2000)
La Mode (1829–54)
La Mode Artistique (1869–99)
Modes et Travaux (1919–)
La Mode Pratique (1891–1951)
La Mode Illustrée (1860–1937)
Die Modenwelt (1865–1932)
Le Moniteur de la Mode (1843–1913)
Monocle (2007–)
Myra's Journal of Dress and Fashion (1852–79)
Nova (1965–75)
Numéro (1998)
Nylon (1999–)
O32c (2001–)
La Parisienne (1865–70)
Le Petit Courrier des Dames (1831–68)
Le Petit Echo de la Mode (1879–1977)
Petticoat (1966–75)
Pictorial Review (1899–1939)
POP (2000–)
Porter (2014–)
Purple/Purple Fashion (1992–)
The Queen (1861–1970)
Red (2007–)
La Revue de La Mode (1872–[1888] 1913)
Seventeen (1944–)
Six (1988–91)
Sleaze/Sleaze Nation (1996–2004)
Der Styl (1922–4)
La Sylphide (1840–85)
Tank (1998–)
Tatler (1901–)
Teen Vogue (2003–)
Time (1923–)
Townsend's Quarterly Selection of Costumes (later monthly; 1823–88)
L'Uomo Vogue (1968–)
Vanity (1981–83)
Vanity Fair (1913–)
Vestoj (2009–)
Visionnaire (1991–)
Vogue (1892–)
W (1972–)
Woman (1937–)
Woman's Journal (1927–2001)
The Woman's World (1886–90)
Wonderland (2004–)

World of Fashion and Continental Feuilletons (1824–51)
Zeitschrift für historische Waffen und Kostümkunde (1921–44)

Newspapers

Daily Mail (1896–)
Daily Mirror (1832–)
The Daily Telegraph (1855–)
Le Figaro (1826–)
The Guardian (1821–)
The Independent (1986–)
The International Herald Tribune (1887–)
Le Monde (1944–)
The New York Times (1851–)
The Observer (1791–)
La Presse (1854–1933)
The Sunday Times (1822–)
The Times (1788–)
The Wall Street Journal (1889–)

Websites/blogs

www.blondesalad.com
www.businessoffashion.com
www.facehunter.org
www.fashionista.com
www.garancedore.fr
www.jak&jil.com
www.libertylondongirl.com.
www.manrepeller,com
www.net-a-porter.com
www.nymag.com/daily/fashion (The Cut)
www.showstudio.com
www.style.com
www.stylebubble.co.uk
www.thedebrief.co.uk
www.vestoj.com

Trade journals

Ambassador Magazine (1946–72)
Draper's Record (1887–)
L'Officiel de la Couture et de la Mode (1921–)
Women's Wear Daily (*WWD*) (1910–)

Publications and interviews

Abnett, Kate (2015), "Condé Nast to transform Style.com into a Global E-Commerce Player." The Business of Fashion (April 27). Available online: www.businessoffashion. com/articles/bof-exclusive/bof-exclusive-conde-nast-to-transform-style-com-into-global-e-commerce-player (accessed April 27, 2015).

Adburgham, Alison (1966), *View of Fashion*, London: Allen and Unwin.

Adburgham, Alison (1972), *Women in Print: Writing Women and Women's Magazines from the Restoration to the Accession of Victoria*, London: Allen and Unwin.

Adburgham, Alison (1981), *Shops and Shopping 1800–1914,* London: Allen and Unwin.

Agins, Terri (2001 [1999]), *The End of Fashion: How Marketing Changed the Clothing Business Forever*, New York: Harper Collins.

Aguilar, Gisela (2013), "Fashion Criticism Panel: A Report and Recording of the Event." Available online: http://www.fashionprojects.org/?cat=102 (accessed April 5, 2016).

Allen, Marit (2005), Interview in A. O'Neill (ed.), *An Oral History of British Fashion*, Tape 3 (F17403), © British Library.

Amed, Imran (2010), "Digital Scorecard: Burberry 3D Livestream", The Business of Fashion (February 25). Available online: www.businessoffashion.com/articles/digital-scorecard/digital-scorecard-burberry-3d-live-stream (accessed August 14, 2014).

Amed, Imran (2013), *The Business of Fashion Special Edition* (Autumn).

Amed, Imran (2014), *The Business of Fashion Companies and Culture Issue* (Spring).

Angeletti, Norberto and Alberto Oliva (2006), *In Vogue: The Illustrated History of The World's Most Famous Fashion Magazine*, New York: Abrams.

Armstrong, Lisa (2014), Interview with Author.

Arnold, Rebecca (2001), *Fashion, Desire and Anxiety: Image and Morality in the 20th Century*, London: I. B. Tauris.

Aronson, Amy (2002), *Taking Liberties: Early American Woman's Magazines and their Readers,* Westport, CT: Praeger.

Aylmer, Olivia (2016), "Keeping in Touch." Available online: www.vestoj.com/keeping-in-touch/ (accessed April 7, 2016).

Baldaia, Suzanne (2005), "Space Age Fashion" in L. Welters and P. Cunningham (eds), *Twentieth-Century American Fashion*, 169–90, Oxford: Berg.

Ballard, Bettina (1960), *In My Fashion*, New York: David McKay.

Ballaster, Ros, Margaret Beetham, Elizabeth Frazer, and Sandra Hebron (1991), *Women's Worlds: Ideology, Femininity and the Woman's Magazine*, London: Macmillan.

Banner, Lois (1983), *American Beauty*, New York: Knopf.

Barnes, Colin (1988), *The Complete Guide to Fashion Illustration*, London: Macdonald.

Barthes, Roland (1990 [1967]), *The Fashion System*, trans. Mathew Ward and Richard Howard, Berkley: University of California Press.

Bartlett, Djurdja (2006), "In Russia at Last and Forever, The First Seven Years of Russian *Vogue*." Fashion Theory: The Journal of Dress Body and Culture 10 (1/2): 175–203.

Bartlett, Djurdja (2013), "Coco Chanel and Socialist Fashion Magazines" in *Fashion Media Past and Present*, D. Bartlett, S. Cole, and A. Rocamora (eds), 46–57, London: Bloomsbury.

Bartlett, Djurdja, Shaun Cole, and Agnès Rocamora (eds) (2013), *Fashion Media Past and Present*, London: Bloomsbury.

Baudelaire, Charles (1968 [1863]), "Le Beau, La Mode et Le Bonheur" in *Le Peintre de La Vie Moderne,* 547, OEuvres Complètes, Paris: Editions du Seuil.

Baudelaire, Charles (1981), *Baudelaire: Selected Writings on Art and Artists*, trans. P. E. Charvet, Cambridge: Cambridge University Press.

Baudelaire, Charles (1995 [1863]), "The Painter of Modern Life" in *The Painter of Modern Life and Other Essays*, trans. Thom Mayne, 1–41, London: Phaidon.

Baudot, François (2001), *Fashion and Surrealism*, New York: Assouline.

Beard, Alice (2002), "'Put in Just for Pictures': Fashion Editorial and the Composite Image in *Nova* 1965–1975." *Fashion Theory: The Journal of Dress, Body and Culture* 6 (1): 25–44.

Beard, Alice (2013), "Fun with Pins and Rope: How Caroline Baker Styled the 1970s" in Djurdja Bartlett, Shaun Cole, and Agnès Rocamora (eds), *Fashion Media: Past and Present*, 22–34, London: Bloomsbury.

Beaton, Cecil (1954), *The Glass of Fashion*, London: Weidenfeld and Nicolson.

Beaton, Cecil and Joséphine Rose (1994), *Cecil Beaton: 50 ans de collaboration avec Vogue*, Paris: Herscher.

Beetham, Margaret (1996), *A Magazine of Her Own? Domesticity and Desire in the Woman's Magazine, 1800–1914*, London and New York: Routledge.

Beetham, Margaret and Kay Boardman (eds) (2001), *Victorian Women's Magazines: An Anthology*, Manchester: Manchester University Press.

Benaïm, Laurence (1996), "Paris, the Beseiged Capital of Ready-to-Wear," *Le Monde*, October 8.

Benjamin, Walter (2000), "Fashion" in *The Arcades Project*, trans. Howard Eiland and Kevin Mclaughlin, 62–81, Cambridge, MA and London: Belknap.

Benwell, Bethan (ed.) (2003), *Masculinity and Men's Lifestyle Magazines*, Oxford: Blackwell.

Berger, John (1972), *Ways of Seeing*, London: Penguin.

Best, Kate N. (2007), *Splitting the Cultural Seams: The Discourse on Female Appearance in the Fashion Periodical and Novel of the Second Empire*, PhD thesis, University of London.

Best, Kate N. (2012a), "Text and Image in the Fashion Periodical of the Second French Empire" in *Text and Image in Modern European Culture*, N. Grigorian, T. Baldwin, and M. Rigaud-Drayton (eds), 101–14, West Lafayette, IN: Purdue Press.

Best, Kate N. (2012b), "Women's Work: Regulatory Rituals of Dressing in the Second Empire Periodical." *Dix-neuf* 16 (1): 74–86.

Blackman, Cally (2007), *100 Years of Fashion Illustration,* London: Laurence King.

Blaszczyk, Regina L. (2007), "Rethinking Fashion" in R. L. Blaszczyk (ed.), *Producing Fashion: Commerce, Culture, and Consumers*, 1–18, Philadelphia: The University of Pennsylvania Press.

Blum, Dilys E. (2003), *Shocking: The Art and Life of Elsa Schiaparelli*, Philadelphia, PA: Philadelphia Museum of Art.

Bolter, Jay D. (2001), *Writing Space: Computers, Hypertext and The Remediation of Print*, London: Routledge.

Bond, Shannon (2014), "Condé Nast Spins Off Shopping Magazine" (August 11). Available online: www.ft.com/cms/s/0/85390816-21a3-11e4b14500144feabdc0. html#axzz3B40iN7iv (accessed August 12, 2014).

Bonnet, Frédéric. (2004), "Ordinary or Extraordinary" in S. Richoux-Bérard and F. Bonnet (eds), *Glossy*, 174–5, Marseille: Musée de la Mode de Marseille.

Bonvoisin, Samra–Martine and Michèle Maignien (1986), *La Presse Féminine*, Paris: PUF.

Borelli, Laird O.S. (1997), "Dressing Up and Talking About It: Fashion Writing in Vogue 1968–1993." *Fashion Theory: The Journal of Dress, Body and Culture* 1 (3): 247–60.

Boucher, François (1959), *Crinolines et calèches 1855–1867*, Paris: Éditions Rombaldi.

Bourdieu, Pierre (1993), "Haute Couture and Haute Culture" in *Sociology in Question*, trans. Richard Nice, London: Sage.

Bourdieu, Pierre (1995), *The Field of Cultural Production*, trans. Randal Johnson, Cambridge: Polity Press.

Bourdieu, Pierre (2010 [1984]), *Distinction*, trans. Richard Nice, New York and London: Routledge.

Bourdieu, Pierre and Yvette Desault (1975), "Le Couturier et sa Griffe: Contribution à une théorie de la magie." *Actes de la recherche en sciences sociales* 1 (1): 7–36.

Bradford, Julie (2015), *Fashion Journalism*, London and New York: Routledge.

Braithwaite, Brian and Joan Barrell (1988 [1979]), *The Business of Women's Magazines*, London: Kogan Page.

Breazeale, Kenon (2000), "In Spite of Women: *Esquire* Magazine and the Construction of the Male Consumer," in J. Scanlon (ed.), *The Gender and Consumer Culture Reader*, 226–44, New York and London: New York University Press.

Breward, Christopher (1992), *Images of Desire: The Construction of the Feminine Consumer in Women's Fashion Journals 1875–1890,* MA dissertation, RCA London.

Breward, Christopher (1995) *The Culture of Fashion: A New History of Fashionable Dress,* Manchester: Manchester University Press.

Breward, Christopher (2003), *Fashion*, Oxford: Oxford University Press.

Breward, Christopher (2004), *Fashioning London: Clothing and the Modern Metropolis*, Oxford: Berg.

Breward, Christopher and David Gilbert (eds) (2006), *Fashion's World Cities*, Oxford: Berg.

Breward, Christopher and Claire Wilcox (2012) *The Ambassador Magazine: Promoting British Textiles and Fashion*, London: V&A.

Brooke, Eliza (2014), "Vogue Makes its Instagram Shoppable with Liketoknow.It" (May 29 2014). Available online: www.fashionista.com/2015/05/vogue-makes-instagram-shoppable (accessed July 15, 2014).

Bruton, Jane (2014), Interview with author.

Bruzzi, Stella and Pamela Church Gibson (eds) (2013 [2000]), *Fashion Cultures Revisited: Theories, Exploration and Analysis*, London: Routledge.

Burman, Barbara (ed.) (1999), *The Culture of Sewing: Gender, Consumption and Home Dressmaking*, Oxford: Berg.

Burrell, Ian (2014), "Fears Rise That Tablets Won't Save Magazines as Digital Sales Fall." *Independent* (August 14). Available online: http://www.independent.co.uk/news/media/online/fears-rise-that-tablets-wont-save-magazines-as-digital-sales-fall-9669532.html (accessed August 18, 2014).

Butler, Judith (1993), *Bodies That Matter: On the Discursive Limits of Sex,*London and New York: Routledge.

Butler, Judith (1999 [1990]), *Gender Trouble: Feminism and the Subversion of Identity*, London and New York: Routledge.

Cage, E. Claire (2009), "The Sartorial Self: Neoclassical Fashion and Gender Identity in France 1797–1804." *Eighteenth-Century Studies* 42 (2): 193–215.

Caizergues, Pierre, Pierre Chanel, and Annie Gudéras (eds) (2002), *Cocteau et la mode*, Paris: Passage du Marais.

Calefato, Patrizia (2004), *The Clothed Body*, trans. Lisa Adams, Oxford: Berg.

Callahan, Maureen (2014), *Champagne Supernovas: Kate Moss, Marc Jacobs, Alexander McQueen, and the '90s Renegades Who Remade Fashion*, London: Simon & Schuster.

Carter, Ernestine (1974), *With Tongue in Chic*, London: Michael Joseph.

Carter, Ernestine (1977), *The Changing World of Fashion 1900 to the Present*, London: Weidenfeld & Nicolson.

Cashmore, Ellis (2006), *Celebrity/Culture*, London and New York: Routledge.

Cavallero, Dani and Alexandra Warwick (2001 [1998]), *Fashioning the Frame: Boundaries, Dress and the Body*, Oxford: Berg.

Certo-Ware, Renata (2014), "Fashion Magazines are Missing the Mark with Shoppable Content", Business of Fashion (July 21). Available online: www.businessoffashion. com/2014/07/op-ed-fashion-magaiznes-missing-mark-shoppable-content.html (accessed July 23, 2014).

Chapus, Eugène (1855), *Manuel de l'homme et de la femme comme il faut*, Paris: Librairie Nouvelle.

Chase, Edna Woolman and Ilke Chase (1954), *Always in Vogue*, London: Victor Gollanz.

Cheang, Sarah (2013), "To The Ends of the Earth: Fashion and Ethnicity in the Vogue Fashion Shoot," in D. Bartlett, S. Cole and A. Rocamora (eds), *Fashion Media Past and Present*, 35–45, London: Bloomsbury.

Chilvers, Simon (2012), "French Vogue Embraces the Digital Age With Website Re-launch." *Guardian* (February 6). Available online: www.theguardian.com/fashion/fashion-blog/2012/feb/06/french-vogue-relaunch (accessed February 9, 2015).

Church Gibson, Pamela (2012), *Fashion and Celebrity Culture*, London: Berg.

Clark, Judith (2006), *Anna Piaggi: Fashion-ology*, London: V&A.

Cline, Sharon E. (2008), *Fémininité à la Française: Femininity, Social Change and French National Identity*, PhD thesis, University of Wisconsin.

Coddington, Grace (2012), *Grace: A Memoir*, London: Chatto and Windus.

Coffin, Judith (1996), *The Politics of Women's Work: The Paris Garment Trades 1750–1905*, Princeton, NJ, and Chichester: Princeton University Press.

Cohen, Margaret and Christopher Prendergast (eds) (1995), *Spectacles of Realism: Gender, Body, Genre*, Minneapolis and London: University of Minnesota Press.

Coleman, Elizabeth-Ann (1990), "Pouvu Que Vos Robes Vous Aillent," *Femmes Fin de Siècle 1885–1895*, 133–45, Paris: Musée de la Mode et du Costume.

Coleridge, Nicholas (1988), *The Fashion Conspiracy: A Remarkable Journey Through The Empires of Fashion*, London: Heinemann.

Coleridge, Nicholas and Stephen Quinn (eds) (1987), *The Sixties in Queen*, London: Ebury Press.

Collins, Amy F. (2004), "The Lady, The List, The Legacy." *Vanity Fair* (March 31). Available online: www.vanityfair.com/news/2004/04/eleanor-lambert200404 (accessed June 12, 2012).

Collins, Lucy (2013), "On Fashion Futures: An Interview with Suzy Menkes." *Fashion Criticism* 4: 65–70, New York: Fashion Projects.

Colombani, Marie-Françoise (2005), *Elle 1945–2005: Une histoire des femmes*, Paris: Filipacchi.

Cone, Annabelle and Dawn Marley (eds) (2010), *The Francophone Women's Magazine: Inside and Outside of France*, New Orleans: University Press of the South.

Conekin, Becky, E. (2010 [2008]), "Lee Miller's Simulaneity: Photographer and Model in the pages of Inter-War *Vogue*," in Eugénie Shinkle (ed.), *Fashion as Photograph: Viewing and Reviewing Images of Fashion*, 70–83, London: I. B. Tauris.

Corner, Frances (2014), *Why Fashion Matters*, London: Thames and Hudson.

Cowles, Fleur and Dominic Dunne (2014), *The Best of Flair*, New York: Rizzoli.

Craik, Jennifer (2003 [1993]), *The Face of Fashion: Cultural Studies in Fashion*, London and New York: Routledge.

Crane, Diana (2000), *Fashion and Its Social Agendas: Class Gender and Identity in Clothing*, Chicago, IL: University of Chicago Press.

Crewe, Ben (2003), *Representing Men: Cultural Production and Producers in the Men's Magazine Market*, Oxford: Berg.

Cronberg, Anja A. (2013a) "Hamish Bowles, International Editor at Large, American Vogue". *Vestoj: On Fashion and Power* 4: IV–IX, London: UAL.

Cronberg, Anja A. (2013b) "Irene Silvagni, Former Creative Director of Yohji Yamamoto." *Vestoj: On Fashion and Power* 4: L–LV, London: UAL.

Cronberg, Anja A. (2016), "Fashion Writing: On Fighting the System." Available online: www.vestoj.com/fashion-writing-on-fighting-the-system/ (accessed April 6, 2016).

Cullen, Oriole (2014). "The Sozzani Sisters," in S. Stanfill (ed.), *The Glamour of Italian Fashion Since 1945*, 261–5, London: V&A.

Cunningham, Patricia A., Heather Mangine, and Andrew Reilly (2005), "Television and Fashion in the 1980s," in L. Welters and P. Cunningham (eds), *Twentieth-Century American Fashion*, 209–28, Oxford: Berg.

Damon-Moore, Helen (1994), *Magazines for the Millions: Gender and Commerce in Ladies' Home Journal and the Saturday Evening Post 1880–1910*, Albany: State University of New York Press.

Davis, Mary E. (2008 [2006]), *Classic Chic: Music, Fashion and Modernism*, Berkeley: University of California Press.

Davray-Piekolek, Renée (1990a), "Femmes Fin de Siècle." *Femmes Fin de Siècle 1885–1895*, 11–27, Paris: Musée de la Mode et du Costume.

Davray-Piekolek, Renée (1990b), "Les Modes Triomphantes 1885–1895," *Femmes Fin de Siècle 1885–1895*, 29–65, Paris: Musée de la Mode et du Costume.

Day, Julia (2005), "Emap Hires Top Team for Sassy Women's Weekly." *Guardian* (January 20). Available online: www.theguardian.com/media/2005/jan/20/ emap. pressandpublishing (accessed February 20, 2015).

Dellis Hill, Daniel (2004), *As Seen in Vogue: A Century of American Fashion in Advertising*, Dallas: Texas Tech University Press.

Derrick, Robin and Robin Muir (eds) (2002), *Unseen Vogue: The Secret History of Fashion Photography*, London: Little Brown.

Derrick, Robin and Robin Muir (2007), *Vogue Covers: On Fashion's Front Page*, London: Little Brown.

Dessins de Mode: Jules David 1808–1892 et son temps (1987), Paris: Mairie de VI Arrondissement.

Devlin, Polly (1979), *Vogue Book of Fashion Photography*, London: Thames and Hudson.

Diderich, Joelle (2014), "Advertising Executive Buys Numéro Magazine." *Women's Wear Daily* (July 25). Available online: wwd.com/media-news/fashion-memopad/ advertising-executive-buys-numro-magazine-7812573/ (accessed August 15, 2014).

Dolan, Alice (2011), "An Adorned Print: Print Culture, Female Leisure and the Dissemination of Fashion in France and England, around 1660–1779." *V&A Online Journal* 3. Available online: www.vam.ac.uk/content/journals/research-journal/ issue-03/an-adorned-print-print-culture,-female-leisure-and-the-dissemination-of-fashion-in-france-and-england,-c.-1660-1779 (accessed February 10, 2015).

Downton, David (2010), *Masters of Fashion Illustration*, London: Laurence and King.

Durrani, Arif (2014a), "Publisher Says 'F*ck the Begrudgers' as Vogue Hits All Time High in September" (August 4). Available online: www.mediaweek.co.uk/article/1306407/ publisher-says-fck-begrudgers-vogue-hits-all-time-high-september (accessed August 4, 2014).

Durrani, Arif (2014b), "Magazine ABCs Top 100 at a Glance" (August 14). Available online: www.mediaweek.co.uk/article/1307934/magazine-abcs-top-100-glance (accessed August 18, 2014).

Edwards, Tim (2003), "Sex, Booze and Fags: Masculinity, Style and Men's Magazines," in B. Benwell (ed.), *Masculinity and Men's Lifestyle Magazines*, 132–46, Oxford: Blackwell.

Eldridge, Lisa (2015), *Face Paint: The Story of MakeUp*, New York: Abrams.

Emery, Joy S. (2014), *A History of the Paper Pattern Industry: The Home Dressmaking Fashion Revolution*, London and New York: Bloomsbury.

Endres, Kathleen L. and Therese Lueck (eds) (1995), *Women's Periodicals in the United States: Consumer Magazines*, Westport, CT: Greenwood Press.

English, Bonnie (2013 [2007]), *A Cultural History of Fashion in the 20th and 21st Centuries*, London: Bloomsbury.

Evans, Caroline (2003), *Fashion at the Edge: Spectacle, Modernity and Deathliness*, New Haven, CT, and London: Yale University Press.

Evans, Caroline (2005), "Multiple, Movement, Model, Mode: The Mannequin Parade 1900–1929," in C. Breward and C. Evans (eds), *Fashion and Modernity*, 125–46, Oxford: Berg.

Evans, Caroline (2013 [2000]), "Yesterday's Emblems and Tomorrow's Commodities: The Return of the Repressed in Fashion Imagery Today," in S. Bruzzi and P. Church Gibsons (eds), *Fashion Cultures Revisited*, 77–102, New York and London: Routledge.

Evans, Caroline (2013), *The Mechanical Smile: Modernism and the First Fashion Shows in France and America, 1900–1929*, New Haven, CT, and London: Yale University Press.

Evans, Caroline and Minna Thornton (1989), *Women and Fashion: A New Look*, London: Quartet.

Falluel, Fabienne (1990), "Les Grands Magasins et la Confection Féminine," *Femmes Fin de Siècle 1885–1895*, 75–91, Paris: Musée de la Mode et du Costume.

Fawcett, Hilary (2004), "Romance, Glamour and the Exotic: Femininity and Fashion in Britain in the 1900s," in A. Heilmann and M. Beetham (eds), *New Woman Hybridities: Femininity, Feminism, and International Consumer Culture, 1880–1930*, 145–57, New York and London: Routledge.

Ferguson, Marjorie (1983), *Forever Feminine: Women's Magazines and the Cult of Femininity*, London: Gower.

Feydeau, Ernest A. (1866), *Du Luxe, des femmes, des mœurs, de la littérature et de la vertu*, Paris: Michel Lévy Frères.

Finkelstein, Joanne (2007), *The Art of Self Invention: Image and Identity in Popular Visual Culture*, London: I. B. Tauris.

Finley, Ruth E. (1931), *The Lady of Godey's: Sarah Josepha Hale*, Philadelphia: J. B. Lippincott and Company.

Fisher, Alice (2009), "Uncertain Times For Style Bible as US *Vogue* Struggles to Reach New Generation." *Observer* (January 11). Available online: www.theguardian.com/lifeandstyle/2009/jan/11/vogue-fashion-wintour-publishing (accessed February 11, 2014).

Flaubert, Gustave (2003 [1856]), *Madame Bovary*, trans. Geoffrey Wall, London: Penguin.

Foley, Bridget (ed.) (2011), *WWD. 100 Years. 100 Designers*, New York: Fairchild Publications.

Fortassier, Rose (1988), *Les Ecrivains Français et la Mode, de Balzac à nos jours*, Paris: PUF.

Fortunato, Paul. L. (2007), *Modernist Aesthetics and Consumer Culture in the Writings of Oscar Wilde*, London and New York: Routledge.

Foucault, Michel (1971), *L'Ordre du discours*, Paris: Gallimard.

Foucault, Michel (1988 [1966]), *History of Sexuality 3: The Care of The Self*, trans. Robert Hurley, Harmondsworth: Allen and Lane.

Foucault, Michel (2001), *Dits et Ecrits II 1976–1988*, Paris: Gallimard.

France, Louise (2007), "What's in it For Me? *Grazia*'s World Uncovered." *Guardian* (March 11). Available online: www.theguardian.com/lifeandstyle/2007/mar/11/features.woman4 (accessed February 11, 2014).

Frankel, Susannah (2004), "Nick Knight: Interview," in S. Richoux-Bérard and F. Bonnet (eds), *Glossy*, 192, Marseille: Musée de la Mode de Marseille.

Freeman, Sarah (1977), *Isabella and Sam: The Story of Mrs Beeton*, London: Victor Gollanz.

Freud, Sigmund (1991 [1977]), "The Taboo of Virginity," in *On Sexuality: Three Essays on the Theory of Sexuality and Other Works,* trans. James Strachey, ed. Angela Richards, Penguin Freud Library, Vol. 7, London: Penguin.

Friedman, Vanessa (2014), Interview with the author.

Frisa, Maria Luisa (2014), "Portrait/Self Portrait: Image of Fashion," in S. Stanfill, (ed.), *The Glamour of Italian Fashion Since 1945*, 136–61, London: V&A.

Frizot, Michel (ed.) (1998), *A New History of Photography*, London: Könnemann.

Furbank, P. N. and A. M. Cain (2004), *Mallarmé on Fashion: A Translation of the Fashion Magazine La Dernière Mode with Commentary*, Oxford: Berg.

Fury, Alex (2013), "Uncompromising Positions," in A. O'Neill (ed.), *Isabella Blow: Fashion Galore!,* 150–7, New York: Rizzoli.

Gallagher, Rachael (2008), "*Grazia* Follows ABC Rise With New Appointments." *Press Gazette* (August 27). Available online: www.pressgazette.co.uk/node/41994 (accessed August 14, 2014).

Ganeva, Mila (2011 [2008]), *Women in Weimar Fashion: Discourses and Displays in German Culture 1918–1933*, London: Camden House.

Garb, Tamar (1998), *Bodies of Modernity: Figure and Flesh in fin-de-siècle France*, London: Thames and Hudson.

Gaudriault, Raymond (1983), *La Gravure de Mode Féminine en France*, Paris: Editions d'Amateur.

Gay-Fragneaud, Pauline and Patricia Vallet (2004a), "The History of Fashion Reviews from Their Origins to the 19th Century," in S. Richoux-Bérard and F. Bonnet (eds), *Glossy*, 178–80, Marseille: Musée de la Mode de Marseille.

Gay-Fragneaud, Pauline and Patricia Vallet (2004b), "Répertoire et Notices Historiques des Revues de Mode," in S. Richoux-Bérard and F. Bonnet (eds), *Glossy,* 65–79, Marseille: Musée de la Mode de Marseille.

Gilbert, David (2013), "A New World Order? Fashion and Its Capitals in the Twenty-first Century," in S. Bruzzi and P. Church Gibson (eds), *Fashion Cultures Revisited*, 11–30, New York and London: Routledge.

Gill, Miranda (2009), *Eccentricity and the Cultural Imagination in Nineteenth-century Paris*, Oxford: Oxford University Press.

Gingeras, Alison. M. (ed.) (2011 [2005]), *Guy Bourdin*, London: Phaidon.

Givhan, Robin (2014), "The Golden Era of 'Fashion Blogging' is Over." *The Cut* (April 21). Available online: www.nymag.com/thecut/2014/04/golden-era-of-fashion-blogging-is-over.html (accessed August 14, 2014).

Glynn, Prudence (1978), *In Fashion: Dress in the Twentieth Century*, London: Allen and Unwin.

Godfrey, John (1990), *A Decade of i-Deas: The Encyclopaedia of the '80s*, London: Penguin.

Goldenberg, Kira (2013), "Fashion Critics Defend Their Craft." *The Columbia Journalism Review* (March 13). Available online: www.cjr.org/behind_the_news/fashion_criticism_panel.php (accessed April 7, 2016).

Golsorkhi, Masoud (2014), Interview with Tallulah Bullock.

Golsorkhi, Masoud (2015), "Mexico Moment." *Tank* 8 (3): 20.

Gordon, Beverly (2005), "Showing the Colors: America," in J. M. Atkins (ed.), *Wearing Propaganda: Textiles on the Home Front in Japan, Britain and the United States, 1931–1945*, 239–55, New Haven, CT: Yale University Press.

Gough-Yates, Anna (2003), *Understanding Women's Magazines: Publishing, Markets and Readerships*, London: Routledge.

Grant, Alice (1988), *Fashion Magazines from the 1890s–1980s: An Account Based on the Holdings of the National Art Library*, London: NAL.

Green, Felicity (2014), *Sex, Sense and Nonsense: Felicity Green on the 60s Fashion Scene*, Woodbridge: ACC Editions.

Green, Stephanie (1997), "Oscar Wilde's 'The Woman's World.'" *Victorian Periodicals Review* 30 (2): 102–20.

Greimas, Algirdas J. (2000), *La Mode en 1830*, Paris: PUF.

Guenther, Irene (2004), *Nazi Chic: Fashioning Women in the Third Reich*, Oxford: Berg.

Gundle, Stephen (2008), *Glamour: A History*, Oxford: Oxford University Press.

Hack, Jefferson and Jo-Ann Furniss (eds) (2001), *Making It Up As We Go Along: A Visual History of the Magazine that Broke All the Rules*, New York: Rizzoli.

Haden-Guest, Anthony (2006), "The queen is dead." *Guardian* (February 11). Available online: www.theguardian.com/media/2006/feb/12/ pressandpublishing. observermagazine (accessed September 12, 2013).

Hahn, Hazel H. (2009), *Scenes of Parisian Modernity: Culture and Consumption in the Nineteenth Century*, New York: Palgrave Macmillan.

Hahn, Kim H. Y. and Eun-Jung Lee (2014), "Effect of Psychological Closeness on Consumer Attitudes Towards Fashion Blogs: The Moderating Effect of Fashion Leadership and Interpersonal LOV." *Journal of Global Fashion Marketing* 5 (2): 103–21.

Hall-Duncan, Nancy (1979), *The History of Fashion Photography*, New York: Alpine Book Company.

Harris, Sahron M. and Ellen Gruber Garvey (eds) (2004), *Blue Pencils, Hidden Hands: Women Editing Periodicals 1830–1910*, Boston, MA: North Eastern University Press.

Harrison, Martin (1991), *Appearances: Fashion Photography since 1945*, London: Cape.

Hartshorn, William and Merry Foresta (1990), *Man Ray in Fashion*, New York: International Center of Photography.

Harvey, John (1995), *Men in Black*, London: Reaktion.

Haye, Amy de la and Cathie Dingwall (1998), *Surfers, Soulies, Skinheads and Skaters: Subcultural Style from the Forties to the Nineties*, London: V&A.

Hebdige, David (1988 [1979]), *Subculture: The Meaning of Style (New Accents)*, New York and London: Routledge .

Higonnet, Anne (1992), *Berthe Morisot's Images of Women*, Cambridge, MA: Harvard University Press.

Higonnet, Anne (1995), "Real Fashion: Clothes Unmake the Working Woman," in M. Cohen and C. Prendergast (eds), *Spectacles of Realism*, 137–63, Minneapolis: University of Minnesota Press.

Hillman, David and Harri Peccinotti (eds) (1993), *Nova 1965–1975*, London: Pavilion.

Hiner, Susan (2010), *Accessories to Modernity: Fashion and the Feminine in Nineteenth-century France*, Philadelphia: University of Pennsylvania Press.

Hirschberg, Lynn (2012), "Our Crowd," in S. Tonchi (ed.), *W: The First 40 Years*, 11, New York: Abrams.

Holgate, Mark (1994), *Couture and Culture on the News Stand: Vogue and Harper's Bazaar 1945–1960*, MA diss., Royal College of Art, London.

Holland, Vyvyan (1955), *Hand-coloured Fashion Plates, 1770–1899*, London: Batsford.

Hollander, Anne (1978), *Seeing through Clothes*, New York: The Viking Press.

Hollander, Anne (2005) *Richard Avedon: Woman in the Mirror*, New York: Abrams.

Horwood, Catherine (2005), *Keeping Up Appearances: Fashion and Class between the Wars*, Stroud: Sutton.

Horyn, Cathy (2006), "Babeth's Feast," *New York Times* (August 27). Available online: http://www.nytimes.com/2006/08/27/style/tmagazine/t_w_1548_1549_talk_jill_. html?_r=0 (accessed August 18, 2014).

Houssaye, Arsène (1869), *Les Parisiennes*, 4 vols, Paris: E. Dentu.

Howard, Vicki (2015), *From Main Street to Mall: The Rise and Fall of the American Department Store*, Philadelphia: The University of Pennsylvania Press.

Howell, Georgina (2000), *Vogue Women*, London: Pavilion.

Howell, Geraldine (2012), *War Time Fashion: From Haute Couture to Homemade, 1939–1945*, London and New York: Bloomsbury.

Hughes, Kathryn (2006 [2005]), *The Short Life and Long Times of Mrs Beeton*, London: Harper Collins.

Hulanicki, Barbara and Martin Pel (2014), *The Biba Years 1963–1975*, London: V&A.

Hume, Marion (1993), "Fashion: The New Mood," *Independent* (May 4): 44, 45, 48.

Jackson, Betty (2015), Interview with the author.

Jannarone, John (2014), "Hearst's Magazine Chief is Still Hot on Print Deals," (July 31). Available online: www,cnbc,com/id/101880556 (accessed August 1, 2014).

Jenkins, Henry.(2006), *Convergence Culture: Where Old and New Media Collide*, New York: New York University Press.

Jobling, Paul (1999), *Fashion Spreads: Word and Image in Fashion Photography since 1980*, Oxford: Berg.

Jobling, Paul (2005), *Man Appeal: Advertising, Modernism and Menswear*, Oxford: Berg.

Johnson, Tom (2014), "Magazine ABCs Show Net Circulation Increase in First Half of 2014," *Printweek* (August 21). Available online: www.printweek.com/print-week/news/1146110/ magazine-abcs-net-circulation-increase-half-2014 (accessed August 21, 2014).

Joist, Héloïse (2004), "The Economics of the Fashion Press," in S. Richoux-Bérard and F. Bonnet (eds), *Glossy*, 171–2, Marseille: Musée de la Mode de Marseille.

Jones, Dylan (1995), "Fashion: An Elle of a Decade," *Independent* (October 22). Available online: www.independent.co.uk/arts-entertainment/fashion-an-elle-of-a-decade-1575491.html (accessed August 8, 2014).

Jones, Dylan (2014), Interview with the author.

Jones, Jennifer (2004), *Sexing La Mode: Gender, Fashion and Commercial Culture in Old Regime France*, Oxford: Berg.

Jones, Terry (ed.) (2001), *Smile i-D: Fashion and Style; the Best from 20 Years of i-D*, Köln: Taschen.

Jones, Terry and Edward Enninful (eds) (2010), *i-D Covers 1980–1990*, Köln: Taschen

Kaiser, Ulrich (2002), *The Effects of Website Provision on the Demand for German Women's Magazines*, Cambridge, MA: NBER.

Kansara, Vikram A. (2010), "Fashion Pioneers: Nick Knight Says Heart and Mind Are the Key to Fashion Imagemaking", Business of Fashion (December 2). Available online: www.businessoffashion.com/articles/people/fashion-pioneers-nick-knight-says-heart-and-mind-are-the-key-to-fashion-imagemaking (accessed August 14, 2014).

Kawamura, Yuniya (2005), *Fashion-ology: An Introduction to Fashion Studies*, Oxford: Berg.

Kelly, Rebecca J. (2005), "Fashion in the Gilded Age: A Profile of Newport's King Family," in L. Welters and P. Cunningham (eds), *Twentieth Century American Fashion*, 9–32, Oxford: Berg.

Keyser, Catherine (2010), *Playing Smart: Women Writers and Modern Magazine Culture*, New York: Rutgers University Press.

Khan, Natalie (2012), "Cutting The Fashion Body: Why The Fashion Image is No Longer Still." *Fashion Theory: The Journal of Dress. Body and Culture* 16 (2): 235–49.

Kirkham, Pat (2005), "Keeping Up Home Front Morale: Beauty and Duty in Wartime Britain," in J. M. Atkins (ed.), *Wearing Propaganda: Textiles on the Home Front in Japan, Britain, and the United States, 1931–45*, 205–27, New Haven, CT: Yale University Press.

Kismaric, Susan and Eva Respiri (2010 [2008]), "Fashioning Fiction in Photography Since 1990," in Eugénie Shinkle (ed.), *Fashion as Photograph: Viewing and Reviewing Images of Fashion*, 29–45, London: I. B. Tauris.

Kitch, Carolyn L. (2001), *The Girl on the Magazine Cover: The Origins of Visual Stereotypes in the American Mass Media*, Chapel Hill: University of North Carolina Press.

Klein, Alyssa V. (2014), "Is Instagram Killing Personal Style Blogs?" Fashionista (June 13). Available online: www.fashionista.com/2014/06/will-instagram-kill-fashion-blogs (accessed August 15, 2014).

Kleinert, Anne-Marie (1980), *Die Frühen Modejournal im Frankreich. Studien zur Literatur der Mode von den Anfängen bis 1848*, Berlin: Eric Schmidt Verlag.

Kleinert, Anne-Marie (2001), *Le Journal des Dames et des Modes, ou le Conquête de L'Europe Féminine (1797–1839)*, Stuttgart: Jan Thorbecke Verlag.

Kline, David and Dan Burstein (2005), *Blog! How the Newest Media Revolution is Changing Politics, Business and Culture*, New York: CDS Books.

Kluger, Richard (1986), *The Paper: The Life and Death of The New York Herald Tribune*, New York: Random House.

Köhler, Angelika (2004), "The Image of the New Woman in American Cartoons," in A. Heilmann and M. Beetham (eds), *New Woman Hybridities: Femininity, Feminism, and International Consumer Culture, 1880–1930*, 158–78, New York and London: Routledge.

König, Anna (2003), "Glossy Words: An Analysis of Fashion Writing in British Vogue." *Fashion Theory: The Journal of Dress, Body and Culture* 10 (1/2): 205–24.

La Ferla, Ruth (2014), "Garance Doré: A Half but Whole," *New York Times* (May 7). Available online: http://www.nytimes.com/2014/05/08/fashion/garance-dore-the-style-blogger-snatches-the-spotlight.html?_r=1 (accessed August 14, 2014).

Landers, James (2010), *The Improbable First Century of Cosmopolitan Magazine*, Colombia, MO: University of Missouri Press.

Langley-Moore, Dorothy (1971), *Fashion Through Fashion Plates 1771–1970*, London: Ward Lock.

Le Bourhis, Katell (1989), "The Elegant Fifties: When Fashion Was Still a Dictate" in S. de Pietri and M. Leventon (eds), *New Look to Now: French Haute Couture 1947–1987*, New York: Rizzoli.

Lehmann, Ulrich (2000), *Tigersprung: Fashion in Modernity*, Cambridge, MA: MIT Press.

Lehmann, Ulrich (2009), "Le mot dans la mode: Fashion and Literary Journalism in Nineteenth-century France," in J. Brand and J. Teunissen (eds), *Fashion and Imagination: About Clothes and Art*, 296–313, Arnhem, Netherlands: ArtEZ Press.

Lehuu, Isabelle (2000), *Carnival on the Page: Popular Print Media in Antebellum America*, Chapel Hill: University of North Carolina Press.

Leith, Luke (2014), "Porter Magazine: Enter the Gatecrasher," *Daily Telegraph* (February

5). Available online: http://www.telegraph.co.uk/luxury/womens-style/23888/porter-magazine-enter-the-gatecrasher.html (accessed March 8, 2014).

Levine, Joshua (2011), "Brand Anna," *Wall Street Journal* (March 26). Available online: www.wsj.com/articles/SB10001424052748704893604576200722939264658 (accessed August 16, 2014).

Levinson, Paul (2012), *New New Media*, Boston, MA: Pearson.

Lewis, Reina (2013), "The Modest Blogosphere: Establishing Reputation, Maintaining Independence," in D. Bartlett, S. Cole, and A. Rocamora (eds), *Fashion Media Past and Present*, 165–74, London and New York: Bloomsbury.

Lipovetsky, Gilles (1994 [1991]), *The Empire of Fashion: Dressing Modern Democracy*, trans. Catherine Porter, Princeton, NJ: Princeton University Press.

Lock, Simon P. (2013), "Rewiring Fashion Week." *The Business of Fashion Special Edition* (Autumn): 33.

Lynge-Jorlén, Ane (2009), "Between the Edge and the Elite," PhD thesis, University of the Arts, London.

Lynge-Jorlén, Ane (2012), "Between Frivolity and Art: Contemporary Niche Fashion Magazines." *Fashion Theory: The Journal of Dress, Body and Culture* 16 (1): 7–28.

Mackenzie Stuart, Amanda (2013), *Empress of Fashion: A Life of Diana Vreeland*, London: Harper Collins.

Marien, Mary W. (2006 [2002]), *Photography: A Cultural History*, London: Laurence King.

Martin, Penny (2002), "English Style Photography," in C. Breward, B. Conekin, and C. Cox (eds), *The Englishness of English Dress*, 173–88, Oxford: Berg.

Martin, Penny (2010 [2008]), "Interview," in Eugénie Shinkle (ed.), *Fashion as Photograph: Viewing and Reviewing Images of Fashion*, London: I. B. Tauris.

Martin, Penny (2014), Interview with Tallulah Bullock.

Martin, Richard (1989), *Fashion and Surrealism*, London: Thames and Hudson.

Massoni, Kelley (2010), *Fashioning Teenagers: A Cultural History of Seventeen Magazine*, Walnut Creek, CA: Left Coast Press.

Matthews David, Alison (2006), "Vogue's New World: American Fashionability and the Politics of Style." *Fashion Theory* (1–2): 13–38.

McCarthy, Mary (1980 [1950]), "Up the Ladder from *Charm* to *Vogue*," in M. McCarthy, *On the Contrary*, 174–92, London: Weidenfeld & Nicolson.

McCracken, Ellen (1993), *Decoding Women's Magazines: From Mademoiselle to MS*, Basingstoke: Macmillan.

McCracken, Grant (1986), "Culture and Consumption: A Theoretical Account of the Structure and Movement of the Cultural Meaning of Consumer Goods." *Journal of Consumer Research* 13 (1): 71–84.

McDowell, Colin (1994), *The Designer Scam*, London: Hutchinson.

McDowell, Colin (ed.) (1995), *The Literary Companion to Fashion*, London: Sinclair Stevenson.

McDowell, Colin (1997), *Forties Fashion and the New Look*, London: Bloomsbury.

McDowell, Colin (2014), Interview with the author.

McIllvanney, Siobhan (2010), "*Le Journal des Dames et des Modes* (1797–1839): A Pioneering Presence in the History of the French Women's Press," in A. Cone and D. Marley (eds), *The Francophone Women's Magazine: Inside and Outside of France*, 3–23, New Orleans: University Press of the South.

McLoughlin, Linda (2000), *The Language of Magazines*, London: Routledge.

McNeil, Peter and Sanda Miller (2014), *Fashion Writing and Criticism: Theory, Writing and Practice*, London and New York: Bloomsbury.

McRobbie, Angela (1991), *In the Culture Society: Art, Fashion and Popular Music*, London: Routledge.

McRobbie, Angela (1998) *British Fashion Design: Rag Trade or Image Industry?* London: Routledge.

Medine, Leandra (2014), Interview with Tallulah Bullock.

Menkes, Suzy (2011), "From Rags to Riches," *New York Times* (October 7). Available online: http://tmagazine.blogs.nytimes.com/2011/10/07/from-rags-to-riches/?_r=0 (accessed August 18, 2014).

Menkes, Suzy (2013a), "The Circus of Fashion," *New York Times* (February 10). Available online: www.nytimes.com/2013/02/10/t-magazine/the-circus-of- fashion.html (accessed August 18, 2014).

Menkes, Suzy (2013b), "The New Speed of Fashion," *New York Times* (August 23). Available online: www.nytimes.com/2013/08/23/t-magazine/the-new-speed-of-fashion.html (accessed August 18, 2014).

Mermet, Emile (1879), *La Publicité en France: Guide Pratique Annuaire pour 1879,* Paris: A Chaix et Cie.

Mesure, Susie (2010), "Fluff Flies as Fashion Writers Pick a Catfight with Bloggers", *Independent* (January 30). Available online: www.independent.co.uk/life-style/fashion/news/fluff-flies-as-fashion-writers-pick-a-cat-fight-with-bloggers-1884539.html (accessed August 14, 2014).

Millbank, Caroline R. (1989), *New York Fashion: The Evolution of American Style*, New York: Abrams.

Miller, Micheal B. (1981), *The Bon Marché: Bourgeois Culture and the Department Store,* Boston, MA: Princeton University Press.

Miller, Sanda (2013), "Taste, Fashion and the French Magazine," in D. Bartlett, S. Cole, and A. Rocamora (eds), *Fashion Media Past and Present*, 13–21, London and New York: Bloomsbury.

Mirabella, Grace (1995), *In and Out of Vogue: A Memoir*, New York: Doubleday.

Moeran, Brian (2008), "Economic and Cultural Production as a Structural Paradox: The Case of International Fashion Magazines." *International Review of Sociology* 18 (2): 267–81.

Mohrt, Françoise (1979), *25 ans de Marie Claire de 1954–1979*, Paris: Marie Claire.

Montfort, Pascal de (2004), "The Fashion Image: Absent Dress," in S. Richoux-Bérard and F. Bonnet (eds), *Glossy*, 166–7, Marseille: Musée de la Mode de Marseille.

Morienval, Jean (1934), *Les Créateurs de la grande presse en France*, Paris: Editions du Spes.

Mort, Frank (1996), *Cultures of Consumption: Masculinities and Social Space in the Late Twentieth Century*, London and New York: Routledge.

Mulier, Thomas (2015), "Richemont Confirms Net-a-Porter Yoox Merger." Available online: www.businessoffashion.com/articles/news-analysis/richemont-confirms-net-a-porter-yoox-merger (accessed March 31, 2015).

Mulvagh, Jane (1989), *Vogue History of 20th Century Fashion*, London: Viking.

Musgrave, Eric (2014), Interview with Tallulah Bullock.

Needham, Gary (2013), "The Digital Fashion Film," in S. Bruzzi and P. Church Gibson (eds), *Fashion Cultures Revisited,* 103–11, London and New York: Routledge.

Newton, Helmut (2013 [2004]), *Helmut Newton*, London: Thames and Hudson.

Niemojewski, Rafal B. (2004), "Fashionable Magazines: A New Type of Magazine; A New Viewpoint on Fashion," in S. Richoux-Bérard and F. Bonnet (eds), *Glossy*, 180–1, Marseille: Musée de la Mode de Marseille.

Nixon, Sean (1996), *Hard Looks: Masculinities, Spectatorship and Contemporary Consumption*, London and New York: Routledge.

North, Michael (2003), *"Material Delight and The Joy of Living"*: *Cultural Consumption in the Age of Enlightenment in Germany*, trans. Pamela Selwyn, London: Ashgate.

Ogersby, Bill (2003), "A Pedigree of The Consuming Male: A Genealogy of The American American 'Leisure Class,'" in B. Benwell (ed.), *Masculinity and Men's Lifestyle Magazines*, 57–85, Oxford: Blackwell.

Okker, Patricia (2003), *Social Stories: The Magazine Novel in Nineteenth-century America*, Charlottesville: University of Virginia Press.

Okker, Patricia (2008 [1995]), *Our Sister Editors: Sarah J. Hale and the Tradition of Nineteenth-century American Women Editors*, Athens: University of Georgia Press.

Oliver, William (2012), *Style Feed: The World's Top Fashion Blogs (selected by Susie Bubble)*, Munich: Prestel.

O'Neill, Alistair (2005), "Cuttings and Pastings," in C. Breward and C. Evans (eds), *Fashion and Modernity*, 175–89, Oxford: Berg.

O'Neill, Alistair (2013 [2000]), "Fashion Photography: Communication, Criticism and Curation from 1975," in S. Bruzzi and P. Church Gibson (eds), *Fashion Cultures Revisited: Theories, Exploration and Analysis*, London and New York: Routledge.

O'Neill, Alistair (2013), *Isabella Blow: Fashion Galore!*, New York: Rizzoli.

Orvell, Miles (1989), *The Real Thing: Imitation and Authenticity in American Culture, 1880–1940*, Chapel Hill: University of North Carolina Press.

Owen, William (1991), *Modern Magazine Design*, New York: Rizzoli.

Palmer, Alexandra (2001), *Couture and Commerce: The Transatlantic Fashion Trade*, Vancouver: University of British Columbia Press.

Parkin, Molly (1993), *Moll: The Making of Molly Parkin*, London: Victor Gollanz.

Patterson, Martha H. (2008 [2005]), *Beyond the Gibson Girl: Re-imagining The American New Woman 1895–1915*, Urbana and Chicago: University of Illinois Press.

Paulicelli, Eugenia (2004), *Fashion under Fascism: Beyond the Black Shirt*, Oxford: Berg.

Pelletan, Eugène (1869), *La Femme au XIXe siècle*, Paris: Librairie Pagnerre.

Perrot, Philippe (1996 [1981]), *Fashioning the Bourgeoisie: A History of Clothing in the 19th Century*, trans. Richard Bienvenu, Princeton, NJ: Princeton University Press.

Pertuis, Karen De (2010 [2008]), "Beyond Perfection: the Fashion Model in the Age of Digital Manipulation," in Eugénie Shinkle (ed.), *Fashion as Photograph: Viewing and Reviewing Images of Fashion*, 168–81, London: I. B. Tauris.

Peterson, Theodore (1956), *Magazines in the Twentieth Century*, Urbana: University of Illinois Press.

Piaggi, Anna (1998), *Fashion Algebra*, trans. Cecilia Treves, London: Thames and Hudson.

Pietri, Stephen de and Melissa Leventon (eds) (1989), *New Look To Now, French Haute Couture 1947–1987*, New York: Rizzoli.

Pochna, Marie-France (2004), "The Dior Phenomenon in the Fashion Press," in S. Richoux-Berard and F. Bonnet (eds), *Glossy*, 164–5, Marseille: Musée de la Mode de Marseille.

Pochna, Marie-France (2008), *Christian Dior*, trans. Joanna Savill, New York: Overlook Duckworth.

Polan, Brenda (2006), "Fashion Journalism," in T. Jackson and D. Shaw (eds), *The Fashion Handbook*, 154–71, London: Routledge.

Pouey, Charles du (1869), *Causerie critique sur la femme*, Tarbes: Th. Telmon.

Pouillard, Veronique (2007), "In the Shadow of Paris: French Haute Couture and Belgian Fashion Between The Wars," in Regina Lee Blaszczyk (ed.), *Producing Fashion: Commerce, Culture and Consumers*, 62–81, Philadelphia: The University of Pennsylvania Press.

Pouillard, Veronique (2013), "Fashion For All?" *Journalism Studies* 14 (5): 716–29.

Puccinelli, Elena (2014), "Communication in the Fashion System," in S. Stanfill (ed.), *The Glamour of Italian Fashion Since 1945*, 240–7, London: V&A.

Purdy, Daniel L. (1998), *The Tyranny of Elegance: Consumer Cosmopolitanism in the Era of Goethe*, Baltimore, MD: John Hopkins University Press.

Quant, Mary (2012), *Mary Quant: Autobiography*, London: Headline.

Radner, Hilary (2000), "On the Move: Fashion Photography and The Single Girl in the 1960s," in S. Bruzzi and P. Church Gibson (eds), *Fashion Cultures Theory, Exploration and Analysis*, 128–42, London: Routledge.

Rappaport, Erika D. (2001), *Shopping for Pleasure: Women in the Making of London's West End*, Princeton, NJ: Princeton University Press.

Reed, Christopher (2006), "The Vogue That Dare Not Speak Its Name: Sexual Subculture During the Editorship of Dorothy Todd, 1922–1926." *Fashion Theory: The Journal of Dress, Body & Culture* 10 (1/2): 39–72.

Reed, David (1997), *The Popular Magazine in Britain and The United States. 1880–1960*, London: British Library.

Reinarch, Simona S. (2013), "Fashion Films, Blogs and E-Commerce: The Puzzle of Fashion Distinction in China," in D. Bartlett, S. Cole, and A. Rocamora (eds), *Fashion Media Past and Present*, 144–54, London and New York: Bloomsbury.

Ribeiro, Alieen (2005), *Fashion and Fiction: Dress in Art and Literature in Stuart England*, New Haven, CT: Yale University Press.

Richardson, Angelique (2004), "The Birth of National Hygiene and Efficiency: Women and Eugenics in Britain and America 1865–1915," in A. Heilmann and M. Beetham (eds), *New Woman Hybridities: Femininity, Feminism, and International Consumer Culture, 1880–1930*, 240–62, New York and London: Routledge.

Richoux-Bérard, Sylvie (2004), "Do It," in S. Richoux–Bérard and F. Bonnet (eds), *Glossy*, 176–7, Marseille: Musée de la Mode de Marseille.

Richoux-Bérard, Sylvie and Frédéric Bonnet (eds) (2004), *Glossy*, Marseille: Musée de la Mode de Marseille.

Ridder, Jolein de and Marianne Van Remoortel (2012), "From Fashion Colours to Spectrum Analysis: Negotiating Femininities in Mid-Victorian Women's Magazines." *Women's History Review* 21 (1): 21–36.

Robbins, Trina (2004), "Nell Brinkley and the New Woman," in A. Heilmann and M. Beetham (eds), *New Woman Hybridities: Femininity, Feminism, and International Consumer Culture, 1880–1930*, 179–89, New York and London: Routledge.

Rocamora, Agnès (2001), "High Fashion and Pop Fashion: The Symbolic Production of Fashion in *Le Monde* and the *Guardian*." *Fashion Theory: The Journal of Dress, Body & Culture* 5 (2): 123–42.

Rocamora, Agnès (2009a), *Fashioning the City: Paris, Fashion and The Media*, London: I. B. Tauris.

Rocamora, Agnès (2009b), "Blogs de mode: les nouveaux espaces du discours de mode." *Sociétés: Revue des Sciences Humaines et Sociales* 2 (104): 105–14.

Rocamora, Agnès (2011) "Personal Fashion Blogs: Screens and Mirrors in The Digital Age." *Fashion Theory: The Journal of Dress, Body & Culture* 15 (4): 407–24.

Rocamora, Agnès (2012), "Hypertextuality and Remediation in the Fashion Media: The Case of Fashion Blogs." *Journalism Practice* 6: 92–106.

Rocamora, Agnès (2013), "How New are The New Media? The Case of Fashion Blogs," in D. Bartlett, S. Cole, and A. Rocamora (eds), *Fashion Media Past and Present*, 155–64, London and New York: Bloomsbury.

Rocamora, Agnès and Alistair O'Neill (2010 [2008]), "Fashioning the Street: Images of the Street in the Fashion Media," in E. Schinkle (ed.), *Fashion as Photograph: Viewing and Reviewing Images of Fashion*, 185–99, London: I. B. Tauris.

Roche, Daniel (1996 [1989]), *The Culture of Clothing: Dress and Fashion in the Ancien Regime*, trans. Jean Birrell, Cambridge: Cambridge University Press.

Rose, Josephine (2012), *Cecil Beaton in Vogue*, London: Thames and Hudson.

Rowlands, Penelope (2005), *A Dash of Daring: Carmel Snow and Her Life in Fashion, Art and Letters*, New York and London: Simon and Schuster.

Ruane, Christine (2007), "Spreading the Word: The Development of the Russian Fashion Press," in R. L. Blaszczyk (ed.), *Producing Fashion: Commerce, Culture and Consumers*, 21–41, Philadelphia: University of Pennsylvania Press.

Sama, Catherine M. (2004), "Liberty, Equality, Frivolity: An Italian Critique of Fashion Periodicals." *Eighteenth-Century Studies* 37 (3): 389–414.

Sand, George (1868), *Mademoiselle Merquem,* Paris: Michel Lévy Frères.

Saner, Ermine (2015), "Porter's Lucy Yeomans: 'It's all About the Woman, Listening to Her, Asking Her What She Wants,'" *Guardian* (February 8). Available online: www.theguardian.com/media/2015/feb/08/porter-magazine-editor-lucy-yeomans (accessed February 12, 2105).

Savi, Lucia (2014), "La Moda In Vogue," in S. Stanfill, *The Glamour of Italian Fashion Since 1945*, 249–53, London: V&A.

Scanlon, Jennifer (1995), *Inarticulate Longings: The Ladies' Home Journal, Gender and The Promise of Consumer Culture*, New York and London: Routledge.

Scanlon, Jennifer (2000), "Advertising Women: The J Walter Thompson Company's Women's Editorial Department," in J. Scanlon (ed.), *The Consumer Culture Reader*, 201–25, New York and London: New York University Press.

Scanlon, Jennifer (2009), *Bad Girls Go Everywhere: The Life of Helen Gurley Brown*, Oxford: Oxford University Press.

Schiaparelli, Elsa (2007 [1954]), *Shocking Life: The Autobiography of Elsa Schiaparelli*, London: V&A Publishing.

Schiro, Anne-Marie (1984), "Eugenia Sheppard, Fashion Columnist Dies," *New York Times* (November 12). Available online: www.nytimes.com/1984/11/12/obituaries/eugenia-sheppard-fashion-columnist-dies.html (accessed March 21, 2014).

Schweitzer, Marlis (2007), "American Fashions For American Women: The Rise and Fall of Fashion Nationalism," in R. L. Blaszczyk (ed.) *Producing Fashion: Commerce, Culture and Consumers*, 62–81, Philadelphia: University of Pennsylvania Press.

Seebohm, Caroline (1982), *The Man Who Was Vogue*, New York: Viking Press.

Seligman, Kevin L. (1996), *Cutting For All: The Sartorial Arts, Related Crafts, and The Paper Pattern*, Carbondale and Edwardsville: Southern Illinois University Press.

Sharp, Ingrid E. (2004), "Riding the Tiger: Ambivalent Images of the New Woman in the Popular Press of the Weimar Republic," in A. Heilmann and M. Beetham (eds), *New Woman Hybridities: Femininity, Feminism, and International Consumer Culture, 1880–1930*, 118–42, New York and London: Routledge.

Sherman, Lauren (2015), "From Fashion Cycle to Fashion Feed" The Business of Fashion (March 9). Available online: www.businessoffashion.com/articles/intelligence/fashion-cycle-fashion- feed (accessed March 9, 2015).

Shevelow, Kathryn (1989), *Women and Print Culture: The Construction of Femininity in the Early Periodical*, London: Routledge.

Shinkle, Eugénie (2010 [2008]), *Fashion as Photograph: Viewing and Reviewing Images of Fashion*, London: I. B. Tauris.

Shinkle, Eugénie (2013), "Fashion's Digital Body: Seeing and Feeling in Fashion

Interactives," in D. Bartlett, S. Cole, and A. Rocamora (eds), *Fashion Media Past and Present*, 175–83, London and New York: Bloomsbury.

Silverman, Debora L. (1986), *Selling Culture: Bloomingdales, Diana Vreeland, and the New Aristocracy of Taste in Reagan's America*, New York: Pantheon.

Simmel, Georg (1971 [1904]), *On Individuality and Social Forms*, ed. D. Levine, Chicago, IL: University of Chicago Press.

Simon, Marie (1995), *Fashion in Art: The Second Empire and Impressionism,* Paris: Zwemmer.

Skov, Lisa (2011), "Dreams of a Small Nation in a Polycentric Fashion World." *Fashion Theory: The Journal of Dress Body and Culture* 15 (2): 137–56.

Skov, Lisa and Marie Riegels Melchior (eds) (2011), *Fashion Theory: The Journal of Dress, Body and Culture* 15 (2).

Smedley, Elliott (2013 [2000]), "Escaping to Reality: Fashion Photography in the 1990s," in S. Bruzzi and P. Church Gibson (eds), *Fashion Cultures Revisited*, 161–74, London and New York: Routledge.

Solca, Luca (2015), "LVMH vs Kering: Which Player is Best Positioned for Growth?" The Business of Fashion (February 23). Available online: http://www.businessoffashion. com/articles/intelligence/lvmh-vs-kering (accessed February 23, 2015).

Spanier, Gideon (2013), "Monocle's Tyler Brûlé, I Don't Care about Social Media and iPads," *London Evening Standard* (April 10). Available online: http://www.standard. co.uk/business/media/monocles-tyler-br-l-i-don-t-care-about-social-media-and-ipads-8567111.html (accessed August 18, 2014).

Stanfill, Sonnet (ed.) (2014), *The Glamour of Italian Fashion Since 1945*, London: V&A.

Steele, Valerie (1994), "Italian Fashion and America," in G. Celant (ed.), *Italian Metamorphosis*, New York: Guggenheim.

Steele, Valerie (1997), "Anti-fashion: The 1970s." *Fashion Theory: The Journal of Dress, Body and Culture* 1 (3): 279–96.

Steele, Valerie (1998 [1988]), *Paris Fashion: A Cultural History*, Oxford: Berg.

Steigrad, Alexandra (2015), "Cathy Horyn is Back in Fashion," *Women's Wear Daily* (January 12). Available online: www.com/globe-news/fashion-memopad/cathy-horyn-is-back-in-fashion-8101794/ (accessed January 12, 2015).

Stewart, Mary L. (2008), *Dressing Modern Frenchwomen: Marketing Haute Couture, 1919–1939*, Baltimore, MD: Johns Hopkins University Press.

Stoeffel, Kat (2014), "Finally, 'Serious' Women are Standing Up for Fashion Magazines", The Cut (July 21). Available online: www.nymag.com/thecut/2014/07/serious-woman-are-standing-up-for-fashion-mags.html (accessed July 23, 2014).

Sullerot, Evelyne (1966), *Histoire de La Presse Féminine,des origins à 1848*, Paris: Armand Colin.

Summers, Leigh (2001), *Bound to Please: A History of the Victorian Corset*, Oxford: Berg

Sumner, David E. (2010), *The Magazine Century: American Magazines Since 1900*, Bern: Peter Lang.

Sunyer, John (2014), "Lunch with the FT: Jefferson Hack," *Financial Times* (August 8). Available online: www.ft.com/cms/s/2/fc444a8a-1cab-11e4-88c3-00144feabdc0.html (accessed August 9, 2014).

Tay, Jinna (2009), "'Pigeon-eyed Readers': The Adaptation and Formation of a Global Asian Fashion Magazine." *Continuum: Journal Of Cultural and Media Studies* 23 (2): 245–56.

Tétart-Vittu, Françoise (1990), "Le Chic Parisien, Images et Modèles dans la Presse Illustrée," *Femmes Fin de Siècle, 1885–1895*, 93–102, Paris: Musée de la mode et du costume.

Tétart-Vittu, Françoise (1992), *Au Paradis des Dames: nouveautés, modes et confections 1810–1870*, Paris: Musées.

Thessander, Marianne (1997), *The Feminine Ideal*, London: Reaktion Books.

Tiersten, Lisa (2001), *Marianne in the Market: Envisioning Consumer Society in Fin-de-Siècle France*, Berkeley and Los Angeles: University of California Press.

Tiffany, John. A. (2011), *Eleanor Lambert: Still Here*, New York: Pointed Leaf Press.

Titton, Monica (2013), "Styling The Street—Fashion Performance, Stardom and Neo-Dandyism in Street Style Blogs," in S. Bruzzi and P. Church Gibson (eds), *Fashion Cultures Revisited*, London and New York: Routledge.

Tonchi, Stefano (ed.) (2012), *W: The First 40 Years*, New York: Abrams.

Troy, Nancy J. (2003), *Couture Culture: A Study in Modern Art and Fashion*, Cambridge, MA: MIT Press.

Troy, Nancy J. (2012), "Art," in A. Geczy and V. Karaminas (eds), *Fashion and Art*, 29–40, London and New York: Berg.

Tungate, Mark (2012 [2005]), *Fashion Brands: Branding Style from Armani to Zara*, London and Philadelphia, PA: Kogan Page.

Tzortzis, Andreas (2007), "A New Type Breed of Fashion Magazine Comes into Vogue," *New York Times* (August 20). Available online: www.nytimes.com/2007/08/20/style/20ihtfberlin.1.7180694.html?pagewanted=all&_r0 (accessed August 9, 2014).

Uhlirova, Marketa (2013), "The Fashion Film Effect," in D. Bartlett, S. Cole, and A. Rocamora (eds), *Fashion Media Past and Present*, 118–32, London and New York: Bloomsbury.

Veblen, Thorstein (2009 [1899]), *The Theory of the Leisure Class*, ed. Martha Banta, Oxford: Oxford University Press.

Veillon, Dominique (2002), *Fashion Under the Occupation*, trans. M. Kochan, Oxford: Berg.

Vincent, Monique (2005), *Le Mercure Galant: Présentation de la première revue feminine d'information et de culture 1672–1710*, Paris: Honoré-Champion.

Völkel, Anika (2006), *Die Modezeitschrift: Vom Journal des Luxus und der Moden zu Brigitte und Elle,* Hamburg: Kovac.

Voss, Kimberley W. and Lance Speere (2013), "Fashion as Washington Journalism History: Eleni Epstein and Her Three Decades at the *Washington Star*." *Media History Monographs* 16 (3). Available online: http://facstaff.elon.edu/dcopeland/mhm/mhmjour16-3.pdf (accessed March 21, 2014).

Vreeland, Alexander and Polly Mellen (eds) (2013), *Vreeland Memos: The Vogue Years*, New York: Rizzoli.

Waddell, Rankin (2010 [2008]), "Interview," in Eugénie Shinkle (ed.), *Fashion as Photograph: Viewing and Reviewing Images of Fashion*, 87–99, London: I. B. Tauris.

Walker, Nancy. A (ed.) (1998), *Women's Magazines 1940–1960: Gender Roles and the Popular Press*, Boston, MA: Bedford/St. Martin's Press.

Walker, Nancy A. (2000), *Shaping Our Mother's World: American Women's Magazines*, Jackson: University Press of Mississippi.

Wallace, Benjamin (2014), "What's so Alluring About a Woman Known as Man Repeller?" The Cut (February 8). Available online: nymag.com/thecut/2014/02/man-repeller-leandra-medine-profile.html# (accessed August 15, 2014).

Waller, Jane and Michael Vaughan-Rees (eds) (1987), *Women in Wartime: The Role of Women's Magazines 1939–1945,* London: Macdonald Optima.

Wargnier, Stéphane (2004), "In Praise of the Intermediary," in S. Richoux-Bérard and F. Bonnet (eds), *Glossy*, 164–5, Marseille: Musée de la Mode de Marseille.

Warhol, Andy and Pat Hackett (1981 [1980]), *POPISM: The Warhol Sixties*, London: Hutchinson.

Warner, Helen (2014), *Fashion on Television: Identity and Celebrity Culture*, London and New York: Bloomsbury.

Wawrzyniak, Martynka (ed.) (2008), *Purple Anthology 1992–2006*, New York: Rizzoli.

Webb, Iain R. (2009), *Foale and Tuffin. The Sixties. A Decade in Fashion*, Woodbridge: ACC Editions.

Webb, Iain R. (2013), *BLITZ: As seen in Blitz—Fashioning '80s Style*, Woodbridge: ACC Editions.

Weill, Georges (1934), *Le Journal. Origines, évolution et rôle de la presse périodique*, Paris: La Renaissance du Livre.

White, Cynthia (1970), *Women's Magazines 1693–1968*, London: Michael Joseph.

White, Erica M. (2009), *Representations of the True Woman and the New Woman in Harper's Bazaar*, Graduate thesis, Iowa State University.

White, Nicola (2000), *Reconstructing Italian Fashion: America and the Development of the Italian Fashion Industry*, Oxford: Berg.

Wilcox, Claire (ed.) (2008), *The Golden Age of Couture*, London: V&A.

Wilkins, Saskia (2014), Interview with Tallulah Bullock.

Williams, Rosalind H. (1982), *Dream Worlds: Mass Consumption in Late Nineteenth-century France*, Berkeley and Los Angeles: University of California Press.

Wilson, Elizabeth. (2003 [1985]), *Adorned in Dreams: Fashion and Modernity*, London: Virago.

Wilson, Elizabeth (2006), "Urban Fashion," in C. Breward and D. Gilbert (eds), *Fashion's World Cities*, 33–9, Oxford: Berg.

Winship, Janice (1987), *Inside Women's Magazines*, London and New York: Pandora Press.

Wurst, Karin A. (1997), "The Self-fashioning of the Bourgeoisie in Late-eighteenth-century German Culture: Bertuch's *Journal des Luxus und der Moden*." *The Germanic Review: Literature, Culture, Theory* 3 (72): 170–82.

Yan, Yan and Kim Bissell (2014), "The Globalization of Beauty: How Ideal Beauty is Influenced by Globally Published Fashion and Beauty Magazines." *Journal of Intercultural Communication Research* 43 (3): 194–214.

Yi, David (2014), "Magazine Circulation Figures Slip 1.9% in First Half of 2014," *Women's Wear Daily* (August 11). Available online: www.com/globe-news/fashion-memopad/not-the-entire-picture-7834298/ (accessed August 12, 2014).

Ying, Jeffrey (2015), "We Chat Publishing is Changing China's Media Landscape," Business of Fashion (April 28). Available online: www.businessoffashion.com/articles/global-currents/wechat-publishing-changing-chinas-mediascape (accessed April 28, 2015).

York, Peter (1980), *Style Wars*, London: Sidgwick and Jackson.

Zahm, Olivier (eds) (2008), *Purple Anthology*, New York: Rizzoli.

Zika, Anna (2006), *Is alles eitel? Zur Kulturgeschichte deutschsprachiger Modejournal zwischen Aufklärung und Zerstruung 1750–1950*, Weimar: VDG.

Zimmerman, Edith (2012), "99 Ways to Be Naughty in Kazakhstan: How Cosmo Conquered the World," *New York Times* (August 3). Available online: www.nytimes.com/2012/08/05/magazine/how-cosmo-conquered-the-world.html?_r=0 (accessed September 8, 2013).

Zuckerman, Mary Ellen (1998), *History of Popular Women's Magazines in the United States 1792–1995*, Westport, CT: Greenwood Press.

INDEX

This index categorizes fashion journalism primarily by other terms, and further by proper names, in all chapters. Terms are indexed in full, or by commonly known abbreviation. An "f." indicates a figure; an "n." indicates an endnote.

Cheung, Angelica 244
chic 54, 55, 71
China 223, 245
"Chronique Mondaine" 69
Church Gibson, Pamela 235
Clark, Ossie 163
class 23, 30, 126
    democratization and 56–7, 109
    regulatory tone 115
    see also middle classes; upper classes
Clothes Show 200
Cockburn, Anna 211
Cocteau, Jean 2f., 86, 150
Coddington, Grace 160, 172, 211, 236, 237
    narratives and 209
Coleridge, Nicholas 201
Colette 84–5f., 86
Coller Davis, Tobé 86
Comme des Garçons 203
Company 222
Condé Nast 161–2, 201, 202, 216, 219, 220,
        221, 225, 236, 238, 240, 244, 246
conglomeration 193, 194–5, 221, 222
Conran, Jasper 208
consumption and consumerism 6, 37,
        52–3, 192
    art and 74
    censure 30, 42
    disparity 117, 174, 190, 191f.
    taste 55
    see also advertising
Cool Britannia 193, 211
La Corbeille 49
corbeilles (wedding baskets) 52
Cosmopolitan 161, 162
    beauty and 184
    feminism 185–6
    globalization 222
    scope 184, 185, 186
    sexual factors 184
Council of Fashion Designers of America
        (CFDA) 143
Courrèges, André 165, 170–1
couture 69, 90, 160
    arbiters and 87f., 88
    art and 80, 82–3, 86
    democratization and 105, 130
    exhibition 78–9
    fakes and 140, 142

hierarchy and 139
occupation and 95–6
propaganda 79–80, 100
scope 86, 88, 95, 125, 133, 139
secrecy and 135
sports 88–9
suppression and 96
covers and cover girls 3, 46, 55, 116, 125
Cowan, John 163
Cowles, Fleur 128
Crawford, Cindy 200
Crescent, Francine 181
Cronberg, Anja 4, 244, 248
Cunard, Nancy 87
Cunningham, Patricia et al. 200

Dahl-Wolfe, Louise 151
Dalí, Salvador 86
Die Dame 97
Dames de Vogue 74, 89
dandyism 29, 47
Daves, Jessica 86
David, Jules 48f., 51
Davis, George 128
Day, Corinne 189, 206, 207
Dazed and Confused 190, 209, 211
Delineator, The 40
democratization 7, 8f., 17, 105, 109, 112,
        113, 220–1
    censure 56–7, 109
    class 23
    disparity 221
    distinction and 7, 130
    personality type and 119
    regulatory tone and 119, 126
    taste and 127
    see also blogging; globalization
Denza, Vanessa 165
department stores 35, 40
La Dernière Mode 29, 30
Derrick, Robin 206–7
designers 89, 143, 189, 201, 203
Dessès, Jean 146
Details 194
Didion, Joan 127, 245
Dimanches de la Femme 105
Dior, Christian 138
    fakes and 140
    Margrave dress 140

Gucci 192
Guerlain 35
Gurley Brown, Helen 161, 184, 185–6

Hack, Jefferson 209, 219
Hackett, Dennis 168
Hale, Sara Josepha 38, 40, 62, 64
Hall-Duncan, Nancy 11, 92, 134, 153
Hamnett, Katherine 193
Harlech, Amanda 206, 228
Harper's and Queen 179, 189
Harper's Bazaar 2f., 16, 41, 64, 86, 137f.,
    147, 148, 151, 243
    advertising 90, 144
    art and 83, 93, 144–5
    disparity 93
    economy 58
    femininity 152
    luxury 41
    memoir 84–5f.
    news and 145
    propaganda 101
    race 180–1
    regulatory tone 148
    scope 41, 93, 149–50
    shopping services 41
    taste 50
Harrison, Martin 160, 168, 171, 176, 180
Hasselblad 134
health and well-being 122, 162
Hearst Magazines 86, 93, 219, 222, 244
Hearst, William Randolph 75, 90, 93, 181
Herald Tribune 146–7, 202–3
Higonnet, Anne 37
Holgate, Mark 134
Hollywood 74, 90, 94–5, 103 n.21,
    214–15
    censure 95
    exposé and 120
    luxury and 118–19, 120
    terminology and 94
Hollywood Patterns 94
Honey 161, 174, 175f., 176, 184
Horst 86
Horyn, Cathy 248–9
house magazines 82
Howell, Georgina 166
"How Fashion became Big Business" 112
Hoyningen-Huené, George 12f., 86

Hulanicki, Barbara 163
Hume, Marion 208, 210
Hutton, Lauren 173

i-D 189, 190, 204, 205f., 206
identifactory fantasies 9–10, 26, 45, 46,
    57, 59–60
    the actress 69, 70f.
    censure 46, 54
    dolly bird 174, 175f., 176
    The Gibson Girl 62–4, 65f.
    La Jeune Fille 9, 60, 61f., 62
    mother figure 57, 58
    The New Woman 54, 64, 66, 88–9
    single girl 160, 174
    see also celebrity; models; *La*
        Parisienne; upper classes
illustrators 82, 83
Incorporated Society of London Fashion
    Designers 155
industrialization 16
"Inside Fashion" 146–7
InStyle 215–16
The International Best Dressed List 142
Interview 167f., 168
IPC 161
Italian fashion press 25, 97, 100, 193, 195

Jackson, Betty 193, 200, 201, 247, 248,
    249–50
Jackson, Winefride 146
Jacobs, Marc 237
Jagger, Bianca 166, 167f.
Jalouse 220
Jardin des Modes 138
La Jeune Fille 9, 60, 61f., 62
Jill 208
Jones, Dylan 204, 206, 207, 210, 213, 220,
    223, 248
    future and 243
Jones, Terry 204
Le Journal des Dames et des Modes 25–7
Le Journal des Demoiselles 60
Le Journal des Jeunes Personnes 61f.
Journal des Luxus und der Moden 23, 24f.,
    25, 43 n.11
Juda, Elsbeth (Jay) 155–6, 156f.
Juda, Hans 155, 156
Junior Bazaar 151

propaganda 76f., 78, 79–80, 96, 100, 102
  disparity 100
  economy 75, 101
  fakes and 79
  gender 97, 98f., 100, 101
  home front and 80
  scope 73, 75, 78, 97, 100–1
  taste 79
  terminology and 78, 97
Prouvost, Jean 119
Purple 190, 239

Quant, Mary 163, 164f., 170
Queen, The 56, 58, 67, 69, 159, 169f., 170
  class 56
  disparity 67, 170–1
  domestic ideals 58
  economy 77
  emancipation and 67
  propaganda and 75, 76f., 80
  scope 168, 170, 171
Quick, Harriet 189

Rabanne, Paco 165
race 180–1
Radner, Hilary 174
Rankin 209, 211
Rappaport, Erika 55
rationing 75, 77, 101, 102
Rave 161
Raymond, Emmeline 32, 38, 58
Ray-Vogue School 86
Reed, Paula 234–5
Rendlesham, Clare (Lady) 170–1
Rénier, Martine 89
La Revue de la Mode 55
Rich, Marcus 245
Richemont 193
riding dress 48f.
Rive Gauche 160
Rodic, Yvan 223
Roitfeld, Carine 181, 226, 236, 238
Rolling Stones 170
romance 118
Rourke, Micky 212f.
Rousteing, Olivier 225
Rowlands, Penelope 150–1

Sade 205f., 206

Saint Laurent, Yves 124, 160, 163, 203, 226
Sand, George 46
Santé 162
Sassoon, Vidal 166
Saturday Review, The 59
Savage, Jon 207
Scanlon, Jennifer 185
Schiaparelli, Elsa 2f., 12f., 86, 89
Schritte zu schonen schreiten 98f.
Schuman, Scott 232
seasons 22, 248
Self 162
service magazines 106, 109, 115, 117
  democratization 112
  economy 117
  expertise and 111–12
  gender 118
  interaction with readers 116
  own shops 117–18
  see also advertising
Settle, Alison 89, 112, 135, 146
Seventeen 106, 108, 112
Seventh Avenue 90, 140
sexual factors 52, 60, 62, 160, 184, 185
  censure 42, 54
  consumption and 174
  disparity 9
  domestic failure and 59
  irreverence 184
  tight lacing 59
sharing magazines 27
Shaver, Dorothy 125, 149, 156
Shaw, Sandie 176
Sheppard, Eugenia 134, 136, 146–7
Shinkle, Eugénie 6
shopping services 40, 41
SHOWstudio 220, 227–8
Shrimpton, Jean 164f., 166
Sieff, Jeanloup 124, 170
Silvagni, Irene 244
Simms, David 189
Simpson, Babs 149
Simpson, Wallace 88
single girl 160, 174
Six 203
Slaughter, Audrey 176
slimness 89
smartness 89